The Industrial Archaeology and Industrial History of South Western England

A Bibliography

The Industrial Archaeology and Industrial History of South Western England

A Bibliography

Compiled by
John Greenwood

MERTON PRIORY PRESS

First published 1999

Published by
Merton Priory Press Ltd
67 Merthyr Road, Whitchurch
Cardiff CF14 1DD

© John Greenwood 1999

ISBN 1 898937 28 1

Printed by
Hillman Printers (Frome) Ltd
Handlemaker Road
Marston Trading Estate
Frome, Somerset BA11 4RW

Contents

Introduction	1
Bibliographies Consulted	3
Periodicals Cited	4
Other Volumes in this Series	12

South Western England

General	13
Agriculture	14
Architecture and Buildings	17
General	17
Domestic	17
Industrial	17
Engineering	17
General	17
The Brunels	18
Fisheries	19
Glassmaking	20
Iron and Steel	20
Leather and Footwear	20
Limeburning	20
Mining	20
General	20
Arsenic	21
China Clay	22
Coal	22
Copper and Tin	23
Granite	25
Iron, Lead, Silver, Zinc, Other	25
Papermaking	26
Posts and Communications	26
Pottery and Ceramics	26
Public Utilities	26
Electricity	26
Gas	27
Water	27
Shipbuilding	27
Textiles	27
Transport	29
General	29
Canals and Rivers	29

Railways	31
General and Western Region since 1948	31
Avon & Gloucester Railway	32
Bath & Weymouth Railway	32
Bristol & Exeter Railway	32
Bristol & Gloucester Railway	32
Bristol & South Wales Union Railway	32
Great Western Railway	32
London & South Western Railway	39
Midland & South Western Junction Railway	40
North Devon & Cornwall Junction Railway	41
Somerset & Dorset Railway	41
Weston, Clevedon & Portishead Railway	41
Roads and Road Transport	41
Bridges	42
Ports and Shipping	42
Other Industries	44

Bristol

General	45
Agriculture	49
Architecture and Buildings	49
General	49
Domestic	49
Industrial	49
Aircraft Manufacture	50
Brewing	51
Brickmaking	51
Building	51
Chemicals	52
Clock and Watchmaking	52
Engineering	52
Food and Wine Supply	54
Glass Making	55
Leather and Footwear	56
Limeburning	56
Metals	56
Mining and Quarrying	57
Paper Making	58
Posts and Communications	58
Pottery and Ceramics	58
Printing and Publishing	60
Public Utilities	61
Electricity	61

Gas	61
Water	61
Shipbuilding	61
Slave Trade	62
Soapmaking	63
Textiles	63
Tobacco Trade	64
Tobacco Pipes	64
Transport	65
General	65
Canals	65
Railways	65
Roads and Road Transport	66
Bridges	67
Ports and Docks	67
Other Industries	70
Ballooning	71

Cornwall

General	72
Agriculture	73
Architecture and Buildings	75
Domestic	75
Industrial	76
Engineering	77
General	77
Engines and Engine Houses	77
Cornish Engineers and Engineering Firms	80
Boulton & Watt	80
Harvey's	81
Holman's	81
Hornblower Family	81
Perran's	81
Trevithick	82
West	84
Woolf	84
Other Engineers and Engineering Firms	84
Explosives	84
Fisheries	85
Gold and Pewter	86
Limeburning	86
Mining	86
China Clay	86
Metals	87

Stone and Slate Quarrying	105
Other Types of Extraction	106
Paper Making	106
Posts and Communications	106
Pottery and Ceramics	106
Printing and Publishing	107
Public Utilities	107
Ship and Boat Building	107
Textiles	108
Transport	108
General	108
Canals and Rivers	108
Railways	109
Roads and Road Transport	111
Ports and Shipping	111
Other Industries	113

Devon

General	115
Agriculture	118
Architecture and Buildings	122
General	122
Domestic	122
Industrial	123
Eddystone Lighthouse	125
Brewing and Cider Making	126
Clock and Watchmaking	126
Engineering	126
General	126
Engines and Engine Houses	127
Newcomen, Savery and their Engines	127
Other Engineers and Engineering Firms	129
Fisheries	130
Gold, Silver and Pewter	130
Gunpowder	131
Mining	131
Arsenic	131
China Clay	131
Granite and Other Stone	132
Metals	132
Coal and Lignite	140
Slate	140
Paper Making	141
Posts and Communications	141

Pottery and Ceramics	141
William Cookworthy	142
Printing and Publishing	143
Public Utilities	144
General	144
Electricity	144
Gas	144
Water	144
Shipbuilding	145
Textiles	147
Transport	148
Canals	148
Railways	149
Roads and Road Transport	152
Bridges	154
Ports, Harbours and Shipping	156
Air Transport	159
Other Industries	159

Dorset

General	161
Agriculture	161
Architecture and Buildings	164
General	164
Domestic	164
Industrial	164
Brewing	165
Brickmaking	166
Building	166
Clock and Watchmaking	166
Engineering	166
Fisheries	166
Limeburning	166
Quarrying	166
Posts and Communications	167
Pottery and Ceramics	167
Rope Making	168
Shipbuilding	169
Textiles	169
Transport	169
Railways	169
Roads and Road Transport	170
Bridges	171
Ports, Docks and Shipping	171

Other Industries	172

Gloucestershire

General	173
Agriculture	175
Ammunition	177
Architecture and Buildings	177
General	177
Domestic	177
Industrial	177
Bell Founding	179
Brewing	179
Clock and Watchmaking	179
Engineering	180
Glass Making	180
Gold	181
Iron and Steel	181
Leather and Footwear	182
Limeburning	183
Match Making	183
Mining and Quarrying	183
Paper Making	184
Pin Making	184
Pottery and Ceramics	185
Posts and Communications	185
Printing and Publishing	185
Public Utilities	185
Ship and Boat Building	186
Textiles	186
Transport	188
General	188
Canals and Rivers	188
Railways	190
Roads and Road Transport	191
Other Industries	192

Somerset

General	194
Agriculture	195
Architecture and Buildings	197
Domestic	197
Industrial	198
Brewing and Cider Making	199
Brickmaking	199

Clock and Watch Making	200
Engineering	200
Footwear and Leather	201
Gunpowder	201
Ironworking	201
Limeburning	202
Mining and Quarrying	202
Paper Making	205
Posts and Communications	205
Pottery and Ceramics	206
Public Utilities	206
Electricity	206
Gas	207
Water	207
Salt	207
Textiles	207
Transport	208
Canals	208
Railways	209
Roads and Road Transport	211
Bridges	211
Piers, Ports, Ships and Shipping	212
Other Industries	213

Wiltshire

General	214
Agriculture	214
Architecture and Buildings	217
Domestic	217
Industrial	218
Building and Civil Engineering	219
Clock and Watchmaking	219
Engineering and Ironmaking	219
Gunmaking	220
Mining and Quarrying	220
Pottery and Ceramics	221
Printing and Publishing	221
Public Utilities	222
Electricity	222
Gas	222
Water	222
Textiles	222
Transport	224
Canals	224

Railways	224
Roads and Road Transport	226
Aviation	227
Other Industries	227

Index of Authors and Personal Names	229
Subject Index	247

Introduction

This is the fifth and final volume of my bibliographical survey of the industrial history and industrial archaeology of England. It was commenced when I was still employed as a librarian at the Open University but had to wait for its completion until my retirement. When I started, the county of Avon was still in existence so that, with the abolition of that county, some restructuring of the bibliography was undertaken, with 'Bristol' being retained as a separate section and all general references to Avon included in it. References relating to particular places other than Bristol formerly in Avon have been placed under Somerset or Gloucestershire as appropriate.

The format of the bibliography follows that of my previous books, primary division being by county and then by industry within each county.

Area covered. The area covered by this bibliography is Bristol and the counties of Cornwall, Devon, Dorset, Gloucestershire, Somerset and Wiltshire, that is, all those counties which have not been included in my previous bibliographies. Where a book or article covers two or more counties, it is usually placed in the 'South Western England' section at the beginning of the work.

Type of material included. The only types of material specifically excluded from this bibliography are government publications and newspaper articles. The only major category of non-published material included is higher degree theses, first degree dissertations being omitted. Other non-published theses and articles have been included where I thought appropriate, but where I have done so I have attempted to give the location where the document may be consulted.

Subject coverage. The definition of industry which I adopted as a guideline for my work is 'Any human activity producing a good or service for sale'. From this definition I have specifically excluded education, the health services, retailing, the financial services, the entertainments industry, and illegal activities such as smuggling.

This project was originally conceived as a bibliography of industrial archaeology. I soon realised that industrial archaeology could not be separated from industrial history as a whole and the scope of the bibliography was widened. Nevertheless the industrial archaeology aspect has been retained and thus what might be termed the 'human side' of industry—industrial relations, industrial accidents, etc.—has not been covered in any depth.

As in all my previous bibliographies I must stress that the foregoing are *guidelines* used in the compilation of this work. I do not believe it possible to adhere rigidly to rules when compiling a book of this kind.

Conclusion. With this volume I conclude the project started many years ago, started because in my work as a librarian I had discovered a large gap in the bibliography of industrial history, especially for those years before the abstracting services were established. I cannot and do not claim that my work has the depth and comprehensiveness of such works as George Ottley's *Bibliography of British Railway History* but my aim was to produce a useful contribution to the bibliography of the economic history of this country and go some way to filling the gap I had discovered. If I have succeeded in that aim, I shall be content.

Acknowledgements. In the preparation of this volume I have visited the public libraries of all the counties listed above and the Science Museum Library on numerous occasions. To the staff of all these libraries I give my thanks for their help. I also thank very warmly the staff of the Open University Library, Milton Keynes, who have given me their usual cheerful help both before and after my retirement. Above all I thank my dear wife Joan, but for whose encouragement this last volume may never have been completed.

Cranfield, Beds. John Greenwood
March 1999

Bibliographies Consulted

In compiling this work, I made use of many sources of information, great and small. Bibliographies which were especially helpful included the following, to the authors of all of which I give grateful acknowledgement.

Bibliography of British history. Tudor period, 1485-1603 (Oxford University Press, 1959)

Bibliography of British history. Stuart period. 1603-1714 (Oxford University Press, 1970)

Bibliography of British history 1789-1851 (Oxford University Press, 1977)

Bibliography of British history 1851-1914 (Oxford University Press, 1976)

R. Burt and P. Waite, *Bibliography of the history of British metal mining* (University of Exeter in association with the Association of Mining History Organisations, 1988)

E.H. Goddard. *Wiltshire bibliography* (Wiltshire Education Committee, 1929)

R.A.M. Green, *A bibliography of printed works relating to Wiltshire 1920-1960* (Trowbridge, Wiltshire County Council, Library and Museum Service, 1975)

P. Hamilton-Leggett, *The Dartmoor bibliography 1534-1991* (Devon Books in association with Dartmoor National Park, 1992)

J. Hibbs, 'The history of the motor bus industry: a bibliographical survey', *J. Transp. Hist.* II 1973–4 41-55

G. Ottley, *A bibliography of British railway history* (2nd ed., HMSO, 1982); *Supplement* (HMSO, 1988)

A.P. Woolrich, 'Notes on the bibliography of industrial Bristol', *BIAS J.* II 1969 30-32

Periodicals Cited

The following periodicals are cited at least once in this bibliography. The list is intended solely as an aid to identifying the full title from the abbreviation. No attempt has been made to trace changes in individual titles.

Acta Mus. Agric.	Acta Museorum Agriculturae
Agric. Hist. Rev.	Agricultural History Review
Agriculture	Agriculture
Amateur Histn.	Amateur Historian
American Neptune	American Neptune
Ann. des Mines	Annales des Mines
Ann. Philosophy	Annals of Philosophy
Ann. Rep. Lundy Soc.	Annual Report of the Lundy Society
Ann. Reps. R. Cornwall Polytech. Soc.	Annual Reports of the Royal Cornwall Poytechnical Society
Ann. Rep. Trans. Plymouth Inst. Devon Cornwall Nat. Hist. Soc.	Annual Report and Transactions of the Plymouth Institute and the Devon and Cornwall Natural History Society
Ann. Sci.	Annals of Science
Antiq. Horol.	Antiquarian Horology
Antiq. J.	Antiquaries Journal
Antiquity	Antiquity
Apollo	Apollo
Archaeologia	Archaeologia
Archaeol. J.	Archaeological Journal
Archaeol. Rev.	Archaeological Review
Archive	Archive
Agriculture	Agriculture
Ark	Ark
Back Track	Back Track
Bath Hist.	Bath History
Belfry Bull.	Belfry Bulletin. Journal of the Bristol Exploration Society
BIAS J.	BIAS Journal (Bristol Industrial Archaeology Society)
Br. Caver	British Caver
Br. Mining	British Mining
Br. Numismatic J.	British Numismatic Journal
Bristol Avon Archaeol.	Bristol and Avon Archaeology
Br. Rlwy. J.	British Railway Journal
Broadsheet	Broadsheet
Builder	The Builder

Bull. Assoc. Ind. Archaeol.	Bulletin of the Association for Industrial Archaeology
Bull. Bus. Hist. Soc.	Bulletin of the Business Historical Society
Bull. Geol. Soc. Gr. Britain	Bulletin of the Geological Society of Great Britain
Bull. Hist. Metall. Gp.	Bulletin of the Historical Metallurgy Group
Bull. Postal Hist. Soc.	Bulletin of the Postal History Society
Bull. Rlwy. Loco. Hist. Soc.	Bulletin of the Railway and Locomotive Historical Society
Bull. Welsh Med. Pott. Res. Gp.	Bulletin of the Welsh Medieval Pottery Research Group
Bus. Archives	Business Archives
Bus. Hist.	Business History
Bus. Hist. Rev.	Business History Review
Camborne School of Mines J.	Camborne School of Mines Journal
Canal & Riverboat	Canal and Riverboat
Cartographic J.	Cartographic Journal
Cave Sci.	Cave Science
Caxtonian	Caxtonian
CBA Group 9 Bull.	CBA Group 9 Bulletin
Cheltenham Loc. Hist. Soc. J.	Cheltenham Local History Society Journal
Chem. & Ind.	Chemistry and Industry
Chem. in Britain	Chemistry in Britain
Cirencester Archaeol. Hist. Soc. Ann. Rep.	Cirencester Archaeological and Historical Society Annual Reports
Connoisseur	Connoisseur
Construction Hist.	Construction History
Cornish Archaeol.	Cornish Archaeology
Country Life	Country Life
Cornish Mag.	Cornish Magazine
Cornish Stud.	Cornish Studies
Dartmoor Mag.	Dartmoor Magazine
Dartmoor Tinworking Res. Gp. Newsl.	Dartmoor Tinworking Research Group Newsletter
Dean Archaeol.	Dean Archaeology
Devon Archaeol.	Devon Archaeology
Devon Cornwall N. & Q.	Devon and Cornwall Notes and Queries
Devon County J.	Devon County Journal
Devon Histn.	Devon Historian
Devon Yrbk.	Devonian Yearbook
Dock Harbour Authority	Dock and Harbour Authority
Dorset County J.	Dorset County Journal
Dorset Yrbk.	Dorset Yearbook
Econ. Geog.	Economic Geography
Econ. Hist. Rev.	Economic History Review

Econ. J.	Economic Journal
Edinburgh J. Sci.	Edinburgh Journal of Science
Edinburgh New Phil.	Edinburgh New Philosophy
Elect. Engr.	Electrical Engineer
Eng. China Clay Rev.	English China Clay Review
Eng. Hist. Rev.	English Historical Review
Engineer	Engineer
Engineering	Engineering
Esso Farmer	Esso Farmer
Exmoor Rev.	Exmoor Review
Flight Int.	Flight International
Folk Life	Folk Life
Foundry Trade J.	Foundry Trade Journal
Furniture Hist.	Furniture History
Galpin Soc. J.	Galpin Society Journal
Geog. J.	Geographical Journal
Geog. Mag.	Geographical Magazine
Geog. Teacher	Geographical Teacher
Geography	Geography
Glass Circle	Glass Circle
Glass Technol.	Glass Technology
Glevensis	Glevensis. The Gloucester and District Archaeological Research Group Annual Review
GSIA J.	GSIA Journal (Gloucestershire Society for Industrial Archaeology)
GSIA Newsl.	GSIA Newsletter
Glos. Comm. Council Loc. Hist. Bull.	Gloucestershire Community Council Local History Bulletin (Title varies slightly)
Glos. Countryside	Gloucestershire Countryside
Glos. Hist.	Gloucestershire History
Glos. Hist. Stud.	Gloucestershire Historical Studies
Hatcher Rev.	Hatcher Review
Hist. Metall.	Historical Metallurgy
Hist. Stud.	History Studies
Hist. Today	History Today
Ind. Archaeol.	Industrial Archaeology
Ind. Archaeol. Rev.	Industrial Archaeology Review
Ind. Heritage	Industrial Heritage
Inst. Br. Geogr. Trans. Pap.	Institute of British Geographers. Transactions and Papers
Int. Stationary Steam Eng. Soc. Bull.	International Stationary Steam Engine Society Bulletin
J. Bath & W. Eng. Soc.	Journal of the Bath & West of England Society

J. Br. Archaeol. Assoc.	Journal of the British Archaeological Association
J. Bristol Somerset Soc. Archit.	Journal of the Bristol and Somerset Society of Architects
J. Ceram. Hist.	Journal of Ceramic History
J. Cerberus Spelaeolog. Soc.	Journal of the Cerberus Spelaeological Society
J. Econ. Hist.	Journal of Economic History
J. Eur. Econ. Hist.	Journal of European Economic History
J. Glass Stud.	Journal of Glass Studies
J. Hist. Farm Bldgs. Gp.	Journal of the Historic Farm Buildings Group
J. Hist. Geog.	Journal of Historical Geography
J. Hist. Metall Soc.	Journal of the Historical Metallurgy Society
J. Ind. Archaeol.	Journal of Industrial Archaeology
J. Interdisc. Econ.	Journal of Interdisciplinary Economics
J. Interdisc. Hist.	Journal of Interdisciplinary History
J. Iron Steel Inst.	Journal of the Iron and Steel Institute
J. Land Agents Soc.	Journal of the Land Agents Society
J. Marine Biol. Assoc.	Journal of the Marine Biology Association
J. Min. Agric.	Journal of the Ministry of Agriculture
J. Pewter Soc.	Journal of the Pewter Society
J. Portsmouth Coll. Tech. Ind. Archaeol. Soc.	Journal of the Portsmouth College of Technology Industrial Archaeology Society
J. Rlwy. Canal Hist. Soc.	Journal of the Railway and Canal Historical Society
J. R. Aeronautical Soc.	Journal of the Royal Aeronautical Society
J. R. Agric. Soc.	Journal of the Royal Agricultural Society
J. R. Instn. Cornwall	Journal of the Royal Institution Cornwall
J. R. Soc. Arts	Journal of the Royal Society of Arts
J. Soc. Archit. Histns.	Journal of the Society of Architectural Historians
J. Soc. Glass Technol. Trans.	Journal of the Society of Glass Technology, Transactions
J. Somerset Mines Res. Gp.	Journal of the Somerset Mines Research Group
J. Statist. Soc. London	Journal of the Statistical Society of London
J. Transp. Hist.	Journal of Transport History
J. Trevithick Soc.	Journal of the Trevithick Society
J. Watford Dist. Ind. Hist. Soc.	Journal of the Watford and District Industrial History Society
Kingston Geogr.	Kingston Geographer
Landscape Hist.	Landscape History
Library	Library
Loc. Pop. Stud.	Local Population Studies
Loc. Hist. Rec.	Local History Record
Local Histn.	Local Historian
Loco. Mag.	Locomotive Magazine

Loco. Mag. Rlwy. Carr. Wagon Rev.	Locomotive Magazine and Railway Carriage and Wagon Review
London & Edinburgh Phil. Mag.	London & Edinburgh Philosophical Magazine
Machine Shop Mag.	Machine Shop Magazine
Mag. Nat. Hist.	Magazine of Natural history
Mar. Mirr.	Mariner's Mirror
Marit. Hist.	Maritime History
Marit. S-W	Maritime South West
Med. Archaeol.	Medieval Archaeology
Mem. N. Cavern Mine Res. Soc.	Memoirs of the Northern Cavern & Mine Research Society
Metallurgia	Metallurgia
Min. Hist.	Mining History: Bulletin PDMHS (Peak District Mines Historical Society)
Min. Mag.	Mining Magazine
Min. Mag. & Rev.	Mining Magazine and Review
Mining Smelting Mag.	Mining and Smelting Magazine
Min. Proc. Instn. Civ. Engrs.	Minutes of the Proceedings of the Institution of Civil Engineers
Mine Quarry	Mine and Quarry
Mine Quarry Engng.	Mine and Quarry Engineering
Min. Wld.	Mining World
N. & Q.	Notes and Queries
Nat. West Q. Rev.	National Westminster Quarterly Review
Notes and Gleanings	Notes and Gleanings
New Civ. Engr.	New Civil Engineer
New Regard	New Regard
Northern Univ. Geog. J.	Northern Universities Geographical Journal
Old Cornwall	Old Cornwall
Panel Hist. Engng. Works Newsl.	Panel for Historical Engineering Works Newsletter
Phil. Mag.	Philosophical Magazine
Phil. Trans. R. Soc.	Philosophical Transactions of the Royal Society
Plymouth Mineral Min. Club J.	Plymouth Mineral and Mining Club Journal
Plymouth Mineral Min. Club Newsl.	Plymouth Mineral and Mining Club Newsletter
Post-Med. Archaeol.	Post-Medieval Archaeology
Pottery Gaz.	Pottery Gazette
Proc. Cotteswold Nat. Field Club	Proceedings of the Cotteswold Naturalists Field Club
Proc. Devon Archaeol. Soc.	Proceedings of the Devon Archaeological Society
Proc. Dorset Field Club	Proceedings of the Dorset Field Club

Proc. Dorset Nat. Hist. Archaeol. Soc. — Proceedings of the Dorset Natural History and Archaeological Society
Proc. Geologists Assoc. — Proceedings of the Geologists Association
Proc. Huguenot Soc. London — Proceedings of the Huguenot Society of London
Proc. Instn. Civ. Engrs — Proceedings of the Institution of Civil Engineers
Proc. Instn. Mech. Engrs. — Proceedings of the Institution of Mechanical Engineers
Proc. Inst. Mining Engrs. — Proceedings of the Institute of Mining Engineers
Proc. Mining Inst. Cornwall — Proceedings of the Mining Institute of Cornwall
Proc. R. Soc. — Proccedings of the Royal Society
Proc. S. Wales Inst. Engrs. — Proceedings of the South Wales Institute of Engineers
Proc. Somerset Archaeol. Nat. Hist. Soc. — Proceedings of the Somerset Archaeology and Natural History Society
Proc. Univ. Bristol Spelaeol. Soc. — Proceedings of the University of Bristol Spelaeological Society
Proc. Ussher Soc. — Proceedings of the Ussher Society
Progress — Progress
Public Admin. — Public Administration

Q. Min. Rev. — Quarterly Mining Review
Q. Rev. — Quarterly Review
Quarry — The Quarry
Quarry Managers J. — Quarry Managers' Journal

Reps. Mines Assoc. Devon Cornwall — Reports of the Mines Association of Devon and Cornwall
Reps. R. Cornwall Polytechnic Soc. — Reports of the Royal Cornwall Polytechnic Society
Reps. Trans. Devons. Assoc. — Reports and Transactions of the Devonshire Association
Rev. Bordeaux et Dépt. Gironde — Revue Historique de Bordeaux et du Département de la Gironde
Rlwy. Gaz. — Railway Gazette
Rlwy. Mag. — Railway Magazine
Rlwy. Loco Hist. Soc. Bull. — Railway and Locomotive Historical Society Bulletin
Rlwy. Wld. — Railway World
Rural Hist. — Rural History

S. Hist. — Southern History
Sands Clays Min. — Sands, Clays and Minerals
Shrops. Min. Club Yrbk. — Shropshire Mining Club Yearbook
SIAS J. — SIAS Journal (Somerset Industrial Archaeoloogy Society)
Somerset Archaeol. Nat. Hist. — Somerset Archaeology and Natural History
Somerset Countryman — Somerset Countryman
Somerset Dorset N. & Q. — Somerset and Dorset Notes and Queries

Somerset Ind. Archaeol. Soc. Bull.	Somerset Industrial Archaeology Society Bulletin
Somerset Mines Res. Gp. J.	Somerset Mines Research Group Journal
Somerset Yrbk.	Somerset Yearbook
Stationary Power	Stationary Power
Syren & Shipping	Syren and Shipping
Tamar. J.	Tamar Journal
Text. Hist.	Textile History
Three Banks Rev.	Three Banks Review
Trans. Bristol Glos. Archaeol. Soc.	Transactions of the Bristol and Gloucestershire Archaeological Society
Trans. Br. Ceram. Soc.	Transactions of the British Ceramic Society
Trans Cornish Inst. Engrs.	Transactions of the Cornish Institute of Engineers
Trans. Cornish Inst. Min. Mech. Metall. Engrs.	Transactions of the Cornish Institute of Mining Mechanical and Metallurgical Engineers
Trans. Eng. Ceram. Circle	Transactions of the English Ceramic Circle
Trans. Essex Archaeol. Soc.	Transactions of Essex Archaeological Society
Trans. Fed. Instn. Min. Engrs.	Transactions of the Federated Institution of Mining Engineers
Trans. Geol. Soc.	Transactions of the Geological Society
Trans. Geol. Survey	Transactions of the Geological Survey
Trans. Instn. Civ. Engrs.	Transactions of the Institution of Civil Engineers
Trans. Instn. Min. Metall.	Transactions of the Institution of Mining and Metallurgy
Trans. Manchester Geol. Soc.	Transactions of the Manchester Geological Society
Trans. Min. Assoc. & Inst. Cornwall	Transactions of the Mining Association and Institute of Cornwall
Trans. N. Cavern Mine Res. Soc.	Transactions of the Northern Cavern and Mine Research Society
Trans. N. Eng. Inst. Min. Engrs.	Transactions of the North of England Institute of Mining Engineers
Trans. Newcomen Society	Transactions of the Newcomen Society
Trans. Plymouth Instn.	Transactions of the Plymouth Institution
Trans. Proc. Torquay Nat. Hist. Soc.	Transactions and Proceedings of the Torquay Natural History Society
Trans. R. Geol. Soc. Cornwall	Transactions of the Royal Geological Society of Cornwall
Trans. R. Hist. Soc.	Transactions of the Royal Historical Society
Trans. R. Instn. Naval Archit.	Transactions of the Royal Institution of Naval Architects
Trans. Soc. Engrs.	Transactions of the Society of Engineers
Trans. Woolhope Nat. Field Club	Transactions of the Woolhope Naturalists Field Club
Trans. Worcester Archaeol. Soc.	Transactions of the Worcestershire Archaeological Society

Transp. Hist.	Transport History
Univ. Birmingham Hist. J.	University of Birmingham Historical Journal
Vernac. Archit.	Vernacular Architecture
Virginia Mag. Hist. & Biog.	Virginia Magazine of History and Biography
Waterways Wld.	Waterways World
Western Power	Western Power
Wheals Mag.	Wheals Magazine
Wilkinson Stud.	Wilkinson Studies
Wills Works Mag.	Wills Works Magazine
Wilts. Archaeol. Nat. Hist. Mag.	Wiltshire Archaeological and Natural History Society Magazine
Wilts. Archaeol. Nat. Hist. Bi-Annual Bull.	Wiltshire Archaeological and Natural History Society Bi-Annual Bulletin
Wilts. Folklife	Wiltshire Folklife
Wilts. Ind. Archaeol.	Wiltshire Industrial Archaeology
Wilts N. & Q.	Wiltshire Notes and Queries
Wool Knowledge	Wool Knowledge
World Archaeol.	World Archaeology
Zeit. Agrargesch. und Agrarsozial.	Zeitschrift von Agrargeschichte und Agrarsoziologie

Other Volumes in this Series

By John Greenwood

The Industrial Archaeology and Industrial History of Northern England: A Bibliography (1985).

The Industrial Archaeology and Industrial History of the English Midlands: A Bibliography (1987).

The Industrial Archaeology and Industrial History of London: A Bibliography (1988).

The Industrial Archaeology and Industrial History of South Eastern England: A Bibliography (1990).

South Western England

GENERAL

1. F. Booker, *Industrial archaeology of the Tamar Valley.* 2nd ed. (Newton Abbot, David & Charles, 1971) 303p.

2. F. Booker, 'The Tamar Valley', *Ind. Archaeol.* IV 1967 1–7

3. C.A. Buchanan and R.A. Buchanan, *The Batsford guide to the industrial archaeology of Southern Central England: Avon County, Gloucestershire, Somerset, Wiltshire.* (Batsford, 1980) 208p.

4. R. Burt, ed., *Industry and society in the South-West.* (Exeter, University, Exeter Papers in Economic History, no. 3, 1970) 110p.

5. N. Cossons, *Industrial monuments in the Mendips, South Cotswold and Bristol region.* (Bristol, City Museum, 1967)

   Bristol Archaeological Research Group, Field guide no. 4

6. H.C. Darby and R.W. Finn, eds., *The Domesday geography of south-west England.* (Cambridge, University Press, 1967) 469p.

7. B. Earl.'A new look at West of England industrial archaeology', *J. Trevithick Soc.* no. 13 1986 17–32

8. S. Fisher and M. Havinden, 'The long-term evolution of the economy of South-West England: from autonomy to dependence', *in* M.A. Havinden *et al.*, eds., *Centre and periphery. Brittany and Cornwall & Devon compared.* (Exeter University Press, 1991) 76–85

9. M. Havinden, 'The Southwest: a case for de-industrialisation', *in* M. Palmer, ed., *The onset of industrialisation: papers presented at a conference on the Teaching of Regional and Local History in Universities and Colleges, held at Nottingham University, Dec. 1976.* (Nottingham University, Dept. of Adult Education, 1976) 5–11

10. K. Hudson, 'Industrial archaeology in the South-West', *Cornish Archaeol.* no. 3 1964 80–3

11. K. Hudson, *Industrial archaeology of Southern England.(Hampshire, Wiltshire, Dorset, Somerset and Gloucestershire east of the Severn)* 2nd ed. (Newton Abbot, David & Charles, 1968) 286p.

12. D. Jones, 'Early industry in the Tamar Valley', *J. Portsmouth Coll. Tech. Ind. Archaeol. Soc.* no. 1 1968 11–15

13. W.E. Minchinton, ed., *Capital formation in South-west England.* (Exeter University, Exeter Papers in Economic History no. 9 1978) 61p.

14. W.E. Minchinton, ed., *Population and marketing: two studies in the history of the South-West.* (Exeter, University, Exeter Papers in Economic History, no. 11, 1976) 139p.

15. R.A. Otter, *Civil engineering heritage: Southern England.* (Thomas Telford, 1994) 294p.

    The area covered includes Cornwall, Devon, Somerset, South Wiltshire and Dorset

16. *Pigot and Co.'s National Commercial Directory of Cornwall, Dorsetshire,*

Devonshire, Somersetshire, Wiltshire. (Michael Winton, 1993) 181p. Facsimile of 1830 ed.

17 J. Potter, *External investment and the manufacturing economy of Devon and Cornwall.* (Ph.D. thesis, Cambridge University, 1992)

18 A.H. Shorter, W.L.D. Ravenhill and K.J. Gregory, *Southwest England.* (London, Nelson, 1969) 340p.

19 W.J. Sivewright, ed., *Civil engineering heritage. Wales and Western England.* (Thomas Telford, 1986) 230p.

20 D.J. Spooner, *Industrial development in Devon and Cornwall, 1939–67.* (Ph.D. thesis, Cambridge University, 1972)

21 Westward Television, *This is our land ... tracing the economic history of the South West of England, with programme material prepared and presented by ... academic staff of the University of Exeter, produced by Adrian Brown.* (1968) 28p.

22 A.P. Woolrich, 'Swedish travellers', *BIAS J.* IV 1971 28–31

Lists the names and activities of various Swedes who visited the South-West in the 18th century

AGRICULTURE

23 G.F. Baker, 'The potato crop failures in the south-west of England, 1845–47', *Devon Cornwall N. & Q.* XXX Part IV 1965–7 97–102

24 J. Benson, 'Medieval vine culture in Devon and Cornwall', *Devon Cornwall N. & Q.* XXI no. 6 1941 281–2

25 J.H. Bettey, 'Livestock trade in the West Country in the seventeenth century', *Somerset Archaeol. Nat. Hist.* CXXVII 1983 123–8

26 G.G.S. Bowie, 'Northern wolds and Wessex downlands: contrasts in sheep husbandry and farming practice, 1770–1850', *Agric. Hist. Rev.* XXXVIII 1990 117–26

The downlands of Southern Wiltshire, East Dorset, Berkshire and Hampshire

27 R.F.T. Chiplin, *The rural landscape of the Blackmore Vale, c. 1840.* (M.A. thesis, Exeter University, 1969)

28 B. Cole, 'Threshing days in the Tamar Valley', *Tamar J.* no. 2 1979–80 42–6

29 W.D. Conybeare, *The Western Agriculturalist, edited by G.P.R. Pulman.* (1846)
Copy in the Devon and Exeter Institution, Exeter

30 A.K. Copus, *Changing markets and the response of agriculture in South West England 1750–1900.* (Ph.D. thesis, University of Wales, Aberystwyth, 1987)

31 Sir H.T. De La Beche, 'On the connection between geology and agriculture in Cornwall, Devon and West Somerset', *J. R. Agric. Soc.* III 1842 21–36

32 T.R.B. Dicks, *The South-Western peninsular of England and Wales: studies in agricultural geography, 1550–1900.* (Ph.D thesis, University of Wales, Aberystwyth, 1964)

33 D. Evans, 'Replanting the cherries and apples of the Tamar Valley', *Tamar J.* no. 17 1995 4–10

34 J.J.A. Fox, 'Outfield cultivation in Devon and Cornwall: a reinterpretation', *in* M. Havinden, *ed., Husbandry and marketing in the South-West, 1500–1800.* (Exeter, University, Exeter Papers in Economic History, 8, 1973) 19–38

35 H.S.A. Fox, 'Peasant farmers, patterns of settlement and *pays*: transformations in the landscapes of Devon and Cornwall during the later Middle Ages', *in* R. Higham, *ed., Landscape and townscape in the South West.* (Exeter, University, Exeter Studies in History no. 22, 1989) 41–73

36 H. Fox, *A study of the field systems of Devon and Cornwall.* (Ph.D thesis, Cambridge University, 1971)

37 G.E. Fussell, '"High farming' in South-western England 1840–80', *Econ. Geog.* XXIV no. 1 1948 53–73

38 G.E. Fussell, 'A western counties farmer in 1700', *J. Min. Agric.* XXXIX 1933 123–9, 641–49

Edward Lisle

39 R. Gallup, 'Vine growing and wine making in the Tamar Valley', *Tamar J.* no. 9 1987 8–14

40 A. Gilg, 'The changing structure of agriculture in Cornwall and Devon, 1958–1986: concentration via peripheralisation', *in* M.A. Havinden, J. Queniart and J. Stanyer, *eds., Centre and periphery: Brittany and Cornwall & Devon compared.* (Exeter, University Press, 1991) 153–63

41 T. Gray ed., *'Harvest failure in Cornwall and Devon'. The Book of Orders and the Corn Surveys of 1623 and 1630–31.* (Exeter University, Institute of Cornish Studies, Sources of Cornish History vol. 1, 1992) 117p.

42 J.B. Harley and E.A. Stuart, 'George Withiel: a West Country surveyor of the late seventeenth century'. *Devon Cornwall N. & Q.* XXXV no. 2 1982 45–8; no. 3 1983 95–114

43 G.V. Harrison, 'The South-West: Dorset, Somerset, Devon and Cornwall', in J. Thirsk, *ed., The agrarian history of England and Wales v. 1 1640–1750: Regional farming systems.* (Cambridge, University Press, 1984) 358–89

44 N. Harvey, 'Edmund Rack and the Bath and West', *J. Land Agents Soc.* XLVII no. 11 1948 284–5

45 M.A. Havinden, *ed., Husbandry and marketing in the South-West, 1500–1800.* (Exeter, University, Exeter Papers in Economic History, no. 8, 1973) 74p.

46 M.A. Havinden and C.M. King, *eds., The south-west and the land.* (Exeter, University, Exeter Papers in Economic History, no. 2, 1969)

47 N. Hicks, *Farming in the West Country.* (David Rendel, 1968) 117p.

48 K. Hudson, *The Bath and West: a bicentenary history.* (Bradford-on-Avon, Moonraker Press, 1976) 251p.

49 K. Hudson, 'The membership of the Bath and West Society during its first 200 years', *Acta Mus. Agric.* XII nos. 1 & 2 1977 50–6

50 G. Jarrett, 'The Devon & Cornwall longwool', *Esso Farmer* XXIX 1977 no. 1 26–31

51 A. Jewell, 'Some cultivation techniques in the South-West of England', *in* W.E. Minchinton eds., *Agricultural improvement: medieval and modern.* (Exeter University, Exeter Papers in Economic History no. 14 1981) 95–111

52 S.G. Kendall, *Farming memoirs of a West Country yeoman*. (London, Faber, 1944) 247p.

Life in Somerset and Wiltshire in the second half of the nineteenth century.

53 A. Langsford, 'The flower growing industry in the Tamar Valley', *Tamar J.* no. 18 1996 10–12

54 R. Lennard, 'Domesday plough-teams: the south-western evidence', *Eng. Hist. Rev.* LX no. 237 1945 217–33

55 W. Marshall, *The rural economy of the West of England including Devonshire and parts of Somersetshire, Dorsetshire and Cornwall*. 2v. (London, 1796)

Reprinted by David & Charles, Newton Abbot, 1970

56 W.E. Minchinton, *ed., Agricultural improvement: medieval and modern.* (Exeter University, Exeter Papers in Economic History no. 14, 1981) 137p.

57 W.E. Minchinton, *ed., Farming and transport in the South-West.* (Exeter, University, Exeter Papers in Economic History, no. 5, 1972) 69p.

58 C.S. Orwin and R.J. Sellick, *The reclamation of Exmoor Forest.* (Newton Abbot, David & Charles, 1970) 312p.

First published in 1929 as *The land reclamation and farming systems on Exmoor*

59 R.R. Pymm, 'Memories of fruit growing in the Tamar Valley', *Tamar J.* no. 8 1986 29–34

60 R.R. Rawson, 'The open fields in Flintshire, Devonshire and Cornwall', *Econ. Hist. Rev.* 2nd ser. VI no. 1 1953 51–4

61 O.J. Reichel, 'Hulham Manor: a sketch historical and economical', *Reps. Trans. Devons. Assoc.* XXVII 1895 404–36

62 F. Rose-Troup, 'Medieval vine culture in Devon and Cornwall', *Devon Cornwall N. & Q.* XXI no. 4 1940 177–80

63 F. Rose-Troup, 'Open field system terms', *Devon Cornwall N. & Q.* XXI no. 4 1940 174–6

Discusses no. 61 and queries some of the author's statements

64 A.H. Shorter, 'Ridge and furrow in Devon and Cornwall', *Devon Cornwall N. & Q.* XXIV 1950 3–6

65 R.G.F. Stanes, *ed.*, 'A georgicall account of Devonshire and Cornwalle in answer to some queries concerning agriculture, by Samuel Colepresse, 1667', *Rep Trans. Devons Assoc.* XCVI 1964 269–301

66 R. Stanes, *The Old Farm: a history of farming life in the West Country.* (Exeter, Devon Books, 1990) 174p.

67 M. Thompson, 'A history of the West Country breeds of sheep', *Ark* XI no. 4 1984 118–21

68 S.A.H. Wilmot, *Landownership, farm structure and agrarian change in south-west England, 1800–1900: regional experience and national ideals.* (Ph.D. thesis, Exeter University, 1988)

ARCHITECTURE AND BUILDINGS
General
69 N.J.G. Pounds, 'Buildings, building stones and building accounts in south-west England', in D. Parsons, *ed., Stone quarrying and building in England A.D. 43–1525.* (Chicester, Phillimore in association with the Royal Archaeological Institute, 1990) 228–37

Domestic
70 W. Minchinton, 'Industrial housing in the West Country', *S. Hist.* VIII 1986 94–111

Industrial
For engine houses see under Engineering—General
See also no. 121

71 H.L. Douch, 'Windmills in Cornwall and Devon', *Devon Cornwall N. & Q.* XXXI 1968 56–59

72 W. Minchinton and J. Perkins, *Tidemills of Devon and Cornwall.* (Exeter University, Exeter Papers in Industrial Archaeology, 1972) 30p.
Also published in *Devon Cornwall N. & Q.* XXXI no. 8 1970 246–50 and *Devon Cornwall N. & Q.* XXXII no. 1 1971 1–7

73 A.H. Shorter, 'A classification of old mills in Devon and Cornwall', *Devon Cornwall N. & Q.* XXIII 1949 277–80

74 J.D.U. Ward, 'Tithe barns of the south-west', *Agriculture* LXV no. 4 1958 195–8

75 J.F. Wellington, 'Water power in West Country mining', *Tamar J.* no. 7 1985 5–13

76 E.H.D. Williams, 'Curing chambers and corn kilns in South-West England', *Somerset Archaeol. Nat. Hist.* CXXXIV 1990 233–42

ENGINEERING
General
77 K. Brown, 'Engine houses in South-West Britain', *Min. Hist.* XIII no. 2 1996 123–9

78 Bristol and West of England Engineering Manufacturers Association, *Golden jubilee; the first fifty years.* (The Association, 1986)

79 W.R.M. Caff, *The history of the development of the steam engine to the year 1850, with special reference to the work of west-country engineers.* (M.Sc. thesis, London University (External), 1937)

80 K.H. Rogers, *The Newcomen engine in the West of England.* (Bradford-on-Avon, Moonraker Press, 1976) 63p.

81 B. de Soyres, 'The birth and growth of engineering in the West Country', *Proc. Instn. Mech. Engrs.* CXXXIX 1938 539–45

The Brunels

For all references to I.K. Brunel, see the author index. For his engineering achievements, see the subject index and contents list. For the Rotherhithe Tunnel and the Great Eastern, *consult the London volume in this series.*

82 R. Beamish, *Memoir of the life of Sir Marc Isambard Brunel.* 2nd ed. (London, Longmans, 1862) 359p.

83 D. Beckett, *Brunel's Britain.* (Newton Abbot, David & Charles, 1980) 256p.

84 I.K. Brunel, *The life of Isambard Kingdom Brunel, civil engineer. 1st edition, reprinted with an introduction by L.T.C. Rolt.* (Newton Abbot, David & Charles, 1971)

His autobiography, originally published 1870.

85 A. Buchanan, S.K. Jones and K. Kiss, 'Brunel and the Crystal Palace', *Ind. Archaeol. Rev.* XVII no. 1 1994 7–21

86 R.A. Buchanan, 'The overseas projects of I.K. Brunel', *Trans. Newcomen Soc.* LIV 1982–3 145–66

87 A. Buck, *The little giant: a life of I.K.Brunel.* (Newton Abbot, David & Charles, 1986) 320p.

88 S.E. Buckley, *Isambard Kingdom Brunel.* (London, Harrap, 1949) 64p.

89 J.M. Campbell, 'Some new Brunel letters', *J. Transp. Hist.* III 1957–8 201–4

90 P. Clements, *Marc Isambard Brunel.* (London, Longmans, 1970) 270p.

91 J. Falconer, *What's left of Brunel.* (Shepperton, Dial House, 1994) 160p.

92 D. Fowler, 'Character insight', *New Civ. Engr.* no. 889 29 Mar. 1990 42–5

Article on I.K. Brunel's personal papers, acquired by Bristol University.

93 W. Frohling, 'The treatise 'On Draught' in William Youatt's book The Horse: an anonymous publication of Isambard Kingdom Brunel', *Trans. Newcomen Soc.* LVIII 1986–7 141–51

94 E. Garnett, *The master engineers.* (London, Hodder & Stoughton, 1954) 223p.

Biographies of Sir Marc Brunel and his son I.K. Brunel

95 P. Hay, *Brunel, his achievements in the transport revolution.* (Reading, Osprey Publishing, 1973) 134p.

96 P. Hay, *Brunel: engineering giant.* (London, Batsford, 1985) 134p.

97 'Isambard Kingdom Brunel', *Proc. R. Soc.* X 1860 vii–xi

Obituary notice

98 Lady C. Gladwyn, 'The Isambard Brunels', *Proc. Instn. Civ. Engrs.* L 1971 1–14

99 D. Jenkins and H. Jenkins, *Isambard Kingdom Brunel, engineer extraordinary.* (Hove, Priory Press, 1977) 96p.

100 R. Jenkins, 'Letters of Marc Isambard Brunel, annotated by Rhys Jenkins', *Trans. Newcomen Soc.* V 1924–5 91–6

101 L.W. Meynell, *Builder and dreamer: a life of Isambard Kingdom Brunel.* (London, Bodley Head, 1952) 192p.

102 W.E. Minchinton, 'I.K. Brunel, engineer, 1859', *Hist. Today* XXIX 1979 824–31

103 Lady C.B. Noble, *The Brunels, father and son.* (London, Cobden-Sanderson, 1938) 279p.

104 R. Powell, *Photography and the making of history: Brunel's kingdom.* (Watershed Publications, 1985) 80p.

105 J. Pudney, *Brunel and his world.* (London, Thames & Hudson, 1974) 128p.

106 Sir A Pugsley, ed., *The works of Isambard Kingdom Brunel: an engineering appreciation.* (London, Institution of Civil Engineers, and University of Bristol, 1976) 222p.

Contents: R.A. Buchanan, I.K. Brunel: engineer; Sir H. Harding, Tunnels; Sir A. Pugsley, Clifton Suspension Bridge; O.S. Nock, Railways; J.B.B. Owen, Arch bridges; L.G. Booth, Timber works; J.B. Caldwell, The three great ships; Sir H. Shirley-Smith, Royal Albert Bridge, Saltash; T.M. Charlton, Theoretical work

107 'Relics of Sir Marc Isambard Brunel and Henry Maudsley', *Engineering* CLVII 1944 347–8

108 L.T.C. Rolt, *Isambard Kingdom Brunel: a biography.* (London, Longmans, 1957) 345p.

Reprinted by Penguin, 1980

109 R.J. Salter, *The great engineer: the story of Isambard Kingdom Brunel.* (London, Lutterworth Press, 1963) 94p.

110 R.R. Sellman, *Isambard Kingdom Brunel.* (London, Methuen Educational, 1971) 31p.

111 S. Smiles, 'The Brunels', *Q. Review* CXII 1862 1–39

112 R. Tames, *Isambard Kingdom Brunel, 1806–1859: an illustrated life of Isambard Kingdom Brunel.* (Aylesbury, Shire Publications, 1972) 48p.

113 A. Vaughan, *Isambard Kingdom Brunel: engineering knight-errant.* (London, Murray, 1991) 301p.

FISHERIES

114 H. Fox, 'Observations in further illustration of the history and statistics on the pilchard fishery', *Ann. Reps. R. Cornwall Polytech. Soc.* Rep. 46 1878 73–119

115 K. Matthews, *The West Country–Newfoundland fisheries (chiefly in the seventeenth and eighteenth centuries).* (D.Phil. thesis, Oxford University, 1969)

116 J. Rule, 'The home market and the sea fisheries of Devon and Cornwall in the nineteenth century', *in* W.E. Minchinton, ed., *Population and marketing: two studies in the history of the south-west.* (Exeter, University, Exeter Papers in Economic History, no. 11, 1976) 123–39

117 A. Southward, G. Boalch and L. Maddock, 'The herring and pilchard fisheries in Devon and Cornwall', *in* D.J. Starkey *ed., Devon's coastline and coastal waters: aspects of man's relationship with the sea.* (Exeter University, Exeter Maritime Studies no. 3, 1988)

118 W.B. Stephens, 'The West Country ports and the struggle for the Newfoundland fisheries in the 17th century', *Reps. Trans. Devons. Assoc.* LXXXVIII 1956 90–101

119 J.N. Taylor, 'Elver fishing on the River Severn', *Folk Life* III 1965 55–60

GLASSMAKING
120 F. Buckley, 'West-country glasshouses', *J. Soc. Glass Technol.* XIII 1929 124–9

IRON AND STEEL
121 M. Bodman, 'A gazetter of ironfounders with waterwheels surviving in the West Country', *Somerset Ind. Archaeol. Soc. Bull.* nos. 74–5 1997 3–11, 10–15

122 T. Daff, 'Charcoal-fired blast furnaces: construction and operation', *BIAS J.* VI 1973 4–12

123 D. Matthew and G. Matthew, 'Iron furnaces in South-Western England', *Eng. Hist. Rev.* XLVIII 1933 91–6

LEATHER AND FOOTWEAR
124 P.R. Mounfield, 'The footwear industry in the South-West of England: 1850 to 1950', *BIAS J.* no. 28 1995 3–14

125 A.H. Shorter, 'The tanning industry in Devon and Cornwall 1550–1850', *Devon Cornwall N. & Q.* XXV no. 1 1952 10–16

'– Additional notes', XXV no. 1 80–1, 109

LIMEBURNING
126 D. Evans, 'The techniques of limeburning', *Devon Cornwall N. & Q.* XXXVI 1987 34–5

127 W.E. Minchinton, *A limekiln miscellany: the South-west and South Wales.* (Exeter Industrial Archaeology Group, 1984) 28p.

128 E. Taylor, 'Three regional styles of limekiln', *BIAS J.* XXI 1989 19–22

MINING
General
129 B. Atkinson, *Mining sites in Cornwall and south-west Devon.* (Dyllansow Truran, 1988) 86p.

130 R. Burt, P. Waite, and R. Burnley, *Devon and Somerset mines, metalliferous and associated minerals 1845–1913.* (Exeter, University, Dept. of Economic History, in association the Northern Mines Research Society, 1984) 136p.

131 Sir R.P. Collier, *A treatise on the laws relating to mines chiefly as to the peculiar mining customs of Devon and Cornwall.* (1849)

132 J.H. Collins, *Handbook to the mineralogy of Cornwall and Devon.* 2nd ed.

(Truro, Heard & Sons, 1892)

Reprinted by Bradford Barton, Truro, 1969

133 J.H. Collins, 'A list of minerals found in Cornwall and Devon, with notes supplementary to the author's 'Handbook'', *J.R. Inst. Cornwall* XVIII 1911 425–61

134 J.H. Collins, *Observations on the West of England mining region. Being an account of the mineral deposits and economic geology of the region.* (Redruth, Cornish Mining Classics, 1988) 683p.

Reprint of the 1912 edition. Originally v. 14 of *Trans. R. Geol. Soc. Cornwall*

135 J.H. Collins, 'The mining districts of Cornwall and West Devon', *Proc. Inst. Mining Engrs* I 1873 39–118

136 *Devon and Cornwall handbook of mines with map and chart, compiled by Westlake and Laws (stock and share brokers).* (Plymouth, *Western Morning News*, 1910) 40p.

137 C. Nicholas, 'Developments in economic geology in South West England: a review of the 1970s', *Proc. Ussher Soc.* V no. 1 1980 4–6

138 T. Spargo, *The mines of Cornwall & Devon: statistics and observations.* 2nd ed. (London, 1868)

Copy in Exeter Reference Library

139 J. Taylor, 'On the economy of the mines of Cornwall and Devon', *Trans. Geol. Soc.* XII 1814 309–27

Reprinted in R. Burt, ed., *Cornish mining: essays on the organisation of Cornish mines and the Cornish mining economy.* (Newton Abbot, David & Charles, 1969) 15–29

140 C. Thomas, *Mining fields of the West: being a practical exposition of the principal mines and mining districts in Cornwall and Devon* (Truro, Bradford Barton, 1967) 100p.

Reprint of 1871 edition.

141 C. Thomas, 'Remarks on mining in Cornwall and Devon', *Ann. Reps. R. Cornwall Polytech. Soc.* Rep. 22 1854 28–35

142 R. Tredinnick, *A review of Cornish and Devon mining enterprise, 1850 to 1856 inclusive.* (London, Thompson & Vincent, 1857) 158p.

143 J. Wellington, 'Water power in West Country mining', *Tamar J.* no. 7 1985 5–13

144 R.N. Worth, 'Historical notes concerning the progress of mining skill in Devon and Cornwall', *Ann. Reps. R. Cornwall Polytech. Soc.* Rep. 40 1872 63–122

145 H.R. Young, 'Surface water and mining in the West Country', *Min. Mag.* LXX no. 6 1944 329–38

Arsenic

146 O.A. Baker, 'Notes on the Tamar Valley arsenic industry', *Plymouth Mineral Min. Club Newsl.* II no. 2 1971 12–13

147 R. Burt, 'Arsenic—its significance for the survival of South Western metal mining in the late nineteenth and early twentieth centuries', *J. Trevithick Soc.* no. 15 1988 5–25

148 R. Burt and M. Timbrell, 'Diversification as a response to decline in the mining industry: arsenic and South-Western metal production 1850–1914', *J. Interdiscip. Econ.* II 1987 31–54

149 R. Burt and M. Timbrell, 'Multiple products and the economics of the mining industries; the case of arsenic production in south-west England, 1850–1914', *J. Eur. Econ. Hist.* XX 1991 379–406

150 B. Earl, 'Arsenic winning and refining methods in the West of England', *J. Trevithick Soc.* no. 10 1983 9–29

151 R.W. Toll, 'Arsenic in West Devon and East Cornwall', *Min. Mag.* LXXXIX no. 2 1953 83–8

China Clay

See also no. 321

152 C.M. Bristow and C.S. Exley, 'Historical and geological aspects of the china clay industry of South-West England', *Trans. R. Geol. Soc. Cornwall* XXI pt. 6 1994 247–314

153 J.M. Coon, 'The china clay industry', *Ann. Reps. R. Cornwall Polytech Soc.* n.s. VI pt. 1 1927 56–68

154 J.M. Coon, 'Development of mechanical appliances on china clay works', *Ann. Reps. R. Cornwall Polytech Soc.* n.s. III pt. 2 1916 100–12

155 J.M. Coon, 'Granite and china clay', *Ann. Reps. R. Cornwall Polytech Soc.* n.s. VI pt. 3 1929 282–300

156 E.H. Davison, 'China-clay industry of Western England', *Pottery Gaz.* LIII 1928 1622

157 E.H. Davison, 'The geology and economics of the china clay deposits of the West of England', *Trans. R. Geol. Soc. Cornwall* XVI no. 3 1930 113–16

158 J.A. Hocking, 'The china clay trade of the United Kingdom', *Northern Univ. Geog. J.* I 1960 20–8

159 K. Hudson, *The history of the English China-Clays: fifty years of pioneering and growth.* (Newton Abbot, David & Charles, 1969) 189p.

160 N.J.G. Pounds, 'The china clay industry of southwest England', *Econ. Geog.* XXVIII 1952 20–30

161 A.D. Selleck, *The china clay of Devon and Cornwall.* (1948)
Typescript. Copy in Plymouth Central Library.

162 C. Thurlow, *China clay from Cornwall and Devon: an illustrated account of the modern china clay industry.* 2nd ed. (St Austell, Cornish Hillside Publications, 1997) 46p.

163 R.N. Worth, 'The clays and fictile manufactures of Cornwall and Devon', *Ann. Reps. R. Cornwall Polytech. Soc.* Rep. 55 1887 51–68

Coal

164 J. Anstie, *The coal fields of Gloucestershire and Somersetshire and their resources.* (London, 1873)
Reprinted by Kingsmead Bookshop, Bath, 1969

165 W. Buckland and W.D. Conybeare, 'Observations of the South-western coal district of England', *Trans. Geol. Survey* 2nd ser. I no. 2 1824 210–316

166 J.F. Davis, *The Forest of Dean and Bristol-Somerset coalfields—A comparative study in industrial geography during the nineteenth and twentieth centuries.* (Ph.D thesis, London University, 1959)

167 W. Fairley, *Glossary of terms used in the coal mining districts of (first) South Wales; (second) Bristol and Somerset.* (1868)

168 L.R. Moore and A.E. Trueman, 'The Bristol and Somerset coalfields, with particular reference to proposals for future development', *Proc S. Wales. Inst. Engrs.* LVII 1941 160–247, 303–5

Copper and Tin

See also nos. 129–45

169 'An accompt of some mineral observations touching the mines of Devon and Cornwall; wherein is described the art of trayning a load; the art of digging the ore; and the way of dressing and of blowing tin: communicated by an inquisitive person, that was much conversant in those mines', *Phil. Trans. R. Soc.* VI 1671 2096–113

170 R.L. Atkinson, *Tin and tin mining.* (Princes Risborough, Shire Books, 1985)

171 O.A. Baker, *Ore mining in the Tamar Valley.* (1961–2)

Typescript. Copy in Plymouth Central Library

172 W.G. Baker, 'Stannary parliament', *Plymouth Mineral Mining Club J.* VII no. 2 1976 3–5

173 D.B. Barton, *A historical survey of the mines and mineral railways of east Cornwall and west Devon.* (Truro, Truro Bookshop, 1964) 102p.

174 D.B. Barton, *A history of copper mining in Cornwall and Devon.* 3rd ed. (Truro, Barton, 1978)

175 R.H. Bird, 'Notes on subterranean temperatures in metal mines', *Br. Mining* no. 3 1976 16–20

176 J. Brooke, 'Stannary tales', *Br. Mining* no. 8 1978 16–21

177 J. Brooke, *Stannary tales, the shady side of mining.* (Truro, Twelveheads Press, 1980) 92p.

178 R. Burt, 'The mineral statistics of the United Kingdom: an analysis of the accuracy of the copper and tin returns for Devon and Cornwall', *J. Trevithick Soc.* no. 8 1981 31–46

179 R. Chadwick, 'Trading in ores 1600–1900', *Tamar J.* no. 5 1983 18–29

180 J.H. Collins, *Principles of metal mining.* (Sheffield, Mining Facsimiles, 1985) 149p.

Reprint of 1875 ed.

181 J.H. Collins, 'Seven centuries of tin production in the West of England', *Trans. Min. Assoc & Inst. Cornwall* III 1892 173–93

182 J.H. Collins, 'Tin and tungsten in the West of England', *Mining Mag.* XIII 1915 207–10

The same title appears in *Ann. Reps. R. Cornwall Polytech. Soc.* n.s. III pt. 2

1916 89–99

183 H.G. Dines, *The metalliferous mining region of South West England*. 2v. 2nd ed. (London, HMSO, 1969)

184 B. Earl, "Melting tin' in the West of England: a study of an old art', *Hist. Metall.* XIX no. 2 1985 153–61; 'Part 2', XX no. 1 1986 17–32

An account of the experimental smelting of tin.

185 *General rules and orders for regulating the practice, fees and costs on appeals to the Lord Warden of the Stannaries from the Court of the Vice-Warden, with an appendix, referring to the statutes under which the rules and orders are made.* (1870)

186 S. Gerrard, 'The early south-western tin industry: an archaeological view', *Mining Hist.* XIII no. 2 1996 67–83

187 J.A. Goodridge, *The historical geography of the copper mining industry in Devon and Cornwall from 1800 to 1900*. (Ph.D. London University (External), 1967)

188 T. Greeves, 'The good life?—the West Country tinner AD c. 1500–c. 1700', *J. Trevithick Soc.* no. 20 1993 39–47

189 J. Hatcher, *English tin production and trade before 1500*. (Oxford, Clarendon Press, 1973) 219p.

190 G. Henwood, *The metalliferous deposits of Devon and Cornwall*. (Penzance, Pope Vilbert, 1843) 512p.

Forms v. 5 of the *Trans. R. Geol. Soc. Cornwall*, 1843

191 R. Jenkins, 'Copper smelting in England: revival at the end of the seventeenth century', *Trans. Newcomen Soc.* XXIV 1943–45 73–80

192 G.R. Lewis, *The stannaries: a study of the medieval tin miners of Cornwall and Devon* (Truro, Barton, 1966) 299p.

Originally published by Houghton Mifflin, Boston, MA, 1906 as Harvard Economic Studies v. 3

193 P. Newman, *ed.*, 'The archaeology of mining and metallurgy in South West-Britain', *Min. Hist.* XIII no. 2 1996

Special issue of the journal.

194 *The old lawes and statutes of the Stannarie made in the yeare 1574.*

Microfilm, Early English Books 1475–1640, Reel 1234.

195 A. Patrick, 'Copper production in the Tamar Valley in the eighteenth century', *Tamar J.* no. 5 1983 35–42

196 T. Pearce, *The laws and customs of the Stannaries in ... Devon and Cornwall; revised and corrected according to the ancient and modern practice.* (1725)

Copy in West Country Studies Library, Exeter

197 R.R. Pennington, *Stannary law: a history of the mining law of Devon and Cornwall.* (Newton Abbot, David & Charles, 1973) 229p.

198 J.R. Pike, *Britain's metal mines: a complete guide to their laws, usage, localities and statistics.* 6th ed. (Sheffield, Mining Facsimiles, 1987) 66p.

Facsimile of 1871 ed.

199 G.A. Rowe, The mines of Tamarside', *Tamar J.* no. 6 1984 37–47

200 C. Salter, 'Seventeenth century tin-mining techniques', *Plymouth Mineral Min. Club J.* X no. 2 1979 11–12; 'Part 2', XI no. 1 1980 7–8; 'Part 3', XII no. 1 1981 11–12, 14

201 C.J. Schmitz, 'Capital formation and technological change in South West England metal mining in the nineteenth century', *in* W.E. Minchinton, ed., *Capital formation in South West England.* (Exeter, University, Papers in Economic History, no. 9 1978)

202 R. Smith, 'An analysis of the processes for smelting tin', *Min. Hist.* XIII no. 2 1996 91–99

203 P.H. Stanier, 'The copper ore trade of south west England in the nineteenth century', *J. Transp. Hist.* V 1979 18–35

204 J.H. Trounson, 'Metal mining in the West of England', *Bull Hist. Metall. Group* IV no. 1 1970 2–3

205 R.F. Tylecote, E. Photos and B. Earl, 'The composition of tin slags from the south west of England', *World Archaeol.* XX no. 3 1989 434–50

Granite

206 G.F. Harris, *Granites and our granite industries.* (London, Crosby Lockwood, 1888) 142p.

207 C.J. Harvey, 'Tamar quarries', *Tamar J.* no. 3 1980–81 17–19

208 P.H. Stanier, *The granite industry of south-west England, 1800–1980: a study in historical geography.* (Ph.D. thesis, Southampton University, 1985)

209 P. Stanier, 'Granite quarry cranes of Cornwall and Devon: vanishing industrial archaeology', *J. Trevithick Soc.* no. 19 1992 18–31

210 P. Stanier, 'The granite quarrying industry in Devon and Cornwall. Part One 1800–1910', *Ind. Archaeol. Rev.* VII 1985 171–189; 'Part Two 1910–85', IX no. 1 1986 7–23

Iron, Lead, Silver, Zinc and other types of Mining

211 M. Atkinson, *Iron ore mining in mainland Britain in the nineteenth and early twentieth centuries and its links with the iron and steel industry, with particular reference to Cleveland, Cumbria and the south western counties of England.* (Ph.D. thesis, Exeter University, 1981)

212 R. Burt and I. Wilkie, 'Manganese mining in the South-West of England', *J. Trevithick Soc.* no. 11 1984 18–40

213 J.H. Collins, 'Notes on the principal lead-bearing lodes of the West of England', *Trans. R. Geol. Soc. Cornwall* XXI 1904 683–718

214 J.H. Collins, 'The precious metals in the West of England', *J. R. Inst. Cornwall* XVI 1903 103–19

215 H. Dewey, *Lead, silver-lead and zinc ores of Cornwall, Devon and Somerset.* (London, 1921) 72p.

216 N. Dickinson, 'Uranium and radium in South West England', *Plymouth Mineral Mining Club J.* XI no. 2 1980 4–8

217 R. Rumbold, 'Radioactive minerals in Cornwall and Devon', *Min. Mag.* XCI no. 1 1954 16–27

218 P.G.L. Vipan, 'Lead and zinc mining in South-West England', *in The future of non-ferrous mining in Great Britain and Ireland.* (London, Institution of Mining and Metallurgy, 1959) 337–53

PAPERMAKING

219 A.H. Shorter, 'Paper making in Devon and Cornwall', *Geography* XXIII 1938 164–76

220 A.H. Shorter, 'Papermaking in S.W. England', *in 7th International Congress of Paper Historians, Trinity College, Oxford, Sept. 1967.* (Oxford, Simmons, 1967) 131–2

221 A.H. Shorter, 'Papermills in Devon and Cornwall', *Devon Cornwall N. & Q.* XXIII no. 4 1947 97–103

'– further evidence', XXIII no. 7 1948 193–8

222 W.B. Stephens, 'The origin of the paper-making industry in the South-West of England', *Devon & Cornwall N. & Q.* XXVII 1956 no. 3 6–7

POSTS AND COMMUNICATIONS

223 M. Brayshaw, 'Royal post-horse routes in South-West England in the reign of Elizabeth I and James I', *Reps. Trans. Devons. Assoc.* CXXIII 1991 79–103

224 D.B. Cornelius, *Devon and Cornwall, a postal survey, 1500–1791.* (Reigate, Postal History Society, 1973) 65p.

225 A.W. Robertson, 'The 'Ship letter' ports of Lyme Bay', *Bull. Postal Hist. Soc.* no. 101 1959 49–52; no. 102 1959 59–62; no. 103 1959 73–7

POTTERY AND CERAMICS

226 J.P. Allan and P. Pope, 'A new class of south-west English pottery in North America', *Post-Med. Archaeol.* XXIV 1990 51–9

227 C.J. Arnold, 'The clay tobacco-pipe industry: an economic study', *in* D.P.S. Peacock, *ed., Pottery and early commerce: characterization and trade in Roman and later ceramics.* (London, Academic Press, 1977) 313–36

This study is confined to the South-West.

PUBLIC UTILITIES
Electricity

228 CEGB South West Region, *Power in the South West and South Wales.* (Bristol, The Board, 1981) 32p.

229 P. Lamb, 'Early days of electricity in the South-West', *BIAS J.* XVI 1983 15–19

230 South Western Electricity Board, *The first five years, 1948–1953.* (The Board,

1953)

231 S.F. Steward, *Twenty-five years of South-Western Electricity: a short history of a state industry.* (South-Western Electricity Board, 1973) 44p.

Gas

232 H. Nabb, *A history of the gas industry in south-west England before 1949.* (Ph.D. thesis, Bath University, 1986)

Water

233 F. Booker and J. Mildren, *The great drought in the South West: the inside story.* (Exeter University, Dept. of Economic History, and Exeter Ind. Archaeol. Group, Occ. Pap. no. 1) 115p.

SHIPBUILDING

234 V.C. Boyle, 'West Country shipyard practice in the days of wooden ships', *Mar. Mirr.* XLV 1959 227–33

235 R.S. Craig, 'British shipping and British North American shipbuilding in the early nineteenth century, with special reference to Prince Edward's Island', in H.E.S. Fisher, ed., *The South West and the sea: papers of a seminar on the maritime history of the South West of England.* (Exeter, The University, Exeter Papers in Economic History, no. 1, 1968) 21–43

236 S. Jones, 'Merchant shipbuilding in the North East and South West of England, 1870–1913', in S. Fisher *ed., British shipping and seaman, 1630–1960: some studies.* (Exeter University, Exeter Papers in Economic History, no. 16, 1984)

237 R.T. Paige, *The Tamar Valley at work: James Goss—a century of shipbuilding and life in the Tamar Valley.* (Tavistock, Dartington Amenity Research Trust, 1978) 80p.

238 D. Starkey, 'Shipbuilding in the South West during the Napoleonic War', *Marit. S-W* no. 6 1993 5–15

239 D.J. Starkey, 'The shipbuilding industry of Southwest England, 1790–1913', in S. Ville, *ed., Shipbuilding in the United Kingdom in the nineteenth century: a regional approach.* (St John's, Newfoundland, International Maritime Economic History Association, Research in Maritime History no. 4, 1993) 75–110

TEXTILES

240 J. Anstie, *A letter to the Secretary of the Bath Agricultural Society on the subject of a premium for the improvement of British wool.* (1791)

241 J. Anstie, *Observations on the importance and necessity of introducing improved machinery into the woollen manufactory; more especially as it affects the counties of Wilts., Gloucester and Somerset.* (1803)

242 A.B. Archer, 'The history and development of the West of England cloth trade', *Proc. Cotteswold Nat. Field Club* XXXV 1966 28–33

243 A.B. Archer, 'Wool and its importance in the social and economic development in Britain', *Proc. Cotteswold Nat. Field Club* XXXVI 1971–2 66–9

244 K.E. Barford, 'The West of England cloth industry: a seventeenth-century experiment in state control', *Wilts. Archaeol. Nat. Hist. Mag.* XLII 1922–4 531–42

245 R.P. Beckinsale, 'Factors in the development of the Cotswold woollen industry', *Geog. J.* XC no. 4 1937 349–62

246 I. Ellis, *A historical geography of the Cotswold woollen industry in the nineteenth and early twentieth centuries*. (M.A. thesis, University of Wales, 1946)

247 W.G. Hoskins, *The rise and decline of the serge industry in the south-west of England, with special reference to the eighteenth century*. (M.Sc. thesis, London University (External), 1929)

248 R.H. Kinvig, 'The historical geography of the West Country woollen industry', *Geog. Teacher* VIII 1916 243–54, 290–306

Reprinted separately. Copy in Wiltshire Local History Library, Trowbridge.

249 J. de L. Mann, *The cloth industry in the West of England from 1640 to 1880*. (Oxford, Clarendon Press, 1971) 371p.

Republished by Alan Sutton, 1987

250 J. de L. Mann, 'The later history of the West of England woollen trade', *Proc. Cotteswold Nat. Field Club* XXXV 1968 pt. 2 103–6

251 J.R. Morris, *The West of England woollen industry, 1750–1840*. (M.Sc. thesis, London University, 1934)

252 W. Partridge, *A practical treatise on dying of woollen, cotton and skein silk, with the manufacture of broadcloth and cassimere including the most improved methods in the West of England*. (London, London School of Economics, Pasold Research Fund, 1989) 263p.

First published 1823

253 K.G. Ponting, *A history of the West of England cloth industry*. (London, Macdonald, 1957) 168p.

254 K.G. Ponting, '19th-century textile invention in the West of England', *BIAS J.* XV 1982 32–6

255 K.G. Ponting, *The special characteristics of the West Country woollen industry*. (International Wool Secretariat, Wool Education Society Lectures, 1956) 20p.

256 K.G. Ponting, 'The structure of the Somerset–Wiltshire border woollen industry 1816–40', *in* N.B. Harte and K.G. Ponting eds., *Textile history and economic history; essays in honour of Miss Julia de Lacy Mann*. (Manchester, University Press, 1973) 163–95

257 K.G. Ponting, 'The West of England cloth industry', *in* J.G. Jenkins, ed., *The wool textile industry in Great Britain*. (Routledge, 1972)

258 K.G. Ponting, 'The west of England cloth trade', *Wool Knowledge* II no. 8 1952 5–7, 21–3; no. 9 1953 15–18

259 K. Ponting, *The woollen industry of South-West England*. (Bath, Adams & Dart, 1971) 214p.

260 A.J. Randall, *Labour and the Industrial Revolution in the West of England*

woollen industry. (Ph.D. thesis, Birmingham University, 1979)

261   K.H. Rogers, *Warp and weft: the Somerset and Wiltshire woollen industry.* (Buckingham, Barracuda, 1986) 144p.

262   K.H. Rogers, *Wiltshire and Somerset woollen mills.* (Edington, Pasold Research Fund, 1976) 265p.

263   C.D. Ross, *The influence of the West Country wool trade on the social and economic history of England.* (International Wool Secretariat, Wool Education Society Lectures, 1955) 16p.

264   J. Stephan, 'Wool gathering: the Cistercians and the woollen industry', *Ann. Reps. Trans. Plymouth Inst. & Devon Cornwall Nat. Hist. Soc.* XXI 1947–49 124–30

265   J. Tann, 'The employment of power in the West of England wool textile industry, 1790–1840', *in* N.B. Harte and K.G. Ponting, eds., *Textile history and economic history; essays in honour of Miss Julia de Lacy Mann.* (Manchester, University Press, 1973) 196–224

266   L.F.J. Walronde, 'Wool, woolmen and weavers', *in* C. Hadfield and A.M. Hadfield, eds., *The Cotswolds: a new study.* (Newton Abbot, David & Charles, 1973) 178–203

267   *Woollen Trade and Manufactures of Wiltshire, Gloucester and Sommerset: Printed Particulars of the state and mode of working these mills.* (1803)

TRANSPORT
General

268   D. Viner, comp., *Transport in the Cotswolds: from old photographs.* (Nelson, Hendon Publishing, 1980) 40p.

Canals and Rivers

269   V. Bowyer, *Along the canal: the Kennet and Avon from Bath to Bradford-on-Avon.* (Bath, Ashgrove, 1985) 62p.

270   A. Burton, *The Kennet and Avon Canal.* 3rd ed. (Devizes, Kennet & Avon Canal Trust, 1990) 44p.

271   R. Clammer and A. Kittridge, *Passenger steamers of the River Dart and Kingsbridge estuary.* (Chatham Paddle Steamer Preservation Society in association with Twelveheads Press, 1987) 72p.

272   K.R. Clew, *The Dorset and Somerset Canal: an illustrated history.* (Newton Abbot, David & Charles, 1971) 116p.

273   K.R. Clew, *The Kennet & Avon Canal: an illustrated history.* 3rd ed. (Newton Abbot, David & Charles, 1985) 224p.

274   K. Clew, 'No cause for celebration', *Waterwys. Wld.* XIV no. 11 1985 38–46
      Canals owned by the GWR

275   H. Conway-Jones, *Working life on Severn & canal: reminiscences of working boatmen.* (Gloucester, Alan Sutton, 1990) 184p.

276   M. Corfield, 'John Ward and the Kennet and Avon Canal', *BIAS J.* XIV 1981

28–35; 'Part 2', XV 1982 20–8

277 J.G. Espley and W.E.D. Young, *The Thames and Severn Canal.* (Gazebo Books, 1969)

278 A.H. Faulkner, *Severn Canal and Cadbury's.* (Rothwell, Robert Wilson, 1981) 48p.

279 J. Green, 'Description of the perpendicular lifts for passing boats from one level of canal to another, as erected on the Grand Western Canal', *Trans. Instn. Civ. Engrs.* II 1838 185–91

280 E.C.R. Hadfield, 'Canals between the English and the Bristol Channels', *Econ. Hist. Rev.* XII 1942 59–67

281 C. Hadfield, *The canals of South West England.* 2nd ed. (Newton Abbot, David & Charles, 1985) 206p.

282 C. Hadfield, 'James Green as canal engineer', *J. Transport Hist.* I no. 1 1953 44–56

Green was active throughout the South-West, especially on the Grand Western Canal.

283 H. Harris and M. Ellis, *The Bude Canal.* (Newton Abbot, David & Charles, 1972) 192p.

284 H. Harris, *The Grand Western Canal.* Rev. ed. (Tiverton, Devon Books, 1996)) 222p.

285 H. Household, *The Thames & Severn Canal.* 2nd ed. (Newton Abbot, David & Charles, 1983) 258p.

286 H. Household, 'The Thames and Severn Canal', *J. Transp. Hist.* VII no. 3 1966 129–40

287 H.G.W. Household, 'Early engineering on the Thames and Severn Canal', *Trans. Newcomen Soc.* XXVII 1949–51 43–50

288 A. Kittridge, *Passenger steamers on the River Tamar.* (Twelveheads Press, 1984) 98p.

289 L.H. Merrett, 'The Grand Western Canal—an expensive gamble', *Transp. Hist.* VIII 1977 99–105

290 J. Rendell.'The Bude Canal and its relation to the Tamar', *Tamar J.* no. 8 1986 21–6

291 J.M. Richardson, *An authentic description of the Kennet & Avon Canal and observations upon the present state of the inland navigation of the South-Western counties of England.* (Kennet & Avon Canal Trust, 1969) 30p.

Originally published 1811

292 A. Richardson, 'Water supplies to the Kennet & Avon Canal (with especial reference to its eventual reopening)', *J. Rlwy. Canal Hist. Soc.* XXVIII 1984–6 155–60

293 J. Russell, *The Kennet & Avon Canal: a journey from Newbury to Bath in 1964.* (Millstream Books, 1997) 136p.

A photographic record

294 D.J. Viner, *The Thames and Severn Canal: a survey from historical photographs.* (Nelson, Hendon Publishing, 1975) 45p.

295 T.S. Willan, 'The river navigation and trade of the Severn Valley 1600–1750',

Econ. Hist. Rev. VIII 1937 no. 1 68–79

296　W.E.D. Young, *The Thames and Severn Canal*. (Gazebo Press, 1968–9)

Railways
General and Western Region since 1948

297　G.F. Allen, *The Western since 1948*. (London, Ian Allan, 1979) 160p.

298　M. Arlett, *Southern steam in the South and West*. (Oxford Publishing Co., 1992) 159p.

299　P. Armstrong, *Western Region allocations: all steam and diesel locomotives allocated to the Western Region*. (1953)

　　Copy in Exeter Central Library

300　S. Austin, *Atlantic Coast express*. (London, Ian Allan, 1989) 112p.

301　G. Body, *The Severn Tunnel: an official history of the building and operation of Britain's longest main line railway tunnel*. (British Rail (Western) and Avon-Anglia, 1986)

302　G. Body, *Western handbook: a digest of GWR and WR data*. (Weston-super-Mare, British Rail (Western Region), and Avon-Anglia, 1985) 64p.

　　v. 2 of two volumes published to mark the sesqui-centenary of the GWR

303　D. Brooke, 'The other costs of railway building—a note on navvy casualties in South-Western England', *J. Rlwy. Canal Hist. Soc.* XXIX pt. 8 July 1989 393–7

304　R. Christiansen, *Thames and Severn*. (Newton Abbot, David & Charles, Regional Histories of Railways of Great Britain, vol. 13 1982) 205p.

305　R. Cowles, *The making of the Severn railway tunnel*. (Gloucester, Sutton, 1989)

306　M. Dart, *The last days of steam in Plymouth and Cornwall*. (Alan Sutton, 1990) 144p.

307　L. Endacott, *Steam in the West*. (Newton Abbot, David & Charles, 1974) 96p.

　　Chiefly illustrations

308　M. Esau, *Steam into Wessex*. new ed. (London, Ian Allan, 1991) 105p.

309　T. Fairclough and E. Shepherd, *Mineral railways of the West Country*. (Truro, Barton, 1975) 96p.

310　H. George, *Roaming the Western rails*. (London, Ian Allan, 1980) 25p.

311　R. Handford Worth, *Early Western railroads: an 1888 description of nine railway locations in S.W. England*. (Weston-super-Mare, Avon-Anglia, 1982) 16p.

312　C.F. Klapper, *Sir Herbert Walker's Southern Railway*. (London, Ian Allan, 1973) 295p.

313　C.G. Maggs, *Railways of the Cotswolds*. (Cheltenham, Peter Nicholson, 1981) 96p.

314　L. Popplewell, *A gazetteer of the railway contractors and engineers of the West Country, 1830–1914*. (Ferndown, Melledgen Press, 1983) 44p.

315 L. Popplewell, *A gazetteer of the railway contractors and engineers of central Southern England 1840–1914.* (Ferndown, Melledgen Press, 1982) 41p.

316 R.C. Riley, *Railway history in pictures: the West Country.* (Newton Abbot, David & Charles, 1972) 112p.

317 K. Robertson, *Somerset and Avon railways in old photographs* (Stroud, Alan Sutton, 1990) 143p.

318 S. Rocksborough-Smith, *Main lines to the West.* (London, Ian Allan, 1981) 127p.

319 G. Shelton, 'George Carr Glyn and the railways', *Three Banks Rev.* no. 46 1960 42–3

320 D. St J. Thomas, *A regional history of the railways of Great Britain. v. 1 The West Country.* 6th ed. (Newton Abbot, David & Charles, 1988) 313p.

321 J.A.M. Vaughan, *An illustrated history of West Country china clay trains.* (Poole, Haynes, 1987) 112p.

Avon & Gloucester Railway

322 C.R. Clinker, 'The Avon and Gloucestershire Railway', *BIAS J.* XIV 1981 22–4

Bath & Weymouth Railway

323 C.G. Maggs, *The Bath to Weymouth line including Westbury to Salisbury.* (Trowbridge, Oakwood Press, 1982) 74p.

Bristol & Exeter Railway

324 G. Measom, *The official illustrated guide to the Bristol and Exeter, North and South Devon, Cornwall, and South Wales Railways.* 2nd ed. 1861 280p.
Reprinted by the Oxford Illustrated Press, 1973

325 H. Rake, 'The Bristol and Exeter Railway', *Rlwy. Mag.* X 1902 144–52

Bristol & Gloucester Railway

326 C.G. Maggs, *The Bristol and Gloucester Railway and the Avon and Gloucestershire Railway.* (Lingfield, Oakwood Press, 1989) 66p.

Bristol & South Wales Union Railway

327 D.S. Barrie, 'The Bristol & South Wales Union Railway', *Rlwy. Mag.* LXXIX 1936 423–7

328 J. Norris, *The Bristol and South Wales Union Railway.* (Railway and Canal Historical Society, 1985) 30p.

Great Western Railway

For the GWR in a specific county see under that county
See also nos. 510–11

329 C.J. Allen, *Salute to the Great Western.* (London, Ian Allan, 1970) 64p.

Chiefly illustrations

330 C. Awdry, *Brunel's broad gauge railway: commemorating the centenary of the GWR's gauge conversion.* (Sparkford, Oxford Publishing, 1992) 144p.

331 G.F. Bannister, *Great Western steam off the beaten track.* (Truro, Barton, 1975) 96p.

332 C. Barman, *The Great Western Railway's last look forward.* (Newton Abbot, David & Charles, 1972) 113p.

First Published as *Next station—London* (London, Allen & Unwin, 1947)

333 G. Beale, 'The 'standard' buildings of William Clarke *Br. Rlwy. J.* I 1983–5 266–76; II 1986 41–2

Clarke was engineer of several railways subsequently absorbed into the GWR

334 R.J. Blenkinsop, *Shadows of the Great Western.* (Oxford, Oxford Publishing Co., 1972) 96p.

Chiefly illustrations

335 F. Booker, *The Great Western Railway: a new history.* (Newton Abbot, David & Charles, 1977) 206p.

336 J.C. Bourne, *[The history and description of the Great Western Railway.] Bourne's Great Western Railway: a reproduction of the history and description of the Great Western Railway—from drawings taken expressly for this work and executed in lithograph* (Newton Abbot, David & Charles, 1969)

Originally published in 1846

337 D. Breckon, *Don Breckon's Great Western Railway.* (Newton Abbot, David & Charles, *c.* 1986) 80p.

338 D. Brock, *Small coal and smoke rings: a fireman on the Great Western.* (London, Murray, 1983) 149p.

339 D. Brooke, 'The equity suit of McIntosh v. the Great Western Railway. The 'Jarndyce' of railway litigation', *J. Transp. Hist.* 3rd ser. XVII no. 2 Sept. 1996 133–49.

340 'Brunel's broad-gauge', *Loco. Mag.* XLVIII no. 598 1942 104–6

341 T. Bryan, *The golden age of the Great Western Railway, 1895–1914.* (Sparkford, Stephens, 1991)

342 R. Carpenter, *An Edwardian album of Great Western passenger classes.* (Upper Bucklebury, Wild Swan, *c.* 1983) 56p.

Chiefly illustrations.

343 G. Channon, 'The Great Western Railway under the British Railways Act of 1921', *Bus. Hist. Rev.* LV 1981 188–216

344 G. Channon, 'The recruitment of directors to the board of the Great Western Railway, I', *J. Transp. Hist.* 3rd ser. XVII no. 1 Mar. 1996 1–19

345 R.H. Clark, *An historical survey of selected Great Western stations: layouts and illustrations.* (Poole, Oxford Publishing, 1976–81) 3v.

v. 4 by C.R. Potts. (*c.* 1985) 224p.

346 J.V.S. Cocks, 'The Great Western Railway and the development of Devon and Cornwall', *Devon Cornwall N. & Q.* XXXVI 1987 9–20

347 B.K. Cooper, *Great Western Railway handbook.* (London, Ian Allan, 1986)

112p.

348 L. Day, *Broad Gauge: an account of the origins and development of the Great Western broad gauge system with a glance at broad gauges in other lands.* (London, HMSO, 1985) 44p.

349 S. Day-Lewis, *Bulleid: last giant of steam.* 2nd ed. (London, Allen & Unwin, 1977)

350 M. Esau, *Spirit of the Great Western.* (Oxford Publishing Co., 1981)

351 T. Fairclough and A. Wills, eds., *Great Western steam through the years.* (Truro, Barton, 1976 & 1978) 2v.

Chiefly illustrations

352 M. Fenton, 'The Brimscombe bankers', *Br. Rlwy. J.* Special GWR edition 1985 64–83

Banking locomotives on the Sapperton Incline

353 D. Fraser, D. Green and B. Scott, *The Great Western Railway in the 1930s.* (Southampton, Kingfisher, 1985) 92p.

Photographs from the collection of G.H. Soole.

354 J. Gardner, *Castles to warships: on the Great Western footplate.* (London, Murray, 1986) 224p.

355 G.H. Gasson, *Nostalgic days: further reminiscences of a Great Western fireman.* (Oxford Publishing Co., 1980)

356 G.H. Gibbs, *The birth of the Great Western Railway: extracts from the diary and correspondence of George Henry Gibbs, edited by Jack Simmons.* (Bath, Adams & Dart, 1971) 96p.

357 J.C. Gibson, *Great Western locomotive design: a critical appreciation.* (Newton Abbot, David & Charles, 1984) 157p.

358 D. Gooch, *Memoirs & diary, transcribed ... and edited by R.B. Wilson.* (Newton Abbot, David & Charles, 1972) 386p.

359 P. Grafton, *Men of the Great Western.* (London, Allen & Unwin, 1979) 94p.

360 'G.W.R. Bristol and Exeter, locomotoves and rolling stock' *Engineer* 16 Dec. 1910 24p. supplement

361 *GWR engines: names, numbers, types and classes: a reprint of the engine books of 1911, 1928 and 1946, with some pages from that of 1938.* (Newton Abbot, David & Charles, 1971) 220p.

362 *Great Western Progress 1935–1935.* (*The Times*, 1935) 180p.

Reprinted from the Great Western Railway centenary number of *The Times.* Reprinted by David & Charles, 1972

363 *Great Western Railway illustrated guide. Introduction by Geoffrey Kitchenside.* (Newton Abbot, Devon Books, 1985) 32p.

Reprint of extracts from a guide book published by Morton & Co. in 1870s.

364 *Great Western timetable of 1885* (1886)

Reprinted by Oxford Publishing Co., 1971

365 'Great Western Railway. Special Centenary Number', *Rlwy. Gaz.* 30 Aug. 1935 52p.

366 D. Griffith, *Locomotive engineers of the GWR.* (Wellingborough, Stephens,

1987)

367 R. Griffiths, *GWR sheds in camera.* (Sparkford, Haynes, 1987) 158p.
Chiefly illustrations

368 M. Hale, *Twixt London and Bristol.* (Poole, Oxford Publishing, 1985) 100p.
The GWR.

369 B. Haresnape, *Great Western Railway, 1923–47.* (London, Ian Allan, 1983) 56p.

370 M. Harris, *Great Western coaches from 1890.* 3rd ed. (Newton Abbot, David & Charles, 1985) 160p.

371 E.G.F. Haswell, *Great Western shed diagrams.* (London, Ian Allan, 1969) 100p.

372 C. Hawkins, *An illustrated history of Great Western Railway engine sheds.* (Upper Bucklebury, Wild Swan, c. 1987) 378p.

373 H. Holcroft, *The Armstrongs of the Great Western: their times, surroundings and contemporaries.* (*Railway World*, 1953) 140p.

374 H. Holcroft, *An outline of Great Western locomotive practice 1837–1947.* (Hampton Court, Locomotive Publishing, 1957) 168p.

375 B. Hollingsworth, *Great Western adventure.* (Newton Abbot, David & Charles, c. 1981) 174p.

376 J.G. Hosegood, *Great Western Railway travelling post offices.* (Upper Bucklebury, Wild Swan, 1983) 76p.

377 J. Hubbard, *No steam without a fire: memories of life on the footplate at Wolverhampton, Kidderminster and Newton Abbot.* (Wolverhampton, Uralia Press, 1978) 108p.
The autobiography of John Hubbard, railwayman with the GWR.

378 P. Karau, ed., *Great Western branch line termini.* (Poole, Oxford Publishing Co., 1985) 123, 128p.
Originally published in two volumes 1977–8

379 R. Kennedy, *Steam on the Great Western: Severn and Cotswolds.* (London, Ian Allan, 1993) 144p.

380 A.R. Kingdom, *The Great Western at the turn of the century.* (Oxford, Oxford Publishing Co., 1976) 112p.

381 I. Krause, *Great Western branch line album.* (Shepperton, Ian Allan, 1969) 112p.
Chiefly illustrations

382 C. Leigh, *GWR country stations.* (London, Ian Allan, 1981) 128p.

383 C. Leigh, *GWR country stations, 2.* (London, Ian Allan, 1984) 112p.

384 C. Leigh, *Rail routes in Devon and Cornwall.* (London, Ian Allan, 1982) 112p.

385 C. Leigh, *The Western before Beeching.* (London, Ian Allan, 1990) 111p.

386 N. Lockett, *Great Western steam in the West Country.* (Haynes, 1990) 120p.

387 E.T. Lyons, *An historical survey of Great Western Railway engine sheds, 1837–1947.* (Oxford Publishing Co., 1979) 216p.

388 E.T. MacDermot, *History of the Great Western Railway.* 2v. in 3 (1927–31)

v. 1 1833–1863 (480p.)

v. 2 1863–1921 (362p.)

v. 3 1923–47, by O.S. Nock (Ian Allan, 1967) 268p.

Vols. 1 and 2 revised by C.R. Clinker and republished in 1964 by Ian Allan.

389 N. MacDonald, *The Western Way.* (Transport Publications, 1983) 176p.

390 C.G. Maggs, *Principal stations.* (London, Ian Allan, 1987) 144p.

Studies the most important stations built by the Great Western Railway.

391 A.H. Malan, *Broad Gauge finale. Compiled from photographs and notes by the Rev. A.H. Malan.* (Upper Bucklebury, Wild Swan, 1985) 70p.

392 G. Measom, *Official illustrated guide to the Great Western Railway.* (Newbury, Berkshire County Library, and Countryside, 1985) 64p.

Facsimile of 1860 ed.

393 G. Measom, *The official illustrated guide to the Great Westen Railway ... [and, The official illustrated guide to the Bristol and Exeter, North and South Devon, Cornwall and South Wales Railways].* (Oxford, Oxford Illustrated Press, 1973) various pagination

Facsimile of 1861 ed., published by Griffin, Bohn and Co.

394 *Mogg's Great Western Railway and Windsor, Bath and Bristol Guide: accompanied by a large ... map of the line; etc.* (1841) 48p.

395 K. Montague, *GWR Great Western.* (Headington, Oxford Publishing Co., 1976) 64p.

396 J. Mosse, 'The *Firefly* locomotive of 1839', *Trans. Newcomen Soc.* LXII 1990–1 97–112

397 J. Mosse, 'The *Firefly* project', *BIAS J.* XVII 1984 32–5

A project to build and run a replica of the *Firefly*.

398 O.S. Nock, *Engine 6000: the saga of a locomotive.* (Newton Abbot, David & Charles, 1972) 108p.

399 O.S. Nock, *Fifty years of Western express running.* (Bristol, Everard, 1954) 353p.

400 O.S. Nock, *The Great Western Railway: an appreciation.* (Cambridge, Heffer, 1951) 185p.

401 O.S. Nock, *The Great Western Railway in the 19th century* (London, Ian Allan, 1962) 200p.

402 O.S. Nock, *The Great Western Railway in the 20th century.* (London, Ian Allan, 1964) 208p.

403 O.S. Nock, ed., *The GWR Stars, Castles & Kings.* (Newton Abbot, David & Charles, 1980) 304p.

404 O.S. Nock, *G.W.R. steam.* (Newton Abbot, David & Charles, 1972) 239p.

405 O.S. Nock, *The locomotives of R.E.L. Maunsell, 1911–37.* (Bristol, Everard, 1954) 192p.

406 O.S. Nock, *Tales of the Great Western Railway: informal recollections of a near-lifetime's association with the line.* (Newton Abbot, David & Charles, 1984) 176p.

407 J. Norris *and others, Edwardian enterprise: a review of the Great Western*

Railway in the first decade of this century: a series of essays by John Norris, Gerry Beale and John Lewis. (Didcot, Wild Swan, 1987) 202p.

408 H. Parris, 'Sir Daniel Gooch: a biographical sketch', *J. Transp. Hist.* n.s. III 1976 203–16

409 G. Perry, ed., *The book of the Great Western.* (London, Times Newspapers, 1970) 94p.

Chiefly illustrations

410 A. Platt, *The life and times of Daniel Gooch.* (Alan Sutton, 1987) 218p.

411 F.J.C. Pole, *Felix Pole—His Book.* (London, Town & Country Press, 1968) 233p.

Pole was general manager of the GWR

412 C.R. Potts, *An historical survey of selected Great Western stations: layout and illustrations. v. 4* (Poole, Oxford Publishing Co., 1985) 224p.

413 Railway Correspondence and Travel Society, *The locomotives of the Great Western Railway. Parts 1–14.* (1951–74)

414 *A railway traveller's reasons for adopting uniformity of gauge, addressed to I.K. Brunel, Esq.* (London, Joseph Cundall) 24p.

415 P. Rees, *C.R.M. Talbot and the Great Western Railway.* (Swansea, West Glamorgan County Council, 1985) 4p.

416 P. Rees, *The Royal Road: 150 years of enterprise.* (Weston-super-Mare, British Rail (Western Region) and Avon Anglia, 1985) 68p.

417 K. Robertson, *150 Great Western years.* (Southampton, Kingfisher, 1985) 56p.

Lavishly illustrated.

418 K. Robertson and D. Abbott, *GWR: the Badminton line: a portrait of a railway.* (Gloucester, Sutton, 1988) 233p.

419 T.W.E. Roche, *More Great Westernry.* (Bracknell, Town & Country Planning, 1969) 91p.

420 T.W.E. Roche, *Plymouth and Launceston—description of a branchline.* 2nd ed. (Teddington, Branch Line Handbooks, 1965) 32p.

421 J.W.P. Rowledge, *G.W.R. locomotive allocations: first and last sheds, 1922–67.* (Newton Abbot, David & Charles, 1986)

422 J.H. Russell, *Great Western miscellany.* (Oxford, Oxford Publishing Co., 1978–9) 2v.

423 J.H. Russell, comp., *Great Western wagon plans: taken from official plans and scale drawings.* (Oxford, University Press, 1976) 137p.

424 J.H. Russell, *Great Western wagons appendix.* (Oxford, Oxford Publishing Co., 1974) 193p.

425 J.H. Russell, *An illustrated history of Great Western diesel railcars.* (Upper Bucklebury, Wild Swan, 1985) 148p.

Supplement by P. Karau and J. Copsley. (1985) 24p.

426 J.H. Russell, *A pictorial record of Great Western coaches. Part 1, 1838–1913.* (Oxford Publishing Co. 1972) 240p.

Part 2 1903–1948. (1973) 273p.

427 J.H. Russell, *A pictorial record of Great Western engines.* (Oxford Publishing

Co., 1975) 2v.

Chiefly illustrations

428 J.H. Russell, *A pictorial history of Great Western wagons.* (Oxford Publishing Co., 1971) 138p.

Chiefly illustrations

429 W.J. Scott, *The great Great Western.* (Wakefield, E.P. Publishing, 1972) 88p.

Facsimile of 1903 ed.

430 G.A. Sekon, *pseud.*, *A history of the Great Western Railway, being the story of the broad gauge.* (London, Digby, Long, 1895)

Republished by Sutton, Gloucester, 1988

431 P.W.B. Semmens, *A history of the Great Western Railway.* (London, Allen & Unwin)

v. 1 *Consolidation, 1923–29* (1985) 102p.

v. 2 *The Thirties, 1930–39* (1985) 96p.

v. 3 *Wartime and the final years, 1939–48.* (1985) 102p.

432 M. Sharman, *The broad gauge of the Great Western Railway, the Bristol & Exeter Railway and the North and South Devon Railways: a selection of 7mm. locomotive drawings.* (Oxford, Oakwood Press, 1985) 4p. + 84 diagrams

Reprinted from *The Locomotive Engineer*

433 J. Simmons, 'South Western v. Great Western: railway competition in Devon and Cornwall', *J. Transp. Hist.* IV no. 1 1959–60 13–36

434 Sir W. Stanier, *George Jackson Churchward, chief mechanical engineer, Great Western Railway: the man and his work.* (1955)

Typescript. Copy in Exeter Central Library.

435 Sir W. Stanier, 'George Jackson Churchward, chief mechanical engineer, Great Western Railway', *Trans. Newcomen Soc.* XXX 1955–7 1–12

436 A.K. Steele, *Great Western broad gauge album.* (Oxford, Oxford Publishing Co., 1972) 80p.

Chiefly illustrations

437 B. Stephenson, *Great Western steam at its zenith.* (London, Ian Allan, 1985) 80p.

An album of photographs 1892–1939.

438 D. St J. Thomas and P. Whitehouse, *The great days of the GWR.* (Nairn, David St John Thomas, 1991) 224p.

439 D. St J. Thomas, *The great way west: the history and romance of the Great Western Railway's route from Paddington to Penzance.* (Newton Abbot, David & Charles, 1975) 96p.

440 Tamar Bridge Joint Committee, *Tamar Bridge.* (1962) 32p.

Copy in West Country Studies Library, Exeter

441 R.E. Toop, *Great Western; steam south of the Severn.* (Truro, Barton, 1973) 95p.

442 P.Q. Treloar, *The Earle Marsh album.* (Birstol, BIAS, Firefly Project. *c.* 1984)

Reproduction of photographs collected by Douglas Earle Marsh in the 1890s of early GWR locomotives.

443 W.A. Tuplin, *Great Western power.* (London, Allen & Unwin, 1975)
444 W.A. Tuplin, *Great Western saints and sinners.* (London, Allen & Unwin, 1971)
445 W.A. Tuplin, *Great Western steam.* (London, Allen & Unwin, 1958) 193p.
446 A. Vaughan, *Great Western portrait, 1913–1921.* (1971)
Chiefly illustrations
447 A. Vaughan, *The Great Western at work, 1921–1939.* (Sparkford, Stephens, 1993) 192p.
448 A. Vaughan, *Grime & glory: tales of the Great Western 1892–1947.* (Gloucester, Sutton, 1987) 192p.
449 A. Vaughan, *Grub, water and relief: tales of the Great Western 1835–1892.* (London, John Murray, 1985) 178p.
450 A. Vaughan, *GWR junction stations.* (London, Ian Allan, 1988) 112p.
451 A. Vaughan, *The heart of the Great Western.* (Peterborough, Silver Link, 1994) 224p.
452 A. Vaughan, *A pictorial record of Great Western signalling.* (Poole, Oxford Publishing Co., 1984) 156p.
453 A. Vaughan, *A pictorial record of Great Western architecture.* (Sparkford, Oxford Publishing Co., 1991) 442p.
454 A. Vaughan, *Signalman's morning.* (London, John Murray, 1981) 177p.
455 A. Vaughan, *Western diesels in camera.* (Shepperton, Ian Allen, 1977)
456 A. Vaughan, *Western Region diesel pictorial.* (Railway Pictorial Pub. Co., 1980) 48p.
457 T.A. Walker, *The Severn Tunnel, its construction and difficulties, 1872–1887.* 3rd ed. (Bath, Kingsmead Bookshop, 1969) 240p.
Reprint of 1891 ed.
458 P. Whitehouse and D.St J. Thomas, eds., *The Great Western Railway: 150 glorious years.* (Newton Abbot, David & Charles, 1984) 208p.
459 J. Whiteley and G. Morrison, eds., *The Great Western remembered.* (Poole, Oxford Publishing Co., 1985) 205p.
460 A. Williams, *Brunel and after, the romance of the Great Western Railway.* (GWR, 1925)
461 C.L. Williams, *Great Western steam miscellany.* (Truro, Barton, 1977) 96p.
462 R.B. Wilson, *Go Great Western: a history of G.W.R. publicity.* (Newton Abbot, David & Charles, 1970)

London & South Western Railway

463 D.L. Bradley, *An illustrated history of LSWR locomotives.* (Upper Bucklebury, Wild Swan, 1985–7) 3v.
464 H.C. Casserley, *London & South Western locomotives.* (London, Ian Allen, 1971) 184p.
465 B.K. Cooper and R. Antell, *A tribute to the London & South Western Railway.*

(London, Ian Allan, 1988)

466 C.H. Ellis, *The South-Western Railway: its mechanical history and background, 1838–1922.* (London, Allen & Unwin, 1956) 256p.

467 J.N. Faulkner and R.A. Williams, *The London and South Western Railway in the twentieth century.* (Newton Abbot, David & Charles, 1988) 224p.

468 S. Fay, *A Royal Road: being the history of the London and South-Western Railway from 1825 to the present time.* (Wakefield, E.P. Publishing, 1973)
Originally published 1883

469 R. Hardingham, ed., *Celebrating 150 years of the LSWR.* (Southampton, Kingfisher Railway Productions, 1988)

470 *A list of published drawings pertaining to the London & South Western Railway.* 6th ed. (South Western Circle, c. 1991) 84p.

471 G. Measom, *The official illustrated guide to the London and South Western Railway, including branch lines and continuations, etc.* (1858)

472 H.H. Meik, 'How the London and South Western Railway reached Waterloo', *Rlwy. Mag.* XLVI 1920 254–6

473 O.S. Nock, *The London and South-Western Railway.* (Shepperton, Ian Allan, 1972) 166p.

474 W.T. Perkins, 'The London and South-Western Railway; its history and progress', *Rlwy. Mag.* XXVIII 1911 443–55

475 Railway Correspondence and Travel Society, *The locomotives of the London and South Western Railway; by D.L. Bradley. Part 1.* (1965)

476 K. Robertson, *London & South Western Railway: 150 years of the L&SWR.* (Ledbury, Amber Graphics, 1990) 64p.

477 G.A. Sekon, pseud., *The London & South-Western Railway: half a century of railway progress.* (Weston-super-Mare, Avon Anglia, 1989) 94p.

478 M. Sharman, comp., *The London and South Western Railway: a selection of 7mm. locomotive drawings.* (Oakwood Press, 1989)

479 R.A. Williams, *The London and South Western Railway: the formative years.* (Newton Abbot, David & Charles, 1968) 267p.

Midland & South Western Junction Railway

480 D. Barrett, B. Bridgeman and D. Bird, *A M&SWJR album: a pictorial history of the Midland and South Western Junction Railway. v. 1 1872–1899.* (Swindon, Red Brick Publishing, 1981) 82p.

481 D.S. Barrie, 'The Midland and South Western Junction Railway', *Rlwy. Mag.* LXX 1932 157–66, 255–66

482 D. Bartholomew, *Midland & South Western Junction Railway. v. 1* (Upper Bucklebury, Wild Swan, 1982) 238p.

483 B. Bridgeman and others, *Swindon's other railway. The Midland & South Western Junction Railway 1900–1985.* (Swindon, Red Brick Publishing, 1985) 88p.

484 C.G. Maggs, *The Midland and South Western Junction Railway.* (Newton Abbot, David & Charles, 1967) 160p.

485 T.B. Sands, *The Midland and South Western Junction Railway*. (Lingfield, Oakwood Press, 1959) 48p.

North Devon & Cornwall Junction Railway

486 C.F.D. Whetmath and D. Stuckey, *North Devon and Cornwall Junction Railway: Torrington-Halwill*. New ed. (Bracknell, Forge, 1980) 48p.

Somerset and Dorset Railway

See also nos. 3547, 3556, 3563, 3567–8

487 E.C.B. Ashford, 'Modern locomotives of the Somerset and Dorset Railway' *Rlwy. Mag.* LXIX 1931 235–45

488 R. Atthill, *The picture history of the Somerset & Dorset Railway*. (Newton Abbot, David & Charles, 1970) 112p.

489 R. Atthill, *The Somerset & Dorset Railway with contributions on locomotives etc., by O.S. Nock*. 2nd ed. (Newton Abbot, David & Charles, 1985)

490 D.S. Barrie and C.R. Clinker, *The Somerset and Dorset Railway*. 3rd ed. (Lingfield, Oakwood Press, 1978) 76p.

491 D. Beale, *Southbound with the 'Pines': a collection of Somerset & Dorset footplate memories*. (Washford, Somerset & Dorset Railway Trust, 1985) 48p.

492 M. Hawkins, *The Somerset & Dorset: then and now*. (Wellingborough, Stephens, 1986) 267p.

493 H.L. Hopwood, 'The Somerset and Dorset Joint Railway', *Rlwy. Mag.* XL 1917 305–14

494 C.W. Judge and C.R. Potts, *An historical survey of the Somerset and Dorset Railway: track layouts and illustrations*. (Oxford Publishing Co., 1979) 135p.

495 C.G. Maggs, *The last years of the Somerset & Dorset*. (London, Ian Allan, 1991) 128p.

496 L. Popplewell, *The Somerset and Dorset Railway: a Victorian adventure in alignment*. (Bournemouth, Melledgen, 1988) 154p.

497 H. Rake, 'Why the Somerset and Dorset became a joint railway', *Rlwy. Mag.* XVI 1905 116–27

Weston, Clevedon & Portishead Railway

See also nos. 3553, 3571, 3575, 3580

498 C.G. Maggs, *The Weston, Clevedon & Portishead Railway*. (Lingfield, Oakwood Press, 1964) 48p.

Roads and Road Transport

499 R.C. Anderson and G. Frankis, *History of Royal Blue Express Services*. (Newton Abbot, David & Charles, 1970) 218p.

500 R.C. Anderson and G.G.A. Frankis, *A history of Western National*. (Newton Abbot, David & Charles, 1979) 202p.

501 M. Brayshaw, 'Royal post-horse routes in south-west England in the reigns of Elizabeth I and James I', *Rep. Trans. Devons. Assoc.* CXXII 1991 79–103

502 J. Davy, *Practical hints for the improvement of parish roads in general, more particularly those in the West of England.* (1830)

Copy in Exeter Central Library

503 H. Eardley-Wilmot, 'Leland's Road and a telling house: S.W. Exmoor', *Devon Cornwall N. & Q.* XXXIV 1981 329–33

504 D. Gerhold, *Transport before the railways: Russell's London flying wagons.* (Cambridge, University Press, 1993) 316p.

Based on the records of T. Russell & Co., one of the largest hauliers operating between the West Country and London.

505 P.W. Gentry, *The tramways of the west of England.* Rev. ed. (Light Railways Transport League, 1960) 176p.

506 F.H.W. Green, 'Motor-bus centres in South-West England, considered in relation to population and shopping facilities', *Inst. Br. Geogr. Trans. Pap.* 1948 59–68

507 C. Harper, *The Exeter road: the story of the west of England highway.* (Chapman & Hall, 1899) 318p.

508 C.G. Harper, *The Portsmouth road: the sailors' highway.* Rev. ed. (1923) 266p.

509 F.A. Hosier, 'The measured mile', *Old Cornwall* IX 1984 544–56

Milestones in Conwall and Devon

510 P.J. Kelley, *Road vehicles of the Great Western Railway.* (Oxford, Oxford Publishing Co., 1973) 128p.

511 P.J. Kelley, *Great Western road vehicles appendix.* (Oxford, Oxford Publishing Co., c. 1982) 152p.

Chiefly illustrations

512 G.N. Wright, *Roads and trackways of Wessex.* (Ashbourne, Moorland Publishing Co., 1988) 191p.

Bridges

513 P.S.A. Berridge, *The girder bridge: after Brunel and others.* (London, R. Maxwell, 1969) 172p.

514 E. Jervoise, *The ancient bridges of Wales and Western England.* (EP Publishing, 1976)

515 J.M. Rendel, 'Particulars of the construction of the floating bridge late established across the Hamoaze, between Torpoint in the County of Cornwall and Devonport in Devonshire', *Trans. Instn. Civil Engrs.* II 1838 213–27

Ports and Shipping

516 M.R. Bouquet, *Westcountry sail: merchant shipping, 1840–1960.* (Newton Abbot, David & Charles, 1971) 112p.

517 W.R. Childs, 'The commercial shipping of South-Western England in the later fifteenth century', *Mar. Mirr.* LXXXIII no. 3 1997 272–92

518 E.A.G. Clark, *The estuarine ports of the Exe and Teign, with special reference to the period 1660–1880: a study in historical geography.* (Ph.D. thesis, London University,(External), 1957)

519 E.A.G. Clark, *The ports of the Exe estuary, 1660–1860: a study in historical geography*. (Exeter, University Press, 1960)

520 J.G. Commin, *Early-Stuart mariners and shipping: the maritime surveys of Devon and Cornwall, 1619–35*. (Exeter, Devon and Cornwall Record Society, n.s. v. 33, 1990) 171p.

521 R.S. Craig, *Shipping in the South-West in its national context 1800–1914*. (Exeter University, Exeter Papers in Economic History, no. 7, 1973)

522 C.L.D. Duckworth and G.E. Langmuir, *West Country steamers*. 3rd ed. (Prescot, Stephenson, 1966) 206p.

523 G. Farr, *West Country passenger steamers*. 2nd ed. (Newton Abbot, David & Charles, 1967) 355p.

524 G. Farr, 'Custom House ship registers of the West Country', *in* H.E.S. Fisher, ed., *The South West and the sea: papers of a seminar on the maritime history of the South West of England*. (Exeter University, Exeter Papers in Economic History, no. 1, 1968) 57–71

525 S. Fisher, ed., *British shipping and seamen, 1630–1960: some studies*. (Exeter University, Dept. of Economic History, 1984)

Studies in the West Country and North-East England

526 H.E.S. Fisher, ed., *Ports and shipping in the South-West: papers presented at two seminars on the maritime history of the South-West of England, held at Dartington Hall, 19–20 October 1968 and 18–19 October 1969*. (Exeter University, Exeter Papers in Economic History, no. 4, 1971) 174p.

527 H.E.S. Fisher, 'The South-West and the Atlantic trades', *in* H.E.S. Fisher, ed., *The South West and the sea: papers of a seminar on the maritime history of the South West of England*. (Exeter University, Exeter Papers in Economic History, no. 1, 1968) 7–14

528 H.E.S. Fisher, ed., *The South West and the sea: papers of a seminar on the maritime history of the South West of England*. (Exeter University, Exeter Papers in Economic History, no. 1, 1968) 73p.

529 H.E.S. Fisher and W.E. Minchinton, eds., *Transport and shipowning in the Westcountry*. (Exeter University, Exeter Papers in Economic History no. 7, 1973) 71p.

530 H.E.S. Fisher, ed., *West country maritime and social history: some essays*. (Exeter University, Exeter Papers in Economic History no. 13, 1980) 159p.

531 D. Gardiner, ed., *A calendar of early Chancery proceedings relating to West Country shipping 1388–1493*. (Devon & Cornwall Record Society, n.s. vol. 21 1976) xix + 131p.

532 J.M. Gilman, 'Some Bristol Channel trading sloops', *Mar. Mirr.* L 1964 6–25

533 T. Gray, ed., *Early Stuart mariners and shipping: the maritime surveys of Devon and Cornwall, 1619–35*. (Devon & Cornwall Record Society, n.s. vol. 33, 1990) 170p.

534 B. Greenhill, 'Aspects of late nineteenth-century rural shipowning in South Western Britain', *in* K. Matthews and G. Panting, eds., *Ships and shipbuilding in the North Atlantic region*. (St John's, Memorial University of Newfoundland, 1978).

535 B. Greenhill, 'The story of the Severn trow', *Mar. Mirr.* XXVI 1940 286–92

536 B. Greenhill, 'Westcountrymen in Prince Edward's Isle', *in* H.E.S. Fisher, *ed., The South West and the sea: papers of a seminar on the maritime history of the South West of England.* (Exeter University, Exeter Papers in Economic History no. 1, 1968) 15–19

537 H.O. Hill, 'West Country barges', *Mar. Mirr.* XLVIII 1962 215–20

538 M. Langley and E. Small, *Estuary and river ferries of south-west England.* (Wolverhampton, Waine Research Publications, 1984) 148p.

539 I.D. Merry, *The shipping and trade of the River Tamar.* (National Maritime Museum, 1980) 2v.

540 V.F.L. Millard, *Ships of Devon and Cornwall, 1652–1942.* (Isleworth, Kenilworth Nautical Pub. Co., 1942) 80p.

541 G. Mote, *The Westcountrymen: ketches and trows of the Bristol Channel.* (Bideford, Badger Books, 1986) 96p.

542 R.M. Nance, 'Trows past and present', *Mar. Mirr.* II 1912 201–5

543 A. Patrick, 'Tamar traffic in the nineteenth century', *in The new maritime history of Devon* v. 2 60–7. See no. 2578

544 *The ports of the Bristol Channel.* (J.S. Virtue & Co., 1893) 273p.

545 W.J. Slade and B. Greenhill, *Westcountry coasting ketches.* (Greenwich, Conway Maritime Press, 1974) 136p.

546 M. Stammers, *West Coast shipping.* 2nd ed. (Aylesbury, Shire Publications, 1983) 88p.

547 P.J. Stuckey, 'Trows on the back', *Marit. S-W* no. 3 111–14

OTHER INDUSTRIES

548 J.S. Attwood, *Booksellers and printers in Devon and Cornwall in the seventeenth and eighteenth centuries.* (Exeter, Privately printed, 1917) 10p.

549 H.H. Cotterell, *Bristol and West Country pewterers.* (Bristol Museum & Art Gallery, 1918) 37p.

Copy in Exeter Central Library.

550 W.E. Minchinton, 'The British cider industry since 1870', *Nat. West. Q. Rev.* Nov. 1975 55–67

Bristol

GENERAL

551 B.W.E. Alford, 'The economic development of Bristol in the nineteenth century: an enigma?', *in* P. McGrath and J. Cannon, *eds., Essays in Bristol and Gloucestershire history* (Bristol, Bristol & Gloucestershire Archaeological Society, 1976) 252–83

552 B.J. Atkinson, 'An early example of the decline of the industrial spirit? Bristol enterprise in the first half of the nineteenth century', *S. Hist.* IX 1987 71–89

553 J.H. Bettey, 'Some major influences on the post-medieval landscape of the Bristol region', *Landscape Hist.* V 1983 123–8

554 J. Bettey, 'Trades and working conditions in Bristol in 1865', *BIAS J.* XV 1982 5–7

555 N. du Q. Bird, 'Dorset apprentices in Bristol, 1532–1565', *Somerset Dorset N. & Q.* XXXIII Sept. 1994 309–10

556 M. Bodman, 'Bristol I.A. references from old local newspapers', *BIAS J.* no. 24 1992 23–36

557 *Bristol Times & Mirror, Bristol's many industries.* (Bristol, 1922)

558 *Bristol Times & Mirror, Work in Bristol: a series of sketches of the chief manufactories in the city.* (Bristol, 1883)

Copy in Bristol Local History Collection

559 J.N.N. Britton, *The Bristol industrial region: a study of the location and structure of manufacturing industry in Gloucestershire, Somerset and west Wiltshire since 1945.* (Ph.D. thesis, London University, 1966)

560 R.A. Buchanan, *The industrial archaeology of Bristol.* (Historical Association, Bristol Branch, Pamphlet no. 18, 1967) 20p.

561 R.A. Buchanan and N. Cossons, *Industrial archaeology of the Bristol region.* (Newton Abbot, David & Charles, 1969) 335p.

562 R.A. Buchanan and N. Cossons, *Industrial history in pictures: Bristol.* (Newton Abbot, David & Charles, 1970) 112p.

563 C.R. Cane, *The trade between Bristol and Ireland, 1791–3.* (M.A. thesis, Exeter University, 1976)

564 E.M. Carus-Wilson, *The Merchant Adventurers of Bristol in the 15th century.* (Historical Association, Bristol Branch, Local History Pamphlet no. 4, 1962) 19p.

565 E.M. Carus-Wilson, 'The overseas trade of Bristol', *in* E. Power and M.M. Postan, *Studies in English trade in the fifteenth century.*(London, Routledge, 1933) 155–62

566 E.M. Carus-Wilson, *The overseas trade of Bristol in the later Middle Ages; a study of English commerce, 1399–1485.* (M.A. thesis, London University, 1926)

567 E.M. Carus-Wilson, *ed., The overseas trade of Bristol in the later Middle*

Ages. 2nd ed. (Merlin Press, 1967) 338p.

568 A. Chatwin, 'A Bristol plan identified', *BIAS J*. IX 1976 17–19
A plan of part of the north bank of the River Avon.

569 J. Cornwell, 'Industrial archaeology and the Avon Ring Road', *BIAS J*. XXI 1989 12–18

570 N. Cox, 'Imagination and innovation of an industrial pioneer: the first Abraham Darby', *Ind. Archaeol. Rev*. XII no. 2 1990 127–44
Concerns Darby's career in Bristol and Coalbrookdale.

571 J. Day, *A guide to the industrial heritage of Avon*. (Association for Industrial Archaeology, 1987) 52p.

572 P. Elkin, 'Bristol Industrial Museum', *BIAS J*. X 1977 18

573 W.L. Goodman, 'Bristol apprentice registers 1532–1658: a selection of enrolments of mariners', *Mar. Mirr*. LX 1974 27–31

574 J. Green, P. Ollerenshaw and P. Wardley, *Business in Avon and Somerset. A survey of archives*. (Business History Centre, Bristol Polytechnic, 1991) 206p.

575 L.V. Grinsell, *The history and coinage of the Bristol mint*. (Bristol, City of Bristol Museum and Art Gallery, 1986) 60p.

576 C.E. Harvey and J. Press, eds., *Studies in the business history of Bristol*. (Bristol, Bristol Academic Press, 1988) 278p.

This book consists of: C. Harvey and J. Press, 'Industrial change and the economic life of Bristol since 1800'; S. Diaper, 'J.S. Fry & Sons: growth and decline in the chocolate industry, 1753–1918'; P. Ollerenshaw, 'The development of banking in the Bristol region, 1750–1914'; D. Bateman, 'The growth of the printing and packaging industry in Bristol, 1800–1914'; P. Davis, C. Harvey and J. Press, 'Locomotive building in Bristol in the age of steam, 1837–1958'; C. Harvey and J. Press, 'Sir George White and the urban transport revolution in Bristol, 1875–1916'; G. Channon, 'Georges and brewing in Bristol'; G. Stone, 'Rearmament, war and the performance of the Bristol Aeroplane Company, 1935–45'; J. Press, 'G.B. Britton and footwear manufacturing in Bristol and Kingswood, 1870–1973'; C. Harvey, 'Old traditions, new departures: the later history of the Bristol & West Building Society'.

577 *Calendar of the Bristol apprentice book 1532–1565. Part I 1532–1542* (Bristol Record Society, vol. 14, 1949)

578 *Calendar of the Bristol apprentice book 1532–1565. Part II 1543–1551* (Bristol Record Society, vol. 33, 1980)

579 *Calendar of the Bristol apprentice book 1532–1565. Part III 1552–1565* (Bristol Record Society, vol. 43, 1992)

580 R.H. James, 'Industry and environment in medieval Bristol', *in Waterfront archaeology: proceedings of the 3rd international conference ... held at Bristol, 1988* (CBA Research Report, 74, 19–26)

581 S.J. Jones, 'The growth of Bristol: the regional aspect of city development', *Inst. Br. Geogr. Trans. Pap*. no. 11 1946 57–83

582 S.J. Jones, 'The historical geography of Bristol', *Geography* XVI 1931 175–86

583 M.D. Kanaris, *Demo-economic growth in the Bristol regional system, early 1950s to mid 1970s.* (Ph.D. thesis, Reading University, 1985)

584 J. Latimer, *History of the Society of Merchant Adventurers of the City of Bristol.* (Bristol, Arrowsmith, 1903) 345p.

585 J. Latimer, 'The Mercers' and Linen Drapers' Company of Bristol', *Trans. Bristol Glos. Archaeol. Soc.* XXVI 1903 288–92

586 E.W. Lennard, 'Some intimate Bristol connections with the overseas empire', *Geography* XVI 1931 111–21

587 E.B.C. Lillingston, 'Bristol Huguenots', *Proc. Huguenot Soc. London* XVII no. 3 1944 267–88

588 J. Loomie, 'Sir William Semple and Bristol's Andalucian trade 1597–1598' *Trans. Bristol. Glos. Archaeol. Soc.* LXXXII 1963 177–87

589 P. McGrath, *John Whitson and the merchant community of Bristol.* (Historical Association, Bristol Branch, 1970) 23p.

590 P. McGrath, *The merchant venturers of Bristol: a history of the Society of Merchant Venturers of the City of Bristol from its origins to the present day.* (Bristol, The Society, 1975) 629p.

591 P. McGrath, *ed., Merchants and merchandise in seventeenth-century Bristol.* 2nd ed. (Bristol Record Society, vol. 19 1968) 315p.

592 P. McGrath, *Records relating to the Society of Merchant Venturers of the City of Bristol in the seventeenth century.* (Bristol Record Society, vol. 17, 1952) 276p.

593 P. McGrath, 'The Society of Merchant Venturers and the Port of Bristol in the 17th century', *Trans. Bristol Glos. Archaeol. Soc.* LXXII 1953 105–28

594 R. Mayo, *The Huguenots in Bristol.* (Historical Association, Bristol Branch, 1985) 31p.

595 C. Merrett, *The trade between Bristol and northern Europe, 1770–80.* (M.A. thesis, Exeter University, 1974)

596 W.E. Minchinton, 'Bristol—metropolis of the West in the eighteenth century', *Trans. R. Hist. Soc.* 5th ser. IV 1954 69–89

597 W.E. Minchinton, *ed., The trade of Bristol in the eighteenth century.* (Bristol Record Society, vol. 20, 1957) 210p.

598 K. Morgan, *Bristol and the Atlantic trade in the eighteenth century.* (Cambridge, Cambridge University Press, 1993) 281p.

An article with the same title appears in *Eng. Hist. Rev.* no. 424 July 1992 626–50

599 S.A.C. Penn, 'A fourteenth-century Bristol merchant', *Trans. Bristol & Glos. Archaeol. Soc.* CIV 1986 183–6

600 J. Powell, 'Bristol and Coalbrookdale', *BIAS J.* XIX 1986 8–14

601 A.J. Pugsley, *Contributions towards the study of the economic development of Bristol in the eighteenth and nineteenth centuries.* (M.A. thesis, Bristol University, 1921)

602 H. Rees, 'The growth of Bristol', *Econ. Geog.* XXI 1945 269–75

603 H. Reid, *Bristol & Co., the story of Bristol's long running businesses from 1710 to the present day.* (Bristol, Redcliffe Press, 1987) 124p.

604 Y. Renouard, 'Les relations de Bordeaux et de Bristol au moyen âge', *Rev. Bordeaux et Dépt. Gironde* VII 1957 97–112

605 F.R. Rogers, 'Bristol and Colchester: a seventeenth-century relationship', *Trans. Essex Archaeol. Soc.* XXIV 1951 53–5

606 F.R. Rogers, *The Bristol craft gilds during the 16th and 17th centuries.* (M.A. thesis, Bristol University, 1949)

607 D.H. Sacks, *Trade, society and politics in Bristol 1500–1640.* (London, Garland, 1985) 2v.

608 D.H. Sacks, *The widening gate: Bristol and the Atlantic economy.* (Berkeley, University of California Press, 1992) 464p.

609 P.K. Stembridge, 'A Bristol-Coalbrookdale connection: The Goldneys', *BIAS J.* XIX 1986 14–20

610 W.B. Stephens, 'Trade trends at Bristol, 1600–1700', *Trans. Bristol Glos. Archaeol. Soc.* XCIII 1974 156–61

611 Sir L.G. Taylor, 'The Merchant Venturers of Bristol', *Trans. Bristol Glos. Archaeol. Soc.* LXXI 1952 5–12

612 M. Thomas, *The heritage book of Nailsea.* (Baron Birch, 1993) 104p.

Largely concerned with industrial development.

613 N.C.P. Tyack, *The trade relations of Bristol with Virginia in the seventeenth century.* (M.A. thesis, Bristol University, 1930)

614 J. Vanes, ed., *Documents illustrating the overseas trade of Bristol in the sixteenth century.* (Bristol Record Society vol. 31, 1979) 196p.

615 J.M. Vanes, *The overseas trade of Bristol in the sixteenth century.* (Ph.D. thesis, London University, 1975)

616 F. Walker, 'Economic growth on Severnside', *Trans. Inst. Br. Geogr.* no. 37 1965 1–13

617 P. Wakelin and J. Day, 'Joseph Harris in Bristol, 1748', *BIAS J.* XV 1982 8–12

References to industrial activities from Harris's journal.

618 F. Walker, 'The industries of Bristol', *Econ. Geog.* XXII 1946 174–92

619 R. Webber, 'Ashton Gate: industrial development of a suburb', *BIAS J.* XVIII 1985 5–9

620 J. Winstone, *Bristol trade cards: remnants of prolific commerce.* (Reece Winstone Archive & Publishing, 1993) 132p.

621 P.T.M. Woodland, 'Bristol merchants and the overseas trade in cider c. 1773–1818', *Trans. Bristol Glos. Archaeol. Soc.* CVI 1988 173–88

622 T. Woolrich, 'Bristol and the 1851 Exhibition', *BIAS J.* VII 1974 20–4

623 A.P. Woolrich, 'An American in Gloucestershire and Bristol: the diary of Joshua Gilpin 1796–7', *Trans. Bristol Glos. Archaeol. Soc.* XCII 1973 169–89

624 A. Wordsworth, *The import trade of Bristol, 1768–70, with particular regard to the American colonial and West Indian trades.* (M.A. thesis, Exeter University, 1981)

AGRICULTURE

625 C. Miller, 'Whitfield Example Farm: a Victorian model', *BIAS J.* XVI 1983 20–7

626 M.A. Thomas, *Agriculture and industry in Nailsea and district 1780–1880.* (M.Phil thesis, Bristol University, 1986)

ARCHITECTURE AND BUILDINGS
General

627 A. Gomme, M. Jenner and B. Little, *Bristol: an architectural history.* (London, Lund Humphries for Bristol & West Building Society, 1979) 452p.

Domestic

628 N.A. Ferguson, *Working class housing in Bristol and Nottingham, 1868–1919.* (Ann Arbor, University Microfilms, 1978) 273p.

Copy in Bristol University Library

629 L. Hall, *The rural houses of North Avon and South Gloucestershire 1400–1720.* (City of Bristol Museum & Art Gallery, Monograph no. 6, 1983) 316p.

630 C. Powell and R. Wilkes, 'Blindbacks for brassworkers', *BIAS J.* VIII 1975 26–8

Workers' housing.

Industrial

631 J. Bartlett, ''The Snuff Mill', Stapleton' *BIAS J.* no. 25 1992 21–7

632 M. Bodman, 'Mills at Stapleton—from newspaper sources', *BIAS J.* no. 25 1992 27

633 M. Bodman, 'Mills on the Congresbury Yeo and its tributaries', *BIAS J.* no. 26 1993 8–14

634 M. Bodman, 'Mills on the Winford Brook', *BIAS J.* no. 27 1994 3–10

635 G. Briscoe, 'Bristol's old lead shot tower', *Ind. Archaeol.* XVII 1983 35–46

636 J. Broome, 'Tucking mill', *BIAS J.* XX 1988 2–3

A fulling mill near Midford.

637 D. Cocks, 'The WCA warehouse', *BIAS J.* VII 1974 4–8

The Western Counties Agricultural Co-operative Association at Redcliff.

638 J. Day, 'The Albert Mill survey', *BIAS J.* VII 1974 10–19

A water mill

639 H.B. Hopkins, 'Cog mill on the River Frome', *BIAS J.* XIII 1980 18

The author links his article with nos. 642–4.

640 H.B. Hopkins, 'Frampton Cotterell Mill', *BIAS J.* XIV 1981 25–7

641 J. Mosse, 'Redcliff Shot Tower', *BIAS J.* no. 2 1969

642   O. Ward and J. Cornwell, 'BIAS excavations at Kings Mill', *BIAS J.* IV 1971 24–5
643   O. Ward, 'The mills of the Bristol Frome', *BIAS J.* II 1969 24–6
      A longer article with the same author and title appears in *BIAS J.* XI 1978 27–33
644   O. Ward, 'Millstones at Willsbridge Mill', *BIAS J.* XXV 1992 28–32

AIRCRAFT MANUFACTURE

See also nos. 904–9, 2904

645   A.R. Adams, *Good company: the story of the Guided Weapons Division of British Aircraft Corporation.* (British Aircraft Corporation, 1976)
646   C.H. Barnes, *Bristol aircraft since 1910.* (London, Putnam, 1964) 415p.
647   C.H.Barnes, 'Bristol and the aircraft industry', *BIAS J.* V 1972 4–10
648   P. Fearon, 'The formative years of the British aircraft industry, 1913–1924', *Bus. Hist. Rev.* XLIII 1969 487
649   Sir R. Fedden, 'The first 25 years of the Bristol Engine Department', *J. R. Aeronautical Soc.* LXV 1961 332–52
650   S. Gillett, 'Rolls Royce West Works', *BIAS J* no. 29 1996 23–9
651   G. Green, *British Aerospace: a proud heritage.* (Wotton-under-Edge, The Author, 1988) 128p.
652   G. Green, *Bristol aerospace since 1910.* 2nd ed. (Wotton-under-Edge, The Author, 1990) 128p.
653   D. Greenman, *75 years of Bristol aerospace.* (Bristol, Royal Aeronautical Society, 1985) 48p.
654   K. Hayward, *The British aircraft industry.* (Manchester, University Press, 1989) 192p.
655   J. Hobbs, *Bristol helicopters: a tribute to Raoul Hafner.* (Bristol, Frenchay Publications, 1984) 157p.
656   D. Littlefield, *A history of the Bristol Britannia: the whispering giant.* (Tivcerton, Halsgrove, 1992) 158p.
657   J. Lovering, *The development of the aerospace industry in Bristol, 1910–1984.* (University of Bristol, Dept. of Geography, School for Advanced Urban Studies, Project Working Paper 3, 1984) 51p.
658   D. Luff, *Bulldog: The Bristol Bulldog fighter.* (Shrewsbury, Airlife, 1987) 180p.
659   J.S. Pudney, *Bristol fashion: some account of the earlier days of Bristol aviation.* (Putnam, 1960) 102p.
660   'Rolls-Royce, Bristol, 1920–1980', *Flight Int.* 26 July 1980 245–8
661   Rolls-Royce Heritage Trust, *Rolls Royce in Bristol.* (Bristol, *c.* 1993)
662   D.A. Russell, ed., *The Book of Bristol Aircraft.* (Leicester, Harborough Publishing, 1946) 140p.
663   Sir A. Russell, *A span of wings: memoirs of a working life in aircraft design encompassing a span from biplanes to Concorde—Bristol fashion.*

(Shrewsbury, Airlife Publications, 1992) 202p.

664 *Shadow to Shadow: a history of the Bristol Aeroplane Banwell Shadow Factory and Bristol Aerojet (BAJ) 1941–91* (Weston-super-Mare, BAJ Coatings Ltd, 1993) 49p.

665 G. Stone, 'Rearmament, war and the performance of the Bristol Aeroplane Company, 1935–45' *in* C.E. Harvey and J. Press, eds., *Studies in the business history of Bristol.* (Bristol, Bristol Academic Press, 1988) 187–212

BREWING

666 Bristol Brewery Georges & Co., *144 years of brewing 1788–1932.* (The Brewery, 1938) 99p.

667 Bristol United Breweries Ltd, *A century of 'Good Health'.* (Bristol, 1937)

668 G. Channon, 'Georges and brewing in Bristol' *in* C.E. Harvey and J. Press, eds., *Studies in the business history of Bristol.* (Bristol, Bristol Academic Press, 1988) 165–86.

669 R. Fulligar, 'Malting at Marshfield', *BIAS J.* XXII 1990 8p.

670 L. Wiltshire, *History of the Bristol Brewery, Georges & Co. Ltd. 1788–1961 and subsidiary companies prior to acquisition by Courage, Barclay & Simonds* (1967)

Typescript. Copy in Bristol City Library Local Collection

BRICKMAKING

671 M. Doughty and O. Ward, 'Shortwood Brickworks', *BIAS J.* no. 8 1975 11–13

In the parish of Pucklechurch, north of Bristol.

672 E. Hammersley, 'The brickmakers of Avon: the quarry and checkweigher returns', *BIAS J.* no. 25 1992 17–20

673 S.B. Pippard, 'Hollybrook bricks', *BIAS J.* no. 15 1982 28–31

Hollybrook Brick Co. Ltd, Bristol

674 O. Ward and W. Harris, 'Charfield block, tile and brick works', *BIAS J.* XIII 1980 31–6

BUILDING

675 R. Day, 'Ferro-concrete: the construction industry enters the 20th century', *BIAS J.* XIII 1980 26–30

676 S.A.C. Penn, 'A hidden workforce: building workers in 14th-century Bristol', *Trans. Bristol Glos. Archaeol. Soc.* CIX 1991 171–8

677 C.G. Powell, 'Case studies and lost tribes: the Bristol firm of James Diment and Stephens, Bastow & Co.', *Construction Hist.* I 1985 25–35

678 C.G. Powell, 'He that runs against time: the life expectancy of building

firms in nineteenth-centry Bristol', *Construction Hist.* II 1986 61–7

679 C. Powell, 'Large but largely forgotten: the Victorian building industry', *BIAS J.* XIII 1980 22–5

680 C. Powell, ''Widows and others' on Bristol building sites: some women in nineteenth-century construction', *Local Histn.* XX no. 2 May 1990 84–7

681 J.R. Ward, 'Speculative building at Bristol and Clifton, 1783–93', *Bus. Hist.* XX 1978 3–18

CHEMICALS

682 J.E.L. Bowcott, 'The industrial background of the Bristol area', *Chem. in Britain* no. 2 1966 65–70

683 T.H. Butler, *The history of Wm Butler & Co. (Bristol) Ltd, 1843–1943.* (Bristol, The Firm, 1954) 92p.

Coal tar merchants.

684 J. Davidson, 'The initial development of Severnside Works', *Chem. & Ind.* 28 Nov. 1964 1968–77

The works of ICI.

685 'Early development of the chemical industry in Bristol', *Chem. & Ind.* LVII 1938 121–3; 148–50; 180–3; 200–3

686 R. Holland, 'Alkali production at the Netham', *BIAS J.* XVI 1983 28–30

687 R. Holland, 'Fertilisers, farming and philanthropy—the Proctor story', *BIAS J.* XXII 1990 23–36

A revised version of no. 689.

688 R. Holland, 'Fertilisers, farming and philanthropy: an update', *BIAS J* no. 29 1996 44–5

689 R. Holland, 'The Netham Chemical Co. Ltd: alkali production in Bristol', *Chem. & Ind.* 3 June 1985 366–71

690 R. Holland, 'Tar distillation at Crew's Hole', *BIAS J.* no. 13 1980 6–8

CLOCK AND WATCHMAKING

See also no. 3007

691 H.E. Morton and C.R. Hudleston, 'Bristol gold and silversmiths and clock and watchmakers', *Trans. Bristol Glos. Archaeol. Soc.* LX 1938 198–227

692 H.E. Nott and C.R. Hudleston, 'An 18th-century clock at the Council House, Bristol; with notes on clock and watchmakers in Bristol', *Trans. Bristol Glos. Archaeol. Soc.* LVII 1935 176–91

ENGINEERING

See also nos. 757–75

693 M. Bone, 'Boulton & Watt steam engines in Bristol and Bath', *BIAS J.* no.

28 1995 24–9

694 C.T.G. Boucher, 'The Clifton hydraulic power scheme: an early work by James Brindley', *J. Rlwy. Canal Hist. Soc.* VII 1961 90–3

695 *Bristol Wagon & Carriage: Illustrated Catalogue, 1900. The Bristol Wagon & Carriage Works Co. Ltd* (New York, Dover Publications, 1994) 178p.

696 R.A. Buchanan, 'Brunel in Bristol', *in* P. McGrath and J. Cannon, eds., *Essays in Bristol and Gloucestershire history* (Bristol, Bristol and Gloucestershire Archaeological Society, 1976) 217–51

697 R.A. Buchanan, *Nineteenth-century engineers in the port of Bristol.* (Historical Association, Bristol Branch, 1971) 19p.

698 R.A. Buchanan and M. Williams, *Brunel's Bristol.* (Bristol & West Building Society and Redliffe Press, 1982) 96p.

699 J.R. Clew, *The Douglas motor cycle 'The best twin'.* Rev. ed. (Yeovil, Foulis, 1981) 250p.

Based in Bristol.

700 A.B. Cooper, 'Mechanical engineering around Bristol', *Proc. Instn. Mech. Engrs.* CLXVI 1952 278–82

701 C.P. Davis, *Locomotive building in Bristol: the Avonside Ironworks (1837–1882).* (B.A. Dissertation, Bristol University, 1979)

Copy in Bristol University Library

702 P. Davis, C. Harvey and J. Press, 'Locomotive building in Bristol in the age of steam, 1837–1958' *in* C.E. Harvey and J. Press, eds., *Studies in the business history of Bristol.* (Bristol, Bristol Academic Press, 1988) 109–36

703 G. Farnsworth, *Golden jubilee: the first 50 years.* (Bristol & West of England Engineering Manufacturers Association, 1986) 51p.

704 T. Fisher and D. Jones, 'Steam in the Underfall Yard', *BIAS J.* IX 1976 12–19

A survey of the Tangye engine in the Underfall Yard.

705 J. Lysaght & Co., *The Lysaght Century 1857–1957* (Bristol, The Firm, 1957) 64p.

706 A.G. Pugsley, 'Engineering in Bristol', *in* C.M. MacInnes and W.F. Whittard, eds. *Bristol and its adjoining counties* (Bristol, W.J. Arrowsmith, 1955) 269–79

707 J. Sawtell, 'Hospital steam engines in the Bristol region', BIAS J. II 1969 20–33

708 R. Stiles, 'Rogers & Co., Bristol boilermakers', *BIAS J.* XXIII 1991 27–42

709 H.S. Torrens, 'Engineering enterprise in Bath and Bristol', *Ind. Archaeol. Rev.* XI no. 2 1989 196–209

710 H.S. Torrens, 'Winwoods of Bristol: Part One 1767–1788', *BIAS J.* XIII 1980 9–17

711 O. Ward, 'Winwood & Co., Bristol', *BIAS J.* no. 29 1996 46

712 G. Watkins, 'Steam power in Bristol', *BIAS J.* XIV 1981 6–15

713 M. Watts, 'Animal-powered machinery in the Bristol region', *BIAS J.* no. 9 1976 32–4

714 M. Watts, 'John Padmore's cranes at Bath and Bristol', *BIAS J*. no. 8 1975 17–19

715 W.A. Young, 'A stockbook of 1828 and other finds', *Trans. Newcomen Soc.* XVIII 1939 193–203

An early stockbook of James Meredith & Co. of Kingston, ironmongers and founders

FOOD AND WINE SUPPLY

716 T. Bowen , 'A short history of the R.N. Coate cider works at Nailsea, 1925–1974', *BIAS J*. no. 27 1994 25–9

717 A. Crawford, *Bristol and the wine trade*. (Historical Association, Bristol Branch, 1984) 28p.

718 S. Diaper, 'J.S. Fry & Sons: growth and decline in the chocolate industry, 1753–1918' *in* C.E. Harvey and J. Press, *eds., Studies in the business history of Bristol*. (Bristol, Bristol Academic Press, 1988) 33–54

719 A. Grant, *Bristol and the sugar trade*. (Harlow, Longmans, 1981) 96p.

720 I.V. Hall, 'The Daubenys: one of the most energetic sugar baker families in eighteenth-century Bristol at the Temple St and Halliers Lane refineries. Part 1 under George Daubeny I', *Trans. Bristol Glos. Archaeol. Soc.* LXXXIV 1965 113–40

721 I.V. Hall, 'The Daubenys: the second and third generations of the family at the Halliers Lane Refinery under George II (1714–1760) and George III. (1742–1806) Part 2.', *Trans. Bristol Glos. Archaeol. Soc.* LXXXV 1966 175–201

722 I.V. Hall, 'John Knight, junior, sugar refiner at the Great House on St Augustine's Back (1654–1679) Bristol's second sugar house', *Trans. Bristol Glos. Archaeol. Soc.* LXVIII 1949 110–64

723 I.V. Hall, 'Temple St Sugar House under the first partnership of Richard Lane and John Hine, 1662–1678', *Trans. Bristol Glos. Archaeol. Soc.* LXXVI 1957 118–40

724 I.V. Hall, 'Whitson Court Sugar House, Bristol, 1665–1824', *Trans. Bristol Glos. Archaeol. Soc.* LXV 1944 1–97

725 I.V. Hall, *The sugar trade of England with special attention to the sugar trade of Bristol*. (M.A. thesis, Bristol University, 1925)

726 G. Harrison, *Bristol Cream*. (London, Batsford, 1955) 162p.

A history of John Harvey & Sons Ltd.

727 D. Jones, *Bristol's sugar trade and refining industry*. (Historical Association, Bristol Branch, 1996) 28p.

728 J. Mostyn, 'Plenty of brave wines: trading at Bristol through the ages', *Country Life* XII 1986 1662–84

729 R. Stiles, 'The Old Market sugar refinery 1684–1908', *BIAS J*. II 1969 10–17

730 G. Wagner, *The chocolate conscience*. (London, Chatto & Windus, 1987) 178p.

The chocolate manufacturing businesses of Fry, Cadbury and Rowntree.

GLASS MAKING

731 B.W.E. Alford, 'The flint and bottle glass industry in the early 19th century: a case study of a Bristol firm', *Bus. Hist.* X 1968 12–21

Phoenix Glassworks

732 'A Bristol glassworks *c*. 1730', *in* P. McGrath, ed., *A Bristol miscellany*. (Bristol Record Society, vol. 37, 1985) 15–20

The inventory and valuation of the property of Humphrey Perrott, crown glass and bottle manufacturer.

733 F. Buckley, 'The early glass houses of Bristol', *J. Soc. Glass Technol. Trans.* IX 1925 36–61

734 Sir H. Chance, 'The Nailsea glass works', *Pottery Gaz.* Jan. 1958 111–13

735 Sir H. Chance, 'Records of the Nailsea glass works', *Connoisseur* July 1967 168–72

736 H.E. Dommett, 'Nailsea and the glass-works', *BIAS J.* XVIII 1985 32–36; 'Part 2', XIX 1986 32–8; 'Part 3', XX 1988 29–37

737 H. St G. Gray, 'Nailsea glass', *Connoisseur* June 1911 85–98

738 H. St G. Gray, 'Notes on the Nailsea glass works', *Connoisseur* LXV 1923 127–33

739 B.J. Greenhill, 'Nailsea Glass Works', *BIAS J.* no. 4 1971 26–7

740 O. Jones, 'The contribution of the Ricketts' mould to the manufacture of the English wine bottle, 1820–1850', *J. Glass Stud.* XXV 1983 167–77

741 Z. Josephs, 'The Jacobs of Bristol, glassmakers to King George III', *Trans. Bristol Glos. Archaeol. Soc.* XCV 1977 98–101

742 A.C. Powell, 'Glass making in Bristol', *Trans. Bristol Glos. Archaeol. Soc.* XLVII 1925 211–57

743 F.G. Webb, *Bristol glassmakers*. (University of Bristol, Dept. of Extra-Mural Studies, 1968, Notes on Bristol History, no. 8)

744 C. Weeden, 'The Bristol bottlemakers', *Chem. & Ind.* 1978 378–81

745 C. Weeden, 'The Bristol glass industry: its rise and decline', *Glass Technol.* XXIV 1983 241–58

746 C. Weeden, 'Bristol glassmakers: their role in an emergent industry', *BIAS J.* no. 17 1984 15–29

747 C. Weeden, 'The problems of consolidation in the Bristol flint glass industry', *Glass Technol.* XXII 1981 236–8

748 C. Weeden, 'The Ricketts Family and the Phoenix Glasshouse, Bristol', *Glass Circle* IV 1982 84–101

749 C. Weeden, 'William Cookworthy and Bristol blue glass', *Glass Technol.* XXXI no. 6 1990 256–65

750 C. Witt, C. Weeden and A.P. Schwind, *Bristol glass*. (Bristol, Redcliffe Press, 1984) 94p.

751 C. Witt, *Introducing Bristol glass*. (Bristol, Redcliffe Press, 1984) 32p.

LEATHER AND FOOTWEAR

752 M. Bodman, 'Woollard tannery—and the Bergne Family', *BIAS J.* no. 25 1992 37–9

753 G.B. Britton & Sons, *Cobblers' tale*. Rev. ed. (Bristol, Abson Press, 1963) 2v.

754 J. Press, 'G.B. Britton and footwear manufacturing in Bristol and Kingswood, 1870–1973' *in* C.E. Harvey and J. Press, *eds., Studies in the business history of Bristol.* (Bristol, Bristol Academic Press, 1988) 213–37

LIMEBURNING

755 E. Taylor, 'Limekilns in Avon', *BIAS J.* XVII 1984 5–8

756 G.M. Yeates, 'The limekilns of Clevedon', *BIAS J.* XIII 1980 19–21

METALS

757 'Avonmouth zinc smelting', *Min. Mag.* Aug. 1975 79–87

758 E.J. Cocks and B. Walters, *A history of the zinc smelting industry in Britain.* (London, Harrap, 1968) 224p.

Published on the occasion of the half-century of the Imperial Smelting Corporation at Avonmouth.

759 J. Day, *Bristol brass. A history of the industry.* (Newton Abbot, David & Charles, 1973) 240p.

760 J.M. Day, 'The Bristol brass industry: furnace structures and their associated remains', *Hist. Metall.* XXII no. 1 1988 24–41

761 J. Day, 'The continental origins of Bristol brass', *Ind. Archaeol. Rev.* VII no. 1 1984 32–56

762 J. Day, 'The Costers: copper-smelters and manufacturers', *Trans. Newcomen Soc.* XLVII 1974–6 47–58

763 J. Day, 'The language of Bristol brass', *BIAS J.* I 1968 17–19

The same title also appears in *Bull. Hist. Metall. Gp.* II no. 2

764 J. Day and the BIAS Survey Group, 'The old brass mills, Saltford', *BIAS J.* IX 1976 20–3

765 D. Eveleigh, *Brass & brassware.* (Princes Risborough, Shire Publications, 1995) 32p.

766 B. Ferrner, *Ferrner's journal 1759–1760—an industrial spy in Bath and Bristol, edited by Tony Woolrich.* (Eindhoven, De Archaeologische Pers, 1986) 55p.

Ferrner, a Swede, was especially interested in William Champion's method of zinc distillation in spelter works.

767 I.S. Harlow, *The 125th anniversary of Robert Harlow & Son Ltd,* (Stockport, Harlow & Sons, 1958) 14p.

Brass manufacturers. Copy in Bristol University Library

768 R. Jenkins, 'The copper works at Redbrook and at Bristol', *Trans. Bristol Glos. Archaeol. Soc.* LXIII 1942 145–67

769 R. Jenkins, 'The zinc industry in England: the early years up to about 1850', *Trans. Newcomen Soc.* XXV 1945–7 41–52

Centres on William and John Champion of Bristol

770 J. Mosse, 'Redcliff shot tower', *BIAS J.* II 1969 4–5

771 'Saltford brass mill, Saltford, Avon'', *Post-Med. Archaeol.* XXX 1996 312

772 B. de Soyres, 'History and particulars of the brass battery process', *Trans. Newcomen Soc.* XXVIII 1951–3 131–5

The battery process, established in the Bristol district, consisted in beating brass sheets in such a way as to dish up the flat plate into a brass pan.

773 H.R. Schubert, 'The wire-drawers of Bristol, 1312–1797', *J. Iron Steel Inst.* CLIX no. 1 1948 16–22

774 H.S. Torrens, *Men of iron; the history of the McArthur Group.* (Bristol, McArthur Group, 1984) 76p.

775 'Warmley Brass Works, Warmley, Avon', *Post-Med. Archaeol.* XXX 1996 312

MINING AND QUARRYING

776 P. Brown, *The Bristol and South Gloucestershire coalfield.* (Bristol, P. Brown, 1994) 56p.

777 M. Chapman, 'Priston 'Coal Adventure' 1792–94', *BIAS J.* no. 25 1992 6–10

778 J. Cornwell, *Collieries of Kingswood and South Gloucestershire.* (Cowbridge (Glam.), D. Brown & Sons, 1983) 83p.

779 J. Cornwell, 'Excavation and conservation work at the Golden Valley Colliery, Bitton', *BIAS J.* no. 23 1991 3–26

780 L.J. Cunningham, *A brief history of coal mining in Clutton.* (Clutton Local History Group, 1985)

781 H.C. Dommett, 'The Nailsea coalfield—Phase 1', *BIAS J.* no. 28 1995 15–23

782 R.W. Malcolmson, *A set of ungovernable people: the Kingswood colliers in the eighteenth century.* (Kingswood District Council, 1986) 8p.

783 A.H. Parsons, 'My life in Bromley colliery 1917–22', *BIAS J.* no. 3 1970 26–7

784 J. Robson, 'The Clandown Passbye', *BIAS J.* no. 9 1976 7–11

The passbye was an arrangement in the shaft at Clandown Colliery so that double-cage operation was possible.

785 M.J.H. Southway, 'Kingswood coal', *BIAS J.* IV 1971 15–22; 'Kingswood coal. Part 2', *BIAS J.* V 1972 25–31; 'The Bedminster Connection. Kingswood Coal. Part Three', *BIAS J.* IX 1976 4–6

786 R. Styles, 'Kingswood coalfield—the Rudgeway drainage level', *Glos. Hist. Stud.* X 1979 50–5

787 D. Vinter, 'The archaeology of the Bristol coalfield', *J. Ind. Archaeol.* I 1964 37–47

788 D. Vinter, *Some coalpits in the neighbourhood of Bristol and Kingswood.* (Dursley, F. Bailey, 1964) 24p.
A republication of no. 787

789 A.P. Woolrich, 'A report on Church Farm Colliery, Mangotsfield in 1875', *BIAS J.* XXI 1989 3–11

PAPER MAKING

790 B. Attwood, 'The BIAS paper mills survey', *BIAS J.* III 1970 11–21

791 B. Attwood, 'Some comments on the art of papermaking', *BIAS J.* II 1969 6–7

792 C. Bemrose, 'Bathford paper mill', *BIAS J.* XIX 1986 5–7

POSTS AND COMMUNICATIONS

793 D. Briggs, *The Bristol Post Office in the Age of Rowland Hill, 1837–64.* (Historical Association, Bristol Branch, 1983)

794 M. Ellis, 'Bristol and the optical telegraph', *BIAS J* no. 28 1995 35–8

795 M. Ellis, 'The introduction of the telephone to Bristol', *BIAS J.* XII 1979 16–24

796 R. Stiles, 'Bristol and the optical telegraph: further details', *BIAS J.* no. 29 1996 43

797 R.C. Tombs, *The Bristol Royal Mail: post, telegraph and telephone.* (Bristol, Arrowsmith, 1899) 295p.

798 R.C. Tombs, *The king's post: being a volume of historical facts relating to the posts, mail coaches, coach roads and railway mail services of and connected with the ancient city of Bristol from 1580 to the present time.* (Bristol, W.C. Hammond, 1905) 251p.

799 I.M. Warn, *Bristol 5th clause and penny posts 1793 to 1840.* (Tonbridge, Postal History Society, 1980) 142p.

POTTERY AND CERAMICS

For clay tobacco pipes see nos. 894–903

800 K.J. Barton, 'A medieval pottery kiln at Ham Green, Bristol', *Trans. Bristol Glos. Archaeol. Soc.* LXXXII 1963 95–126

801 K.J. Barton, 'A note on the distribution of Ham Green Pottery', *Trans. Bristol Glos. Archaeol. Soc.* LXXXI 1967 201–2

802 K.J. Barton, 'Some evidence for two types of pottery manufactured in Bristol in the early 18th century', *Trans. Bristol & Glos. Archaeol. Soc.* LXXX 1961 160–8

803 R.J. Charleston, 'Bristol & Sweden: some Delftware connexions', *Trans. Eng. Ceram. Circle* V no. 4 1963 222–34

804 R.K. Henrywood, *Bristol potters, 1775–1906*. (Bristol, Redcliffe Press, 1992) 96p.

805 R. Jackson, P. Jackson and R. Price, 'Bristol potters and potteries 1600–1800: a documentary history', *J. Ceram. Hist.* no. 12 1982 1–235

806 R.G. Jackson, *Magnus Lundberg and the Redcliff Back Pottery, Bristol*. (Bristol, The Author, 1979) 12p.

807 R. Jackson, P. Jackson and I. Beckey, 'Tin-glazed earthernware kiln waste from the Limekiln Lane Potteries, Bristol', *Post-Med. Archaeol.* XXV 1991 89–114

808 S. Levitt, *Pountneys: the Bristol pottery at Fishponds, 1905–1989*. (Bristol, Redcliffe Press, 1990) 104p.

809 F.S. McKenna, *Champion's Bristol porcelain*. (Leigh-on-Sea, F. Lewis, 1947) 107p.

810 F.S. McKenna, 'William Stephens: Bristol china painter', *Trans. Eng. Ceram. Circ.* IV no. 1 1957 33–44

811 J.V.G. Mallet, 'Cookworthy's first Bristol factory of 1765', *Trans. Eng. Ceram. Circ.* VIII no. 1 1971 212–20

812 K. Marochan, 'Crews Hole Pottery, St George, Bristol', *Trans. Bristol Glos. Archaeol. Soc.* LXXXI 1962 189–93

813 H. Owen, *Two centuries of ceramic art in Bristol: being a History of the Manufacture of 'The True Porcelain' by Richard Champion ... with an account of the Delft, Earthernware and Enamel Glassworks from original sources*. (London, Bell & Dandy, 1873) 419p.

814 W.J. Pountney, *Old Bristol potteries: being an account of the old potters and potteries of Bristol and Brislington between 1650 and 1850, with some pages on the old Chapel of St Anne, Brislington*. (Bristol, J.W. Arrowsmith, 1920) 370p.

815 R. Price, 'Further notes concerning medieval potters', *Bristol Avon Archaeol.* IX 1991 49–50

816 F.B. Proctor, 'Some products of Lowdin's Bristol porcelain factory and their marks', *Apollo* XLIII no. 254 1946 87–90, 93

817 A.J. Toppin, 'The proprietors of the early Bristol china factory: identified as William Miller and Benjamin Lund', *Trans. Eng. Ceram. Circ.* III no. 3 1954 129–40

818 A. Trapnell, *A catalogue of Bristol and Plymouth porcelain, with examples of Bristol glass and pottery, forming the collection made by Mr Alfred Trapnell, with preface by the Rev. A.W. Oxford*. (Bristol, William George's Sons, 1905) *c.* 60p.

Copy in Plymouth Central Library

819 J.P. Way, *A short history of old Bristol pottery and porcelain marks, etc.* (Bristol, J.P. Way, *c.* 1908) 32p.

PRINTING AND PUBLISHING

820   A.A. Allen and A.G. Powell, *Bristol and its newspapers, 1713–1934.* (Bristol, 1934)

821   D. Bateman, 'The growth of the printing and packaging industry in Bristol, 1800–1914', *in* C.E. Harvey and J. Press, *eds., Studies in the business history of Bristol.* (Bristol, Bristol Academic Press, 1988) 83–107

822   D. Bateman, *An examination of the organisation and policy of the Bristol Typographical Society in the second half of the nineteenth century.* (M.A. thesis, Bristol Polytechnic, 1985)

823   D. Bateman, *The 19th-century Bristol printing trade and the role of the Bristol Typographical Society.* (Ph.D. thesis, Bristol Polytechnic, 1991)

824   B.R.M. Darwin, *Robinsons of Bristol, 1844–1944.* (Bristol, Robinson, 1945) 72p.

Paper bag makers.

825   *Early Bristol newspapers. A detailed catalogue of Bristol newspapers published up to and including the year 1800 in the Bristol Reference Library.* (Bristol Reference Library, 1956) 32p.

826   L.F. Feakes, *The location of printing houses: a case study of the Bristol area.* (Ph.D. thesis, Open University, 1986) 2v.

827   H. Mardon, *Landmarks in the history of a Bristol firm 1824–1904* (Bristol, The Firm, 1918) 66p.

Mardon, Son & Hall

828   Mardon, Son & Hall, *Mardons during the war years.* (Bristol, The Firm, 1946)

829   Partridge & Love Ltd, *A brief record of over 50 years of progress.* (Bristol, The Firm, 1951)

830   J.E. Pritchard, 'The earliest Bristol-printed book', *Trans. Bristol Glos. Archaeol. Soc.* LVI 1934 197–9

'A Forme of Common-Prayer' printed 1643

831   W.K. Sessions, *The King's Printer at Newcastle-upon-Tyne in 1639, at Bristol in 1643–1645, at Exeter in 1645–1646: with illustrations and dates of extant printed works.* Rev. ed. (York, Ebor, 1984) 149p.

832   M. Turner and D. Vaisey, *eds., Art for commerce: illustrations and designs in stock at E.S. & A. Robinson, printers, Bristol in the 1880s.* (London, Scholar Press, 1973) 352p.

Facsimile ed. of Robinson's book of stock designs for paper bags and wrapping paper.

833   A.P. Woolrich, *Printing in Bristol.* (Historical Association, Bristol Branch, Local History Pamphlet no. 63, 1986) 21p.

834   J. Wright & Sons, *125 years of printing and publishing, 1825–1950.* (Bristol, Wright, 1952) 22p.

835   J. Wright & Sons, *150 years of printing and publishing.* (Bristol, 1975)

PUBLIC UTILITIES
Electricity

836   P.G. Lamb, *Electricity in Bristol, 1863–1948.* (Historical Association, Bristol Branch, 1981) 60p.

837   P.Lamb, 'Electric arc lamps in Bristol', *BIAS J.* no. 29 1996 38–42

838   P. Lamb, '100 years of public electricity supply in Bristol', *BIAS J.* no. 26 1993 22–5

839   D.G. Tucker, 'The beginnings of electricity supply in Bristol 1889–1902', *BIAS J.* V 1972 11–18

840   G. Watkins, 'Bristol electricity supply', *BIAS J.* III 1970 22–5

Gas

841   H. Nabb, *The Bristol gas industry 1815–1949.* (Historical Association, Bristol Branch, Local History Pamphlet no. 67, 1987) 48p.

842   H. Nabb, *The Bristol Gas Light Company: the Breillat dynasty of engineers.* (Historical Association, Bristol Branch, 1993) 38p.

843   H. Nabb, 'Notes on the site of the Canon's Marsh gasworks, Bristol', *BIAS J.* no. 26 1993 33

844   M.H. Painting, *The development of the gas industry in the Bristol region, 1810–1950.* (Ph.D. thesis, Bath University, 1979)

Water

845   R. Fulligar, 'Hop House—a Victorian water supply system', *BIAS J.* no. 25 1992 33–6

846   F.C. Jones, *Bristol's water supply and its story.* (Bristol, St Stephen's Press, 1946) 52p.

847   D. Large and F. Round, *Public health in mid-Victorian Bristol.* (Historical Association, Bristol Branch, 1974)

848   P. Skinner, 'Pumping Bristol's water: Part One', *BIAS J.* XI 1978 14–19; 'Part Two. Chelvey', XII 1979 12–15

SHIPBUILDING

See also nos. 234–9

849   A. Ball and D. Wright, *SS* Great Britain. (Newton Abbot, David & Charles, 1981) 96p.

850   J. Blake, *Restoring the* Great Britain. (Bristol, Redcliffe Press, 1989) 95p.

851   E. Corlett, *The iron ship: the history and significance of Brunel's* Great Britain. (Bradford-on-Avon, Moonraker Press, 1975)

       The history of the 'SS *Great Britain*' including her salvage and return to Bristol.

852   E.C.B. Corlett, 'The Steamship *Great Britain*', *Trans. R. Instn. Naval Archit.* CXIII 1971 411–37

853 B. Dumpleton and M. Miller, *Brunel's three ships.* (Melksham, Venton, 1974) 169p.

854 G. Farr, *Bristol shipbuilding in the nineteenth century containing a list of the vessels known to have been built in the Port of Bristol, with an introduction, notes on the builders, etc.* (Historical Association, Bristol Branch, pamphlet no. 27, 1971) 25p.

855 G. Farr, *Shipbuilding in the Port of Bristol.* (Greenwich, National Maritime Museum, 1977) 68p.

856 G.E. Farr, *The steamship* Great Britain. 2nd ed. (Historical Association, Bristol Branch, pamphlet no. 11, 1970)

857 G.E. Farr, *The steamship* Great Western: *the first Atlantic liner.* (Historical Association, Bristol Branch, pamphlet no. 8, 1963) 18p.

858 R. Goold-Adams, *The return of the* Great Britain. (London, Weidenfeld & Nicolson, 1976) 226p.

859 R. Goold-Adams, 'The SS *Great Britain* and its salvaging', *J. R. Soc. Arts* CXIX 5176 1971 234–48

860 H. Gregor, *The SS* 'Great Britain'. (Macmillan, 1971) 33p.

861 D. Griffiths, *Brunel's* Great Western. (Wellingborough, Patrick Stephens, 1985) 160p.

862 J.C.G. Hill, *Shipshape and Bristol fashion.* Rev. ed. (Bristol, Redcliffe Press, 1983) 113p.

863 A. King, 'Bristol's other iron ship: steam tug *'Mayflower''*, *BIAS J.* XVI 1983 10–14

864 M.E. Leek, 'The appearance and lead of the rig of the S.S. *Great Britain* in 1845', *Mar. Mirr.* LXII 1976 327–36

865 L.H. Matthews, 'The last of the *'Great Britain''*, *Geog. Mag.* XXVI 1953–4 68–74

866 J. O'Callaghan, *The saga of the steam ship* Great Britain. (London, Hart-Davies, 1971) 190p.

867 K.T. Rowland, *The* Great Britain. (Newton Abbot, David & Charles, 1971) 132p.

868 N. Von Behr, 'The B.D.I.: 'the most perfect [dredger] by far in the world'', *BIAS J.* no. 27 1994 19–24

SLAVE TRADE

869 E. Donnan, *Documents illustrative of the history of the slave trade to America.* (Washington, Carnegie Institute, Publication no. 409, 1930–35; reissued by Octagon Books, New York, 1965) 4v.

870 C.M. MacInnes, *Bristol and the slave trade.* (Historical Association, Bristol Branch, Local History Pamphlet no. 7, 1963) 19p.

871 P. Marshall, *The anti-slave trade movement in Bristol.* (Historical Association, Bristol Branch, Local History Pamphlet no. 20, 1968) 26p.

872 P. Marshall, *Bristol and the abolition of slavery: the politics of emancipation.* (Historical Association, Bristol Branch, pamphlet no. 37, 1975) 28p.

873 D.G. Rees, *The role of Bristol in the Atlantic slave trade, 1710–69.* (M.A. thesis, Exeter University, 1971)

874 D. Richardson, ed., *Bristol, Africa and the eighteenth-century slave trade to America: vol. 1. The years of expansion, 1698–1729* (Bristol Record Society Publications vol. 38, 1986) 203p

875 D. Richardson, ed., *Bristol, Africa and the eighteenth-century slave trade to America: vol 2. The years of ascendancy 1730–1745* (Bristol Record Society Publications vol. 39, 1987) 157p.

876 D. Richardson, ed., *Bristol, Africa and the eighteenth-century slave trade to America: vol.3. The years of decline 1746–1769* (Bristol Record Society Publications vol. 42, 1991) 249p.

877 D. Richardson, ed., *Bristol, Africa and the eighteenth-century slave trade to America: vol.4. The final years, 1770–1807* (Bristol Record Society Publications vol. 47, 1996) 279p.

878 P.D. Richardson, *The Bristol slave trade in the eighteenth century.* (M.A. thesis, Manchester University, 1969)

879 D. Richardson, *The Bristol slave traders: a collective portrait.* (Historical Association, Bristol Branch, pamphlet no. 60, 1985) 32p.

SOAPMAKING

880 Company of Soapmakers, *Proceedings, minutes and enrolments of the Company of Soapmakers, 1562–1642, edited by H.E. Matthews.* (Bristol Record Society, Publications for 1939) 263p.

881 S.J. Diaper, 'Christopher Thomas & Brothers Ltd: the last Bristol soapmakers. An aspect of Bristol's economic development in the nineteenth century', *Trans. Bristol Glos. Archaeol. Soc.* CV 1987 223–32

882 D.T.A. Linday and G.C. Bamber, *Soapmaking past and present: special edition to commemorate 100 years of soapmaking 1876–1976.* (Nottingham, Gerard Bros. Ltd, 1976) 24p.

883 T. O'Brien, 'Christopher Thomas & Brothers Ltd' *Progress* XL 1949 43–8

884 J. Somerville, *Christopher Thomas, soapmaker of Bristol: the story of Christr. Thomas & Bros. 1745–1954.* (Bristol, White Tree Books, 1991) 121p.

TEXTILES

885 F.F. Fox and J. Taylor, eds., *Some account of the Guild of Weavers in Bristol chiefly from MSS.* (Bristol, Printed for private circulation, 1889) 100p.

886 P.K. Griffin, 'The diary of a Bristol merchant, 1850–53', *Trans. Bristol Glos. Archaeol. Soc.* XC 1971 228–30

The diary of John Cousins, woollen merchant.

887 S.J. Jones, 'The cotton industry in Bristol', *Inst. Br. Geogr. Trans. Pap.* XIII 1947 59–79

TOBACCO TRADE

888 B.W.E. Alford, 'Penny cigarettes, oligopoly and entrepreneurship in the U.K. tobacco industry in the late nineteenth century', *in* B. Supple, *ed., Essays in British business history.* (Oxford, Clarendon Press, 1977) 49–68

889 B.W.E. Alford, *W.D. & H.O. Wills and the development of the UK tobacco industry, 1786–1965.* (London, Methuen, 1973) 500p.

890 S.V. Dickinson, *The first sixty years, a history of the Imperial Tobacco Company ... 1902–62* (1965) 134p.

891 *Tobacco and its associations with Bristol, compiled with the compliments of W.D. & H.O. Wills, Bristol.* (Bristol, The Firm, *c.* 1930)

Copy in Bristol University Library

892 N.C.P. Tyack, 'The tobacco trade between Bristol and Virginia, 1600–1700. Part 1', *Wills Works Mag.* VII no. 52 1935 144–8; 'Part 2', VII no. 53 193–200; 'Part 3', VII no. 54 234

893 R. Till, *Wills of Bristol 1786–1901.* (Bristol, Wills, 1954) 74p.

Originally published in *Wills Works Magazine*

Tobacco Pipes

894 R.G. Jackson and R.H. Price, *Bristol clay pipes: a study of makers and their marks.* (Bristol, Bristol City Museum, Research Monograph no. 1, 1974) 152p.

895 A.H. Oswald, 'The archaeology and economic history of English clay tobacco pipes', *J. Br. Archaeol. Assoc.* XXIII 1960 40–102

896 A. Peacey, *The archaeology of the clay tobacco pipe. XIV: The development of the clay tobacco pipe kiln in the British Isles.* (Oxford, Tempus Reparatum, BAR British Series 246, 1996) 295p.

897 R.H. Price and others, *Bristol clay pipe makers.* (Bristol, The Authors, 1979) 320p.

898 R. Price, R. Jackson, P. Jackson, P. Harper and O. Kent, 'The Ring family of Bristol, clay tobacco pipe manufacturers', *Post-Med. Archaeol.* XVIII 1984 263–300

899 R. Price, R. Jackson and P. Jackson, 'Wales and the Bristol clay pipe trade', *Bull. Welsh Med. Pottery Res. Gp.* III 1980 59–72

900 J.E. Pritchard, 'Tobacco pipes of Bristol of the XVIIth century and their makers', *Trans. Bristol Glos. Archaeol. Soc.* XLV 1923 165–91

901 I.C. Walker, *The Bristol clay tobacco-pipe industry.* (Bristol, City Museum, 1971)

902 I.C. Walker, *Clay tobacco-pipes, with particular reference to the Bristol industry.* (Ottawa, National Historic Parks and Sites Branch, History and Archaeology Series, 11a–d, 1977) 4v.

903 D.B. Whitehouse, 'The bore diameter of clay tobacco pipes made at Bristol between 1620 and 1850', *Trans. Bristol Glos. Archaeol. Soc.* LXXXV 1966 202–6

TRANSPORT
General

904   C. Harvey and J. Press, 'Sir George White and the urban transport revolution in Bristol, 1875–1916', *in* C.E. Harvey and J. Press, *eds., Studies in the business history of Bristol.* (Bristol, Bristol Academic Press, 1988) 137–63

905   A. Bradley and J. Press, *eds., Catalogue of the George White papers.* (Bristol, Bristol Academic Press, 1989) 126p.

906   C. Harvey and J. Press, 'The George White papers at Bristol Record Office', *Bus. Archives* no. 54 1987 17–30

907   C. Harvey and J. Press, 'Sir George White: a career in transport, 1874–1916', *J. Transp. Hist.* 3rd ser. IX no. 2 1988 170–89

908   C. Harvey and J. Press, *Sir George White of Bristol 1854–1916.* (Historical Association, Bristol Branch, 1989)

909   G. White, *Tramlines to the stars: George White of Bristol.* (Bristol, Redcliffe Press, 1995) 80p.

The author is White's great-grandson. White was also one of the founders of the aircraft industry in Bristol

Canals

See also no. 694

910   B. Greenhill, 'Sailing barges of the Severn: the rise and fall of the trows', *Country Life* 10 April 1969

911   E. Walls, *The Bristol Avon.* (Bristol, Arrowsmith, 1927) 318p.

Part of the 'Rivers of England'.

Railways

See also nos. 701–2

912   A.W. Arthurton, 'The Camerton and Limpley Stoke Railway', *Rlwy. Mag.* XXIX 1911 33–7

913   Avon County Council, *Railways in Avon: a short history of their development and decline 1832–1982.* (The Council, Planning Dept., 1983) 27p.

914   Avon County Council, *Railway stations and halts in Avon: a photographic record.* (The Council, n.d.)

915   G. Body, *The Severn Tunnel: an official history of the building and operation of Britain's longest main line railway tunnel.* (Weston-super-Mare, British Rail (Western) and Avon-Anglia, 1986) 48p.

916   G. Channon, *Bristol and the promotion of the Great Western Railway.* (Historical Association, Bristol Branch, Pamphlet no. 62, 1985) 32p.

917   C.R. Clinker, 'Bristol Port Railway and Pier', *Rlwy. Mag.* XCIII no. 571 1947 267–70

918   C.R. Clinker, 'Railway development in Bristol', *Rlwy. Mag.* CII 1956 575–80, 663–7, 736–40, 772

919   R. Day, 'Canons Marsh Goods Shed', *BIAS J.* no. 27 1994 37–8

920 P. Harris, *Bristol's railway mania 1862–1864*. (Historical Association, Bristol Branch, pamphlet no. 66, 1987) 23p.

921 M. Harris, ed., *Brunel, the GWR & Bristol*. (London, Ian Allan, 1993) 144p.

922 W. Harris, 'Charfield Station', *BIAS J*. XI 1978 20–21

923 C.G. Maggs, *Rail centres: Bristol*. (London, Ian Allan, 1981) 128p.

924 C.G. Maggs, *The Bristol port railway and pier and the Clifton extension railway*. (Blandford, Oakwood Press, 1975) 59p.

925 C.G. Maggs, 'The Severn Bridge Railway', *Rlwy. Mag*. CVII 1961 22–6

926 C.G. Maggs, 'The Thornbury Branch', *Rlwy. Mag*. CIII 1957 866–8

927 J. Mosse, 'Bristol Temple Meads', *BIAS J*. IV 1971 10–11

928 C.L. Mowat, 'The Bristol and Portishead Pier and Railway', *Rlwy. Mag*. June 1955 371–8

929 M. Oakley, *Railways in Avon*. (Weston-super-Mare, Avon-Anglia, 1986) 48p.

930 K. Thomas, 'Wagons of the A. & G. Dramway', *BIAS J*. XXI 1989 23–7

Avon & Gloucestershire Dramroad

931 J.W. Totterdill, ' ... A peculiar form of construction', *J. Bristol Somerset Soc. Archit*. V 1961 111–12

Deals with the design of Temple Meads station roof.

932 A.R.F. Trew, 'The old Bristol and Gloucestershire Railway', *Rlwy. Mag*. XXV 1909 452–9

933 M. Vincent, *Lines to Avonmouth: a story of railways in the Bristol area*. (Oxford, Oxford Publishing Co., 1979) 158p.

Roads and Road Transport

934 J.B. Appleby, *Bristol trams remembered*. (Westbury-on-Trym, The Author, 1969) 70p.

935 Bristol Omnibus Co. Ltd, *The people's carriage, 1874–1974* (Bristol, 1974)

936 Bristol Tramways & Carriage Co., *Pictorial Bristol and handbook of the Bristol Tramways and Carriage Co*. (Bristol, 1897)

937 N. Cossons, 'Turnpike roads of the Bristol region—a preliminary study', *BIAS J*. I 1968 6–13

938 M.S. Curtis, *Bristol buses in camera*. (London, Ian Allan, 1984) 112p.

939 M. Curtis, *Bristol: a century on the road*. (Falmouth, Glasney Press, 1977) 144p.

940 M.S. Curtis, *Bristol VR*. (London, Ian Allan, 1994) 112p.

Buses built by Bristol Commercial Vehicles, Brislington

941 P. Elkin, 'The Grenville steam carriage', *BIAS J*. X 1977 19

942 P.T. Marcy, 'Bristol's roads and communications on the eve of the Industrial Revolution, 1740–1780', *Trans. Bristol Glos. Archaeol. Soc*. LXXXVII 1969 149–72

943 K. Morgan, *Country carriers in the Bristol region in the late nineteenth century*. (Historical Association, Bristol Branch, Local History Pamphlet no.

64, 1986) 15p.

944   S.A. Rees, 'Turnpike roads of the Bristol area survey: Part 2', *BIAS J.* V 1972 19–24

945   R. Winstone, *Bristol's trams.* (Bristol, The Author, 1974) 84p.

Bridges

946   W.H. Barlow, 'Description of the Clifton Suspension Bridge', *Min. Proc. Instn. Civ. Engrs.* XXVI 1867 243–57

947   G. Body, *Clifton Suspension Bridge—an illustrated history.* (Bradford-on-Avon, Moonraker Press, 1976) 76p.

948   J. Bridges, *Four designs for rebuilding Bristol Bridge ... as also a short description of the method and size of the materials propos'd to be used in the course of this work.* (Bristol, E. Ward, 1760) 59p.

949   A.E. Cottrell, *The history of Clifton Suspension Bridge.* (Bristol, 1928)

950   *History and construction of the Clifton Suspension Bridge: illustrated by view of the bridge and sections of the various parts. With detailed explanations.* (Bristol, J. Wright & Sons, 1864)

951   C.J. Long, *The history of the Clifton Suspension Bridge.* 17th ed. (Bristol, Clifton Suspension Bridge Trust, 1968)

952   R.F.D. Porter Goff, 'Brunel and the design of the Clifton Suspension Bridge', *Proc. Instn. Civ. Engrs.* Part I LVI 1974 303–21

953   F. Stratford, *A short account of the manner proposed for rebuilding of Bristol Bridge etc.,* (Bristol, 1760)

954   W.W. Webb, *A complete account of the origin and progress of the Clifton Suspension Bridge, over the River Avon.* (Bristol, J. Wright, 1864) 62p.

Ports and Docks

955   'The Avonmouth Dock extension', *Engineer* 18 May 1928

956   M. Ballard, *Bristol: sea-port and city, with an introduction and editorial assistance of Berna Clark.* (London, Constable, 1966) 208p.

957   I. Benbrook, *Bristol city docks: a guide to the historic harbour.* (Bristol, Redcliffe Press, 1989)

958   J. Bird, *The major seaports of the United Kingdom.* (London, Hutchinson, 1963) 454p.

Chapter 7. pp. 181–205 Bristol, the Avon and Avonmouth

959   W.D. Bowman, *Bristol.* (London, Geoffrey Bles, 1927) 128p.

Famous ports series

960   B.J.H. Brown, 'Bristol's second outport: Portishead in the nineteenth century', *Transp. Hist.* IV 1970 80–93

961   A. Buchanan, 'The Cumberland Basin, Bristol', *Ind. Archaeol.* VI 1969 325–33

The name was given to the entrance basin of the Bristol floating harbour.

962   R.A. Buchanan, 'The construction of the floating harbour in Bristol, 1804–1809', *Trans. Bristol Glos. Archaeol. Soc.* LXXXVIII 1969 184–204

963 R.A. Buchanan, 'I.K. Brunel and the Port of Bristol', *Trans. Newcomen Soc.* XLII 1969–70 41–56

964 R.A. Buchanan, *Nineteenth-century engineers in the Port of Bristol.* (Historical Association, Bristol Branch, Local History Pamphlet no. 26, 1971) 19p.

965 City Docks Working Group, *Bristol City Docks—maritime walks.* (City of Bristol District Council, 1983)

966 F.E. Cooke, *The economic development of the port of Bristol, 1900–45.* (M.Sc. thesis, London University (External), 1953)

967 N. Coombes, *Passenger steamers of the Bristol Channel: a pictorial record.* (Truro, Twelveheads, 1990) 120p.

968 C.D. Curtis, 'The Port of Uphill', *Somerset Dorset N. & Q.* XXIX 1973

969 J.W. Damer Powell, 'Lists of Bristol ships 1571 and 1572', *Trans. Bristol Glos. Archaeol. Soc.* LII 1930 117–22

970 P.Elkin, *Images of maritime Bristol.* (Derby, Breedon Books, 1995) 197p.
Contains almost 350 pictures of the docks.

971 E.J. Farr *and others, Bristol city docks remembered, 1970–1973.* (Bristol, Bristol Shiplovers Society, 1986) 40p.

972 G. Farr, 'Bristol Channel pilotage: historical notes on its administration and craft', *Mar. Mirr* XXXIX 1953 27–44

973 G.E. Farr, 'The Bristol City Line, of Bristol, England', *American Neptune* XIV 1954 115–35

974 G. Farr, 'Bristol quay bollards', *BIAS J.* III 1970 5–8

975 G.E. Farr, ed., *Records of Bristol ships, 1800–1838. Vessels over 150 tons.* (Bristol Record Society, Publications no. 15, 1950) 296p.

976 G.E. Farr, 'Sea Mills Dock', *Mar. Mirr.* XXV 1939 349–50

977 T. Fisher, D. Jones and R. Day, 'The Port of Bristol Underfall Yard workshops', *BIAS J.* X 1977 4–11

978 T. Fisher and J. Powell, 'The hydraulic system in Bristol City docks', *BIAS J.* XII 1979 6–10

979 G.L. Good, 'The excavation of two docks at Narrow Quay, Bristol, 1978–9', *Post-Med. Archaeol.* XXI 1987 25–126

980 J.C.G. Hill, *Shipshape and Bristol fashion.* 2nd ed. (Liverpool, *Journal of Commerce and Shipping* 1966) 110p?

981 P.W. Hobday, *Bristol city docks: the final years of commercial shipping.* (Liverpool, Jocast, 1982) 41p.
Chiefly illustrations

982 T. Howard, *Report ... on ... dockizing the River Avon.* (Bristol, 1879)

983 D.P. Hussey, *Re-investigating coastal trade; the ports of the Bristol Channel and the Severn Estuary, c. 1695–c. 1704.* (Ph.D. thesis, Wolverhampton University, 1995)

984 F.D.C. Jeffery, 'The Port of Bristol workshops at the Underfall Yard, Bristol', *BIAS J.* I 1968 20–4

985 R.H. Jones, 'The administration of the Port of Bristol', *Public Admin.* XVI

1958 314–23

986 E. Jordan, *The story of Lovell's shipping*. (Bristol, White Tree Books, 1992) 180p.

987 D. Large, ed., *The Port of Bristol, 1848–1884*. (Bristol Record Society, Publications vol. 36, 1984) 221p.

988 J. Lord and J. Southam, T*he floating harbour: a landscape history of Bristol City Docks*. (Bristol, Redcliffe Press, 1983) 128p.

989 B.J.A. McClelland, *The economic and social development of the Port of Bristol 1848–1908*. (M.Sc. thesis, Bath University, 1979)

990 P.V. McGrath, 'Merchant shipping in the 17th century: the evidence of the Bristol Deposition Books', *Mar. Mirr.* XL 1954 282–93; 'Part II', XLI 1955 23–37

991 P.V. McGrath, 'The Merchant Venturers and Bristol shipping in the early seventeenth century', *Mar. Mirr.* XXXVI 1950 69–80

992 C.M. MacInnes, 'The Port of Bristol' *in* H.A. Cronne, T.W. Moody and D.B. Quinn, eds., *Essays in British and Irish history in honour of James Eadie Todd* (London, Frederick Muller, 1949) 200–17

993 J.B. Mackenzie, 'The Avonmouth Dock', *Min. Proc. Instn. Civ. Engrs.* LV 1878–9 3–21

994 W.E. Minchinton, *Politics and the port of Bristol in the eighteenth century: the petitions of the Society of Merchant Venturers 1698–1803*. (Bristol Record Society, vol. 23, 1963) 225p.

995 W.E. Minchinton, *The port of Bristol in the 18th century*. (Historical Association, Bristol Branch, 1962) 24p.

996 W.G. Neale, *At the port of Bristol, vol. 1. Members problems 1848–1899* (Bristol, Port of Bristol Authority, 1968) 219p.

997 W.G. Neale, *At the port of Bristol vol 2. The turn of the tide 1900–1914*. (Bristol, Port of Bristol Authority, 1970) 212p.

998 W.G. Neale, *The tides of war and the Port of Bristol 1914–1918*. (Bristol, Port of Bristol Authority, 1976) 315p.

999 T. Page and J. Hawkshaw, *Report on whether the plan for converting the bed of the Avon into a floating harbour would be practicable* ... (26 July 1860) 4p. + map.

Copy in Bristol City Library

1000 R. Parsons, *The story of Kings: C.J. Kings & Sons 1850 to the present day*. (Bristol, White Tree Books, 1988)

1001 R.M. Parsons, *The white ships: the banana trade at the Port of Bristol*. (Bristol, City of Bristol Museum and Art Gallery, 1982) 93p.

1002 Port of Bristol Authority, Royal Portbury Dock, 1977. *Avonmouth Dock centenary, 1877–1977*. (Bristol, The Authority, 1977) 15p.

1003 J. Powell, 'Brunel Lock and the feeder cut: two unsuccessful attempts at re-opening', *BIAS J.* XVII 1985 12–14

Bristol Docks

1004 J. Press, *The merchant seamen of Bristol, 1747–1789*. (Historical Association, Bristol Branch, 1976) 23p.

1005 W.N. Reid, *History of the Port of Bristol.* (1877)
Copy in Bristol University Library

1006 J. Rich, 'New dock at Pill', *BIAS J.* XVI 1983 31–5

1007 D. Ross-Johnson, 'The Port of Bristol in the past and present', *Dock Harbour Authority* IV 1923–4 299–303

1008 Royal Portbury Dock 1977, *Avonmouth Dock Centenary, 1877–1977.* (Port of Bristol Authority, 1977) 20p.
Pamphlet to commemorate the opening of the Royal Portbury Dock

1009 J.W. Sherborne, *The port of Bristol in the Middle Ages.* 2nd ed. (Historical Association, Bristol Branch, 1971)

1010 F. Shipsides and R. Wall, *Bristol: maritime city.* (Bristol, Redcliffe, 1981) 47p.

1011 F. Shipsides and R. Wall, *Quayside Bristol: city and port in recent years.* (Bristol, Redcliffe, 1992) 104p.

1012 J.R. Stevens, *An examination of the factors which link Bristol dock policy with the development of the tramp shipping of the port, 1840–90.* (M.A. thesis, Bristol University, 1940)

1013 R. Stiles, 'Bristol City docks', *BIAS J.* VI 1973 18–20
A diagram listing sites of industrial archaeological importance

1014 C. Townsend, *Report of the Committee for considering the desirability and practicability of dockizing the River Avon.* (Bristol, 1883)
C. Townsend was the chairman.

1015 J. Vanes, *The Port of Bristol in the sixteenth century.* (Historical Association, Bristol Branch, 1977) 26p.

1016 F. Walker, 'The Port of Bristol', *Econ. Geog.* XV 1939 109–24

1017 D.J. Webb, *The changing industrial geography of the port and city of Bristol since 1861: a study in port function.* (M.Phil. thesis London University, 1967)

1018 C. Wells, *A short history of the Port of Bristol.* (Bristol, Arrowsmith, 1909) 425p.

1019 A.F. Williams, 'Bristol port plans and improvement schemes of the 18th century', *Trans. Bristol Glos. Archaeol. Soc.* LXXXI 1962 138–88

OTHER INDUSTRIES

1020 P. Addison, 'Winford ochre and oxide', *BIAS J.* no. 26 1993 2–7
The Winford ochre industry.

1021 M. Boorer, 'Bristol pewterers from 1810 to 1878', *J. Pewter Soc.* II no. 2 1979 3–5

1022 J. Bryant, 'Ropewalks and ropemakers of Bristol', *BIAS J.* X 1977 12–17

1023 J. Christie-Miller, *Feltmakers: a record of two feltmaking families.* (Stockport, Swain & Co., 1957) 28p.

1024 W.L. Goodman, 'Bristol carpenters' nails, 1492–1586', *Mar. Mirr* LIX

1973

1025 W.L. Goodman, 'Musical instruments and their makers in Bristol apprentice registers, 1536–1643', *Galpin Soc. J.* XXVIII 1974 9–14

1026 J.W. Greenwood, 'The closure of the Tudor mint at Bristol', *Br. Numismatic J.* LI 1981 107–11

1027 S. Gwyn-Smith and G. Grant, *Bengal matches from Bristol: Octavius Hunt Ltd* (Kidlington, Gwyn-Smith, 1987) 54p.

1028 G.E. P. How, 'The goldsmiths of Bristol', *Connoisseur* CLXXXVI 1974 252–5

1029 D. Street, *Not worth a pin: pin-making in the Kingswoood area.* (Avon County Community Environment Scheme, 1986) 12p.

1030 K.M. Walton, 'Eighteenth-century cabinet-making in Bristol', *Furniture Hist.* XII 1976

Ballooning

1031 M. Crane, 'Sadler's balloon ascent from Bristol in 1810', *Avon Past* no. 3 1980 28–32

1032 J. Penny, 'Ballooning in the Bristol region: 1784 to 1786. The opening chapter in the history of local manned flight', *BIAS J.* no. 29 1996 30–7

1033 H.M. Wills, 'Ballooning at Bath: some notable ascents', *BIAS J.* XVI 1983 5–9

Cornwall

GENERAL

See also nos. 1–22

1034 W.G.V. Balchin, *The Cornish landscape*. (London, Hodder & Stoughton, 1983) 234p.

1035 W.J. Bennett, *The settlement of Cornwall with particular reference to the economic aspects of its development 1750–1950*. (M.A. thesis, London University, 1951)

1036 M.O. Coombe, 'The industrial history of Hayle', *J. Ind. Archaeol.* X no. 1 1973 64–76

1037 Cornwall Archaeology Unit, *Minions Survey*. (CAU Reports, 1993) 313p.

Examines the development of industry on south-east Bodmin Moor

1038 J.S. Courtenay, 'A treatise on the statistics of Cornwall', *Ann. Reps. R. Cornwall Polytech. Soc.* 6th Rep. 1838 81–140

Many industries are covered.

1039 D.H. Cullum, *Society and economy in west Cornwall, c. 1588–1750.* (Ph.D. thesis, Exeter University, 1993)

1040 W.H. Curnow, *The industrial archaeology of Cornwall*. (Truro, Tor Mark Press, 1969)

1041 B. Deacon, 'Proto-industrialization and potatoes: a revised narrative for nineteenth-century Cornwall', *Cornish Stud.* 2nd ser. V 1997 60–84

1042 J.J. Fox, 'The relative prosperity of different parts of Cornwall before the opening of the Cornwall Railway, as shown by the excess of births over deaths from 1855 to 1858', *Ann. Reps. R. Cornwall Polytech. Soc.* no. 28, 1860 126–8

1043 W.K.V. Gale, 'Iron in the Cornish Industrial Revolution', *J. Trevithick Soc.* no. 3 1975 22–42

1044 M.J.J.R. Hatcher, *The assessionable manors of the Duchy of Cornwall in the later Middle Ages*. (Ph.D. thesis, London University, 1967)

1045 J. Hatcher, 'A diversified economy: later medieval Cornwall', *Econ. Hist. Rev.* 2nd ser. XXII no. 2 1969 208–27

1046 J. Hatcher, *Rural economy and society in the Duchy of Cornwall, 1300–1500.* (Cambridge, University Press, 1970) 322p.

1047 J. Keast, *'The king of Mid-Cornwall'—the life of Joseph Thomas Treffry (1782–1850).* (Redruth, Dyllansow Truran, 1982) 202p.

A landowner, mineowner, and entrepreneur in harbour building, roads and railways.

1048 D.A. Kneebone, *Fish, tin and copper*. (Redruth, Dyllansow Truran, 1983) 64p.

A general industrial survey of Cornwall

1049 P. Laws, *The industries of Penzance*. (St Austell, Trevithick Society, 1978) 48p.

1050 T.W. McGuinness, *Population changes in Cornwall in relation to economic resources*. (Ph.D. thesis, London University, 1944)

1051 T.W. McGuinness, 'Occupational changes in Cornwall', *Ann. Reps. R. Cornwall Polytech. Soc.* XI no. 2 1943 78–107

1052 N.J.G. Pounds, 'The Domesday geography of Cornwall', *Ann. Reps. R. Cornwall Polytech. Soc.* X no. 1 1942 68–81

1053 N.J.G. Pounds, *The historical geography of Cornwall.* (Ph.D. thesis, London University (External), 1945)

1054 N.J.G. Pounds, 'The movement of population in Cornwall during the 18th century', *Ann. Reps. R. Cornwall Polytech. Soc.* IX no. 5 1941 89–93

1055 W.J. Rowe, *Cornwall in the Age of the Industrial Revolution.* 2nd ed. (St Austell, Cornish Hillside, 1993) 375p.

1056 W.J. Rowe, *The Industrial Revolution in Cornwall, 1740–1870.* (D.Phil. thesis, Oxford University, 1950)

1057 J. Rowe, 'Humphrey Davy and the Cornish contribution to the Industrial Revolution', *J. Trevithick Soc.* no. 6 1978 55–63

1058 A.L. Rowse, *Tudor Cornwall. Portrait of a society.* (London, Cape, 1941) 462p.

A social and economic survey.

1059 M. Tangye, *Portreath: some chapters in its history.* (Redruth, The Author, 1968) 56p.

A general description of Porthreath's industries, including limeburning, shipbuilding, tin streaming, quarrying etc.

1060 A.C. Todd, *Beyond the blaze—a biography of Davies Gilbert.* (Truro, Barton, 1967) 293p.

An early Cornish entrepreneur

1061 A.C. Todd and P. Laws, *The industrial archaeology of Cornwall.* (Newton Abbot, David & Charles, 1972) 288p.

1062 J.C.A. Whetter, 'Cornish trade in the 17th century: an analysis of the port books', *J. R. Instn. Cornwall* n.s. IV 1964 388–413

1063 J. Whetter, *Cornwall in the 17th century. An economic survey of Kernow.* (Padstow, The Lodenek Press, 1974) 219p.

1064 J.C.A. Whetter, *The economic history of Cornwall in the seventeenth century.* (Ph.D. thesis, London University, 1965)

1065 G.B. White, 'A Cawsand capitalist: the Book of William Ellis, I & II', *Devon Cornwall N. & Q.* XXXII 1973 note 174 230–7, note 173 271–5

1066 R.N. Worth, 'The tokens of Cornwall', *J. R. Instn. Cornwall* V 1874–8 28–49

AGRICULTURE

See also nos. 23–68 and 1114, 1240

1067 C.J. Caseldine, 'Environmental change in Cornwall during the last 13000 years', *Cornish Archaeol.* XIX 1980 3–16

1068 V. Chesher and J. Palmer eds., *Three hundred years on Penwith farms.* (Penwith, Penwith Local History Group, 1994)

1069 J. Couch, 'Observations on the harvest in the east part of Cornwall from the years 1816–1852', *Ann. Reps. R. Cornwall Polytech. Soc.* no. 20 1852 68–74

1070 R. Fraser, *General view of the agriculture of the County of Cornwall ... prepared for the Board of Agriculture.* (London, 1794)

1071 G.E. Fussell, 'Cornish farming A.D. 1500–1910', *Amateur Histn.* IV no. 8 1960 338–45

1072 J. Hanson and P. Hanson, *To clothe the fields with plenty.* (Landfall, Landfall Publications, 1997) 64p.

A review of farming in Cornwall at the end of the 18th century, centred on George Wilce of St Kew.

1073 W. Hawk, *Agricultural experiments in Cornwall, 1895–1925.* (Truro, Netherton & Worth, 1929) 251p.

1074 J. Hatcher, 'Non-manorialism in medieval Cornwall', *Agric. Hist. Rev.* XVIII 1970 1–16

1075 N. Hilton, 'The Land's End peninsula: the influence of history on agriculture', *Geog. J.* CXIX 1953 57–72

1076 R. Kain and H. Holt, 'Agriculture and land use in Cornwall, c. 1840', *S. Hist.* III 1981 139–81

1077 W.F. Karkeek, 'On the farming of Cornwall', *J. R. Agric. Soc.* VI 1845 66p.

Reprinted separately. Copy in Cornish Studies Library, Redruth

1078 L. Maker, 'The Callington platform'—Cornish pioneers in agriculture', *Ann. Reps. R. Cornwall Polytech. Soc.* IX no. 5 1941 26–35

James Walter Lawry, Daniel Brent, William Hawk and others.

1079 I.S. Maxwell, 'Cornish farming, c. 1800', *Ann. Reps. R. Cornwall Polytech. Soc.* X no. 1 1942 27–50

1080 M. Overton, 'The 1801 crop returns for Cornwall', *in* M. Havinden, *ed., Husbandry and marketing in the South-West, 1500–1800.* (Exeter University, Exeter Papers in Economic History, no. 8, 1973) 39–62

1081 F.G. Payne, 'An old Cornish plough, and others', *Antiquity* XXI no. 83 1947 151–57

1082 H.M.C. Payne, 'Cornish pounds', *Old Cornwall* IV no. 5 1946 143–47

1083 G.H. Pethybridge, 'The potato blight yesterday and today', *Ann. Reps. R. Cornwall Polytech. Soc.* IX no. 3 1939 48–61

1084 R. Potts, *ed., A calendar of Cornish glebe terriers, 1673–1735.* (Devon & Cornwall Record Society, Publications, n.s. 19, 1974) 209p.

1085 N.J. G. Pounds, 'Barton farming in 18th century Cornwall', *Ann. Reps. R. Cornwall Polytech. Soc.* n.s. VII 1973 55–75

1086 N.J.G. Pounds, 'Food production and distribution in pre-industrial Cornwall', *in* W. Minchinton, *ed., Population and marketing: two studies in the history of the South-West.* (Exeter University, Exeter Papers in Economic History, no. 11, 1976) 107–22

1087 N.J.G. Pounds, 'The Lanhydrock Atlas and Cornish agriculture about 1700', *Ann. Reps. R. Cornwall Polytech. Soc.* 1944 n.s. XI pt. 3 112–25

1088 C. Riddle, *'So useful an undertaking': a history of the Royal Cornwall Show 1793–1993.* (Royal Cornwall Agricultural Association, 1993) 361p.

1089 J. Rowe, 'Cornish agriculture in the age of the Great Depression', *J. R. Instn. Cornwall* n.s. III no. 3 1959 147–62

1090 F.W. Shepherd, 'Agriculture in the Isles of Scilly', *Agriculture* LV 1948–9 528–36

1091 J. Stevens, *A Cornish farmer's diary: selections from the diary of James Stevens of Zennor and Sancreed (1847–1918) edited by P.A.S. Pool*. (Published by the Editor, 1977) 273p.

1092 A.C. Thomas, 'The glebe lands of Camborne', *Ann. Reps. R. Cornwall Polytech. Soc.* 1949 22–52

Includes extracts from terriers of 1601, 1625, 1680, 1727

1093 J. Tucker, *A Cornish farmer's boy*. (Studley, Brewin Books, 1993) 150p.

1094 F.A. Turk, 'The Cornish goat: its type and its past', *J. R. Instn. Cornwall* n.s. VIII no. 3 1980 243–6

1095 C.E. Welch, 'A survey of some duchy manors', *Devon Cornwall N. & Q.* XXIX 1962–4 161–4, 196–200, 214–17, 241–3, 276–9; XXX 1965–7 4–7, 33–6, 67–70, 102–5

1096 J.C.A. Whetter, 'Five Cornish farmers in the 17th century', *Old Cornwall* VII 1967–73 81–90

1097 G.K. Whyatt, *Land use in Cornwall at the end of the seventeenth century*. (M.A. thesis, University of Wales, 1959)

1098 P.D. Wood, 'Open-field strips, Forrabury Common, near Boscastle', *Cornish Archaeol.* no. 2 1963 29–33

1099 G.B. Worgan, *General view of the agriculture of Cornwall ... published by order of the Board of Agriculture*. (London, 1811) 192p.

ARCHITECTURE AND BUILDINGS
Domestic

See also no. 1445

1100 V.M. Chesher and F.J. Chesher, *The Cornishman's house: an introduction to the history of traditional domestic architecture in Cornwall*. (Truro, Barton, 1968) 142p.

1101 V. Chesher, *Industrial housing in the tin and copper mining areas of Cornwall*. (Cornwall, Trevithick Society, 1981) 26p.

1102 F. Chesher, 'The late medieval house at Colquite, St Mabyn', *Cornish Archaeol.* no. 6 1967 57–64

1103 J.W. Tonkin, 'The recording of vernacular architecture in Cornwall', *Cornish Archaeol.* no. 4 1965 51–64

1104 M.E. Weaver, 'Industrial housing in West Cornwall', *Ind. Archaeol.* III no. 1 1966 23–45

1105 M.E. Weaver, 'Notes on a farmhouse complex at Penrice, Karslake Downs', *Cornish Archaeol.* no. 6 1967 64–7

Industrial

For engine houses see under Engineering: Engines and Engine houses
See also nos. 71–6

1106 R. Angove, 'Water power in Cornwall', *Ind. Archaeol.* XVIII 1988 83–8

1107 D.E. Benney, *An introduction to Cornish watermills.* (Truro, Barton, 1972) 104p.

1108 C. Carter, 'Tregaseal River', *J. Trevithick Soc.* no. 22 1995 28–49

Mainly concerned with water-powered projects along the river.

1109 H.L. Douch, 'Coosebean Mill', *J. Trevithick Soc.* no. 2 1974 91–4

1110 H.L. Douch, *Cornish windmills.* (Truro, Blackford, 1963) 69p.

1111 J.N. Douglass, 'The building of the Wolf Rock lighthouse', *J. Trevithick Soc.* no. 12 1985 52–60

1112 C.G. Henderson, 'Cornish tucking mills and windmills', *in his Essays in Cornish History* (Oxford, Clarendon Press, 1935) 204–10

Essays in Cornish History was republished by Barton, Truro, 1963

1113 A. Hitchens Unwin, 'Lower Gweek Mills', *J. Trevithick Soc.* no. 10 1983 70–8

A water-mill

1114 J. Nankervis, '3500 years of farm buildings at Wicca in west Cornwall', *J. Hist. Farm Bldgs Gp* no. 4 1990 14–41

1115 J. Schofield, 'Early blowing-houses at Godolphin', *Cornish Archaeol.* no. 7 1968 107

1116 P.A. Sheppard, 'St Austell ice house', *Old Cornwall* VII 1967–73 232–5

1117 H.E.S. Simmons, *Watermills of Cornwall.* 1977. 6v.

Volumes in the Simmons Collection relating to British windmills and watermills. A photocopy of the original typescript folders is available in the Science Museum Library, London.

1118 H.E.S. Simmons, *Windmills of Cornwall.* 1977.

Part of the volume *The windmills of the Channel Islands, Cheshire, Cornwall and Cumberland* in the Simmons Collection. Photocopy of the original typescript folders is available in the Science Museum Library, London.

1119 P. Stanier, 'Early mining and water power in the Caradon mining district of Eastern Cornwall', *J. Trevithick Soc.* no. 14 1987 32–45

1120 A. Stoyel, 'The Gawns waterwheel, Blisland, Cornwall, England', *in Trans. 4th Symposium of the International Molinological Society, Matlock, Sept. 1977.* (London, Society for the Protection of Ancient Buildings, 1978) 31–3

1121 A.H. Unwin, 'A Cornish windmill', *J. Trevithick Soc.* no. 16 1989 35–49

1122 A.H. Unwin, 'Gearing systems in Cornish grist mills', *J. Trevithick Soc.* no. 14 1987 46–66

1123 A. Unwin, 'The watermills of St Keverne', *J. Roy. Inst. Cornwall* n.s. VII 1977 292–301

ENGINEERING
General

1124 N. Beagrie, 'The St. Mawes ingot', *Cornish Archaeol.* no. 22 1983 107–11

1125 J.B. Cornish, 'The men who made the Cornish mines', *J.R. Inst. Cornwall* XIII 1898 430–34

1126 Sir E. Durning-Lawrence, 'Steam in relation to Cornwall', *J. R. Inst. Cornwall* XVI 1904 161–80

1127 Viscount Falmouth, 'From Watt to Parsons, or the rise of steam power' *J. R. Inst. Cornwall* XXIII 1931-2 426–37

1128 T.R. Harris, 'Engineering in Cornwall before 1775', *Trans. Newcomen Soc.* XXV 1945-7 111–22

1129 J. Hodge, 'The Cornish gauge and J. & F. Pool', *J. Trevithick Soc.* no. 8 1981 70–2

1130 J. Hodge, 'The Holman T100 gas turbine air compressor', *J. Trevithick Soc.* no. 6 1978 64–79

1131 W.T. Hooper, 'The world's debt to Cornish engineers', *J. R. Instn. Cornwall* XXV Appendix 1942 84–95

1132 R. Jenkins, 'Early engineering and ironfounding in Cornwall', *Trans. Newcomen Soc.* XXIII 1942-3 23–35

Same title appears in *Engineering* CLIV 1942 304–5, 325–6

1133 S. Michell, 'Cornish foundries—what they have achieved', *Ann. Reps. R. Cornwall Polytech. Soc.* n.s. VII 1932 193–202

1134 A.F. Sanders and J. Hodge, 'Diesel engine development in Penzance', *J. Trevithick Soc.* no. 8 1981 54–7

Engines and Engine Houses

Including man engines.
See also nos. 77–81

1135 D.B. Barton, *The Cornish beam engine: a survey of its history and development in the mines of Cornwall and Devon from before 1800 to the present day, with something of its use elsewhere in Britain and abroad.* 2nd ed (Truro, Barton, 1966) 285p.

1136 D.B. Barton, *Cornwall's engine houses.* (Tor Mark, 1989) 32p.

1137 R. Bayles, 'The Cornish beam pumping engine at the Dorothea Slate Quarry', *Mem. N. Cavern Mine Res. Soc.* II no. 1 1971 19–20

1138 R. Bayles, 'The Cornish beam engine at Dorothea slate quarry', *Int. Stationary Steam Engine Soc. Bull.* XIV no. 1 Spring 1992

1139 R. Bayles, 'Dorothea Cornish engine', *Int. Stationary Steam Engine Soc. Bull.* XIV no. 3 Autumn 1992

1140 K. Brown, 'The Cornish beam engine: fact and fiction', *J. Trevithick Soc.* no. 17 1990 53–65

Sets out to correct inaccuracies in no. 1135

1141 K. Brown, 'A new light on Austen's 80"', *J. Trevithick Soc.* no. 18 1991 51–63

Maurice Cook's research throws more light on the eventual fate of Austen's

80" engine at Fowey Consols.

1142 K. Brown, 'Prestongrange 70–inch Cornish engine—a myth exploded', *J. Trevithick Soc.* no. 9 1982 42–51

Prestongrange, near Edinburgh.

1143 'The Cornish pumping engine', *Engineer* XXIX–XXXII 1870–1

A series of 20 articles

1144 'The Cornish man-engine', *Mining Smelting Mag.* I June 1862 366

1145 Cornwall Archaeology Unit, *A guide to conserving historic mine buildings.* (CAU Reports) 33p.

1146 B.A. Curtis, 'The Cornish man engine', *Old Cornwall* VII 1967–73 502–6

1147 H. Davey, 'History of the Cornish engine', *Ann. Reps. R. Cornwall Polytech. Soc.* I n.s. 1908–10 281–95

1148 Delta, 'A note on early Cornish mine pumps', *Ind. Archaeol.* XVI 1981 110–15

1149 H.W. Dickinson, *The Cornish engine: a chapter in the history of steam power, descriptions of a series of films produced by the Shell Film Unit with the co-operation of the Cornish Engines Preservation Society.* (Art & Technics, 1950) 46p.

1150 G.J. Drew and J.E. Connell, *Cornish beam engines in South Australian mines.* (South Australia, Dept of Mines & Energy, 1993, Special Publication no. 9)

1151 A. Fraser, 'On the use of the Cornish pumping engine', *Trans. Soc. Engrs.* 1864

Copy in the Cornish Studies Library, Redruth

1152 B.A. Fyfield-Shayler, 'Wendron Forge: an investment in industrial archaeology (Part one)', *Ind. Archaeol.* XIII 1978 129–57

1153 D. Gilbert, 'On the progressive improvements made in the efficiency of steam engines in Cornwall, with investigations of the methods best adapted for imparting great angular velocities', *Phil. Trans. R. Soc.* 1830 121–32

Copy in the Cornish Studies Library, Redruth

1154 H.N. Harvey, 'Cornish boilers', *Min. Assoc. and Inst. Cornwall* IV 1893–5 17–52

Copy in the Cornish Studies Library, Redruth

1155 D.E. Hatton, *How the Cornish engine evolved.* (1993) 12p.

Typescript. Copy in the Cornish Studies Library, Redruth

1156 W.J. Henwood, 'Account of experiments on the performance of some steam engines in Cornwall', *Edinburgh J. Science* VI 1832 246–51

1157 W.J. Henwood, 'Account of the steam engines in Cornwall', *Edinburgh J. Sci.* X 1829 34–49

1158 W.J. Henwood, 'Notes on some recent improvements of the steam engines in Cornwall', *Phil. Mag.* 2nd ser. X 1831 97–103

1159 W.J. Henwood, 'Observations on some late statements by Mr Farey respecting the steam engines of Cornwall', *Phil. Mag.* VII 1830 323–5

Discusses the part played by Arthur Woolf in the development of the steam engine.

1160 W.J. Henwood, 'Observations on the steam engines in Cornwall', *Phil. Mag.*

3rd ser. VIII 1836 20–21

Comment on nos. 1178–9

1161 W.J. Henwood, 'On the expansive action of steam in some of the pumping engines on the Cornish mines', *Trans. Instn. Civ. Engrs.* II 1838 49–60

1162 T. Holman, 'The Cornish Engines Preservation Society', *Ann. Reps. R. Cornwall Polytech. Soc.* n.s. XI pt. 3 1944 37–44

1163 Sir E.D. Lawrence, 'Steam in relation to Cornwall', *J. R. Instn. Cornwall,* 1904 XVI 161–80

1164 P. Laws, *Cornish engines and engine houses in the care of the National Trust.* (National Trust, 1973) 31p.

1165 T. Lean, *On the steam engines in Cornwall.* (Truro, Barton, 1969)

Reprint of *Historical statement of the improvements made in the duty performed by the steam engines in Cornwall from the commencement of the publication of the Monthly Reports.* (1839)

1166 F.W. Michell, 'On the diminished duty of Cornish pumping engines and its remedy', *Ann. Reps. R. Cornwall Polytech. Soc.* no. 63 1895 109–12

1167 C. Noall, 'History of the Cornish man engine. Part 1', *Cornish Mag.* VII no. 3 1964 79–83; 'Part 2', VII no. 4 1964 126–8

1168 H.G. Ordish, *Cornish engine houses, a pictorial survey.* (Truro, D.B. Barton, 1967) 66p.

1169 H.G. Ordish, *Cornish engine houses, a second pictorial survey.* (Truro, D.B. Barton, 1968) 63p.

1170 T. Parsons, 'The Cornish man engine', *Plymouth Mineral Min. Club J.* X no. 1 1979 17–18

1171 R.R. Pennington, 'The Cornish beam engine and patent law', *J. Trevithick Soc.* no. 3 1975 45–55

1172 W. Pole, *Treatise on the Cornish pumping engine in two parts. Part 1.Historical notice of the application of the steam engine to the purpose of draining the mines of Cornwall. ... Part II. Description of the Cornish pumping engine, and its various peculiarities as contrasted with the Boulton and Watt single-acting engine.* (London, John Weale, 1844) 235p.

1173 J.T. Rodda, 'The diminished duty of Cornish pumping engines', *Ann. Reps. R. 7Cornwall Polytech. Soc.* no. 54 1886 171–183

1174 C. Rowe, 'Drawings of the Levant Whim: Part 1—Original Parts', *J. Trevithick Soc.* no. 22 1995 8–27; 'Part 2—Cylinder valves and condenser', no. 23 1996 3–42; 'Part 3—Further drawings and a list of changes during restoration', no. 24 1997 3–20

1175 W.D. Sawyer, 'Beyond Watt: the Cornish engine in its laboratory', *Stationary Power* no. 6 1989 2–37

1176 H.R. Shambrook, 'The Cornish boiler', *Br. Mining* no. 19 1982 46–7

1177 A. Sharpe *and others, Engine house assessment: Mineral Tramways Project.* (Cornwall Archaeological Unit, 1991) 200p.

1178 J. Taylor, 'On the new rotative steam-engine', *Phil. Mag.* 3rd ser. VII 1835 369–70

1179 J. Taylor, 'On the history of rotatory single steam engines working

expansively, in reply to Mr Henwood', *Phil. Mag.* 3rd ser. VIII 1836 136–8
See no. 1160

1180 D.H. Tew, 'The continental origins of the man-engine and its development in Cornwall and the Isle of Man' *Trans. Newcomen Soc.* XXX 1955–7 49–62.

1181 D.H. Tew, 'Man engines in Cornwall', *J. Trevithick Soc.* no. 8 1981 47–53

1182 A.C. Todd, *The Cornish miner in America.* (Truro, Barton, 1967) 279p.

1183 J.H. Trounson, 'Cornish engines and the men who handled them', *J. R. Inst. Cornwall* n.s. V 1967 213–49

1184 J.H. Trounson, 'Cornish stacks and engine houses', *J. Trevithick Soc.* no. 9 1982 73–84

1185 J.H. Trounson, 'Engineering marvels', *J. Trevithick Soc.* no. 7 1979–80 7–33

1186 G.N. von Tunzelmann, 'Technological diffusion during the Industrial Revolution: the case of the Cornish pumping engine', *in* R.M. Hartwell, ed., *The Industrial Revolution,* (Oxford, 1970)

1187 J. Wellington, 'The Cornish rotative beam engine', *Tamar J.* no. 4 1982 12–18

1188 T. Wicksteed, *An experimental inquiry concerning the relative power of, and useful effect produced by the Cornish and Boulton and Watt pumping engines and cylindrical and waggon head boilers.* (London, 1841)

1189 T. Wicksteed, *On the effective power of the high pressure expansive condensing steam engines commonly used in Cornish mines: showing their applicability to the purpose of supplying towns with water.* 2nd ed. (London, John Weale, 1838) 16p.

There is a similar title in *Trans. Instn. Civ. Engrs.* II 1838 61–8

Cornish Engineers and Engineering Firms

See also no. 79

Boulton & Watt

For further references see the Midlands volume in this series.
See also no. 1320

1190 H. Fox, 'Boulton and Watt', *Ann. Reps. R. Cornwall Polytech. Soc.* n.s. I 1908–10 311–28 and 524–39

Letters received by Thomas Wilson of Chacewater, financial agent of Boulton and Watt in Cornwall.

1191 R.L. Hills, 'James Watt in Cornwall', *J. Trevithick Soc.* no. 24 1997 46–60

1192 J. Griffiths, *The third man: the life and times of William Murdoch 1754–1839, the inventor of gas lighting.* (London, Andre Deutsch, 1992) 373p.

1193 A.K.H. Jenkin, 'Boulton and Watt in Cornwall', *Ann. Reps. R. Cornwall Polytech. Soc.* XCIII (n.s. V) 1926 350–64

1194 J. Tann, 'Riches from copper: the adoption of the Boulton & Watt engine by Cornish mine adventurers', *Trans. Newcomen Soc.* LXVII 1995–6 27–52

Harvey's

See also nos. 1696, 1770

1195 *Harvey's of Hayle, Catalogue 1884* (Truro, Barton, 197–)

1196 S. Michell, 'The early history of the Hayle foundry, 1770–1833, based on material collected by the late Stephen Michell of Hayle, edited by J.H. Rowe', *Ann. Reps. R. Cornwall Polytech. Soc.* n.s. VIII pt. 3 1936 40–9

1197 C. Noall, *Harvey's: 200 years of trading.* (Truro, UBM Harvey, 1979) 52p.

1198 E. Vale, *The Harveys of Hayle: engine builders, shipwrights and merchants of Cornwall.* (Truro, D.B. Barton, 1966) 356p.

Holman's

1199 'Engineering in Cornwall: the story of Holman Bros. Ltd, Camborne', *Machine Shop Mag.* 1947 2–8

1200 E.B. Holman, 'Holman's Foundry, St Just in Penwith: reminiscences 1890–1951', *Cornish Stud.* no. 15 1987 29–36

1201 'If it's metal take it to Holman's' *Archive* no. 3 Sept. 1994 49–64

Hornblower Family

1202 T.R. Harris, 'The Hornblower family, pioneer steam engineers', *J. Trevithick Soc.* no. 4 1976 7–44

'Addendum', no 5 1777 66–9

1203 J. Hornblower and J. Winwood, *An address to the Lords ... concerned in the mines of Cornwall.* (1768) c. 20p.

Reprinted in no. 1207

1204 R. Jenkins, 'Jonathan Hornblower and the compound engine', *Trans. Newcomen Soc.* XI 1930–1 138–55

1205 J. Tann, 'Mr Hornblower and his crew: Watt engine pirates at the end of the 18th century', *Trans. Newcomen Soc.* LI 1979–80 95–109

1206 A.C. Todd, 'Davies Gilbert—patron of engineers (1767–1839) and Jonathan Hornblower (1753–1815) *Trans. Newcomen Soc.* XXXII 1959–60 1–13

1207 H.S. Torrens, 'New light on the Hornblower and Winwood compound steam engine', *J. Trevithick Soc.* no. 9 1982 21–41

1208 H.S. Torrens, 'Some newly discovered letters from Jonathan Hornblower (1753–1815)', *Trans. Newcomen Soc.* LIV 1982–3 189–200

Perran's

1209 *Illustrated catalogue of pumping and winding engines etc., manufactured by Williams' Perran Foundry Co. Perranarworthal.* (Trevithick Society, 1974) 36p.

Reprint of 1870 catalogue

1210 W.T. Hooper, 'Perran Foundry and its story', *Ann Reps. R. Cornwall Polytech. Soc.* n.s. IX pt. 3 1939 62–89

1211 W.T. Hooper, 'Summary of the history of Perran Foundry', *Ann. Reps. R.*

Cornwall Polytech. Soc. n.s. VI pt. 3 1929 273–81

Trevithick

1212 J.J. Beckerlegge, 'Trevithick, the Cornish engineer: a centenary study', *Ann. Reps. Trans. Plymouth Inst.* XVII 1928–36 297–304

1213 J. Blight, 'The inventions of Trevithick, with special reference to the locomotive', *Trans. Cornish Inst. Min. Mech. Metall. Engrs* X 1925 99–114

1214 H. Boase, 'On the introduction of the steam engine to the Peruvian mines', *Trans. R. Geol. Soc. Cornwall* I 1818 212–23

Discusses Richard Trevithick's part in providing these engines.

1215 D.W. Davies, 'Richard Trevithick in Costa Rica', *J. Trevithick Soc.* no. 5 1977 7–26

1216 J. Davis, *Memorial edition of the life of Richard Trevithick.* (London, Spon, 1883) 24p.

1217 H.W. Dickinson and A. Titley, *Richard Trevithick, the engineer and the man.* (Cambridge, University Press, 1934) 308p.

Trevithick Centenary Memorial Volume

1218 J.M. Eyles, 'William Smith, Richard Trevithick and Samuel Homfrey: their correspondence on steam engines, 1804–1806', *Trans. Newcomen Soc.* XLIII 1970–1 137–61

Reprinted in in *J. Trevithick Soc.* no. 12 1985 10–35

1219 D. Flinn, 'Richard Trevithick, Arthur Woolf and the Shetland Mining Company', *J. Trevithick Soc.* no. 17 1990 23–30

1220 E.K. Harper, *Cornish giant: Richard Trevithick. The Father of the locomotive-engine.* (London, Spon, 1913) 61p.

1221 J.G.B. Hills, 'Richard Trevithick and refrigeration', *Trans. Newcomen Soc.* XLI 1968–9 169–71

1222 J. Hodge, 'Cornish engineering letters relating to Richard Trevithick and others', *J. Trevithick Soc.* no. 8 1981 58–69

1223 J. Hodge, *Richard Trevithick: an illustrated life of Richard Trevithick, 1771–1833.* (Aylesbury, Shire Publications, 1973) 48p.

1224 J. Hodge, 'Richard Trevithick as the inventor of containerisation for ships', *J. Trevithick Soc.* no. 7 1979–80 103–4

1225 J. Hodge, 'Richard Trevithick—his place in engineering history', *J. Trevithick Soc.* no. 1 1973 9–26

1226 J. Hodge, 'Trevithick's heritage', *J. Trevithick Soc.* no. 12 1985 7–9

1227 L. Ince, 'Richard Trevithick's patent steam engine', *Stationary Power* I 1987 67–75

1228 R. Jenkins, 'An unpublished book on the steam engine: Trevithick', *in The Collected Papers of Rhys Jenkins.* (London, Newcomen Society, 1936) 107?–

Reprinted from the *Engineer* 21 May 1920 519–20. Concerns a projected volume by John Farey on Trevithick and Woolf.

1229 R.J. Law, 'The boilers of Richard Trevithick and Arthur Woolf', *J. Trevithick Soc.* no. 9 1982 9–20

Reprinted from 'A survey of tank boilers down to 1850', *Trans. Newcomen Soc.* XLVIII 1976–7

1230 P. Lead and H. Torrens, 'The introduction of the Trevithick steam engine to north Staffordshire', *J. Trevithick Soc.* no. 8 1981 26–30

1231 P. Lead and H. Torrens, 'Richard Trevithick, the Heath Family and the North Staffordshire connection', *J. Trevithick Soc.* no. 10 1988 59–69

1232 S. Mercer, 'Trevithick and the Merthyr tramroad', *Trans. Newcomen Soc.* XXVI 1947–9 89–103

1233 S. Merry, *Trevithick, the Cornish engineer.* (Padstow, Lodernek Press, 1975)

1234 J.F. Odgers, *Richard Trevithick, 'The Cornish Giant', 1771–1833: memorials and commemorations in Camborne and district.* (The Author, 1956) 40p.

1235 N. Pedlar, 'The Trevithick connection in Japan', *J. Trevithick Soc.* no. 13 1986 60–8

1236 L. St L. Pendred, 'The mystery of Trevithick's London locomotives', *Trans. Newcomen Soc.* I 1920–1 34–49

1237 'Richard Trevithick', *Engineering* CXXXV 1933 439–41

1238 'Richard Trevithick: some unpublished documents', *J. Trevithick Soc.* no. 3 1975 10–21

The documents are an agreement between Trevithick and Uville, an agreement between Uville and his partners, and the will of Richard Trevithick senior.

1239 L.T. C. Rolt, *The Cornish giant. The story of Richard Trevithick, father of the steam locomotive.* (London, Lutterworth Press, 1960) 160p.

1240 J. Rowe, 'Bringing home the sheaves', *J.R. Inst. Cornwall* n.s. X 1990 385–402

Discusses Trevithick's wheat threshing engine and other agricultural innnovations.

1241 C. Thomas, 'Richard Trevithick: new light on his earliest years and family origins', *J. Trevithick Soc.* no. 2 1974 45–53

1242 A. Titley, 'Richard Trevithick and the winding engine', *Trans. Newcomen Soc.* X 1929–30 35–68

1243 A. Titley, 'Trevithick and Rastrick and the single-acting expansive engine', *Trans. Newcomen Soc.* VII 1926–7 42–59

1244 H.S. Toviens, 'A contemporary note on Trevithick's Camborne Road locomotive', *J. Trevithick Soc.* no. 13 1986 77–9

1245 F. Trevithick, *The life of Richard Trevithick, with an account of his inventions.* (London, 1872) 2v.

1246 J.H. Trevithick, 'Richard Trevithick', *Min. Mag.* XXIII 1920 249–51

1247 R. Wailes, 'Richard Trevithick—engineer and adventurer', *in Engineering heritage* v. 1 (Heinemann for Instn. of Mechanical Engineers, 1963) 70–74

1248 L.H. Woodcock, 'Richard Trevithick's first steam-locomotive trial, Christmas 1801', *Trans. Newcomen Soc.* XLIII 1970–1 175–81

West

1249 M.H. Cooke, 'William West of St Blazey', *Br. Mining* no. 25 1984 5–14.

1250 M. Cooke, 'William West on the 80"', *J. Trevithick Soc.* no. 16 1989 79–82

1251 R.N. Worth, *Sketch of the life of William West C.E. of Tredenham*. (1880) 63p. Reprinted by the Institute of Cornish Studies, 1973.

Woolf

1252 T.R. Harris, *Arthur Woolf (1766–1837): the Cornish engineer*. (Truro, Barton, 1966) 112p.

1253 T.R. Harris, 'Arthur Woolf (1766–1837) Cornish engineer and inventor', *Trans. Cornish Inst. Engrs.* XIX 1963–4 15–25

1254 S. Hocking, 'A brief sketch of the life and labours of Arthur Woolf, engineer', *Reps Proc. Miners' Assoc Cornwall & Devon*, 1874 8–22

1255 R. Jenkins, 'A Cornish engineer: Arthur Woolf, 1766–1837', *Trans. Newcomen Soc.* XIII 1932–3 55–73

Other Cornish Engineers and Engineering Firms

1256 T.R. Harris, 'James Sims and the compound engine', *Engineering* CLV 1943 294–5

1257 T.R. Harris, *Sir Golsworthy Gurney 1793–1875*. (Truro, Trevithick Society and Federation of Old Cornwall Societies, 1975) 100p.

An inventor.

1258 T.R. Harris, 'Some lesser known Cornish engineers', *J. Trevithick Soc.* no. 5 1977 27–65

1259 A.B. Hollowood, *Cornish engineers ... with reproductions of contemporary photographs and documents.* (Camborne, Holman Bros., 1951) 96p.

1260 W.H. Jones, *T.W. Bate and the Dunheved Ironworks.* (Redruth, Truran, 1986) 45p.

1261 E. Loam, 'Michael Loam, engineer', *Ann. Reps. R. Cornwall Polytech. Soc.* n.s. VII pt. 1. 1931 142–58

1262 F.B. Michell, *Michell: a family of Cornish engineers 1740–1910*. (Cornwall, Trevithick Society, 1984) 76p.

1263 S. Michell, 'Some minor foundries of Cornwall, based on materials collected by the late Stephen Michell of Hayle, edited by J.H. Rowe', *Ann. Reps. R. Cornwall Polytech. Soc.* n.s. VIII pt. 2 1935 52–60

1264 T.B. Paisley, *The Fowells of St Ives: Engineers.* (St Ives, H.W. Oldman, 1972?)

EXPLOSIVES

See also no. 1554

1265 B. Earl, *Cornish explosives.* (Trevithick Society, 1978)

1266 T.R. Harris, 'A short history of the Cornish explosives industries', *Trans. Cornish Inst. Engrs.* XXVI 1970–1 2–15

FISHERIES

See also nos. 114–19

1267 J. Chester, 'Essay on the pilchard', *Ann. Reps. R. Cornwall Polytech. Soc.* 3 1835 102–7

1268 J. Couch, 'Essay on the natural history of the pilchard', *Ann. Reps. R. Cornwall Polytech. Soc.* no. 3 1835 65–96

1269 C.L. Fox, 'The present position of the Cornish pilchard industry', *Ann Reps. R. Cornwall Polytech. Soc.* n.s. X pt. 2 1943 21–36

1270 M. Geen, 'The St Ives fishing industry', *Old Cornwall* III no. 9 1941 370–5

1271 K. Harris, *Hevva! An account of the Cornish fishing industry in the days of sail.* (Redruth, Dyllansow Truran, 1983) 88p.

1272 F.H. McWilliams, 'Fishing in West Cornwall', *Ann. Reps. R. Cornwall Polytech. Soc.* 126th Rep 1959 20–33

1273 R.M. Nance, 'Some implements and objects connected with Cornish fisheries', *J.R. Inst. Cornwall* XXIV 1933 88–98

1274 D. Nicholls, 'The Cornish sea-urchin fishery', *Cornish Stud.* no. 9 1981 5–18

1275 C. Noall, *Cornish seines and seiners: a history of the pilchard fishing industry.* (Truro, Barton, 1972) 160p.

1276 C. Noall, *Tales of the Cornish fishermen.* (Truro, Tormark Press, 1970)

1277 J. Parsons and N. Parsons, *Cornish fisherboy to master mariner: the life of Henry Blewett 1836–1891.* (Bournemouth Local Studies Pubs., 1995) 4v.

1278 W. Pezzack, 'The Mount's Bay mackerel driver', *J.R. Inst. Cornwall* XXIII 1930 297–99

A type of fishing boat

1279 W. Roberts, 'Quantities of pilchards exported from Cornwall, and prices at which they were sold; from 1815 to 1871', *J.R. Inst. Cornwall* IV 1872 159–60

1280 J. Scantlebury, 'The development of the export trade in pilchards from Cornwall during the sixteenth century', *J.R. Inst. Cornwall* n.s. X 1989 330–59

1281 J. Scantlebury, 'John Rashleigh of Fowey and the Newfoundland cod fishery 1608–20. Part 1', *J.R. Inst. Cornwall* n.s. VIII 1978 61–71

1282 J. Scantlebury, 'Those blessed pilchards', *J. R. Inst. Cornwall* n.s. XIV 1993 pt. 3 248–68

1283 'Seine-fishing at St Ives, Cornwall', *Marit S-W* no. 5 1991 46-53

1284 D. Smart, *The Cornish fishing industry: a brief history.* (Tor Mark Press, 1992) 32p.

1285 M. Tangye, 'A seventeenth-century fish cellar at Porth Godrevy, Gwithian', *Cornish Archaeol.* no. 30 1991 243–52

A device for packing fish.

1286 R. Vallentin, 'A brief account of an attempt at oyster cultivation at Falmouth in 1895–6', *J.R. Inst. Cornwall* XIII 1896 180–6

1287 R. Vallentin, 'Some remarks on an experimental lobster hatchery', *J.R. Inst. Cornwall* XIII 1896 186–90

1288 R. Vallentin, 'A summary of two logbooks kept at Cadgwith, recording the capture of lobsters, crayfish and crabs in 1895', *J.R. Inst. Cornwall* XIII 1896

191–4

1289 N. Wilkinson, 'Studies of Brixham trawlers', *Mar. Mirr.* XLVII 1961 310 + 2 plates

Sketches of these sailing trawlers.

GOLD AND PEWTER

1290 H.L. Douch, 'Cornish goldsmiths', *J.R. Inst. Cornwall* n.s. VI no. 2 1970 121–38

1291 H.L. Douch, 'Cornish pewterers', *J.R. Inst. Cornwall* n.s. VI 1969 65–80

1292 H.H. Mills, 'The West Country goldsmiths', *J.R. Inst. Cornwall* XX 1921 535–58

LIMEBURNING

See also nos. 126–7

1293 N.J.G. Pounds, 'Building and operating accounts of an 18th-century limekiln', *Devon Cornwall N. & Q.* XXXII 1973 237–40

At Morval Barton

MINING

See also nos. 129–218

China Clay

See also nos. 152–63, 321, 1735, 1747, 1752, 1754

1294 W.K. Andrews, '50 years of English China Clays Ltd', *English China Clay Rev.* Spring 1969

1295 M. Arthur, *The autobiography of a china clay worker*. (Old Cornwall Societies, 1995) 96p.

1296 R.M. Barton, *A history of the Cornish china-clay industry*. (Truro, Barton, 1966) 212p.

1297 D. Cock, *A treatise, technical and practical, on the nature, production and uses of china-clay*. (London, Simpkin, Marshall, 1880) 151p.

1298 J.H. Collins, 'The china-clay industry of Cornwall', *Mining Mag.* IV 1911 449–55

1299 C.A.V. Conybeare, ed., *The Rosemellyn China Clay Lease, Roche, Cornwall. Correspondence relating to the transactions between Capt. Charles Eldon Serjeant, landlord and the late Alexander Barrett, lessee, showing the exactions under which the china clay industry has suffered and the need for stringent reforms*. (Truro, Heard & Sons, 1886) 10p.

1300 J.M. Coon, 'China clay industry', *Ann. Reps. R. Cornwall Polytech. Soc.* XCVI no. 6 1927 56–67

1301 W.H. Fitton, 'On the porcelain earth of Cornwall', *Ann. Philosophy* III 1814

180–4

1302 P.C. Herring, J.R. Smith and Corwall Archaeological Unit, *The archaeology of the St Austell china-clay area: an archaeological and historical assessment.* (Truro, Cornwall Archaeology Unit, 1991) 179 [81] p.

1303 'History of the china clay industry', *Quarry Managers' J.* Aug. 1946 99–102

1304 K. Hudson, *The history of English China Clays: fifty years of pioneering and growth.* (Newton Abbot, David & Charles, 1969) 179p.

A business history of English China Clays Ltd, St. Austell

1305 D.H. Knight, 'The china-clay industry of Cornwall', *Ann. Reps. R. Cornwall Polytech. Soc.* 128th Rep. 1961 23–55

1306 J.A. Paris, 'On the stones and clays annually exported from Cornwall for the purpose of architecture, manufactures, and the arts', *Trans. R. Geol. Soc. Cornwall* I 1818 231–6

1307 M. Pemberton, 'Developments in china clay processing', *Mine Quarry* XVIII no. 4 1989 40–3

1308 J.R. Ravensdale, 'The China Clay Labourers' Union', *Hist. Stud.* I 1968 51–62

1309 J.R. Ravensdale, 'The 1913 china clay strike and the Workers' Union', *in* J.H. Porter, *ed., Provincial labour history* (Exeter University, Exeter Papers in Economic History no. 6, 1972)

1310 A.L. Rowse, 'The Cornish china-clay industry', *Hist. Today* XVII 1967 483–86

1311 A. Sharpe, 'The survey of the winding and pumping plant at Trethowel clayworks', *J. Trevithick Soc.* no. 18 1991 85–90

1312 J.R. Smith and Cornwall Archaeology Unit, *Cornwall's china clay heritage.* (Truro, Twelveheads, 1992) 48p.

1313 C. Thurlow, *China clay: traditional mining methods in Cornwall.* (Penrhyn, Tor Mark Press, 1990) 32p.

A largely photographic record.

1314 J. Tonkin, 'An account of Trethowel china clay works', *J. Trevithick Soc.* no. 18 1991 91–107

1315 J. Tonkin, 'The Belowda Beacon clayworking—two forgotten pits', *J. Trevithick Soc.* no. 21 1994 2–21

1316 W. Trethewey, 'History of the china clay industry', *Quarry Managers J.* XXX 1946 99–102, 143–8

1317 P. Varcoe, *China clay: the early years.* (St Austell, Francis Antony Ltd, n.d.) 40p.

Metals

See also nos. 169–205

1318 'An account of the produce of all the copper mines in Cornwall in ore, copper and money for the year ending the 30th June 1815', *Trans. R. Geol. Soc. Cornwall* I 1818 252–63

Note: at the end of vols. 1–6 of *Trans. R. Geol. Soc. Cornwall* there are detailed statistics on the production and sale of tin and copper in Cornwall.

1319 G.C. Allen, 'An eighteenth-century combination in the copper mining industry',

Econ. J. XXXIII 1923 74–85

1320 G.C. Allen, *The history of an eighteenth-century combination in the copper-mining industry.* (M.Comm. thesis, University of Birmingham, 1922)

Matthew Boulton's attempts to control the price of copper from the mines in Cornwall and Anglesey.

1321 C.K.C. Andrew, 'The Cornish miner's petition to Queen Victoria', *Devon Cornwall N. & Q.* XXVI no. 2 1954 58–61

1322 R. von Arx, 'False hopes at New Wheal Speedwell (or: Mr Knight comes to grief)', *Br. Mining* no. 48 1993 86–9

1323 R. von Arx, 'A glimpse at Cape Cornwall Mine', *Br. Mining* XLIII 1991 43–6

1324 R. von Arx, 'A glimpse at East Trevell Mine in Cornwall', *Br. Mining* XLIII 1991 41–2

1325 C. Atkinson, 'The Excelsior tunnel', *Old Cornwall* IX no. 5 1981 246–7

1326 B. Atkinson, 'Industrial archaeology: Portheras Cove to Letcha Cliff', *Plymouth Mineral Min. Club J.* XV no. 1 1984 3–5

1327 B. Atkinson, 'The mines of Perranporth: a recent survey', *Plymouth Mineral Min. Club J.* XII no. 3 1982 3–4, 8

1328 B. Atkinson, *Mining sites in Cornwall.* 2v. (Redruth, Dyllansow Truran, v. 1 1988, v. 2 1994)

1329 B. Atkinson, 'The North Cliff Mines: Chapelporth to Hayle', *Plymouth Mineral Min. Club J.* XII no. 1 1981 4–5, 14

1330 B. Atkinson, 'Portreath's lost mines', *Plymouth Mineral Min. Club J.* XIV no. 3 1984 8–9

1331 B. Atkinson, 'A survey of the lesser known mining sites of Cornwall. List 1: The Liskeard area', *Plymouth Mineral Min. Club J.* XIII no. 3 1983 14–15; 'List 2: Calstock, Callington and Launceston', XIV no. 1 1983 17; 'List 3: St Austell to Saltash', XIV no. 2 1983 13; 'List 4: Around St. Ives', XIV no. 3 1984 16; 'List 5: St Agnes to Perranporth', XV no. 1 1984 11; 'List 6: Wendron to the Porkellis area', XV no. 3 1985 11; 'List 7: Newquay to Perranporth', XVI no. 1 1985 10; 'List 8: The Lizard-Falmouth-Mevagissey', XVI no. 2 1986 12; 'List 9: Padstow-St. Columb and Bodmin', XVI no. 3 1986 11; 'List 10: Hayle, Gwinear-Gwithian', XVII no. 1 1986 7; 'List 11: Penzance to Mounts Bay', XVII no. 2 1987 5; 'List 12: Around Gwennap', XVIII no. 1 1988 9

1332 M. Atkinson and R. Burt, 'Mining in the Duchy of Cornwall', *in* C. Gill, ed., *The Duchy of Cornwall.* (Newton Abbot, David & Charles, 1987)

1333 R.L. Atkinson, *Tin and tin mining.* (Shire Publications, 1985)

1334 D. Austin, G.A.M. Gerrard and T.A.P. Greeves, 'Tin and agriculture in the Middle Ages and beyond: landscape archaeology in St Neot Parish, Cornwall', *Cornish Archaeol.* no. 28 1989 7–251

1335 B.C.L. Bainbridge, 'The tin streaming industry in Cornwall: a survey', *Cornish Archaeol.* no. 7 1968 61–2

1336 B.F. Bainsmith, 'The Fuggan Pit at Little Wheal Speed', *Old Cornwall* V 1951–61 463–4

1337 O.A. Baker, 'Old Gunnislake: tribute to a classic locality', *Plymouth Mineral*

Min. Club Newsl. II no. 3 1971 14–15

1338 C.F. Barclay, 'Some notes on the West Devon Mining District', *Trans. R. Geol. Soc. Cornwall* XVI 1931 157–76

1339 S. Bartlett, *'400 mining men of Liskeard'* (Nantwich, Private Publication, 1987) 28p.

1340 S. Bartlett, *The mines and mining men of Menheniot.* (Truro, Twelveheads, 1994) 144p.

1341 D.B. Barton, *Essays in Cornish mining history.* (Truro, Barton)

    v. 1 1968 198p.

    v. 2 1971 176p.

1342 D.B. Barton, *A guide to the mines of west Cornwall.* 2nd ed. (Truro, Barton, 1965) 51p.

1343 D.B. Barton, *Historic Cornish mining scenes underground.* 2nd ed. (Truro, Barton, 1980) 56p.

Based on the photos of J.C. Burrows, of Camborne, and Herbert Hughes.

1344 D.B. Barton, *Historical survey of the mines and mineral railways of East Cornwall.* (Truro, Barton, 1964) 102p.

1345 D.B. Barton, *A history of tin mining and smelting in Cornwall.* (Truro, Barton, 1967) 302p.

1346 N. Beagrie, 'A bronze 'ox-hide' ingot from Cornwall', *Cornwall Archaeol.* XXIV 1985 160–2

1347 T. Beare, *The bailiff of Blackmoor, 1586: an examination of the history, laws and customs of medieval and sixteenth century tinners.* (Camborne, Penhellick, 1994) 138p.

1348 J. Bennett, 'John Connell Delarne Bevan and the East Cornwall Silver Mining Company', *Br. Mining* XLIII 1991 5–8

1349 A.C. Bizley, 'New Chiverton Mine in the Parish of Perranzabuloe', *Old Cornwall* IX 1983 424–6

1350 J. Blight, 'Mine drainage', *Trans. Cornish Inst. Min. Mech. Metall. Engrs.* IV 1916 9–84

1351 J.R. Blunden, 'The redevelopment of the Cornish tin industry', *in* K.T. Gregory and W.L.D. Ravenhill *Exeter essays in honour of Arthur Davies.* (Exeter, Exeter University, 1971) 169–84

1352 J.R. Blunden, 'The renaissance of the Cornish tin industry', *Geography* LV 1970 331–5

1353 H.S. Boase, 'On the tin-ore of Botallack and Levant', *Trans. R. Geol. Soc. Cornwall* II 1822 383–403

1354 W.C. Borlase, *Historical sketch of the tin trade in Cornwall, from the earliest period to the present day.* (Plymouth, 1874)

1355 J.H. Brock, 'Cornish mining: past present and future', *Tamar J.* no. 12 1990 23–7

1356 J.H. Brock, *South Crofty: Europe's premier tin mine.* (Camborne, South Crofty Ltd, 1984)

1357 J. Brooke, 'The Bubble Company', *Br. Mining* no. 5 1977 6–9

Originally formed to work the land and mines of Carnmoah in Camborne parish.

1358 J. Brooke, 'Cornwall: sites of interest old and new, 1981', *Br. Mining* no. 19 1980–2 55–7

1359 J. Brooke *ed., The Cunnack Manuscript*. (The Trevithick Society, 1993) 76p.
Notes on more than 100 Cornish mines compiled by Richard John Cunnack (1826–1908)

1360 J. Brooke, 'The first investment trust', *J. Trevithick Soc.* no. 17 1990 48–52
West Cornwall Mines Investment Co.

1361 J. Brooke, 'Historical notes on Wheal Jane', *Mem. N. Cavern Mine Res.* Soc. II no. 3 1973 161–2

1362 J. Brooke, 'Not as a general rule', *J. Trevithick Soc.* no. 20 1993 51–4
On the management of Wheal Robins Copper Mine, St Neot.

1363 J. Brooke, 'Thomas Saunders Cave, speculator extraordinary', *Br. Mining* XLIII 1991 9–34

1364 J. Brooke, *The tin streams of Wendron*. (Truro, Twelveheads, 1994) 95p.

1365 J. Brooke, 'Two Cornish companies', *Devon Cornwall N. & Q.* XXXIII no. 8 1977 313

1366 J. Brooke, 'Wheal Buller', *J. Trevithick Soc.* no. 4 1976 65–72

1367 J. Brooke, 'Wheal Fortune in Ludgvan', *J. Trevithick Soc.* no. 23 1996 63–67

1368 J. Brooke, 'Wheal Hermon, St Just 1560–1976', *J. Trevithick Soc.* no. 21 1994 39–43

1369 J. Brooke, 'Wheal Vor and the Gundry bankruptcies', *J. Trevithick Soc.* XIV 1987 67–82

1370 J. Brooke, 'Wheal Zion', *Tamar J.* no. 8 1986 15–20

1371 J. Brooke, 'William Millet Thomas, company promoter', *Br. Mining* no. 48 1993 65–85

1372 A.W. Brooks, 'King Edward Mine, West Cornwall 1897–1921', *Camborne School of Mines J.* 1986 57–68

1373 A.W. Brooks, C.J. Dungey and C.A.J. Munro, 'Recent technical developments at South Crofty and Geevor Mines', *Camborne School of Mines J.* 1984 42–9

1374 D.G. Broughton, 'The Birch Tor and Vitifer tin mining complex', *Trans. Cornish Inst. Engrs.* XXIX 1968–9 25–49

1375 K. Brown and B. Acton, *Exploring Cornish mines* (Landfall Publications)
v. 1 2nd ed. 1996
v. 2 1995.
vol.3 1997

1376 K. Brown, 'Notes on a collier's visit to a Cornish copper mine (1864)' *J. Trevithick Soc.* no. 16 1989 67–73

1377 L.G. Brown, 'Fifty years of Cornish mining', *Trans. Cornish Inst. Engrs.* XVIII 1962–3 17–28

1378 J. Bryant, 'On the remains of an ancient crazing mill in the parish of Constantine', *J.R. Inst. Cornwall* VII 1882 213–14

1379 A. Buckley and A. Sharpe, 'Discoveries at Dolcoath mine', *J. Trevithick Soc.* no. 20 1993 35–8

1380 A. Buckley, 'Who were the tinners? A study of early Tudor tin workers', *J. Trevithick Soc.* no. 24 1997 96–105

1381 J.A. Buckley, *Cornish mining—at surface.* (Penryn, Tor Mark, 1990) 31p.

1382 J.A. Buckley, *The Cornish mining industry: a brief history.* (Penrhyn, Tor Mark, 1992) [1]p.

1383 J.A. Buckley, 'The great country adit: a model of co-operation', *J. Trevithick Soc.* no. 16 1989 2–21

1384 J.A. Buckley, 'The introduction of blasting into Cornish mines', *Wheals Mag.* no. 12 Dec. 1982

1385 J.A. Buckley, 'A Levant mine manager's letter book', *J. Trevithick Soc.* no. 18 1991 108–16

Letters of Ben Nicholas

1386 J.A. Buckley, *A miner's tale: the story of Howard Mankee.* (Redruth, Penhellick, *c.* 1988) 120p.

1387 A. Buckley and B. Earl, 'Preliminary report on the tin and iron working site at Crift Farm', *J. Trevithick Soc.* no. 17 1990 66–77

1388 J.A. Buckley, 'Upheavals among Tudor tinners', *Wheals Mag.* no. 11 Dec. 1981. [1]p.

1389 J.F. Buckley, *A history of South Crofty Mine.* (Truro, Dyllansow Truran, 1981) 208p

1390 J.A. Buckley, *Tudor tin bounds of West Penwith.* (Redruth, Dyllansow Truran, 1987)

1391 L.J. Bullen, 'A day at South Crofty Mine in 1944', *Br. Mining* no. 48 1993 55–64

1392 G. Burke and P. Richardson, 'The adaptability of the Cornish cost book system: a response', *Bus. Hist.* XXV no. 2 1983 193–9

See no. 1398

1393 G.M. Burke, *The Cornish miner and the Cornish mining industry 1870–1921.* (Ph.D. thesis, London University, 1982)

1394 G. Burke and P. Richardson, 'The decline and fall of the cost book system in the Cornish tin industry, 1895–1914', *Bus. Hist.* XXIII no. 1 1981 4–18

1395 G. Burke, 'The decline of the independent bal maiden: the impact of change in the Cornish mining industry', *in* A.V. John ed., *Unequal opportunities: women's employment in England 1800–1918.* (Oxford, Blackwell, 1986) 179–204

1396 J.C. Burrow and J.A. Buckley, *Cornish mining—underground.* (Penryn, Tor Mark Press, 1989) 32p.

1397 J.C. Burrow and W. Thomas, *'Mongst mines and miners: being underground scenes by flashlight illustrating and explaining the methods of working in the Cornish mines about 1895.* (Truro, Barton, 1965) 39p.

Reprint of 1893 ed.

1398 R. Burt and N. Kudo, 'The adaptability of the Cornish cost book system', *Bus. Hist.* XXV no. 1 1983 30–41

See no. 1392

1399 R. Burt, 'Cornish company records in the Guild Hall Library, City of London', *J. Trevithick Soc.* no. 19 1992 32–43

Mining companies

1400 R. Burt, P. Waite and R. Burnley, *Cornish mines: metalliferous and associated minerals, 1845–1913.* (Exeter, University of Exeter, 1987)

1401 R. Burt, ed., *Cornish mining: essays on the organisation of Cornish mines and the Cornish mining economy.* (Newton Abbot, David & Charles, 1969) 210p.

1402 R. Burt, *John Taylor: mining entrepreneur and engineer, 1779–1863.* (Buxton, Moorland, 1977) 318p.

1403 R.O. Burt, 'Mineral recovery from the Old Red River Valley, Cornwall', *Trans. Cornwall Inst. Engrs.* XXV 1969–70 42–57

1404 'Caradon copper mines', *Tamar J.* no. 1 1978 23–8

1405 J. Carne, 'A description of the stream-work at Drift Moor, near Penzance', *Trans. R. Geol Soc. Cornwall* IV 1832 47–69

1406 J. Carne, 'On the discovery of silver in the mines of Cornwall', *Trans. R. Geol Soc. Cornwall* I 1818 118–26

1407 J. Carne, 'On the mineral productions and the geology of the parish of St Just', *Trans. R. Geol. Soc. Cornwall* II 1822 290–358

1408 J. Carne, 'On the period of the commencement of copper mining in Cornwall' and 'On the improvements which have been made in mining', *Trans. R. Geol Soc. Cornwall* III 1827 35–85

1409 J. Carne, 'Statistics of the tin mines in Cornwall and of the consumption of tin in Great Britain', *J. Statist. Soc. London* II 1839 260–8

Reprinted in R. Burt, ed., *Cornish mining: essays on the organisation of Cornish mines and the Cornish mining economy.* (Newton Abbot, David & Charles, 1969) 83–93

1410 J. Carswell, *The prospector: being the life and times of Rudolph Erich Raspe (1737–1794).* (London, Cresset Press, 1950) 277p.

1411 C. Carter, 'The boring machine—introduction of compressed air powered rock drills into the Camborne mines', *J. Trevithick Soc.* no. 20 1993 2–22

1412 F.L. Caunter, *Under the surface.* (St Austell, H.E. Warne, 1957)

1413 R. Cawthorne, ed., *All that remains: a survey of the mines in the Kithill and Callington areas, a century after the heyday of the mining industry in Devon and Cornwall.* (Plymouth, Plymouth Caving Group, n.d.)

1414 G.H. Chilcott, 'Notes on tin ownership in Cornwall', *J.R. Inst. Cornwall* XVII 1907 255–9

1415 R.P. Chops, 'Thomas Bushell and the Cornish mines', *Devon Cornwall N. & Q.* Jan. 1919 152–5

1416 A.J. Clarke and E.W. Rabjohns, 'The history of Wheal Grenville', *Camborne School of Mines J.* 1975 41–52

1417 J.H. Collins, 'Some historical and other notices of mining in the northern part of the Parish of St. Agnes', *Ann. Reps. R. Cornwall Polytech. Soc.* n.s. II 1911–1913 64–74

1418 C. Combes, 'Mémoire sur l'exploitation des mines des Comtses de Cornwall et de Devon', *Ann. des Mines* 3rd ser. V 1834 109, 345, 593

1419 'Copper ore statistics: public ticketings, Cornwall 1814–1856', *Br. Mining* no. 8 1978 40–41

1420 A. Corbyn, 'The method of ore extraction employed at a Cornish tin mine', *Shrops Min Club Yrbk.* 1961–2 36–37

1421 J. Corin, *Levant, a champion Cornish mine.* (Truro, Trevithick Society, 1992) 70p.

1422 Cornish Chamber of Mines, *Mining in Cornwall today.* (Truro, Cornish Chamber of Mines, 1974)

1423 'A Cornish experimental mine', *Mine Quarry Engng.* XXII Dec. 1956 513–15 Holman's.

1424 Cornwall Archaeology Unit, *St Just Mining District Survey.* (CAU Reports) 2v.

1425 Cornwall Archaeology Unit, *Wheal Coates, St Agnes.* (CAU and the National Trust) 37p

1426 'Cornwall: sites of interest—old and new', *Br. Mining* no. 19 1980–2 55–7

1427 'Cornwall's latest tin mine (Mount Wellington)', *Mine Quarry* IV no. 9 Sept. 1975 18–26

1428 P.C. Davey, *Studies in the history of mining and metallurgy to the middle of the seventeenth century, considered in relation to the progress of scientific knowledge and with some reference to mining in Cornwall.* (Ph.D. thesis, London University, 1954)

1429 E.H. Davison, 'The history of Cornish mining in relation to the geology of the area', *Trans. R. Geol Soc. Cornwall* XIV–XV 1926 491–500

1430 B. Deacon, 'Migration and the mining industry in East Cornwall in the mid nineteenth century', *J.R. Inst. Cornwall* n.s. X 1986–7 84–104

1431 P.R. Deakin, J.A. Buckley and R.T. Riekstins, *South Crofty underground.* (Camborne, Penhellick Publications, 1995)

1432 'Developments in mineral processing in the Cornish tin industry', *Camborne School of Mines J.* 1984 50–55

1433 M.G. Dickinson, 'An early tinworks deed: some implications', *Devon Cornwall N. & Q.* XXXIII 1976 185–8

1434 D. Dixon, 'The Richards Family of Tavistock and Mary Tavy', *J. Trevithick Soc.* no. 22 1995 67–76

1435 S.C. Dominy and G.S. Camm, 'The nature and exploitation of narrow tin-bearing veins: a case study from South Crofty Mine, Cornwall, UK', *Br. Mining* no. 57 1996 150–70

1436 M.B. Donald, 'Burchard Kranich (c. 1515–1578) miner and Queen's physician, Cornish mining stamps, antimony and Frobisher's gold', *Ann. Sci.* VI no. 3 308–22

1437 H.L. Douch, ed., 'An early mining agreement', *J. R. Inst. Cornwall* n.s. II no. 2 1954 107–11

1438 H.L. Douch, *East Wheal Rose: the history of Cornwall's greatest lead mine.* (Truro, Barton, 1964) 84p.

1439 B. Earl, *Cornish mining: the techniques of metal mining in the West of England, past and present.* (Truro, Barton, 1968) 118p.

1440 B. Earl and R.F. Tylecote, 'East Cornwall lead-silver smelter at Wheal Langford, Callington (SX 386690)', *J. Trevithick Soc.* no. 15 1988 36–42

1441 E.W.A. Edmonds, 'Great Dowgas Mine, St Stephen', *J. Trevithick Soc.* no. 12 1985 78–84

1442 C.J. Evans, 'Adapt and survive: patterns of tin usage', *Mining Mag.* June 1985 557–61

1443 H.R. Evans, 'A Cornish family of tin-bounders', *Devon Cornwall N. & Q.* XXVIII 1960 209–15, 229–33

The Allen family.

1444 C.E. Everard, 'Mining and shore-line evolution near St Austell, Cornwall', *Trans. R. Geol. Soc. Cornwall* XIX 1959–60 199–219

1445 J. Ferguson, 'The copper slag blocks of Hayle, Cornwall: remains of a late 18th-century industry', *Mining Hist.* XIII no. 2 1996 104–8

These blocks, produced by the Cornish Copper Company, were used for building

1446 H.W. Fisher, 'The stannaries of Cornwall', *J.R. Inst. Cornwall* XVI 1904 292–306

1447 P.W. Flower, *A history of the trade in tin; a short description of tin mining and metallurgy; a history of the origins and progress of the tinplate trade.* (London, G. Bell & Sons, 1880) 219p.

1448 J. Forbes, 'On the temperature of mines', *Trans. R. Geol. Soc. Cornwall* II 1822 159–217

1449 J. Forbes, 'Tour into Cornwall to the Land's End', *J R. Inst. Cornwall* IX 1983 146–206

1450 R.W. Fox, 'On the temperature of mines', *Trans. R. Geol Soc. Cornwall* II 1822 15–28

1451 S. Furze, 'Tin dressing', *Ann. Reps. R. Cornwall Polytech. Soc.* n.s. VIII pt. 3 1936 58–84

1452 S. Furze, 'The evolution of Cornish dressing machinery', *Trans. Cornish Inst. of Min. Mech. Metall Engrs.* X 1925 72–98

1453 B.A. Fyfield-Shayler and C.P. Norton, 'Tolgus tin: sole survivor of the traditional Cornish tin streaming industry', *Ind. Archaeol.* XV 1980 34–66

1454 W.K.V. Gale, 'Tour of Cornish mining sites', *Bull. Hist. Metall Gp.* IV no. 1 1970 10–11

1455 G.A.M. Gerrard, *The early Cornish tin industry: an archaeological and historical study.* (Ph.D. thesis, University of Wales, Lampeter, 1986)

1456 G.A.M. Gerrard, *The excavation of a medieval tin works at West Colliford, St. Neots Parish, Cornwall.* (M.A. thesis, University of Wales, Lampeter, 1983)

1457 S. Gerrard, 'The medieval and early modern Cornish stamping mill', *Ind. Archaeol. Rev.* XII no. 1 1989 9–19

1458 S. Gerrard and A. Sharpe, 'Archaeological survey and excavation at Wheal Prosper Tin Stamps, Lanivet', *Cornish Archaeol.* XXIV 1985 197–211

1459 S. Gerrard, 'Retallack: A late medieval tin-mining complex in the Parish of Constantine, and its Cornish context', *Cornish Archaeol.* XXIV 1985 175–82

1460 S. Gerrard, 'Stream working in medieval Cornwall', *J. Trevithick Soc.* no. 14

1987 7–31

1461 T.E. Gillet, 'The geology of South Crofty Mine', *Trans. N. Cavern Mine Res. Soc.* I no. 2 1964 23–7

1462 J.C. Goodridge, 'The tin-mining industry: a growth point for Cornwall', *Inst. Br. Geogr. Trans. Pap.* no. 38 1966 95–104

1463 J. Goodridge, 'A new life for tin', *Geog. Mag.* Aug. 1985 424–9

1464 R.S. Harker, 'The flooding of Wheal Owles', *Mem. N. Cavern Mine Res. Soc.* Aug. 1965 35–9

1465 J.R. Harris *The Copper King: a biography of Thomas Williams of Llanidan.* (Liverpool, University Press, 1964) 194p.

1466 J.R. Harris and R.O. Roberts, 'Eighteenth-century monopoly: the Cornish Metal Company agreements of 1785', *Bus. Hist.* V no. 2 1962 69–82

1467 T.R. Harris, 'The Cornish Copper Company 1754–1869: copper smelters, merchants, engineers and ironfounders', *J. Trevithick Soc.* no. 6 1978 7–19

1468 T.R. Harris, 'A Cornish industrial undertaking. Some episodes from the history of the Cornish Copper Company with special reference to the Copperhouse Foundry and Engine Works 1819–1869', *Ann. Reps. R. Cornish Polytech. Soc.* n.s. IX pt. 1 1937 82–106

1469 T.R. Harris, *Dolcoath: Queen of Cornish mines.* (Camborne, Trevithick Society, Occ. Pub. no. 1 1974) 108p.

1470 T.R. Harris, 'John Edwards (1731–1807), Cornish industrialist', *Trans. Newcomen Soc.* XXIII 1942–43 13–22

A copper smelter, mine adventurer and merchant.

The same title appears in *Engineering* CLIV 1942 365, 416–17

1471 Sir G. Harrison, *Substance of a report on the laws and jurisdiction of the Stannaries in Cornwall.* (London, 1835) 178p.

Copy in the Cornish Studies Library, Redruth

1472 J. Hatcher, *English tin production and trade before 1550.* (London, Oxford University Press, 1973) 219p.

1473 C. Hawkins, 'Observations on gold found in the tin stream works of Cornwall', *Trans. R. Geol. Soc. Cornwall* I 1818 235–6

1474 J. Hawkins, 'On the process of refining', *Trans. R. Geol. Soc. Cornwall* I 1818 201–11

1475 J. Hawkins, 'On the state of our tin mines, at different periods, until the commencement of the eighteenth century', *Trans. R. Geol. Soc. Cornwall* IV 1832 71–94

1476 E.S. Hedges, *Tin in social and economic history.* (London, Edward Arnold, 1964) 194p.

1477 P. Heffer, *East Pool and Agar: a Cornish mining legend.* (Redruth, Dyllansow Truran, 1985) 60p.

1478 J.S. Henderson, 'Notes on the smelting of tin at Newham, Truro, in the years 1703–1711', *J.R. Inst. Cornwall* no. 19 1912 199–220

1479 J. Henderson, 'On the methods generally adopted in Cornwall in dressing tin and copper ore', *Proc. Instn. Civ. Engrs.* XVII 1857–8

1480 G. Henwood, *Cornwall's mines and miners: nineteenth-century studies by George Henwood*, edited by R. Burt. (Truro, Barton, 1972)

1481 W.J. Henwood, 'On the detrital tin ores of Cornwall', *J. R. Instn. Cornwall* IV 1874 191–254

1482 S. Herbert, 'Life after death for Cornish tin', *Mine Quarry* X no. 3 1981 21–25

1483 P. Herring, 'Mapping the mines and streamworks of Bodmin Moor', *Mining Hist.* XIII no. 2 1996 64–6

1484 J. Higgans, 'Angarack smelting house: its history', *J. Trevithick Soc.* no. 7 1979–80 37–55

1485 J. Hocking jun., 'On tin stamping', *Proc. Mining Inst. Cornwall* I 1877 10

1486 W.T. Hooper, 'List of principal works and memoirs relating to the geology, mining, and engineering of Cornwall', *Sand, Clays, Min.* III 1938 April 233–34

Chronological list of publications 1542–1936 in Falmouth Library.

1487 W.T. Hooper, 'Swanpool mine', *Ann. Reps. R. Cornwall Polytech. Soc.* n.s. VII 1932 179–84

1488 W. Hosking, 'Mining development scheme for the Camborne–Redruth northern area', *Trans. Corn. Inst. Min. Mech. Metall. Engrs.* X 1925 7–22

1489 W.J. Houston, 'The Tolgus Tin Stamping Co. Ltd., Redruth, Cornwall', *Mem. N. Cavern Mine Res. Soc.* Aug. 1965 32–5

1490 B. Howard, 'The Vice-Warden and the Truro files', *J. Trevithick Soc.* no. 21 1994 33–8

Consideration of the role of the Vice-Warden of the Stannaries

1491 J. Hunter, 'Visit to Wheal Jane tin mine', *Br. Mining* no. 3 1976 8–10

1492 C.C. Jenkins, 'Early tin smelting in Cornwall', *Old Cornwall* V 1951–61 269–73

1493 C.C. James, 'Great Wheal Vor', *Trans. R. Geol. Soc. Cornwall* XVII no. 4 1944–5 194–207

1494 C.C. James, 'Mine temperatures in West Cornwall', *Trans. R. Geol Soc. Cornwall* XVII 1950 164–73

1495 G. Jars, *Voyages métallurgiques ou recherches et observations ...* (1781) 3v.

v. 3 3me mémoire. Sect. V. Mine de cuivre de Whéal Spernon à Redruth dans la province de Cornouailles. pp. 86–7

7me mémoire. Sect. VII. Mines d'étain et de cuivre de la province de Cornouaille en Angleterre. pp. 186–92

Sect. VIII. Mine d'étain et cuivre de Pednandrea en Angleterre. pp. 192–4

Sect. IX. Mine d'étain de Godolophin Ball. pp. 194–202

Sect X. De l'exploitation des mines d'étain de Cornouailles. pp. 202–7

Sect. XI. Des bocards et laveries, et de la vente des minérais. pp. 207–12

Sect XII. De la fonte des minérais d'étain et ceux de cuivre. pp. 212–19

Sect. XIII. Machines à feu d'une nouvelle construction, qui dans le même temps qu'elles élevent les eaux des mines, servent à fondre du minérai. pp.219–22

Sect XIV. Séconde fonderie pour les mines de cuivre de la province de Cornouailles. pp. 222–3 (This foundry was in fact located near Bristol).

1496 A.K.H. Jenkin, 'Cornish history in mine plans and cost books', *J.R. Inst. Cornwall* XXII 1928 422–4

1497 A.K.H. Jenkin, *The Cornish miner. An account of his life above and underground from early times.* 3rd ed. (London, Allen & Unwin, 1962) 252p.

Also reprinted by David & Charles.

1498 A.K.H. Jenkin, *Mines and miners of Cornwall.* (Truro, Truro Bookshop)

    1. *Around St Ives.* (1961) 50p.

    2. *St Agnes-Perranporth.* (1962)

    3. *Around Redruth.* (1962)

    4. *Penzance-Mounts Bay.* (1962)

    5. *Hayle, Gwinear and Gwithian.* (1963)

    6. *Around Gwennap.* (1963)

    7. *Perranporth-Newquay.* (1963)

    8. *Truro to the Clay District.* (1964)

    9. *Padstow, St Columb and Bodmin.* (1964)

    10. *Camborne-Illogan.* (1965)

    11. *Marazion, St Hilary and Breage.* (1965)

    12. *Around Liskeard.* (1966)

    13. *The Lizard-Falmouth-Mevagissy.* (1967)

    14. *St Austell to Saltash.* (1967)

    15. *Calstock, Callington and Launceston.* (Federation of Old Cornish Societies, 1969)

    16. *Wadebridge, Camelford and Bude.* (Federation of Old Cornish Societies, 1970)

    Index to vols. 1–16. (St Austell, Old Cornwall Publications, 1979)

Several of these books have been reprinted by Forge Books, Bracknell

1499 A.K.H. Jenkin, 'The history of Great Wheal Vor', *J.R. Inst. Cornwall* XXIII 1930 300–24

1500 A.K.H. Jenkin, 'The rise and fall of Wheal Alfred', *J. R. Instn. Cornwall* n.s. III no. 3 1959 124–37

A copper mine, 1800–16

1501 A.K.H. Jenkin, 'Tin and copper mining in Cornwall in early days', *Engineer* CXLI 1926 465

1502 A.K.H. Jenkin, *Wendron tin.* (Helston, Wendron Forge Ltd, 1978) 64p.

1503 R. Jenkins, 'Hammer mills in Cornwall', *Trans. Newcomen Soc.* XVIII 1937–8 270–1

1504 P. Joseph, 'After the fire: the industrial archaeology of the Botallack cliffs', *J. Trevithick Soc.* no. 23 1996 68

1505 P. Joseph, 'St Just United Mine, 1862–1866', *J. Trevithick Soc.* no. 24 1997 21–45

1505 R.J. Law, 'A glimpse of the Cornish mineral industry in 1873', *J. Trevithick Soc.* no. 4 1976 57–61

Short passage from the writings of Rudolph Erich Raspe, a German

1506 *Laws of the Stannaries of Cornwall 1753, with a new introduction by R.R. Pennington.* (Trevithick Society, 1974) 126p.

1507 N.G. Le Boutillier, *South Crofty mine: geology and mineralisation.* (J.A. Buckley, 1997) 32p.

1508 R. Le Marchant, 'The dressing of copper ores', *Tamar J.* no. 9 1987 4–7

1509 R. Le Marchant, 'Leats and watercourses in the Marwellham area', *Tamar J.* no. 4 1982 21–6

1510 R. Le Marchant, 'The reopening of George and Charlotte Mine', *Tamar J.* no. 2 1979–80 46–9

1511 R. Le Marchant, 'Evidence of pumping at George and Charlotte Mine', *Tamar J.* no. 3 1980–1 24–6

1512 R. Le Marchant, 'Tin streaming', *Tamar J.* no. 10 1988 30–3

1513 J.R. Leifchild, *Cornwall: its mines and miners.* (London, Frank Cass, 1968) 303p.

Reprint of the 1908 edition

1514 Sir C. Lemon, 'Statistics of the copper mines of Cornwall', *J. Statist. Soc. London* I 1838 65–84

Reprinted in R. Burt, ed., *Cornish mining: essays on the organisation of Cornish mines and the Cornish mining economy.* (Newton Abbot, David & Charles, 1969) 49–82

1515 B. Llewellyn, 'A survey of the deeper tin zones in a part of the Carn Brea area, Cornwall', *Trans. Inst. Min. Metall.* LV 1945–6 505–23

1516 H. Louis, 'On the origin of the cost book system', *Ann. Reps. R. Cornwall Polytech. Soc.* n.s. IV pt. 1 1918 232–7

1517 J. Maclean, 'The tin trade of Cornwall in the reigns of Elizabeth and James compared with that of Edward I', *J. R. Inst. Cornwall* IV 1874 187–90

1518 P. Mayer, 'Calstock and Bere Alston silver lead mines in the first quarter of the 14th century', *Cornish Archaeol.* no. 29 1990 79–95

1519 J. Maynard, 'Remarks on two cross-sections through Carne Brae Hill and the neighbouring mines', *Ann. Reps. R. Cornwall Polytech. Soc.* no. 41 1873 190–203

1520 G. McDonnell, 'Further investigations at Crift Farm, Lanlivery', *J. Trevithick Soc.* no. 20 1993 48–50

1521 G. McDonnell, A Hoaen and H. Loney, 'The Crift Farm project, Second Interim Report, December 1994', *J. Trevithick Soc.* no. 22 1995 50–7

'Crift is a unique site that offers the opportunity to excavate a tin smelting site that utilised simple technology'

1522 T.W. McGuinness, *Changes in the population in west Cornwall with the rise and decline of mining.* (M.Sc. thesis, London University, 1938)

1523 T.W. McGuinness, 'Changes of population in West Cornwall with the rise and decline of mining', *Ann. Reps. R. Cornwall Polytech. Soc.* IX no. 4 1940 22–95

1524 T.W. McGuinness, 'Occupational change in Cornwall (over a period of *c.* 100 years)', *Ann. Reps. R. Cornwall Polytech. Soc.* CX 1943 78–107

1525 N. McKenna and B. Atkinson, 'A study of the grylls and bunny adits, Botallack, St Just', *Plymouth Mineral Min. Club J.* XV no. 3 1985 4–5

1526 M.J. Messenger, *Caradon and Looe: the canal, railways and mines.* (Twelveheads, Twelveheads, 1978) 128p.

1527 S. Michell and J.T. Letcher.'Cornish mine drainage', *Ann. Reps. R. Cornwall Polytech. Soc.* 43rd Rep. 1875 133–220

1528 F.B. Michell, 'The development of the copper mining industry in Cornwall and the Industrial Revolution', *Camborne School of Mines J.* 1980 55–9

1529 F.B. Michell, 'The dressing of tin ores (Geevor). Part 1', *Mine Quarry Engng.* XI Jan. 1946 15–19

1530 F.B. Michell, 'The dressing of tin ores (Porkellis & East Pool). Part 2', *Mine Quarry Engng.* XI Feb. 1946 29–36

1531 F.B. Michell, 'Half a century of progress in tin dressing and metallurgy', *Trans. Cornish Inst. Engrs.* XVIII 1962–63 2–15

1532 F.B. Michell, 'The history of mineral processing in Cornwall', *Bull. Hist. Metall. Gp.* IV no. 1 1970 4–9

Same title appears in *Camborne School of Mines J.* 1972 23–8

1533 F.B. Michell, 'Ore dressing in Cornwall 1600–1900', *J. Trevithick Soc.* no. 6 1978 25–32

1534 M.L. Moissenet, *Observations on the rich parts of the lodes of Cornwall: their form and their relations with the directions of the systems. Translated from the French by J.H. Collins.* (London, Simkins, Marshall, 1877) 150p.

1535 J.E. Morgan, 'Iron ropes for the Cornish mines?: technology transfer between Saxony and Falmouth c. 1840', *Mining Hist.* XIII no. 2 1996 10–15

1536 T.A. Morrison. *Cornwall's central mines: the Northern district, 1810–95.* (Penzance, Alison Hodge, 1980) 392p.

1537 W.A. Morris, 'The Ding-Dong mining syndicate 1911–1925', *J. Trevithick Soc.* no. 15 1988 68–74

1538 T.A. Morrison, *Cornwall's central mines: the Southern district 1810–1895.* (Penzance, Alison Hodge, 1983) 495p.

1539 J. Morton, 'The Cornish Copper Company, 1693 to 1697', *J. Trevithick Soc.* no. 7 1979–80 57–75

1540 M.P. Moyle, 'On the temperature of the Cornish mines', *Trans. R. Geol. Soc. Cornwall* II 1822 404–15

1541 E. Newell, 'Cornish miners' petition to Queen Victoria, 1842: a belated reply', *Devon Cornwall N. & Q.* XXXVI pt. 6 1989 204–8

1542 E. Newell, *The British copper ore market in the nineteenth century, with particular reference to Cornwall and Swansea.* (D.Phil. thesis, Oxford University, 1988)

1543 E. Newell, 'Interpreting the Cornish copper standard', *J. Trevithick Soc.* no. 13 1986 36–45

1544 E.W. Newton, 'The mining coinage of Cornwall', *Ann. Reps. R. Cornwall Polytech. Soc.* n.s. V pt. 3 1925 337–49

1545 C. Noall, 'The Cornish bal maiden', *Cornish Mag.* IV no. 6 1961 176–80

1546 C. Noall, *Botallack.* (Truro, Barton, 1972) 170p.

1547 C. Noall, *Geevor*. (Pendeen, Geevor Tin Mines, 1983)

1548 C. Noall, *Levant: the mine beneath the sea.* (Truro, Barton, 1970) 172p. A copper mine 1820–1930.

1549 C. Noall, *The St Ives mining district. 2v.* (Redruth, Dyllansow Truran, v.1 1983, v.2 1993) 118p. and 158p.

1550 C. Noall, *The St Just mining district.* (Truro, Barton, 1973) 179p.

1551 C. Noall, 'The tinners riot of 1729', *Old Cornwall* V 1951–61 396–98, 418–21

1552 M. Palmer and P. Neaverson, 'The Basset Mines: their history and industrial archaeology', *Br. Mining* no. 32 1987 1–68

1553 M. Palmer and P. Neaverson, 'Nineteenth-century tin and lead dressing: a comparative study of the field evidence', *Ind. Archaeol. Rev.* XII no. 1 1989 20–39

1554 J.A. Paris, 'On the accidents which occur in the mines of Cornwall, in consequence of the premature explosion of gunpowder ...', *Trans. R. Geol. Soc. Cornwall* I 1818 78–97

1555 W.H. Pascoe, *C.C.C.: the story of the Cornish Copper Company.* (Redruth, Truran, 1982) 202p.

1556 W.A. Pascoe, 'Cornish mining adventure', *Old Cornwall* V 1951–61 108–18

1557 W.A. Pascoe, 'Notes on the Cornish tin industry', *Mining Mag.* LXXIII no. 2 1945 84–7

1558 W.H. Paynter, *Our old Cornish mines: East Cornwall.* (Liskeard, The Author, 1964) 23p.

1559 J. Penhale, *The mine under the sea.* (Falmouth, J.H. Lake, 1962) 67p.

1560 R.D. Penhallurick, *Tin with antiquity: mining and trade throughout the ancient world with particular reference to Cornwall.* (Institute of Metals, 1986) 271p.

1561 R.R. Pennington, 'The Cornish Metal Company, 1785–1792', *J. Trevithick Soc.* no. 5 1977 76–88

1562 R.R. Pennington, 'The South Wheal Rancis and West Wheal Basset boundary litigation', *J. Trevithick Soc.* no. 7 1979–80 95–102

1563 N.J.G. Pounds, 'German miners in Elizabethan Cornwall', *Geography* XXIX no. 1 1944 25

1564 N.J.G. Pounds, 'Population movement in Cornwall, and the rise of mining in the 18th century', *Geography* XXVIII no. 2 1943 37–46

1565 L.L. Price, *'West Barbary' or Notes on the system of work and wages in the Cornish mines.* (London, Henry Frowde, 1891)

Reprinted in R. Burt, ed., *Cornish mining: essays on the organisation of Cornish mines and the Cornish mining economy.* (Newton Abbot, David & Charles, 1969) 111–92

1566 'Providence Mine, St. Just, Cornwall', *Br. Caver* XXXIX 1964 59–62

1567 J. Provis, 'On the lead ores of Cornwall', *Reps. Mines Assoc. Devon Cornwall* 1874 70–8

1568 W. Pryce, *Mineralogia Cornubiensis: a treatise on minerals, mines and mining ... to which is added, an explanation of the terms and idioms of miners* (Truro, Barton, 1972) 331p.

Reprint of the original 1778 ed.

1569 A. Raistrick, 'Ore dressing in the 18th and early 19th centuries', *Mine Quarry Engng.* IV 1939 161–6

Mainly Cornwall and Yorkshire

1570 J. Rowe, 'The declining years of Cornish tin mining', *in* J.H. Porter, *ed., Education and labour in the South-West* (Exeter University, Exeter Papers in Economic History no. 10, 1975) 59–77

1571 J. Rowe, 'The rise of foreign competition to Cornish tin-mining', *Ann. Reps. R. Cornwall Polytech. Soc.* no. 132 1965 22–39

1572 J.G. Rule, *The labouring miner in Cornwall, c. 1740–1870: a study in social history.* (Ph.D. thesis, Warwick University, 1971)

1573 A. Russell, 'John Hawkins, F.G.S., F.R.H.S., F.R.S., 1761–1841: a distinguished Cornishman and early mining geologist', *J. R. Instn. Cornwall* n.s. II no. 2 1954 98–106

1574 C.J. Schmitz, 'Cornish mine labour and the Royal Commission of 1864', *J. Trevithick Soc.* no. 10 1983 35–45

1575 W.E. Sevier, 'Progress at Geevor tin mine', *Mining Mag.* LXXIII no. 4 1945 201–10

1576 H.R. Shambrook, 'The Caradon and Phoenix mining area', *Br. Mining* no. 20 1982

1577 H.R. Shambrook, 'The Phoenix United Mines, in the parish of Linkinhorne, East Cornwall', *Br. Mining* no. 5 1977 46–53

1578 R. Shambrook, 'Some East Cornwall mines', *Plymouth Mineral Min. Club J.* VII no. 3 1977 15, 19

1579 H.R. Shambrook, 'The Wherry Mine, Penzance, its history and mineral production', *Br. Mining* no. 19 1982 91–4

1580 A. Sharpe, *St Just. An archaeological survey of the mining district.* (Cornwall, Archaeological Unit, 1993) 2v.

1581 J. Sims, 'On the economy of mining in Cornwall' *in* H. English, *The Mining Almanack for 1849.* (London, 1849)

Reprinted in R. Burt, *ed., Cornish mining: essays on the organisation of Cornish mines and the Cornish mining economy.* (Newton Abbot, David & Charles, 1969) 95–107

1582 B.S. Skillen, 'Miners, coiners and conjurers: some Cornish tales', *Br. Mining* no. 41 1990 7–13

1583 B.S. Skillen, 'Nobody like the Captain: men of the mines', *Br. Mining* no. 45 1992 46–56

Discussion of a series of articles by George Henwood in *The Mining Journal* 1857–8 on notable miners.

1584 V. Smale, 'South Terras: Cornwall's premier uranium and radium mine', *J.R. Inst. Cornwall* n.s. II vol. I no. 3 1993 304–22

1585 D. Smith, 'The life and essays of William Vivian, Cornish mining engineer 1817–1879', *Br. Mining* no. 50 1994 100–10

1586 R. Smith, 'An analysis of the processes for smelting tin', *Mining Hist.* XIII no. 2 1996 91–9

1587 W. Smyth, 'On the iron mines of Perran', *Trans. R. Geol. Soc. Cornwall* VII 1865 332–5

1588 T. Spargo, *The mines of Cornwall.* (Truro, Barton, 1959–61)

    v. 1 *The Land's End peninsula* (1959)

    v. 2 *The Camborne area.* (1960)

    v. 3 *The Mount's Bay area.* (1960)

    v. 4 *The Redruth area.* (1961)

    v. 5 *Mid-Cornwall.* (1961)

    v. 6 *East Cornwall.* (1961)

This edition is a reprint of the edition of 1865.

1589 G. Spink, 'South Caradon: victim of man and time', *Plymouth Mineral Min. Club J.* IV no. 3 1974 12–13

1590 S. Staal, 'Calenick crucibles', *Ann. Reps. R. Cornwall Polytech. Soc.* CXXIV 1957 44–54

1591 P. Stanier, *Cornwall's mining heritage.* (Twelveheads, 1988) 48p.

1592 F.J. Stephens, 'Adits and adit-drivers', *Old Cornwall* III no. 7 1940 283–6

1593 F.J. Stephens, 'The ancient mining districts of Cornwall', *Ann. Reps. R. Cornwall Polytech. Soc.* n.s. VII pt. 1 1931 159–78 Liskeard district; VIII pt. 2 1935 35–51 St Austell; IX pt. 1 1937 70–81 north of Truro; IX pt 2. 1938 33–56 parishes of Illogan, St Agnes

1594 F.J. Stephens, 'General notes on ancient mining in Cornwall', *Ann. Reps. R. Cornwall Polytech. Soc.* 1928 162–71

1595 F.J. Stephens, 'Notes on the mining district between Camborne and Redruth, north of the main road', *Trans. R. Geol Soc. Cornwall* XIV–XV 1919 288–307

1596 F.J. Stephens, 'Notes on the Marazion and Perranuthnoe mining districts', *Ann. Reps. R. Cornwall Polytech. Soc.* 1893 LXI–LXIII 117

1597 F.J. Stephens, 'Some old Cornish mine adventurers', *Old Cornwall* III 1941–42 438–42, 479–81, 497–500

1598 F.J. Stephens, 'The Wendron Mining District', *Ann. Reps. R. Cornwall Polytech. Soc.* Rep. 55 1887 125–8

1599 P. Stephens and J. Stengelhofen, 'Tin stream works at Tuckingmill', *J. Trevithick Soc.* no. 1 1973 90–5

1600 A. Stoyel, 'Brea Adit Works, Camborne', *J. Trevithick Soc.* no. 4 1976 45–56

1601 J. Taylor, 'On the economy of mining', *Q. Mining Rev.* X 1837 261–72

    Reprinted in R. Burt, ed., *Cornish mining: essays on the organisation of Cornish mines and the Cornish mining economy.* (Newton Abbot, David & Charles, 1969) 31–48

1602 J. Taylor, R.K. Harrison and K. Taylor, 'Structure and mineralisation at Roskrow United Mine, Ponsanooth, Cornwall', *Bull. Geol. Soc. Gr. Britain* XXV 1966 33–40

1603 C. Thomas, 'A Cornish mine captain: Josiah Thomas of Dolcoath 1833–1901', *Camborne School of Mines J.* LXXXVI 1986 69–75

1604 H. Thomas, *Cornish mining interviews.* (Camborne, Camborne Printing Co., 1896) 351p.

The author was editor of the *Cornish Post and Mining News*.

1605 J. Thomas, 'Description of the operations at Dolcoath Mine', *J. R. Inst. Cornwall* III 1868–70 191–7

1606 J.G. Thomas, 'Notes on some early blowing and smelting sites in the Carn Brea–St Agnes area', *J. Trevithick Soc.* no. 2 1974 71–83

1607 R.A. Thomas, 'Notes on Cornish mines in 1896', *Ann. Reps. R. Cornwall Polytech. Soc.* 64th Rep. 1896 89–94

1608 W. Thomas, 'Abandoned Cornish mines: the mines of St Just', *Ann. Reps. R. Cornwall Polytech. Soc.* n.s. VII pt. 1 1931 32–7

1609 V.J. Tilly, 'The proposed revival of Cornish mining', *Camborne School of Mines J.* 1949 4–9

1610 A. Titley, 'Cornish mining: notes from the account books of Richard Trevithick, Senior', *Trans. Newcomen Soc.* XI 1930–1 26–41

1611 R. Tredinnick, *A review of Cornish copper mining enterprise, with a description of the most important dividend and progressive copper and tin mines of Cornwall and Devon and a detailed account of the Buller and Basset district.* (London, 1858)

1612 G.M.A. Trinick, 'The Tregurtha Down Mines, Marazion 1700–1965', *Ind. Archaeol. Rev.* II 1978 111–28

Primarily tin but also some copper mining.

Same title also appears in *J. Trevithick Soc.* no. 8 1981 7–25

1613 R. Trivett, *An industry of the past.* (Plymouth, Plymouth College of Art & Design, 1981) 30p.

The copper industry

1614 J.H. Trounson, 'The boy who worked up mine', *J. Trevithick Soc.* no. 12 1985 73–74

W.G. Opie of Redruth

1615 J.H. Trounson, *The Cornish mineral industry: past performance and future prospect: a personal view 1937–1951*, edited by Roger Burt and Peter Waite. (Exeter, University of Exeter in association with the National Association of Mining History Organisations, 1989) 197p.

1616 J.H. Trounson, 'The Cornish mineral industry. Part 1', *Mining Mag.* LXVI no. 2 1942 47–52; 'Part 2', LXVI no. 5 1942 195–205; 'Part 3. The St Just and St. Ives mining districts', LXVII no. 3 1942 119–30; 'Part 4 no. 1. The Marazion, Wheal Vor, St Erth, Gwinear and Crowan districts', LXVIII no. 1 1943 9–18; 'Part 4 no. 2. The Marazion, Wheal Vor, St Erth, Gwinear and Crowan districts', LXVIII no. 2 1943 78–85; 'Part 4 no. 3. The Marazion, Wheal Vor, St Erth, Gwinear and Crowan districts', LXIX no. 6 1943 329–42; 'Part 5. The Wendron district', LXXII no. 2 1945 73–83

1617 J.H. Trounson, 'The Cornish mining industry in the 19th and 20th centuries', *J. Trevithick Soc.* no. 11 1984 7–17

1618 J.H. Trounson, *Cornwall's future mines.* (University of Exeter Press, 1993) 164p.

1619 J.H. Trounson, 'Some useful prospects in Cornwall. Part 1', *Min. Mag.* LXXXIV no. 2 1951 73–84; 'Part 2.', LXXXIV no. 3 1951 139–49; 'Part 3.',

LXXXIV no. 4 1951 209–16

1620 J.H. Trounson, *Historic Cornish mining scenes at surface*. (Truro, Barton, 1969) 64p.

1621 J.H. Trounson, *Mining in Cornwall, 1850–1960*. 2v. (Ashbourne, Moorland, 1980)

New edition published by Dyllansow Truran in 1985 and republished by the Trevithick Society 1989.

Lavishly illustrated

1622 J.H. Trounson, 'Practical considerations in developing old Cornish mines', *in Symposium on the future of non-ferrous mining in Great Britain and Ireland*. (1959) Paper 18

Copy in the Cornish Studies Library, Redruth

1623 D.G. Tucker and M. Tucker, 'The story of Wheal Guskus in the Parish of Saint Hilary', *J. Trevithick Soc*. no. 1 1973 49–62

1624 J.F. Turner, 'Developments in mineral processing in the Cornish tin industry', *Camborne School of Mines J*. 1984 50–5

1625 R.F. Tylecote, 'Calenick: a Cornish tin smelter, 1702 to 1891', *Hist. Metall*. XIV no. 1 1980 1–16

1626 R.F. Tylecote, 'The history of the tin industry in Cornwall: some suggested lines of research', *Cornish Archaeol*. no. 5 1966 30–3

1627 J. Vivian, *Tales of the Cornish miners*. (Truro, Tor Mark Press, 1981)

1628 R.B. Warner, 'The Carnanton tin ingot', *Cornish Archaeol*. no. 6 1967 29–31

1629 J.Y. Watson, *Compendium of British mining with statistical notes on the principal mines of Cornwall to which is added the historical uses of metals and a glossary of the terms used in mining*. (1843) 84p.

Republished in 1962 by Truro Bookshop.

1630 J.Y. Watson, *Cornish mining notes, 1861*. (Truro, Truro Bookshop, 1961) 31p.

First published in *Mining J*. 1861

1631 Webb-Geach, *History and progress of mining in the Caradon and Liskeard district*. (1863)

Webb (Stockbroker) and Edward Geach

1632 A.P. Wells, 'On stream analysis at Wheal Jane', *Mining Mag*. Feb. 1983 124–31

1633 'Wheal Owles and Boscean United Mining Co. Ltd, St Just, Penzance', *Mem. N. Cavern Mine Res. Soc*. Aug. 1965 39–40

1634 'What future for Cornish tin. Part 1', *Mine Quarry Engng*. XVI no. 1 1987 7–13; 'Part 2', XVI no. 3 1987 19–21

1635 J. Whitehead, 'Geevor tin mine', *Camborne School of Mines J*. 1954 31–44

1636 W.F. Wilkinson, 'On the dressing of the tin ores in Cornwall', *Trans. Inst. Min. Metall*. 1912–13 225p.

1637 G. Williams, 'Bal Du Mine of West Wheal Reeth', *J. Trevithick Soc*. no. 13 1986 80–3

1638 G. Williams, 'The decline of Great Work and the formation of Wheal Reeth Tin Ltd.', *J. Trevithick Soc*. no. 19 1992 55–85

1639 G. Williams, 'Ding Dong, its origins and early working', *J. Trevithick Soc.* no. 23 1996 45–62
1640 G. Williams, 'Ding Dong—the 19th century and beyond', *J. Trevithick Soc.* no. 24 1997 61–95
1641 G. Williams, 'Georgia Consols', *J. Trevithick Soc.* no. 22 1995 58–66
1642 G. Williams, 'A history of Giew Mine', *J. Trevithick Soc.* no. 11 1984 60–70
1643 G. Williams, 'Parbola Mine', *J. Trevithick Soc.* no. 21 1994 44–60
1644 G. Williams, 'Polrose Mine', *J. Trevithick Soc.* no. 20 1993 58–75
1645 G. Williams, 'Tindene Mine', *J. Trevithick Soc.* no. 15 1988 75–81
1646 G. Williams, 'Tregembo Mine', *J. Trevithick Soc.* no. 17 1990 31–47
1647 G. Williams, 'West Godolphin Mine', *J. Trevithick Soc.* no. 16 1989 50–66
1648 G. Williams, 'West Great Work Mine', *J. Trevithick Soc.* no. 18 1991 66–84
1649 H.V. Williams, *Cornwall's old mines.* (Truro, Tor Mark Press, 1969)
1650 A. Woodrow, 'Andrew Angwin M.Inst.M.M.', *J. Trevithick Soc.* No. 11 1984 71–75

HM Inspector of Mines for Devon and Cornwall, 1880–7

1651 H.R. Young, 'Leaves from Cornish mining history', *Min. Wld.* CXL 1941 62–3, 79–80

Stone and slate quarrying

See also nos. 206–10

1652 E. Bird, 'The effects of quarry waste disposal on beaches on the Lizard peninsula, Cornwall', *J. Trevithick Soc.* no. 14 1987 83–92
1653 Cornwall Archaeology Unit, *Coastal slate quarries: Trebarwith to Tintagel.* (CAU Reports, 199-) 60p
1654 J.H. Collins, *The Henbarrow granite district.* Cornish Hillside Publications, 1992) 58p.

Facsimile of the 1878 ed.

1655 Delabole Slate Ltd, *Prints from the past.* (Delabole Slate Ltd, 1982)

12 photographic studies

1656 J.S. Enys, 'Some remarks on the granite found near Penryn and on the mode of working it', *London & Edinburgh Phil. Mag. & J. Sci.* II 1833
1657 G.F. Harris, *Granites and our granite industries.* (London, Crosby Lockwood, 1888) 142p.
1658 J.M. Kent, 'The Delabole slate quarry', *J. R. Inst. Cornwall* n.s. V 1968 317–23
1659 J. Rapson and Mr Pascoe, 'Cornish slate—Carnglaze quarry', *Ind. Heritage* V no. 2 1987 16–19
1660 P. Stanier, 'The De Lank granite quarry', *Mining Hist.* XIII no. 2 1996 41–46
1661 P. Stanier, 'Granite working in the Cheesewring district of Bodmin Moor, Cornwall', *J. Trevithick Soc.* no. 12 1984 36–51
1662 P.H. Stanier, 'Hazards and frauds on the Cornish slate shipping trade in the 1820s', *Devon Cornwall N. & Q.* XXXIV 1978 29–32

1663 P. Stanier, 'John Freeman and the Cornish granite industry 1840–1965', *J. Trevithick Soc.* no. 13 1986 7–35
'Addendum', no. 14 1987 93–96

1664 C. Vincent, *Delabole slate quarry. Past and present.* (The Author, 1984) 25p.

Other types of extraction

See also nos. 211–18

1665 M. Gregory, 'The production of Cornish radium at South Terras Mine', *Trans. Cornish Inst. Min. Mech. Metall.* Engrs. X 1925 63–70

1666 R. Webber, 'The St Erith sand pits', *Old Cornwall* XII no. 1 1997 32–8

PAPER MAKING

See also nos. 219–22

1667 A.H. Shorter, 'The distribution of paper-making in Cornwall in the 19th century', *Devon Cornwall N. & Q.* XX 1938 2-10

1668 A.H. Shorter, 'Paper-making in Devon and Cornwall', *Geography* XXIII 1938 164-76

1669 A.H. Shorter, 'The paper-making industry in Cornwall', *Ann. Reps. R. Cornwall Polytech. Soc.* 1948 30-41

POSTS AND COMMUNICATIONS

See also nos. 223-5

1670 Marconi Company, *A chapter of Marconi's history, The story of Poldhu.* (Chelmsford, Marconi Co., Booklet no. 7)

1671 Marconi Company, *Imperial and international wireless communications 1909-46.* (Marconi Co., Booklet no. 6)

1672 M.E. Philbrick, 'Postal history of Cornwall before 1840', *Old Cornwall* VIII 425-32

1673 F.J.D. Taylor, *The Goonhilly Project.* (Institution of Electrical Engineers, 1964) 152p.

POTTERY AND CERAMICS

See also nos. 226-7

1674 P.C.D. Brears, 'Techniques of the Truro Pottery', *Folk Life* X 1972 47-54

1675 C.M.E. Collins, 'Porcelain and pottery manufacture in Cornwall', *Ann. Reps. R. Cornwall Polytech. Soc.* 43rd Rep. 1875 59-62

1676 C.M.E. Collins, 'Potteries in Cornwall', *Ann. Reps. R. Cornwall Polytech. Soc.* no. 36 1868 28-43

1677 H.L. Douch, 'Cornish earthernware potters', *J. R. Inst. Cornwall* n.s. VI no. 1 1969 33-64

1678 H.L. Douch, 'Cornish earthenware potters', *J. R. Inst. Cornwall* n.s. VI no. 1 1969 33-64

1679 H.L. Douch, 'The tobacco trade and the manufacture of clay-pipes in Cornwall', *J. R. Inst. Cornwall* n.s. VI no. 2 1970 139-53

1680 L. Miller, 'Wedgwood in Cornwall', *J. Trevithick Soc.* no. 15 1988 27-35

1681 B. Nicholls, 'The Tamar Firebrick and Clay Company', *Ind. Archaeol.* IX 1972 242-264

1682 D.P.S. Peacock, 'The gabbroic pottery of Cornwall', *Antiquity* LXII 1988 302-4

1683 E.A. Rees, 'Cornwall's part in ceramic history', *Ann. Reps. R. Cornwall Polytech. Soc.* n.s. VIII pt. 2 1935 61-75

1684 C. Staal, 'Calenick crucibles', *Ann. Reps. R. Cornwall Polytech. Soc.* 124th Rep. 1957 44-54

1685 R.N. Worth, 'Modern pottery', *Ann. Reps. R. Cornwall Polytech. Soc.* no. 44 1876 46-52

PRINTING AND PUBLISHING

See also no. 548

1686 R.A.J. Potts, 'Early Cornish printers, 1740-1850', *J. R. Inst. Cornwall* n.s. IV no. 3 1963 264-325

1687 N. Tangye, *Cornwall newspapers 18th & 19th century. Gazetteer & finding list.* (Trevithick Society, Institute of Cornish Studies, 1980) 20p.

Also appears in *J. Trevithick Soc.* no. 7 1979–80 76-94

1688 N. Tangye, 'The newspaper in Cornwall: a protracted birth', *Cornish Stud.* no. 7 1979 61-5

PUBLIC UTILITIES

See also nos. 228-33

1689 A. Pearson, 'The coal gas industry at Falmouth 1819-1866', *J. Trevithick Soc.* no. 15 1988 43-52

SHIP AND BOAT BUILDING

See also nos. 234-9

1690 P.T. Craddock and D.R. Hook, 'Cornish copper and naval sheathing: new evidence of an old story', *in* J. Lang *ed., Metals and the sea* (Historical Metallurgy Society, 1990) 49-50

1691 C.J. Davies, 'Shipbuilding on the Isles of Scilly', *J.R. Inst. Cornwall* n.s. X 1988 187-220

1692 J.A. Derriman, 'A West Looe shipbuilding contract of 1686', *Devon Cornwall N. & Q.* XXV 1983

1693 A. Kittridge, 'Steam ferry building in Mount Batten and Turnchapel 1870-

1905', *Marit. S-W* no. 3 1987 21-8

1694 C. Noall and M. McCaughan, 'William Paynter—a renowned boatbuilder of St. Ives', *Marit. S-W* no. 5 1991 34-45

1695 A.S. Oliver, *Boats and boatbuilding in West Cornwall: a study of traditional Cornish fishing craft*. (Truro, Barton, 1971) 96p.

1696 T. Pawlyn, 'The Swansea dredger, 1852', *Marit. S-W* no. 3 1987 15-19

The building of a dredger for Swansea harbour by the Hayle foundry.

1697 W.H. Verran, 'Shipbuilding at Newquay and notes on local vessels', *Mar. Mirr* XXXI 1945 198-209

1698 C.H. Ward-Jackson, *Ships and shipbuilders of a west country seaport: Fowey, 1786-1939*. (Truro, Twelveheads, 1986) 124p.

TEXTILES

1699 H.L. Douch, 'Truro's Kidderminster, Brussels and velvet pile', *J. Trevithick Soc.* no. 3 1975 57-61

1700 J. Smedley, 'A history of the Cornish wool industry and its people', *J.R. Inst. Cornwall* n.s. II 1994 85-109

TRANSPORT
General

1701 Cornwall Record Office, *Turnpikes, canals and ferries*. (Truro, Record Office, Handlist no. 5, 1985) 51p.

Typescript. A list of record office holdings.

1702 J.H. Drew, *Rail and sail to Pentewan, edited by M.J.T. Lewis*. (Truro, Twelveheads, 1986) 48p.

1703 M.J. Messenger, *Caradon and Looe: the canal, railways and mines: the history of the Liskeard and Looe railway and the mines and industries they served*. (Truro, Twelveheads, 1978)

Canals and Rivers

1704 M.J. Messenger, 'The demise of a successful canal', *J. Rlwy. Canal Hist. Soc.* XXII 1976 11-12

The Liskeard & Looe Union Canal

1705 M.J. Messenger, 'The Liskeard and Looe Canal', *J. Trevithick Soc.* no. 1 1973 80-7

1706 M.J. Messenger, 'A note on an early Cornish canal scheme', *J. Trevithick Soc.* no. 2 1974 95-6

1707 N.J.G. Pounds, 'The canal building age in Cornwall', *Ann. Reps. R. Cornwall Polytech. Soc.* n.s. IX no. 4 1940 131-6

1708 J. Riddell, 'St Columb Canal', *Waterways Wld.* XXIII no. 8 1994 74–6

Railways

See also nos. 306, 309, 486, 1526

1709 G.H. Anthony, *The Hayle, West Cornwall and Helston Railways.* (Lingfield, Oakwood Press, 1969)

1710 D.S. Barrie and 'Precursor', 'Railway relics in West Cornwall', *Rlwy. Mag.* LXXIII 1933 391-7

1711 D.B. Barton, *The Redruth and Chasewater Railway, 1824–1915: a history of the Cornish mineral railway and port which served the Great Gwennap Copper Mines.* Rev. ed. (Truro, Barton, 1966) 102p.

1712 A. Bennett, *The Great Western Railway in West Cornwall.* (Southampton, Kingfisher Railway Productions, 1988) 80p.

1713 A. Bennett, *The Great Western Railway in East Cornwall.* (Cheltenham, Runpast, 1990) 79p.

1714 A. Bennett, *The Great Western Railway in Mid Cornwall.* (Southampton, Kingfisher Railway Productions, 1988) 96p.

1715 P.S.A. Berridge, 'Brunel's contribution to bridge engineering', *Engineering* 24 April 1959 538-40

On the centenary of the Royal Albert Bridge, Saltash

1716 G. Biddle, 'The Newquay and Cornwall Junction Railway', *Rlwy. Mag.* XCIX

1717 J. Binding, *Brunel's Cornish viaducts.* (Penryn, Pendragon Books and Historical Model Railway Society, 1993) 146p.

1718 G. Body, *Cornwall railway: the history, route and operation of the BR (Western) main line from Plymouth to Truro and its links on to Penzance, Falmouth and the Cornish coast.* (Weston-super-Mare, British Rail, c. 1984) 36p.

Western at work, no. 4

1719 G. Body, *Riviera Express: the train and its route.* (Bristol, Avon-Anglia Publications, 1979) 32p.

1720 R.P. Brereton, 'Description of the Centre Pier of the Saltash Bridge on the Cornwall Railway, and of the means employed for its construction', *Min. Proc. Instn. Civ. Engrs.* XXI 1861 268-76

1721 R. Burlison, 'The Pentewan Railway', *Back Track* VIII no. 5 Sept.–Oct. 1994

1722 C.R. Clinker, 'The Bodmin and Wadebridge Railway', *J. Trevithick Soc.* no. 1 1973 29-48

1723 C.R. Clinker, 'The East Cornwall Mineral Railway', *Rlwy. Mag.* XCVII 1951

1724 C.R. Clinker, *The railways of Cornwall, 1809-1963: a list of Authorising Acts of Parliament, opening and closing dates ...* (Dawlish, David & Charles, 1963) 32p.

1725 J.B.B. Collins, 'Ancient and modern railways around Bodmin', *Rlwy. Mag.* XVII 1905 135-42

1726 Cornwall Archaeology Unit, *Mineral Tramways Project.* (CAU Reports, 1991) 57p., 7 maps

Mining and transport systems in the Camborne–Redruth–Gwennap area.

1727 R. Crombleholme *and others, Callington railways: Bere Alston–*

Calstock–Callington. 2nd ed. (Bracknell, Forge, 1985) 60p.

1728 A. Fairclough, *Cornwall's railways.* (Penrhyn, Tor Mark, 1990) 40p.

1729 A. Fairclough, *The story of Cornwall's railways.* (Truro, Tor Mark Press, 1970) 47p.

1730 H.L. Hopwood, 'The Great Western Railway in Cornwall', *Rlwy. Mag.* LVII 1925 193–203

1731 H.L. Hopwood, 'The Liskeard and Looe Railway', *Rlwy. Mag.* XLI 1917 316–20

1732 H.L. Hopwood, 'The St Ives branch of the Great Western Railway', *Rlwy. Mag.* LV 1924 337–9

1733 M.J.T. Lewis, *The Pentewan Railway.* Rev. ed. (Truro, Twelveheads, 1981) 92p.

1734 W.W. Mason, 'Trevithick's first rail locomotive', *Trans. Newcomen Soc.* XII 1931–32 85–103

1735 M.J. Messenger, 'Early Cornish mineral railways', *J. Rlwy. Canal Hist. Soc.* XXII 1976

Same title also appears in *J. Trevithick Soc.* no. 5 1977 70–5

1736 M.J. Messenger, 'The Liskeard & Caradon Railway', *J. Trevithick Soc.* no. 6 1978 83

1737 M.J. Messenger, 'Passenger traffic on the Liskeard and Caradon Railway', *J. Rlwy. Canal Hist. Soc.* XIX 1973

1738 M. Messenger, 'The St Germans Quay Tramway', *J. Trevithick Soc.* no. 23 1996 83–8

1739 E. Osler, *History of the Cornwall Railway, 1835–46.* (Weston-super-Mare, Avon Anglia, 1982) 39p.

1740 C. Noall, 'The West Cornwall Railway', *Cornish Mag.* I no. 7 1958 240–2, 264

1741 H. Rake, 'The Cornwall Railway', *Rlwy. Mag.* XI 1902 441–47, 536–41

1743 T.W.E. Roche, *Cornish Riviera Limited: a review of the life of a famous train.* (Bracknell, Town & Country Press, 1969) 24p.

1744 T.W.E. Roche, *The withered arm: reminiscences of the Southern lines west of Exeter.* New ed. (Bracknell, Town & Country Press, 1977) 76p

1745 P.W.B. Semmens, *The withered arm: the Southern west of Exeter.* (Weybridge, Ian Allan, 1988) 48p.

1746 J. Simmons, 'The railway in Cornwall, 1835–1914', *J.R. Inst. Cornwall* n.s. IX 1982 11–29

1747 J.R. Smith, 'Cornwall's white gold', *Rlwy. Mag.* CXXXI 1985 162–4

The railway network built to serve the china clay industry

1748 J.T.R. Snell, 'Engines of the Callington–Bere Alston Railway line', *Tamar J.* no. 14 1992 4–8

1749 C.S. Stock, 'The Redruth and Chacewater Railway', *Rlwy. Mag.* XVI 1905 97–101

1750 'Trevithick's locomotive experiment of 1808', *Engineer* 18 Dec. 1903 589–590

1751 H.A. Vallance, 'The 'Cornishman'', *Rlwy. Mag.* XCII no. 564 1946 203–4, 215

1752 J.A.M. Vaughan, *An illustrated history of West Country china clay trains.* (Poole, Haynes, 1987) 112p.

1753 J.A.M. Vaughan, *The Newquay branch and its branches.* (Sparkford, Haynes, 1991) 192p.

1754 E.A. Wade, *The Redlake tramway and china clay works.* (Truro, Twelveheads, 1982)

1755 C.F.D. Whetmath and D.O. Faulkner, *The Bodmin and Wadebridge Railway.* (Morden, Falcon Publishing Co., 1963) 52p.

1756 R.J. Woodfin, *The centenary of the Cornwall Railway.* (Ely, W. Jefferson, 1960) 193p.

1757 D.J. Wroe, *The Bude branch.* (Southampton, Kingfisher Railway Productions, 1988) 112p.

Roads and Road Transport

See also nos. 499–512

1758 L.F. Barham, *Cornwall's electric tramcars: the history of the Camborne and Redruth system.* (Penrhyn, Glasney Press, 1973) 84p.

1759 L.F. Barham, *Torbay transport: an illustrated study of road passenger vehicles in Torquay and Paignton during the early years of the 20th century.* (Falmouth, Glasney Press, 1979) 112p.

1760 T. Clark, 'Roads and road metalling', *Ann. Reps. R. Cornwall Polytech. Soc.* no. 54 1886 103–9

1761 G.B. Grundy, 'Ancient highways of Cornwall', *Archaeol. J.* XCVIII 1941 165–80

1762 C. Henderson and H. Coates, *Old Cornish bridges and streams.* (London, Simpkin Marshall, 1928) 133p.

1763 C. Noall, *A history of Cornish mail- and stage-coaches.* (Truro, Truro Bookshop, 1963) 116p.

1764 E.M. Philbrick, 'The Redruth to Penzance turnpike roads', *J. Trevithick Soc.* no. 1 1973 63–79

Ports and Shipping

See also nos. 516–47

1765 F. Argau, 'Sailing barges of the Fal estuary', *Mar. Mirr.* LXIV 1978 163–8

1766 F. Argau and R. Bird, 'Falmouth pilot cutters, 1800–1900', *Mar. Mirr.* LXIV 1978 9–12

1767 J. Brooke, 'Sir William Lemon's Quay', *Devon Cornwall N. & Q.* XX 1965–7

1768 J. du Boulay, 'Wrecks in the Isles of Scilly' *Mar. Mirr.* XLVI 1960 88–112

1769 S.M. Campbell, 'The haveners of the medieval dukes of Cornwall and the organisation of the duchy ports', *J. R. Inst. Cornwall* n.s. IV no. 2 1962 113–44

1770 C. Carter, 'The Hayle of Hayle 1893–1933', *J. Trevithick Soc.* no. 9 1982 58–61

A three-masted steel collier.

1771 C. Carter, 'The long career of the 'Rolling Reggie'', *J. Trevithick Soc.* no. 19 1992 44–54

The coaster *Treleigh* operating out of Portreath.

1772 R.C. Curtis, *Roundwood Quay on the River Fal—Trelissick, Feock, Cornwall: a short history.* (Truro, National Trust 1972) 7p.

1773 A. Davies, *The history of the Falmouth working boats.* Rev. ed. (A. Davies, 1995) 261p.

Oyster dredgers of the River Fal.

1774 H.L. Douch, 'The Ellis family and toll charges on Coverack quay', *Ann. Rep. R. Cornwall Polytech. Soc.* CXXI 1954 46–9

1775 J.N. Douglass, 'The building of the Wolf Rock lighthouse', *J. Trevithick Soc.* no. 12 1984

1776 R.H.C. Gillis, 'The pilot gigs of Cornwall and the Isles of Scilly', *J.R. Inst. Cornwall* n.s. V no. 2 1966 173–200

The same title appears in *Mar. Mirr.* LV 1969 117–38

1777 R.H.C. Gillis, 'Porth was once a busy port', *Old Cornwall* VIII 1973 17–20

1778 B. Green, 'The maritime industrial history of Bideford', *J. Trevithick Soc.* no. 9 1972 52–7

1779 B. Greenhill and D.R. MacGregor, 'The *Mary* of Truro: the life story of a coasting smack', *Mar. Mirr.* XLVI 1960 81–7

1780 J.R. Hearn, *The Liberty of the Water of the Tamar, with a schedule of Cornish shipping for 1760–1.* (Saltash, The Author, 1969) 70p.

From *Old Cornwall* VI no. 10 1966 445–51

1781 H.O. Hill, 'East Cornish luggers', *Mar. Mirr.* XXI 1935 225–44

1782 H.O. Hill and B. Greenhill, 'Notes on the Falmouth oyster dredgers', *Mar. Mirr.* XLI 1955 43–6

1783 P.L. Hull, 'The history of Cremyll ferry', *Ann. Reps. R. Cornwall Polytech. Soc.* 130th Rep.1963 22–49

1784 A. Kittridge, *Cornwall's maritime heritage.* (Truso, Twelveheads, 1991) 47p.

1785 A. Kittridge, *Passenger steamers of the River Fal.* (Truro, Twelveheads, 1988) 120p.

1786 A. Kittridge, *Passenger steamers of the River Tamar.* (Truro, Twelveheads, 1984?) 96p. + 98 illus.

1787 J.B. Lamb, 'Fifty years at our ports', *English China Clay Rev.* Spring 1969

1788 R. Larn and B. Larn, *Charlestown: the history of a Cornish port.* (The Authors, Charlestown 1994) 220p.

1789 D. Mudd, *The Falmouth packets.* (Bodmin, Bossiney Books, 1978) 56p.

1790 R.M. Nance, *A glossary of Cornish sea-word, edited by P.A.S. Pool.* (Federation of Old Cornish Societies, 1963) 204p.

1791 R.M. Nance, 'Sea-stones and killicks in West Cornwall', *Mar. Mirr.* III 1913 295–303

Types of primitive anchors

1792 R.M. Nance, 'West Cornwall fishing luggers before 1850', *Mar. Mirr.* XXX 1944 93–108

1793 C. Noall, *Cornish lights and wrecks.* (Truro, Barton, 1968) 170p.

1794 C. Noall, *The story of Cornwall's ports and harbours.* (Truro, Tormark Press, 1970) 48p.

1795 A.H. Norway, 'Private trade on the Falmouth packets', *J.R. Inst. Cornwall* XI 1891 73–83

1796 K.J. O'Donoghue and H.S. Appleyard, *Hain of St Ives.* (Kendal, World Ship Society, 1986) 132p.

A shipping line

1797 D.W. Pascoe, 'Falmouth docks and harbour', *Old Cornwall* IX 1982 351–5

1798 R. Pearse, *Ports and harbours of Cornwall.* (St Austell, H. Warne, 1963) 156p.

1799 P.A.S. Pool, 'The Penzance Harbour Charter of 1512', *J. R. Inst. Cornwall* n.s. VI 1971 230–2

1800 N.J.G. Pounds, 'Ports and shipping of the Fal', *J.R. Inst. Cornwall* n.s. I 1946 43–60

1801 N.J.G. Pounds, 'The ports of Cornwall in the middle ages', *Devon Cornwall N. & Q.* XXIII no. 3 1947 65–73

1802 P.H. Stanier, 'Hazards and frauds on the Cornish slate shipping trade in the 1820s', *Devon Cornwall N. & Q.* XXXIV 1978 29–32

1803 P.H. Stanier, 'Lost mining ports of the South Cornish coast', *Ind. Archaeol. Rev.* III 1978 1–16

1804 W.B. Stephens, 'The foreign trade of Plymouth and the Cornish ports in the early seventeenth century', *Rep. Trans. Devons. Assoc.* CI 1969 125–37

1805 D.M. Trethowan, *The rise and decline of Porthleven harbour, 1810–1960.* (M.A. thesis, Exeter University, 1972)

1806 C.H. Ward-Jackson, *Ships and shipbuilders of a West Country seaport; Fowey 1786–1939.* (Truro, Twelveheads, 1986?) 130p.

1807 C.H. Ward-Jackson, *Stephens of Fowey: a portrait of a Cornish merchant fleet, 1867–1939.* (London, National Maritime Museum, 1980) 115p.

1808 J.C.A. Whetter, 'Cornish trade in the 17th century: an analysis of the port books', *J.R. Inst. Cornwall* n.s. IV no. 4 1964 388–413

OTHER INDUSTRIES

1809 H.M. Brown, *Cornish clocks and clockmakers.* 2nd ed. (Newton Abbot, David & Charles, 1970) 94p.

1810 C. Hockin, *St Austell brewery, established 1851.* (The Brewery, 1981) 48p.

1811 H.R. Hodge, 'The West of England Bacon Co., Redruth', *J. Trevithick Soc.* no. 2 1974 55–70

1812 N.J.G. Pounds, 'The 'soapy stone' and the steatite industry of Cornwall', *Devon Cornwall N. & Q.* XXII no. 13 1945 247–50

1813 J.H. Rowe, ed., 'Some minor industries of Cornwall. Based on materials collected by the late S. Michell, edited by J.H. Rowe', *Ann. Reps. R. Cornwall*

Polytech. Soc. n.s. VIII pt. 2 1935 52–60

1814 A.R. Trudgian, 'The organ builder: John Trudgian's organ factory', *English China Clay Rev.* Summer 1969

1815 W.J. Watton, 'The history of underground photography in Cornwall', *J. Trevithick Soc.* no. 17 1990 2–22

Devon

GENERAL

See also nos. 1–22

1816 J. Andrews, W. Elston and N. Shiel, *Exeter coinage*. (Exeter, Exeter Industrial Archaeology Group, *c.* 1980) 84p.

1817 J.S. Bento, *Description of the three united towns, Plymouth, Stonehouse and Devonport, showing their greatness, industry, religion, trade, etc.* (1829)

Typescript copy in Plymouth Central Library

1818 M. Bone, *Barnstaple's industrial archaeology: a guide.* (Exeter University Industrial Archaeology Group, Exeter Papers in Industrial Archaeology, 1974) 39p.

1819 J.L. Braithwaite, 'The post-war industrial development of Plymouth: an example of the effect of national industrial location policy', *Inst. Br. Geogr. Trans. Pap.* no. 45 1968 39–50

1820 R.D.F. Bromley,'Nineteenth-century economic and population change at Chulmleigh', *Rep. Trans. Devons. Assoc.* CII 1970 121–40

1821 C.G. Brown, ed., *A guide to the industrial archaeology of Plymouth and Millbrook, Cornwall.* 2nd ed. (Plymouth, City Museum and WEA, *c.* 1973) 52p.

1822 W. Burt, *Review of the mercantile, trading and manufacturing state, interests and capabilities of the Port of Plymouth: with miscellaneous additions by other persons, and notes.* (Plymouth, Nettleton, 1816) 278p.

1823 E.M. Carus-Wilson, *The expansion of Exeter at the close of the Middle Ages.* (Exeter, University Press, Hart Memorial Lecture in Local History, 1961, 1963) 35p.

1824 W.R. Childs,'Devon's overseas trade in the late Middle Ages', *in The new maritime history of Devon* vol. 1 79–89 (see no. 2598)

1825 M. Chitty, *Guide to industrial archaeology in Exeter.* (Exeter University Industrial Archaeology Group, Publication no. 1, 1971) 15p.

1826 E.A.G. Clark, 'Three Exeter pioneers in the Italian trade', *in The new maritime history of Devon* vol. 1 242–3 (See no. 2598)

Samuel Milford, Abraham Kennaway, Matthew Lee

1827 W.F. Collier, *The trade of Plymouth.* (1878)

Pamphlet reprinted from the *Trans. Plymouth Institution*

1828 W. Cotton, *An Elizabethan Guild of the City of Exeter. An account of the proceedings of the society of Merchant Adventurers, during the latter half of the 16th century.* (Exeter, William Pollard, 1873) 178p.

Appendices are transcripts from the papers of the Merchant Adventurers Company

1829 W. Crossing, *Crossing's Dartmoor worker, edited and with an introduction by Brian Le Mesurier.* (Newton Abbot, David & Charles, 1966) 163p.

A series of articles originally written for the *Western Morning News* in 1903.

1830 B. Drewe, *Economic growth in Devon, 1066–1332: an original work in local history presented towards the University of London Extra-Mural Diploma in History.* (1971)

Typescript. Copy in Devon & Exeter Institution, Exeter

1831 C. Edginton, *Tiverton's industrial archaeology: a guide.* (Exeter Industrial Archaeology Group & Tiverton Museum, c. 1976) 36p.

1832 *Exeter and its region,* ed. Frank Barlow. (Exeter, University, on behalf of the Local Executive Committee of the British Association, 1969), including:

J. Youings, 'The economic history of Devon 1300–1700' 164–74

W.E. Minchinton, 'The economic history and industrial archaeology of Devon since 1700', 175–93

H.W.B. Luxton, 'Agriculture', 217–39

G.D. Rouse, 'Forestry', 240–3

1833 H.P.R. Finberg, *Tavistock Abbey: a study in the social and economic history of Devon.* (Cambridge, University Press, 1951) 320p.

1834 G.P. Finch, *The experience of peripheral regions in an age of industrialisation: the case of Devon, 1840–1914.* (D.Phil. thesis, Oxford University, 1984)

1835 C. Gaskell-Brown and R. Coleman-Smith,'The archaeology of New Quay, Devon', *Reps. Trans. Devons. Assoc.* CXIV 1982 133–68

1836 C. Gill ed., *Dartmoor, a new study.* (Newton Abbot, David & Charles, 1970) 314p.

Four chapters cover industry, roads, railways and farming activities

1837 D. Griffiths, 'The conservation and management of the industrial landscape within Dartmoor National Park', *Mining Hist.* XIII no. 2 1996 100–3

1838 H. Harris, *The industrial archaeology of Dartmoor.* 4th ed. (Peninsular Press, 1992) 240p.

1839 W.J. Harte,'Some evidence of trade between Exeter and Newfoundland up to 1600', *Reps. Trans. Devons. Assoc.* LXIV 1932 475–84

1840 D.J.B. Hindley, *The economy and administration of the estates of the Dean and Chapter of Exeter Cathedral in the fifteenth century.* (M.A. thesis, Leeds University, 1958)

1841 W.G. Hoskins, 'A Devon yeoman in 1648', *Devon Cornwall N. & Q.* XXII no. 6 1943 162–64

George Maunder of Cruwys Marchand

1842 W.G. Hoskins, 'Devonshire trade in the early eighteenth century', *Devon Cornwall N. & Q.* XX no. 4 1938 151–4

1843 W.G. Hoskins, 'An East Devon yeoman', *Devon Cornwall N. & Q.* XXI no. 6 1941 241-8

The inventory of George Hoskyns, 1625

1844 W.G. Hoskins, *Industry, trade and people in Exeter 1688–1800.* 2nd ed. (Exeter, Exeter University Press, 1968) 189p.

1845 M. Kowaleski, ed., *The local customs accounts of the Port of Exeter, 1266–1321.* (Devon and Cornwall Record Soc., n.s. vol. 36, 1993)

1846 M. Kowaleski, *Local markets and merchants in late fourteenth-century Exeter*

(England). (Ph.D. thesis, Toronto University, 1982)

1847 M. Kowaleski, *Local markets and regional trade in medieval Exeter* (Cambridge, Cambridge University Press, 1995) 442p.

1848 W.T. MacCaffrey, *Exeter, 1540–1640: the growth of an English country town.* 2nd ed. (Cambridge, MA, Harvard University Press, 1975)

1849 F.A. Mace, *The trade and industry of Devonshire in the later middle ages.* (M.A. thesis, London University, 1925)

1850 D. McGrail, 'Economic activity and economic aspects of urban change in the borough of Plympton, 1500–1780', *Devon Histn.* XXXIII 1986 28–34

1851 I. Maxted,'Local studies libraries as rare book collections', *Loc. Stud. Librarian* XVII no. 1 1998 2–7

Gives useful information on Exeter trade directories

1852 W.E. Minchinton and I. Jarman,'Baltic trade with Devon 1784–1795', *Marit. S-W.* no. 2 1986 19–31

1853 W.E. Minchinton, *Devon at work: past and present.* (Newton Abbot, David & Charles, 1974) 112p.

1854 W.E. Minchinton, *Devon's industrial past: a guide.* (Dartington Centre for Education and Research, 1986) 34p.

4th ed of *Industrial archaeology in Devon*

1855 F.W. Morgan, 'The Domesday geography of Devon', *Reps. Trans. Devons. Assoc.* LXXII 1940 305–31

1856 L.M. Nicholls, *The trading communities of Totnes and Dartmouth in the late fifteenth and early sixteenth centuries.* (M.A. thesis, Exeter University, 1960)

1857 J.D. O'Hea, *Economy and society in the Upper Teign Valley 1801–1851, with special reference to Bridford.* (M.A. thesis, Exeter University, 1981)

1858 S.R. Parsons, *The standard of living of the working class in the south-west of England during the Industrial Revolution, with special reference to the county of Devon.* (M.A. thesis, Exeter University, 1977)

1859 H.M. Peskett, 'Tuckers Hall, Exeter: some early guild ordinances', *Devon Cornwall N. & Q.* XXXI 1970 235–45

1860 P. Sampson, 'Culmstock as an industrial town', *Devon Histn.* no. 19 1979 33–4

1861 A.H. Slee, 'Some dead industries of North Devon', *Reps. Trans. Devons. Assoc.* LXX 1938 213–21

1862 R. Stanes, 'Notes on the Culm Valley', *Devon Histn.* no. 19 1979 31–2

1863 W.B. Stephens, *The economic and commercial development of the city and port of Exeter, 1625–88.* (Ph.D. thesis, London University (External), 1954)

1864 W.B. Stephens, *Seventeenth-century Exeter: a study of industrial and commercial development, 1625–1688.* (Exeter, History of Exeter Research Group Monograph no. 9, 1958) 203p.

See also *Devon & Cornwall N. & Q.* XXXI 1968–70 84–5

1865 W.B. Stephens,'The foreign trade of Plymouth and the Cornish ports in the early 17th century', *Reps. Trans. Devons. Assoc.* CI 1969 125–37

1866 W.B. Stephens,'Merchant companies and commercial policy in Exeter, 1625–1688', *Reps. Trans. Devons. Assoc.* LXXXVI 1954 137–60

1867 H.W. Strong, *Industries of North Devon, with new material by B.D. Hughes.* (Newton Abbot, David & Charles, 1971) 224p.

Reprint of 1889 edition

1868 J.L. Tamblin, *The problems of industrial location in Plymouth.* (M.A. thesis, London University, n.d.)

Copy in Plymouth Central Library

1869 Rev. W.H. Thornton, 'Concerning some old habits and decaying industries formerly prevalent in the West of England and more particularly in the county of Devon', *Reps. Trans. Devons. Assoc.* XXXIX 1907 156–78

1870 H. Touchard, 'Le commerce maritime d'Exeter au début du XVme siècle', *in Economies et sociétés au Moyen Age; mélanges offerts à Edouard Perroy* (Paris, Publications de la Sorbonne, Série 'Etudes' t. 5, 1973) 531–7

AGRICULTURE

See also nos. 23–68

1871 N.W. Alcock, 'An east Devon manor in the later Middle Ages. I: 1374–1420. The manor farm' *Reps. Trans. Devons. Assoc.* CII 1970 141–87

'II, Leasing the demesne, 1423–1650', *Reps. Trans. Devons. Assoc.* CV 1973 141–90

1872 N.W. Alcock, Fields and farms in an East Devon parish', *Reps. Trans. Devons. Assoc.* CVII 1975 93–172

1873 C.M.A. Baker, 'The origin of South Devon cattle', *Agric. Hist. Rev.* XXXII 1984 145–58

1874 H.T. Beche, 'On the connection between geology and agriculture in Devon', *J. R. Agric. Soc.* III 1842 21–35

1875 V.G. Beynon, 'The changing structure of dairying in Devon since the 1930s', *Devon Histn.* no. 11 Oct 1975 35–40

1876 S.F. Baldock, 'A report on a preliminary survey of farmhouse cider-making equipment in the county of Devonshire', *Devon Histn.* no. 19 1979 2–8

1877 J.R. Blunden, *Agricultural enterprise on the red loams and culm measures of Devon—an analytical survey.* (Ph.D. thesis, Exeter University, 1965)

1878 D.J. Bonney, 'Former farms and fields at Challacombe, Manston, Dartmoor', *in Exeter Essays in Geography* (Exeter University Press, 1971) 83–91

1879 A. Born, 'Limestone, limekilns and the limeburning industry north and west of Dartmoor', *Reps. Trans. Devons. Assoc.* CXXIII 1991 213–40

1880 G.M. Chapman, 'An eighteenth-century east Devon farm', *Devon Cornwall N. Q.* XXXVI 1988 101–3

1881 R.P. Chope, 'Some old farm implements and operations', *Reps. Trans. Devons. Assoc.* L 1918 268–92

1882 J. Dearing, 'Gorse, man and land use change on Dartmoor: a preliminary investigation', *Reps. Trans. Devons. Assoc.* CIX 1977 135–52

1883 P.V. Denham, 'The Duke of Bedford's Tavistock estate, 1820–38', *Reps. Trans. Devons. Assoc.* CX 1978 19–51

1884 'Devon agriculture in the eighteenth century: the evidence of the Milles MS', in *The South-West and the Land* (Exeter University, Exeter Papers in Economic History no. 2, 1969)

1885 Devon County Agricultural Association, *The centenary book, 1872–1972, compiled by M.C.B. Hoare and Clement Marten.* (1972) 50p.

1886 R. Dyer, 'Tavistock Woodlands Estate. A brief review of some past and current activities', *Tamar J.* no. 11 1989 13–16

Forestry and sawmilling

1887 H.P.R. Finberg, 'A farmer's lease in 1402', *Devon Cornwall N. & Q.* XXIII no. 2 1947 50–1

1888 H.P.R. Finberg, 'The open field in Devonshire', *Antiquary* XXIII 1949 180–7

Reprinted with additions in W.G. Hoskins and H.P.R. Finberg, *Devonshire studies* (Jonathan Cape, 1952) 265–88 *and in* H.P.R. Finberg, *ed., West Country historical studies.* (Newton Abbot, David & Charles, 1969)

1889 G. Finch, 'Devon's farm labourers in the Victorian period: the impact of economic change', *Reps. Trans. Devons. Assoc.* CXIX 1987 85–100

1890 A. Fleming, 'Dartmoor reaves' *Devon Archaeol.* III 1985 1–6

1891 A. Fleming, 'Medieval and post-medieval cultivation on Dartmoor: a landscape archaeologist's view', *Proc. Devon Archaeol. Soc.* LII 1994 101–17

1892 E.G. Fogwill, *The past agricultural utilisation of Dartmoor.* (M.A. thesis, London University, 1952)

1893 E.G. Fogwill, 'Pastoralism on Dartmoor', *Reps. Trans. Devons. Assoc.* LXXXVI 1954 89–114

1894 H.S.A. Fox, 'The chronology of enclosure and economic development in Medieval Devon', *Econ. Hist. Rev.* XXVIII 1975 181–202

1895 H.S.A. Fox, 'Field systems of East and South Devon: I. East Devon', *Reps. Trans. Devons. Assoc.* CIV 1972 81–135

1896 H.S.A. Fox, 'The study of field systems', *Devon Histn.* no. 4 1972 3–11

1897 R. Fraser, *General view of the agriculture of the County of Devon with observations on the means of its improvement: drawn up for consideration of the Board of Agriculture and Internal improvement.* (1794) 75p.

A facsimile reprint of this edition was published in 1970 by Porcupines of Barnstaple

1898 G.E. Fussell, 'Devonshire farming: an American Quaker's walking tour', *Devon County J.* I no. 4 1947 107–8

Elihu Burritt's tour

1899 G.E. Fussell, 'Four centuries of farming systems in Devonshire 1500–1900', *Reps Trans. Devons. Assoc.* LXXXIII 1951 179–204

1900 W.H. Gamlen, 'Agriculture in north-east Devon, fifty to sixty years ago', *Reps. Trans. Devons. Assoc.* XII 1880 380–6

1901 E. Gawne, 'Field patterns in Widecombe Parish and the Forest of Dartmoor', *Reps. Trans. Devons. Assoc.* CII 1970 49–69

1902 J. Grant, *A few remarks on the large hedges and small enclosures of Devonshire, and the adjoining counties.* (1844) 16p.

Copy in West Country Studies Library, Exeter.

1903 Rev. Hawker, 'Devonshire cyder', *Reps. Trans. Devons. Assoc.* XV 1883 237–45

1904 Rev. Hawker, 'The Devonshire farm–labourer now and eighty years ago', *Reps. Trans. Devons. Assoc.* XIV 1882 329–36

1905 R.G. Haynes, 'Vermin traps and rabbit warrens on Dartmoor', *Post-Med. Archaeol.* IV 1970 147–64

1906 M. Havinden, 'Lime as a means of agricultural improvement: the Devon example', *in* C.W. Chalklin and M.A. Havinden, *eds., Rural change and urban growth 1500–1800*. (London, Longmans, 1974) 104–34

1907 J.O. Hitchings, 'A Devonshire estate—a changing landscape?', *J. R. Agric. Soc.* CXLVIII 1987 46–53

1908 W.G. Hoskins, 'The making of the agrarian landscape' *in* W.G. Hoskins and H.P.R. Finberg, *Devonshire studies.* (London, Cape, 1952)

1909 W.G. Hoskins, *The ownership and occupation of the land in Devonshire 1650–1800*. (Ph.D. thesis, London University (External), 1938)

1910 W.G. Hoskins, 'The occupation of land in Devonshire, 1650–1800', *Devon Cornwall N. & Q.* XXI 1941 2–12

1911 W.G. Hoskins, 'The reclamation of the waste in Devon, 1550–1800', *Econ. Hist. Rev.* XIII 1943 80–92

1912 J.E. Kew, *The land market in Devon, 1536–1958.* (Ph.D. thesis, Exeter University, 1967)

1913 Sir R. Lethbridge, 'Apple culture and cider-making in Devonshire', *Reps. Trans. Devons. Assoc.* XXXII 1900 142–94

1914 E.W. Martin, 'A yeoman's diary', *Devon County Mag.* I no. 3 1947 71–2, 74
Based on extracts from William Honnywell's book of accounts, etc., *c.* 1596–1611.

1915 W.E. Minchinton and M. Overton, 'The 1801 crop returns for Devon', *Devon Cornwall N. & Q.* XXXII 1973 197–203

1916 R. Ogden, 'Devon's beekeeping past', *Devon Histn.* no. 49 1994 3–10

1917 N.C. Oswald, 'The ownership of farms and farmlands in Thurlestone and the South Hams in recent times', *Devon Histn.* no. 49 1994 24–7

1918 N.C. Oswald, 'The South Devon breed of cattle', *Reps. Trans. Devons. Assoc.* CXXII 1990 25–40

1919 B. Payne, ed., *Huxtable, the story of a Devon farm* (West Buckland, B. Payne, 1993) 104p.

1920 S. Pearce, 'Early medieval land use on Dartmoor and its flanks', *Devon Archaeol.* III 1985 13–19

1921 A.D.M. Phillips, *Underdraining in England during the 19th century, with special reference to Northamptonshire and Devonshire.* (Ph.D. thesis, London University, 1988)

1922 J. Porter, 'Peter Kropotkin on Devon agriculture', *Devon Histn.* no. 17 1978 25–6

1923 J.H. Porter, 'The 'Revolt of the Field': the Devon response', *S. Hist.* VII 1985 163–78

1924 J.H. Porter, 'Tenant right: Devonshire and the 1880 Ground Game Act', *Agric. Hist. Rev.* XXXIV 1986 188–97

1925 R.R. Pymm, 'Memories of fruit growing in the Tamar Valley', *Tamar J.* no. 8 1986 29–34

1926 F. Retter, *An east Devon farm and its village.* (Exeter, Obelist, 1985) 64p.

1927 R. Robinson, 'Early eighteenth-century cider production at Bearscombe Farm, South Devon', *Devon Histn.* no. 28 1981 15–18

1928 P. Sainsbury, *The transition from tradition to technology: a history of the dairy industry in Devon.* (Tiverton, The Author, 1991) 112p.

1929 A. Sheridan, 'Characteristics of Devon agriculture in the early modern period', *Devon Histn.* no. 44 1992 11–14

1930 A.H. Slee, 'The open fields of Braunton: Braunton Great Field and Braunton Downs', *Reps. Trans. Devons. Assoc.* LXXXIV 1952 142–9

1931 A.H. Shorter, 'Field patterns in Brixham parish, Devon', *Reps. Trans. Devons. Assoc.* LXXXII 1950 271–80

1932 A.H. Shorter, 'Flax growing in Devon in the eighteenth and early nineteenth centuries', *Devon Cornwall N. & Q.* XXIV 1950 41–4

1933 J. Sinclair, *History of the Devon breed of cattle.* (Published for the Devon Cattle Breeders' Society by Vinton & Co., 1893) 392p.

Copy in Exeter Central Library.

1934 E. Stanbrook, *Dartmoor Forest farms: a social history from enclosure to abandonment.* (Devon Books, 1994) 129p.

1935 R. Stanes, 'Landlord and tenant and husbandry covenants in eighteenth-century Devon', *in* W.E. Minchinton ed., *Agricultural improvement: medieval and modern.* (Exeter University, Exeter Papers in Economic History no. 14, 1981) 41–64

1936 R. Stanes, *The old farm: a history of farming life in the West Country.* (Exeter, Devon Books, 1990) 174p.

1937 R.G.F. Stanes, 'Open-field agriculture in south Devon', *Rep. Trans. Devons. Assoc.* XCVI 1964 71–74

1938 W.J. Tamblin, *Geographical factors influencing the development of intensive agriculture in S.W. England with special reference to Plymouth and the Tamar Valley, etc.* (M.A. thesis, 1945)

Copy in Plymouth Central Library

1939 H. Tanner, 'On the farming of Devonshire', *J. R. Agric. Soc.* IX 1848 454–95

1940 K. Ugawa, 'The economic development of some Devon manors in the thirteenth century', *Reps. Trans. Devons. Assoc.* XCIV 1962 630–83

1941 C. Vancouver, *General view of the agriculture of the county of Devon with observations on the means of its improvement.* (London, 1808) 479p.

A facsimile reprint published in 1969 by David & Charles of Newton Abbot

1942 H.H. Walker, 'Some medieval demesne boundaries in Torquay', *Reps. Trans. Devons. Assoc.* XCVII 1965 194–211

1943 A. Watt, *Dairy farming in Devonshire; with a report on dairying in Normandy and Brittany.* (Plymouth, William Brendon & Sons, 1885)

1944 F. Wilkinson, 'The Dartmoor husbandman', *Devons. Histn.* no. 14 1977 5–10

1945 R.E. Wilson, 'Lime burning in East Devon', *Devon Histn.* no. 21 1980 12–16

1946 D.M. Winter, *The survival and re-emergence of family farming: a study of the Holsworthy area of West Devon.* (Ph.D. thesis, Open University, 1987)

1947 R. Wurtzburg, 'The sub-letting of smallholdings on a Devon estate 1788–1834', *Rep. Trans. Devon Assoc.* CXXVI 1994 85–105

ARCHITECTURE AND BUILDINGS
General

1948 R. Chudley, *A history of craft masonry in Devonshire.* (Exmouth, The Author, 1984) 212p.

1949 *Devon's traditional buildings.* (Devon County Council, Planning Dept., 1978) vi + 82p.

1950 C.E. Welch, ed., *Plymouth building accounts of the 16th and 17th centuries.* (Exeter, Devon & Cornwall Record Society, Publications n.s. no. 12, 1967) 117p.

Domestic

See also no. 70

1951 N.W. Alcock, *Dartington houses: a survey.* (Exeter University, Industrial Archaeology Group, Paper no. 3, 1972) 22p.

1952 N.W. Alcock, 'A Devon farm: Bury Barton, Lapford', *Reps. Trans. Devons. Assoc.* XCVIII 1966 105–32

1953 N.W. Alcock and others, 'Devon farm-houses—Part I', *Reps. Trans. Devons. Assoc.* C 1968 13–28; 'Part II. Some Dartmoor houses', CI 1969 83–106; 'Part 3 Moorland and non moorland longhouses' by S.R. Jones CIII 1971 35–75; 'Part 4: Some medieval houses in East and North Devon' by N.W. Alcock and C. Hulland, CIV 1972 35–56; 'Part 5: Some medieval houses in North and Mid-Devon' by C. Hulland, CXII 1980 127–70; 'Part 6 More medieval houses in North and Mid-Devon', CXVI 1984 29–61

1954 N.W. Alcock, 'Devonshire linhays: a vernacular tradition', *Reps. Trans. Devons. Assoc.* XCV 1963 117–30

1955 N.W. Alcock, 'The medieval buildings of Bishop's Clyst', *Reps. Trans. Devons. Assoc.* XCVIII 1966 133–53

1956 M. Brayshay, 'The Duke of Bedford's model cottages in Tavistock 1840–1870', *Reps. Trans. Devons. Assoc.* CXIV 1982 115–31

1957 M. Brayshay, 'Heathcoat's industrial housing in Tiverton, Devon', *S. Hist.* XIII 1991 82–104

1958 S.W. Brown and J. Pidgeon, 'Hatherleigh Farm, Bovey Tracey', *Proc. Devon Archaeol. Soc.* no. 44 1986 184–91

1959 S.W. Brown and M. Laithwaite, 'Northwood Farm, Christow; an abandoned farmstead on the eastern fringe of Dartmoor', *Proc. Devon Archaeol. Soc.* no. 51 1993 161–84

1960 S.D. Chapman, 'Industrial housing in Devon before 1770', *Devon. Histn.* no. 16 1978 17–20

1961 B. Clapp, 'A note on housebuilding in Exeter, 1867–1940', *in* W. Minchinton, *ed., Capital formation in South-West England.* (Exeter University Papers in Economic History, no. 9 1978) 55–61

1962 H.E. Gawne, 'Sweaton farmhouse', *Rep. Trans. Devons. Assoc.* CXXIV 1992 167–73

1963 W.G. Hoskins, 'The development of the small house', *Reps. Trans. Devons. Assoc.* CX 1978 1–8

1964 W.G. Hoskins, 'Stone Farm, Thorverton', *Devon Cornwall N. & Q.* XXIV 1951 145–47

1965 J.M.W. Laithwaite and N.W. Alcock, 'Medieval houses in Devon and their modernisation', *Med. Archaeol.* XVII 1973 100–25

1966 M. Laithwaite, 'Middle Moor, Sowton: a reassessment', *Reps. Trans. Devons. Assoc.* CIII 1971 77–83

A farmhouse

1967 J.M.W. Laithwaite, 'Town houses up to 1700', *in Devon's traditional buildings.* (Devon County Council Planning Dept., 1978) 30–42

1968 M. Laithwaite, 'Two medieval houses in Ashburton', *Proc. Devon Archaeol. Soc.* no. 29 1968 181–94

1969 C.H. Laycock, 'The old Devon farm house, Part I', *Reps. Trans. Devons. Assoc.* LII 1920 158–91; 'Part II', LIV 1923 224–70 and LV 1924 154–81

1970 D. Portman, *Exeter houses, 1400–1700.* (Ph.D. thesis, Exeter University, 1962)

1971 D. Portman, *Exeter houses 1400–1700.* (Exeter University, 1966) 133

1972 J.R.L. Thorp, 'The Quay, Dartmouth: a Devon town-house of 1664', *Proc. Devon Archaeol. Soc.* no. 41 1983 107–22

1973 J.R.L. Thorp, 'Two hall houses in a late medieval terrace, 8–12, Fore St, Silverton', *Proc. Devon Archaeol. Soc.* no. 40 1982 171–80

1974 P.J. Weddell, 'The excavation of medieval and later houses and St Margaret's chapel at Exmouth 1982–1984', *Proc. Devon Archaeol. Soc.* no. 44 1986 107–41

1975 E.H.D. Williams, 'Poltimore farmhouse, Farway', *Reps. Trans. Devons. Assoc.* CVI 1974 215–29

1976 R.E. Wilson, 'Tudor and Merton cottages Sidmouth', *Reps. Trans. Devons. Assoc.* CVI 1974 155–9

1977 R.H. Worth, 'The Dartmoor House', *Ann. Rep. Trans. Plymouth Inst. & Devon Cornwall Nat. Hist. Soc.* XVIII 1936–7 34–47

Industrial

For engine houses see nos. 2029–31; see also nos. 71–6

1978 U.W. Brighouse, 'Milling in Woodbury', *Devon Cornwall N. & Q.* XXXV pt. 2 1982 63–6

1979 P. Castle and P. Castle and others, 'Outcombe tin mill in Sheepstor Parish: a survey of the field remains', *Dartmoor Tinworking Res. Gp. Newsl.* no. 3 July

1992

1980 J. Coad, 'Historic architecture of HM naval base Devonport 1689–1850', *Mar. Mirr.* LXIX 1983 341–92

1981 A.W. Everett, 'The monastic barn at Shiphay, Torquay', *Reps. Trans. Devons. Assoc.* XCVII 1965 157–60

1982 H.S.A. Fox, 'The millstone makers of medieval Dartmoor', *Devon Cornwall N. & Q.* Spring 1994 XXXVII Part 5 153–7

1983 V. Gray, 'Bickleigh Mill on the River Meavy', *Reps. Trans. Devons. Assoc.* CXX 1988 81–6

1984 D. Greenhow, 'More water by the mill: the restoration, machinery and history of Otterton Mill, Devon', *Ind. Archaeol.* XIV 1979 309–25

1985 S.F. Harley, 'Watermills of Pilton', *Devon. Histn.* no. 27 1983 15–21

1986 W.R. Mallett, *A paper on the water power of the Exe Valley.* (1892) 43p.

Copy in West Country Studies Library, Exeter

1987 W.E. Minchinton and J. Perkins, *Tidemills of Devon and Cornwall.* (Exeter University Industrial Archaeology Group, 1971)

1988 W.E. Minchinton, 'More tidemills—and another windmill', *Devon Cornwall N & Q.* XXXVI 1989 175–6

1989 W.E. Minchinton, *Windmills of Devon.* (Exeter University, Dept of Economic History, and Exeter Industrial Archaeology Group, 1977) 56p.

1990 W.E. Minchinton, 'Windmills in Devon', *Devon Cornwall N. & Q.* XXXI no. 3 1968 78–82

1991 W.E. Minchinton and J.W. Perkins, 'Further windmills in Devon', *Devon Cornwall N. & Q.* XXXII 1972 105–9

1992 W.E. Minchinton, 'Yet further Devon windmills', *Devon Cornwall N. & Q.* XXXIV 1980 238–40

1993 P.H. Newton, 'Blagdon cider barn, Paignton', *Rep. Trans. Devons. Assoc.* CXXII 1991 203–11

1994 H. Parsons, 'The Dartmoor blowing-house (some recent investigations)', *Rep. Trans. Devons. Assoc.* LXXXVIII 1956 189–96

1995 M.C. Phillips and R.E. Wilson, 'Water mills in East Devon Part I', *Devon Cornwall N. & Q.* XXXIII 1974 13–17; 'Part II', XXXIII 1974 51–56; 'Part III', XXXIII 1974 80–4; 'Part IV', XXXIII 1975 126–30; 'Part V', XXXIII 1975 170–5; 'Part VI', XXXIII 1976 262–4; 'Part VII', XXXIII 1976 304–6 1977; 'Part VIII', XXXIV 1978 32–3; 'Part IX', XXXIV 1978 75–80; 'Part X', XXXIV 1979 113–19; 'Part XI', XXXIV 1979 139–44

1996 L. Sheldon, 'Devon barns', *Rep. Trans. Devons. Assoc.* LXIV 1932 389–95

1997 L. Sheldon, 'Devon toll-houses', *Rep. Trans. Devons. Assoc.* LXV 1933 293–306

Supplementary list in LXVIII 1936 395

1998 H.E.S. Simmons, *Watermills of Devonshire.* 1977. 10v.

Volumes in the Simmons Collection relating to British windmills and watermills. A photocopy of the original typescript folders is available in the Science Museum Library, London.

1999 H.E.S. Simmons, *Windmills of Devonshire*. 1977.

Part of the volume *The windmills of Devon, Dorset and Durham* in the Simmons Collection relating to British windmills and watermills. A photocopy of the original typescript folders is available in the Science Museum Library, London.

2000 J. Thorpe, ed., *North Devon windmills*. (North Devon Archaeological Society, 1989) 68p.

2001 R.W. Toll, 'Water power in West Devon', *Min. Mag.* LXXVIII no. 3 1948 137–41

2002 M. Watts, 'Farm and threshing mill at Poltimore Farm, Farway, Devon', *Ind. Archaeol. Rev.* XIII no. 2 1991 182–9

Eddystone Lighthouse

2003 R.M. Ballantyne, *The story of the rock, or, Building on the Eddystone*. (London, J. Nisbet, 1879) 127p.

2004 J.S.P. Buckland, 'The first Eddystone lighthouse', *Devon Cornwall N. & Q.* XXXV no. 3 1983 128–30

2005 W.T. Douglass, 'The new Eddystone lighthouse; with an abstract of the discussion upon the paper', *Min. Proc. Instn. Civil Engrs.* LXXV 1883–4 pt. 1

2006 E.P. Edwards, *The Eddystone lighthouses (new and old); an account of the building and general arrangements of the new tower with an abridgement of Smeaton's narrative of the building of the old tower*. (Simpkin, Marshall, 1882) 186p.

2007 E. Marshall, *The first light on the Eddystone: a story of two hundred years ago*. (Seeley & Co., 1894) 179p.

2008 C.H. Navillus, *The Eddystone lighthouses and their history*. (n.d.)

Copy in Plymouth Central Library.

2009 J. Smeaton, *An account of the Eddystone lighthouse and rocks with plates. (Chiefly compiled from Mr Smeaton's large work on the Eddystone Lighthouse.)* (1824)

Copy in Plymouth Central Library.

2010 J. Smeaton, *A narrative of the building, and a description of the construction of the Eddystone Light-house with stone, to which is subjoined an appendix giving some account of the lighthouse on the Spurn Point built upon a sand*. 2nd ed. (1793) 198p.

2011 *The story of John Smeaton and the Eddystone Lighthouse*. (John Nelson, 1884) 117p.

2012 R.H. Weston, *Letters and important documents relative to the Eddystone Lighthouse selected chiefly from the correspondence of the late Robert Weston, Esq., and from his manuscripts*. (1811)

2013 W.H. Wood, *The House in the Sea: the story of the first lighthouse on the Eddystone*. (London, Harrap, 1952) 207p.

BREWING AND CIDER MAKING

2014 T.J. Falla, 'Heavitree breweries', *Devon Cornwall N. & Q.* XXXIV 1980 211–13

2015 A.E. Mettler, 'The Tavistock brewery—Brook Street', *Tamar J.* no. 10 1988 7–17

2016 D. Postles, 'Brewing and the peasant economy: some manors in late medieval Devon', *Rural Hist.* III 1992 133–44

2017 H. Stafford, *A treatise on cyder-making ... with a catalogue of cyder apples of character in Herefordshire and Devonshire.* 2nd ed. (London, D. Henry & R. Cave, 1755) 64p.

Copy in Exeter Central Library

2018 E.V.M. Whiteway, *Whiteway's cyder: a company history.* (Newton Abbot, David & Charles, 1990) 176p.

Whiteways of Whimple

CLOCK AND WATCHMAKING

2019 J.K. Bellchambers, *Devonshire clockmakers.* (Totnes, The Author, 1962) 41p.

2020 C. Ponsford, 'Benjamin Bowring, watchmaker', *Devon Histn.* no. 18 1979 14–16

2021 C.N. Ponsford, and others, *Clocks and clockmakers of Tiverton.* 3rd ed. (Tiverton, W.P. Authors, 1982) 67p.

2022 C.N. Ponsford, *Devon clocks and clockmakers.* (Newton Abbot, David & Charles, 1985) 360p.

2023 C. Ponsford, 'More eighteenth- and early nineteenth-century references to clockmakers', *Devon & Cornwall N. & Q.* XXXIII no. 6 1976 194–6

2024 C.N. Ponsford, *Time in Exeter: a history of 700 years of clocks and clockmaking in an English provincial city.* (Exeter, Headwell Vale Books, 1978) 200p.

2025 I. Rogers, 'Ancient clocks at Barnstaple', *Devon Cornwall N. & Q.* XII 1922 185–6

2026 I. Rogers, 'Some ancient clocks in North Devon', *Devon Cornwall N. & Q* XII 1923 357–64

2027 E.G.S. Saunders, 'Thomas Mudge, Edward Clement and John Rouckleiffe, Devonshire clockmakers', *Reps. Trans. Devons. Assoc.* LXVII 1935 395–7

ENGINEERING

See also nos. 77–81

General

2028 H. Trump, 'Brunel and Teignmouth', *Devon Histn.* no. 17 1978 12–15

Engines and Engine Houses

See also no. 77

2029 R. Le Marchant, 'The man engine and Devon Great Consols mine', *Tamar J.* no. 11 1989 7–12

2030 R.W.M. Nance and R.D. Nance, 'A survey of engine houses on the mines of South Devon', *Mining Hist.* XIII no. 2 1996 109–22

2031 A.R. Pye and K.A. Westcott, *Archaeological survey of the pumping engine-house at Wheal Betsy, Mary Tavy.* (Exeter Museums, Archaeological Field Unit, Rep. 92-08, 1992)

Newcomen, Savery and Their Engines

See also no. 80

2032 J.S. Allen, 'The introduction of the Newcomen engine 1710–1733', *Trans. Newcomen Soc.* XLII 1969–70 169–90; XLIII 1970–1 199–202; XLV 1972–3 223–6

2033 J.S. Allen, 'Some early Newcomen engines and the legal disputes surrounding them', *Trans. Newcomen Soc.* XLI 1968–9 181–202

2034 J.S. Allen, 'Thomas Newcomen (1663/4–1729) and his family', *Trans. Newcomen Soc.* LI 1979–80 11–24

2035 C.O. Becker and A. Titley, 'The valve-gear of Newcomen's engine', *Trans. Newcomen Soc.* X 1929–30 1–14

2036 J.J. Bootsgezel, 'John Calley, the partner of Thomas Newcomen', *Trans. Newcomen Soc.* XI 1930–1 135–7

2037 J.S.P. Buckland, 'Thomas Savery: his steam engine workshop of 1702', *Trans. Newcomen Soc.* LVI 1984–5 1–20

2038 H. Davey, 'The Newcomen engine', *Proc. Instn. Mech. Engrs.* 1903 655–704

2039 H.W. Dickinson, *Thomas Newcomen, engineer, 1663–1729, revised by Percy Russell.* (Dartmouth, Newcomen Association, 1952) 12p.

2040 R.L. Hills, 'A steam chimera: a review of the history of the Savery engine', *Trans. Newcomen Soc.* LVIII 1986–7 27–44

2041 M. Hine, 'The pedigree of Thomas Newcomen', *Trans. Newcomen Soc.* IX 1928–9 105–8

2042 G.J. Hollister-Short, 'Antecedents and anticipations of the Newcomen engine', *Trans. Newcomen Soc.* LII 1980–1 103–17

2043 R. Jenkins, 'The heat engine idea in the seventeenth century: a contribution to the history of the steam engine', *Trans. Newcomen Soc.* XVII 1936–7 1–11

Discounts the conjectural link between Newcomen and Robert Hooke.

2044 R. Jenkins, 'Savery, Newcomen and the early history of the steam engine, Part I', *Trans. Newcomen Soc.* III 1922–3 96–118; 'Part II', IV 1923–4 113–33

Reprinted in *The Collected Papers of Rhys Jenkins.* (London, Newcomen Society, 1936) 48–93

Part 1 also appears in *Rep. Trans. Devon Assoc.* XLV 1913 343–67

2045 R. Jenkins, 'Thomas Newcomen: a note on his handwriting', *Trans. Newcomen Soc.* VII 1926–7 60–2

2046 R. Jenkins, 'Thomas Newcomen and the birth of the steam engine', *Devon Yrbk.* 1913 94–104

2047 R. Jenkins, 'Thomas Savery F.R.S., engineer and inventor', *Devon Yrbk.* 1915 75–84

2048 T. Lidstone, *Some account of the residence of the inventor of the steam-engine.* (London, Longman, 1869)

Copy in the Devon and Exeter Institution, Exeter

2049 C. Matschoss, 'A holograph letter of Newcomen', *Trans. Newcomen Soc.* II 1921–2 115–17

2050 R.A. Mott, 'The Newcomen engine in the eighteenth century', *Trans. Newcomen Soc.* XXXV 1962–3 69–86

2051 L. St L. Pendred, 'An eulogy upon Newcomen', *Trans. Newcomen Soc.* IX 1928–9 99–101

2052 D. Richards, 'Thomas Newcomen and the environment of innovation', *Ind. Archaeol.* XIII 1978 335–6, 345–6

2053 L.T.C. Rolt and J.S. Allen, *The steam engine of Thomas Newcomen.* New ed. (Ashbourne, Landmark Publishing, 1997) 160p.

First published 1963.

2054 L.T.C. Rolt, *Thomas Newcomen: the prehistory of the steam engine.* (Dawlish, David & Charles, 1963) 158p.

2055 T. Savery, *The miner's friend; or, an engine to raise water by fire, described, and of the manner of fixing it in mines, with an account of several other uses it is applicable unto; and an answer to the objections made against it.* (London, 1702) *c.* 19p.

Reproduced in *J.R. Instn. Cornwall* XVI 1904–6 181–209

2056 I.H. Smart, 'The Dartmouth residences of Thomas Newcomen and his family', *Trans. Newcomen Soc.* LX 1988–9 145–60

2057 E.C. Smith, 'Thomas Newcomen: two hundred years of steam power', *Trans. Newcomen Soc.* IX 1928–9 102–12

2058 A. Stowers, 'Thomas Newcomen's first steam engine 250 years ago and the initial development of steam power', *Trans. Newcomen Soc.* XXXIV 1961–2 133–49

2059 A. Stowers, 'The development of the atmospheric steam engine after Newcomen's death in 1729', *Trans. Newcomen Soc.* XXXV 1962–3 87–96

2060 'Thomas Newcomen: a commemorative symposium for the 250th anniversary of his death', *Trans. Newcomen Soc.* L 1978–9 163–218, including:

S. Lindqvist, 'The work of Martin Triewald in England'

I.N. Walden, 'Will it work? (A replica of the 1712 Newcomen engine)'

J.R. Harris, 'Recent research on the Newcomen engine and historical studies'

J. Tann, 'Makers of improved Newcomen engines in the late 18th century'

R.A. Buchanan, 'Steam and the engineering community in the eighteenth century'

J.H. Andrew, 'Some observations on the Thomas Barney engraving of the

1712 Newcomen engine'

A. Smith, 'The Newcomen engine at Passy, France, in 1725'

There is also a list of all the articles relating to Newcomen which have appeared in *Trans. Newcomen Soc.*

2061 W.A. Young, 'Thomas Newcomen, ironmonger: the contemporary background', *Trans. Newcomen Soc.* XX 1939–40 1–15

Other Engineers and Engineering Firms

2062 R.A. Barron, *The Finch Foundry Trust and Sticklepath Museum of Rural Industry.* (*c.* 1984)

2063 E. Budge, 'The Bridge Iron Foundry, Lumburn', *Tamar J.* V 1983 9–12

2064 M.G. Dickinson, 'Eighteenth-century engine builders', *Devon Cornwall N. & Q.* XXXV pt. 3 1983 123–4

2065 A.B. Green, 'James Green, civil engineer, 1781–1849', *Devon Histn.* no. 32 7–14

2066 H. Harris, 'Foundries in nineteenth-century Tavistock', *Devon Histn.* no. 31 Oct 1985 16

2067 C. McCombe, 'Two centuries of casting production in Exeter', *Foundry Trade J.* CLIV 5 May 1983 576–90

Largely a history of Bodley Bros. & Co. Ltd, Exeter, 1790–1967.

2068 J.K. Major, *Finch Brothers Foundry, Sticklepath, Okehampton, Devon.* (Newton Abbot, David & Charles, *c.* 1968) 16p.

2069 K.S. Perkins, 'Nasmyth's steam hammer at Devonport', *Devon Histn.* no. 44 1992 14–20

2070 K.S. Perkins, 'A Westcountry engineer: Charles Greaves 1816–1883', *Devon Histn.* no. 40 1990 14–20

2071 I. Richardson and M. Watts, 'Finch Foundry, Devon', *Ind. Archaeol. Rev.* XVIII no. 1 1995 83–95

2072 P. Roberts, 'The Cruquis engine', *Plymouth Mineral Min. Club J.* XVI no. 1 1985 10

2073 C. Scott, 'An iron foundry in Exeter', *Devon Histn.* no. 41 1990 26–8

FISHERIES

See also nos. 114–19

2074 P. Barton, 'Dartmouth's whaling trade', *Marit. S-W* no. 7 1994 39–46

2075 M.G. Dickinson, ed., *A living from the sea: Devon's fishing industry and its fishermen.* (Exeter, Devon Books, 1987) 87p.

2076 C. Dixon, 'The Exeter Whale Fishery Company, 1754–87', *Mar. Mirr.* LXII 1976 225–31

2077 E.A.S. Eliot, 'An original article on the pilchard fishery at Burrough Island by Colonel Montagu a hundred years ago: with supplementary notes to the present time', *Reps. Trans. Devons. Assoc.* XXXV 1903 430–3

2078 M. Firestone, 'Crab fishermen in South Devon', *Devon Hist.* no. 12 1976 2–5

2079 T. Gray, 'Devon's fisheries and Early-Stuart Northern New England', *in The new maritime history of Devon* vol. 1 139–44 (see no. 2598)

2080 W. Heape, 'Notes on the fishing industry of Plymouth', *J. Marine Biol. Assoc.* old series I 1887 45–95

2081 A.M. Northway, *The Devon fishing industry, 1760–1860*. (M.A. thesis, Exeter University, 1969)

2082 N. Oswald, 'Devon and the cod fishery of Newfoundland', *Reps. Trans. Devons. Assoc.* CXV 1983 19–36

2083 A. Northway, 'The Devon fishing industry in the eighteenth and nineteenth centuries', *in The new maritime history of Devon* v. 2 126–35 (see no. 2598)

2084 J.H. Porter, 'The Exe Bight Oyster Fishery and Pier Company, 1864–72', *Devon Cornwall N. & Q.* XXXV 1986 357–63

2085 M. Porter, 'Devon's fishing industry, 1880–1990', *in The new maritime history of Devon* vol. 2 243–9 (see no. 2598)

2086 P.A. Ribbins, *The decline of the fishing industry at Plymouth*. (196–) Photocopy in Plymouth Central Library.

2087 W. Roach, 'Notes on the herring, long-line and pilchard fisheries of Plymouth', *J. Marine Biol. Assoc* n.s. I 1890 382–90 and II 1891 180–8

2088 A.L. Rowse, 'The dispute concerning the Plymouth pilchard fishery, 1584–91', *Econ. J. Econ. Hist. Suppl.* II 1932 461–72

2089 P. Russell, 'Some historical notes on the Brixham fisheries', *Reps. Trans. Devons. Assoc.* LXXXIII 1951 278–97

2090 A.J. Southward and G.T. Boalch, 'The maritime resources of Devon's coastal waters', *in The new maritime history of Devon* v. 1 51–61 (see no. 2598)

2091 D.J. Starkey, 'Devonians and the Newfoundland trade', *in The new maritime history of Devon* v. 1 163–71 (see no. 2598)

2092 M. Straight, *Report on the Brixham fishing industry*. (1935) Typescript. Copy in Exeter University Library

GOLD, SILVER AND PEWTER INDUSTRIES

See also no. 549

2093 S. Baring-Gould, 'A gold-washing apparatus', *Reps. Trans. Devons. Assoc.* XX 1888 376–7

2094 J.F. Chanter, 'The Barnstaple Goldsmiths' Guild, with some notes on the early history of the town', *Reps. Trans. Devons. Assoc.* XLIX 1917 163–89

2095 J.F. Chanter, 'The Exeter Goldsmiths' Guild', *Reps. Trans. Devons. Assoc.* XLIV 1912 438–79

2096 R. Homer, 'Exeter pewterers from the fourteenth century to about 1750', *Reps. Trans. Devons. Assoc.* CXXVII 1995 57–79

2097 R.F. Homer, 'The pewterers of Devon', *Devon Histn.* no. 38 1989 3–9

2098 R.F. Homer, 'Robert Gaul I and II, Exeter's last pewterers', *Devon Histn.* no. 35 1987 15–17

2099 G. Paley, M.M. Rowe and J.A.H. Wylie, 'The Williams family, gold and silver-smiths of Bristol and their association with the Exeter Assay Office', *Devon Cornwall N. & Q.* XXXVI 1987 20–36

2100 R.S. Rendle, 'The goldsmiths and silversmiths of Plymouth, Devon circa 1600 to 1800', *Reps. Trans. Devons. Assoc.* CXVIII 1986 155–225

2101 S.E. Thomas, 'The Barnstaple pewterers', *Reps. Trans. Devons. Assoc.* CIII 1971 85–102

GUNPOWDER

See also no. 2863

2102 J. Copley, 'Powder Mills—Cherry Brook', *Tamar J.* no. 11 1989 17–21

Manufacture of gunpowder

2103 A.R. Pye and R. Robinson, *An archaeological survey of the gunpowder factory at Powdermills Farm, Postbridge, Devon.* (Exeter Museums, Archaeological Field Unit Report, no. 90.07, 1990)

2104 A. Pye, 'An example of a non-metalliferous Dartmoor industry: the gunpowder factory at Powdermills', *Proc. Devon Archaeol. Soc.* LII 1994 221–40

MINING
Arsenic

See also nos. 146–51

2105 T. Dixon and others, *Gawton Mine and Arsenic Works: the field survey, 1988.* (Exeter Museums, Archaeological Field Unit Report no. 89.02, 1989)

2106 H. Macan, 'The arsenic industry in Devonshire', *Notes and Gleanings* 15 Sept. 1888

2107 A.R. Pye and T. Dixon, 'The arsenic works at Devon Great Consols Mine, Tavistock', *Proc. Devon Archaeol. Soc.* no. 47 1989 79–111

A similar title also published as Exeter Museums, Archaeological Field Unit Report no. 89.08

2108 A. Pye and P. Weddell, 'A survey of the Gawton Mine & Arsenic works, Tavistock Hamlets, West Devon', *Ind. Archaeol. Rev.* XV 1992 62–96

A similar title also appears in *Tamar J.* no. 14 1992 17–27

2109 R.W. Toll, 'The arsenic industry in the Tavistock District of Devon', *Sands, Clay Minerals* April 1938 224–7

2110 P.J. Weddell and A.R. Pye, *Gawton Mine and Arsenic Works: the documentary research, 1988.* (Exeter Museums, Archaeological Field Unit Report no. 89.01, 1989)

China Clay

See also nos. 152–63

2111 P.C. Bradley, 'Clay in Devon', *Trans. Proc. Torquay Nat. Hist. Soc.* VIII no. 1 3–9 1939

2112 'Ball clay mining and quarrying', *Mine and Quarry* XVI no. 5 11–12 and 14–16

At Bovey Tracey, South Devon.

2113 J.A. Bulley, 'The beginnings of the Devonshire ball-clay trade', *Rep. Trans. Devons. Assoc.* LXXXVII 1955 191–204

2114 Devon & Courtney Clay Co. Ltd, *Devon clay.* 3rd ed. (The Company, 1936) 41p.

2115 English Clays, Lovering, Pochin and Co. Ltd, *Lee Moor, a brief history, by J. Penderill-Church.* (196–)

Typescript. Copy in Plymouth Central Library

2116 English Clays, Lovering, Pochin and Co. Ltd, *A short history of china clay production in Devon.* (196–)

Typescript. Copy in Plymouth Central Library

2117 D.A. Holdridge, 'Ball clays and their properties', *Trans. Br. Ceram. Soc.* LV 1956 369–440

2118 M.J. Messenger, *North Devon clay: the history of an industry and its transport.* (Truro, Twelveheads Press, 1982) 104p.

2119 L.T.C. Rolt, *The potters' field: a history of the South Devon ball clay industry.* (Newton Abbot, David & Charles, 1974) 160p.

The firm of Watts, Blake, Bearne & Co. Ltd features in this book

2120 E.A. Wade, *The Redlake tramway, and china clay works.* (Truro, Twelveheads Press, 1982) 84p.

2121 Watts, Blake, Bearne and Co. Ltd, *Devon ball clays and china clays; by V.R.G. Ashcroft-Healey and D. Mitchell; 250th anniversary edition, 1710–1960.* (Newton Abbot, The Firm, 1960) 116p.

Granite and Other Stone

See also nos. 206–10

2122 J.V.S. Cocks, 'The Haytor granite quarries', *Devon Cornwall N. & Q.* XXXII 1971 13–15

See also nos. 2440, 2456, 2465, 2475

2123 H. Harris, 'Nineteenth-century granite working on Pew Tor and Staple Tor, Western Dartmoor', *Reps. Trans. Devons. Assoc.* CXIII 1981 29–51

2124 C.J. Schmitz, 'The granite quarries and mineral mines of Lundy', *BIAS J.* X 1977 23–6

2125 R.F.G. Stanes, 'Devonshire batts. The whetstone mining industry and community of Blackborough, in the Blackdown Hills', *Reps. Trans. Devons. Assoc.* CXXV 1993 71–112

2126 R. Thomas, 'Bickleigh Vale quarries', *Devon Archaeol.* IV 1991 28–32

Metals

See also nos. 169–205

2127 S.R. Aiken, *West Devon mining: the influence of mining on the parish of Tavistock in the 19th century, a study in social and economic geography.*

(1964)

Typesript. Copy in Plymouth Central Library

2128 R. von Arx, 'Haytor and Smallacombe in Dartmoor', *Br. Mining* no. 50 1994 144–8

2129 R. von Arx, 'Vignette on Druid Mine in Devon', *Br. Mining* no. 55 1995 90–3

2130 R. von Arx, 'Wheal Lopes in Devon', *Br. Mining* no. 48 1993 90–2

2131 B. Atkinson, 'South of Tavistock: the mines of the Bere Alston peninsula, the Tavy and the Walkham valleys', *Plymouth Mineral Min. Club J.* XVI no. 2 1986 3–6

2132 M. Atkinson and C. Schmitz, 'Kelly iron mine, near Bovey Tracey', *Devon Histn.* no. 11 1975 27–34

2133 M. Atkinson, R. Burt and P. Waite, *Dartmoor mines: the mines of the granite mass.* (Exeter University, Dept. of Economic History, Industrial Archaeology Group, 1978) 56p.

Reprinted in 1983

2134 M. Atkinson, P. Waite and R. Burt, 'The iron mining industry in Devon', *Br. Mining* no. 19 1982 27–33

2135 O.A. Baker, 'Mining at Tamerton', *Plymouth Mineral Min. Club J.* IV no. 3 1974 16–18

2136 M. Bawden, 'Mines and mining in the Tavistock district', *Reps. Trans. Devons. Assoc.* XLVI 1914 256–64

2137 R. Bayles, 'Great Devon consols', *Trans. N. Cavern Mine Res. Soc.* I no. 1 1961 4–6

2138 K.E. Beer, 'Mineralisation in the Teign Valley', *Rep. Trans. Devons. Assoc.* CX 1978 77–80

2139 D.E. Bick, 'North Devon and Exmoor', *Plymouth Mineral Min. Club J.* III no. 2 1972 3–4

2140 J. Brooke, 'Brixham iron mines', *Devon Cornwall N. & Q.* XXXIII no. 5 1975 180

2141 J. Brooke, 'Devon United Mines', *Plymouth Mineral Min. Club J.* XV no. 3 1985 12

2142 J. Brooke, 'The gold mines of Devon', *Plymouth Mineral Min. Club J.* VII no. 3 1977 5–7; VIII no. 1 1977 3–5; VIII no. 2 1977 3–4

2143 J. Brooke, 'The last years of Devon Great Consols', *J. Trevithick Soc.* no. 9 1982 69–72

2144 J. Brooke, 'The Nascent copper process', *Tamar J.* no. 10 1988 47–48

2145 J. Brooke, 'New light on Devon Great Consols', *Devon Cornwall N. & Q.* XXX no. 7 1966 183–84

2146 J. Brooke, 'South Devon iron mines', *Plymouth Mineral Min. Club J.* VI no. 3 1976 7–8

2147 J. Brooke, 'Who discovered Devon Great Consol', *Br. Mining* no. 5 1977 21–2

2148 J. Brooke, 'Wheal Zion', *Tamar J.* no. 8 1986 15–20

2149 D.G. Broughton, 'Dartmoor tin working: its effect upon scenery and landuse', *Kingston Geogr.* I no. 1 1968 31–9

2150 D.G. Broughton, *A report on the geology, mineralogy and mining in the north eastern part of Dartmoor: from surveys around the moorland area in the vicinity of the town of Chagford.* (1961)
Typescript. Copy in Plymouth Central Library

2151 D.G. Broughton, 'Tin working in the Eastern district of the Parish of Chagford, Devon', *Proc. Geologists Assoc.* LXXVIII 1967 447–62

2152 R. Burnard, 'The antiquity of mining on Dartmoor', *Trans. Plymouth Instn.* 1890–91

2153 P.F. Claughton, 'Fullabrook Mine', *Plymouth Mineral Min. Club J.* VI no. 1 1975 4–5

2154 P. Claughton, 'The Lumburn Leat—evidence for new pumping technology at Bere Ferrers in the 15th century', *Mining Hist.* XIII no. 2 1996 35–40

2155 P. Claughton, 'The medieval silver-lead miner: a preliminary study', *Bull. Peak Dist. Min. Hist. Soc.* XII no. 2 1993 28–30

2156 P.F. Claughton, 'The metalliferous mines of North Devon and Exmoor', *Plymouth Mineral Min. Club J.* IV no. 1 1973 4–9
'Additions and corrections', V no. 1 1974 9–10

2157 P.F. Claughton, 'Mining in the parish of Georgeham, North Devon', *Plymouth Mineral Min. Club J.* VI no. 3 1976 15–16

2158 P.F. Claughton, 'Mining in the parishes of East Buckland and Charles, North Devon', *Br. Mining* no. 39 1989 4–13

2159 P.F. Claughton, 'The mining industry at Combe Martin, North Devon', *Plymouth Mineral Min. Club J.* VII no. 2 1976 13–15; 'Part 2', VII no. 3 1977 11–14; 'Part 3', VIII no. 1 1977 16–18; 'Part 4', VIII no. 2 1977 15–18

2160 P. Claughton, 'Silver-lead—a restricted resource: technological choice in the Devon mines', *in* T.D. Ford and L. Willies, eds., 'Mining before powder', *Bull. Peak Dist. Min. Hist. Soc.* XII no. 3 1994 54–9

2161 J.V.S. Cocks, 'The stannary bounds of Plympton and Tavistock', *Devon Cornwall N. & Q.* XXXII no. 3 1971 76–9
'A correction' XXXII no. 4 1972 124

2162 R.M.L. Cook, T.A.P. Greeves and C.Kilvington, 'Eylesbarrow, 1814–52. A study of a Dartmoor tin mine', *Reps. Trans. Devons. Assoc.* CVI 1974 161–214

2163 M.G. Dickinson, 'Dartmoor mining leats, 1786–1836', *Devon Cornwall N. & Q.* XXXIII no. 4 1975 102–8

2164 D.G. Dixon, *Mining and the community in the parishes of North Molton, South Molton, Molland and Twitchen, Devonshire.* (M.A. thesis, Southampton University, 1983)

2165 B. Earl, 'Tin smelting at Week Ford, Dartmoor; a brief note', *J. Hist. Metall. Soc.* XXIII 1989 119

2166 H.P.R. Finberg, 'Bounds of the Devon stannaries', *Devon Cornwall N. & Q.* XXII no. 4 1942 121–3

2167 H.P.R. Finberg, 'The stannary of Tavistock', *Reps. Trans. Devons. Assoc.* LXXXI 1949 155–84

2168 H.P.R. Finberg, 'An unrecorded Stannary Parliament', *Reps. Trans. Devons. Assoc.* LXXXII 1950 295–310

Proceedings of the Crockerntor assembly, 1600

2169 S. Gerrard, 'The Beckamoor Combe Streamwork Survey', *Dartmoor Tinworking Res. Group Newsl.* no. 3 July 1992

2170 S. Gerrard, 'The Dartmoor tin industry: an archaeological perspective', *Proc. Devon Archaeol. Soc.* LII 1994 173–98

2171 S. Gerrard and T. Greeves, 'Summary report on the excavation of Upper Merrivale tin blowing and stamping mill', *Dartmoor Tinworking Res. Gp Newsl.* no. 2 1992

2172 P. Glanvill, 'Wheal Friendship Mine, Devon', *J. Cerberus Spelaeolog. Soc.* XV no. 4 1985 109–10

2173 J.C. Goodridge, 'Devon Great Consols: a study of Victorian mining enterprise', *Rep. Trans. Devon Assoc.* XCVI 1964 228–68

2174 T. Greeves, 'Adventures with fiery dragons—the Cornish tinner in Devon from the 15th to the 20th century', *J. Trevithick Soc.* no. 19 1992 2–17

2175 T.A.P. Greeves, 'The archaeological potential of the Devon tin industry', *in* D.W. Crossley, *ed., Medieval industry.* (London, Council for British Archaeology, Research Report no. 40, 1981) 85–95

2176 T.A.P. Greeves, *The Devon tin industry, 1450–1750: an archaeological and historical survey.* (Ph.D. thesis, Exeter University, 1981)

2177 T.A.P. Greeves, 'Eighth-century tin smelting on Dartmoor: do we really have the evidence?', *J. Hist. Metall. Soc.* XXIV no. 1 1990 45–6

2178 T.A.P. Greeves, 'Four Devon stannaries; a comparative study of tinworking in the 16th century', *in* T. Gray *et al eds., Tudor and Stuart Devon—the common estate and government.* (Exeter, 1992) 39–74

2179 T.A.P. Greeves, 'The Great Courts or Parliaments of Devon tinners 1474–1786', *Reps. Trans. Devons. Assoc.* CXIX 1987 145–67

2180 T.A.P. Greeves, 'A history of Whiteworks tin mine', *Plymouth Mineral Min. Club J.* XI no. 2 1980 11–16

2181 T.A.P. Greeves, 'Merrivale Bridge Mine, Wheal Fortune and Staple Tor Sett, 1806–1887', *Plymouth Mineral Min. Club J.* VI no. 3 1976 3–5, 11

2182 T.A.P. Greeves, 'A mine in the Deancombe Valley', *Reps.Trans. Devons. Assoc.* CI 1969 197–201

2183 T.A.P. Greeves, 'An outline archaeological and historical survey of tin mining in Devon 1500–1900', *in* W. Wachtler and G. Engewald, *eds., International Symposium zur Geschichte des Bergbaus und Huttenwesens.* Vortrag Band 1. (ICOHTEC, 1980) 73–80

2184 T.A.P. Greeves and E. Greeves, 'A probable tin mill at Claziwell', *Dartmoor Tinworking Res. Gp. Newsl.* no. 12 1997 4–5

2185 T. Greeves, 'Stamping and smelting at Upper Merrivale Tin Mill: preliminary results 1991–1993', *in* T.D. Ford and L. Willies, eds., 'Mining before powder', *Bull. Peak Dist. Min. Hist. Soc.* XII no. 3 1994 76–80

2186 T.A.P. Greeves, 'Steeperton Tor Mine, Dartmoor, Devon', *Reps. Trans. Devons. Assoc.* CXVII 1985 101–27

2187 T. Greeves, *Tin mines and miners of Dartmoor: a photographic record.* Rev. ed. (Exeter, Devon Books, 1986) 86p.

2188 T. Greeves, 'Tin smelting in Devon in the 18th and 19th centuries', *Mining Hist.* XIII no. 2 1996 84–9

2189 T.A.P. Greeves and P. Newman, 'Tin-working and land-use in the Walkham Valley: a preliminary analysis', *Proc. Devon Archaeol. Soc.* LII 1994 199–219

2190 T.A.P. Greeves, 'A tinners' mill in Walkhampton Parish', *Reps. Trans. Devons. Assoc.* CIII 1971 197–9

2191 T.A.P. Greeves, 'Wheal Prosper: a little known Dartmoor tin mine', *Plymouth Mineral Min. Club J.* VI no. 1 1975 6–7

2192 T.A.P. Greeves, 'Wheal Cumpston tin mine, Holne, Devon', *Reps. Trans. Devons. Assoc.* CX 1978 161–71

2193 V. Grey, 'A leat on Roborough Down and an early 17th-century tinners' dispute', *Reps. Trans. Devons. Assoc.* CXXI 1990 71–82

2194 F. Griffith and P. Weddell, 'Ironworking in the Blackdown Hills: results of a recent survey', *Mining Hist.* XIII no. 2 1996 27–34

2195 T.M. Hall, 'On the mineral localities of Devonshire', *Rep. Trans. Devons. Assoc.* II no. 2 1868 332–42

2196 J.R. Hamilton, 'The mines and minerals of Exmoor', *Camborne School of Mines J.* 1950 45–8

2197 H. Harris, 'A Dartmoor ochre works', *Devon Histn.* no. 43 1991 20–5

2198 H.B.M. Harris, 'Manganese mining in West Devon', *Tamar J.* no. 9 1987 20–4

2199 R. Hazard, 'The Devon Great Consols Mine', *Shrops. Min. Club Yrbk.* 1963–4 45–50

2200 G. Hicks, 'The Bere Alston silver lead-mines', *Plymouth Mineral Min. Club J.* IV no. 3 1974 8–9

Reprinted in *Tamar J.* no. 1 1978 20–3

2201 R.F. Homer, 'The Whiddon tin mines, Ashburton', *Reps. Trans. Devons. Assoc.* CXXVIII 1996 155–69

2202 J. Hunter, 'An exercise in mineral exploration: Dartmoor, 1974', *Br. Mining* no. 5 1977 1–6

2203 J. Hunter, 'Hamerdon Ball—rolling again?', *Br. Mining* no. 8 1978 43–8

Possible restart of wolfram mining at Hamerdon Ball.

2204 A.K.H. Jenkin, *Mines of Devon*.

v.1 *The Southern Area*. (Newton Abbot, David & Charles, 1974) 154p.

v.2 *North and East of Dartmoor*. (Exeter, Devon Library Services, 1981) 226p

2205 M.H. Jones, 'Extracts from a Brendon Hill diary', *Exmoor Rev.* no. 3 1961 57–62

2206 M.H. Jones, 'The incline at Brendon Hill', *Exmoor Rev.* no. 28 1987 35–45

2207 M.H. Jones, 'Wartime mining on Exmoor', *Exmoor Rev.* 1979 41–2

2208 J.T. Kingston, *Account of the iron mine at Haytor*. (1828)

Copy in Exeter Public Library

2209 *The lawes and statutes of the Stannarie of Devon*.

Available on microfilm. Early English books 1475–1640, Reel 1304

2210 C.D. Linehan, 'A forgotten manor in Widecombe-in-the-Moor, with notes on its geology, archaeology and mining by H. French', *Rep. Trans. Devons. Assoc.* XCIV 1962 463–92

2211 E.C. Long, 'Anderton tin mine', *Tamar J.* no. 6 1984 11–19
Near Tavistock

2212 M.J. Messenger, 'Bulkamore Iron Mine and its tramway', *Devon Histn.* no. 14 1977 15–16

2213 M.T. Mills, 'The copper mines of Lundy', *23rd Ann. Rep. Lundy Soc.* 1972 59–62

2214 P. Newman, 'The moorland Meavy: a tinners' landscape', *Reps. Trans. Devons. Assoc.* CXIX 1987 223–40

2215 P. Newman, 'Recording the tinworks of Dartmoor Forest', *Mining Hist.* XIII no. 2 1996 143–9

2216 P. Newman, 'Tinners and tenants in South-West Dartmoor. A case study in landscape history', *Reps. Trans. Devon Assoc.* CXXVI 1994 199–238

2217 P. Newman, 'Two small mines in the Newleycombe Valley', *Dartmoor Mag.* no. 8 1987 8–10

2218 P. Newman, 'Week Ford Tin Mills, Dartmoor', *Proc. Devon Archaeol. Soc.* no. 51 1993 185–97

2219 B. Nicholls, 'The Lady Elizabeth Mine, Ermington', *Plymouth Mineral Min. Club J.* XV no. 2 1984 3–6

2220 P. Oxenford, 'Virtuous Lady Copper Mine', *Plymouth Mineral Min. Club J.* IV no. 2 1973 8

2221 J. Pamment and B. Slater, 'An eighteenth century lead-and-silver mine near Newton St.Cyres', *Proc. Devon Archaeol. Soc.* XLVI 1988 149–53

2222 H. Parsons, 'The Dartmoor blowing-house', *Rep. Trans. Devons. Assoc.* LXXXVIII 1956 184–96

2223 W.H. Pascoe, 'The mines of Phillack Parish', *Plymouth Mineral Min. Club J.* XIV no. 1 1983 3–5

2224 A. Patrick, 'Copper production in the Tamar Valley in the 18th century', *Tamar J.* no. 5 35–42

2225 S.R. Pattison, 'A day in the North Devon mineral districts', *Trans. R. Geol. Soc. Cornwall* VII

2226 J.P.R. Polkinghorne, 'The Bridford baryte mine', *Trans. R. Geol. Soc. Cornwall* XVIII 1951 240–54

2227 J.P.R. Polkinghorne, 'Bridford baryte mine, Devon', *Trans. Cornish Inst. Engrs.* IX 1953–4 16–23

2228 W.J. Prew, 'On metals in Devon: a comparative review of origins and principles', *Reps. Trans. Devons. Assoc.* LXXXI 1949 333–40

2229 R.R. Pymm, 'Mill Hill Quarry, Tavistock—a brief visit', *Tamar J.* no. 9 1987 15–19

2230 Lady Radford, 'Notes on the tinners of Devon and their laws', *Reps. Trans. Devons. Assoc.* LXII 1930 225–47

2231 J.V. Ramsden, *The mineral deposits and mines of the Teign Valley, Devonshire.* (1937)

Typescript. Copy in West Country Studies Library, Exeter

2232 J.V. Ramsden, 'Notes on the mines of Devonshire', *Reps. Trans. Devons. Assoc.* LXXXIV 1952 81–104

2233 J.V. Ramsden, *Notes on the mineral deposits of the Teign Valley, Devon.* (1945)

Typescript. Copy in West Country Studies Library, Exeter

2234 B. Redgrave, 'Wheal Betsy: a Dartmoor lead mine', *Dartmoor Mag.* no. 10 1988 18

2235 P.H.G. Richardson, 'Hexworthy tin mine', *Plymouth Mineral Min. Club J.* III no. 3 1972 3–4; IV no. 2 1973 11–13

2236 P.H.G. Richardson, 'Notes on the Old Burning House, near Ilsington', *Plymouth Mineral Min. Club J.* VII no. 3 1977 16–17

2237 P.H.G. Richardson, 'Devon Great Consols after 1903', *Plymouth Mineral Min. Club J.* X no. 1 1979 3–8

A similar title appears in *Tamar J.* no. 2 1979–80 33–42

2238 P.H.G. Richardson, 'The Mary Tavy mines: some recollections, 1932–1982', *Plymouth Mineral Min. Club J.* XIV no. 2 1983 3–8

2239 P.H.G. Richardson, *Mines of Dartmoor and the Tamar Valley after 1913.* (*Br. Mining* vol. 44 May 1992, a monograph of the Northern Mines Research Society) 160p.

2240 P.H.G. Richardson, 'South Devon United Mine, Peter Tavy', *Plymouth Mineral Min. Club J.* XV no. 2 1984 9–13

2241 P.H.G. Richardson, 'Roborough Down Wolfram', *Plymouth Mineral Min. Club J.* XVII no. 1 1986 3

2242 P.H.G. Richardson, 'Small details: snippets from the Devon Great Consols workbooks for the early 1920s', *Plymouth Mineral Min. Club J.* XVII no. 3 1987 7–8

2243 P. Roberts, 'Standon Hill and Wapsworthy', *Plymouth Mineral Min. Club J.* XII no. 2 1981 12

2244 S. Roberts, 'Kelly Mine: the first year', *Plymouth Mineral Min. Club J.* XVII no. 1 1986 9–12

This article and the one following tell of the restoration of this mine by a group of volunteers.

2245 P. Roberts, 'Kelly Mine: the first ten years', *Mining Hist.* XIII no. 2 1996 163–67

2246 S. Roberts, 'East Pool', *Plymouth Mineral Min. Club J.* XVIII no. 1 1988 3–4

2247 J.A.C. Robins, 'Bachelors Hall Tin Mine', *Plymouth Mineral Min. Club J.* XIV no. 3 1984 3–7

2248 J.A.C. Robins, 'The Grimstone and Sortridge Leat', *Tamar J.* no. 10 1988 24–9

2249 J. Robins, *Follow the leat with John Robins: a series of walks along Dartmoor leats and a description of the mines some of them served.* (Tavistock, Privately published, 1984) 184p.

Supplementary notes (1986) pp. 185–228

2250 J. Robins, 'A fresh concept of the leats of Whiteworks Mine', *Dartmoor Mag.*

no. 3 1986 19

2251 J. Robins, 'The Vitifer leat', *Dartmoor Mag.* no. 7 1987 26

2252 J. Rottenbury, 'The Bampfylde Mine', *Exmoor Rev.* 1969 24–9

2253 F.J. Rottenbury, *Geology, mineralogy and mining history of the metalliferous mining areas of Exmoor.* (Ph.D. thesis, Leeds University, 1974)

2254 J. Rottenbury, 'The Mines of Combmartin', *Exmoor Rev.* 1973 47–50

2255 G.A. Rowe, 'The mines of Tamarside—No. 1. Drakewall's Mine', *Tamar J.* no. 3 1980–1 20–3; 'No. 2 Old Gunnislake Mine', no. 4 1982 30–3; 'No. 3 South Hooe Mine', no. 5 1983 7–8; 'No. 4 Devon Great Consols', no. 6 1984 37–47; 'No. 6 Gawton Mine', no. 8 1986 4–6

2256 G.A. Rowe, 'New Great Consols', *Tamar J.* no. 7 1985 26–30

Probably no. 5 of preceding entry.

2257 P.M.G. Russell, 'Manganese mining in Devon', *Devon Cornwall N. & Q.* XXXI 1970 205–13

2258 C.J. Schmitz, 'The early growth of the Devon barytes industry, 1835–75', *Reps. Trans. Devons. Assoc.* CVI 1974 59–76

2259 C.J. Schmitz, 'The development and decline of the Devon barytes industry, 1875–1958', *Reps. Trans. Devons. Assoc.* CIX 1977 117–33

2260 C.J. Schmitz, *The Teign Valley lead mines.* (Sheffield, Northern Cavern & Mines Res. Soc., Individual Survey series no. 6, 1973) 125p.

2261 C.J. Schmitz, 'The Teign Valley silver-lead mines, 1806–1880', *Br. Mining* no. 15, 1980 121p.

A second edition of the preceding entry

2262 J. Scott and G. Gray, *Out of the darkness. A brief history and description of the Old Quarry, Beer.* (Beer Quarry Caves, n.d.) 21p.

2263 R. Shambrook, 'The Devon Great Consolidated Copper Mining Company', *J. Trevithick Soc.* no. 9 1982 62–8

2264 T. Shaw, 'Iron mine at Haytor Vale, Devon', *Br. Caver* XXVI 1955 83–4

2265 J.M. Slader, *Days of renown: the story of mining on Exmoor and the border parishes.* (Bracknell, West Country Publications, 1965) 55p.

2266 R. Smerdon, 'Avon Dam blowing house furnace: some observations and speculations', *Dartmoor Tinworking Res. Gp. Newsl.* no. 12 1997 6–8

2267 R.G.F. Stanes, 'Iron-smelting at Hemyock', *Devon Cornwall N. & Q.* XXXIV 1978 36–7

2268 F.H. Starkey, 'Notes on the Devonport leat and the area around Nun's Cross Farm, Dartmoor', *Devon Cornwall N. & Q.* XXXIV 1979 103–4

2269 D. Stuckey, *Adventurer's slopes: the story of the silver and other mines of Combe Martin in Devon.* (Bracknell, West Country Handbooks, 1965) 25p.

2270 C. Taylor, 'The story of Devon Great Consols Mine 1844–1901', *Tamar J.* no. 10 1988 34–43

2271 R.W. Toll, 'Manganese in West Devon', *Min. Mag.* XCIX no. 1 1958 17–19

2272 R.W. Toll, 'Old silver lead mines in West Devon', *Min. Mag.* LXXVIII no. 6 1948 335–42

2273 R.W. Toll, 'Radioactive minerals in the Tavistock district', *Min. Mag.* LXXXV no. 3 1951 137–42

2274 R. Waterhouse, 'A reconstruction of Upper Merrivale Tin Mill in its final phase of working, *c.* 1700', *Dartmoor Tinworking Res. Gp. Newsl.* no. 7 1994 5–8

2275 G. Williams, 'The decline of Great Work and the formation of Wheal Reeth Tin Ltd', *J. Trevithick Soc.* no. 19 1992 55–85

2276 R. Wilson-North, 'Recording the iron mines of Exmoor', *Mining Hist.* XIII no. 2 1996 137–42

2277 G. Woodcock, 'The East Crebor mining tragedy', *Tamar J.* no. 12 1990 9–12

2278 G. Woodcock, 'The strikes at Devon Great Consols', *Tamar J.* no. 16 1994 5–16

2279 R.N. Worth, 'The ancient stannary of Ashburton', *Reps. Trans. Devons. Assoc.* VIII 1876 311–22

2280 R.H. Worth, 'A blowing house in the parish of Chagford', *Reps. Trans. Devon Assoc.* LIX 1927 343–5

2281 R.H. Worth, 'Blowing houses in the valleys of the Sheepstor Brook and the Glazebrook', *Reps. Trans. Devons. Assoc.* LXIV 1932 273–8

2282 R.H. Worth, 'Blowing houses in the valleys of the Sheepstor Brook, the Meavy, the Erme and the Avon ', *Reps. Trans. Devons. Assoc.* LXV 1933 307–21

2283 R.H. Worth, 'Blowing houses in the valley of the Walkham (Moorland)', *Reps. Trans. Devons. Assoc.* LXIII 1931 361–7

2284 R.H. Worth, 'The Dartmoor blowing house', *Reps. Trans. Devons. Assoc.* LXXII 1940 209–50

2285 R.H. Worth, 'Dartmoor blowing houses: stray notes', *Reps. Trans. Devons. Assoc.* LXI 1929 401; LXX 1938 451–4

2286 R.N. Worth, 'The economic geology of Devonshire', *Reps. Trans. Devons. Assoc.* VII 1875 209–33

2287 R.H. Worth, 'Notes on some Dartmoor blowing houses', *Reps. Trans. Devon Assoc.* LXXII 1940 201–50

' — Supplement', LXXVIII 1946 281–4

2288 R.H. Worth, 'Stray notes on Dartmoor tin-working', *Reps. Trans. Devon Assoc.* XLVI 1914 284–9

2289 R.F. Youell, 'Eastern Exmoor', *Plymouth Mineral Min. Club J.* V no. 1 1974 12–16

Coal and Lignite

2290 R. Acworth, 'The anthracite seams of North Devon', *J. Trevithick Soc.* no. 18 1991 117–25

2291 C.W. Parish, *The creation of an industry.* (Plaistow, Curwen Press, 1947)
The exploitation of the lignite deposit near Bovey Tracey

Slate

2292 F. Booker, 'A medieval quarry puzzle', *Tamar J.* no. 2 1979–80 29–33
Blue slate mining in the Bere Alston peninsula

2293 A. Born, 'Blue slate quarrying in South Devon: an ancient industry', *Ind. Archaeol. Rev.* XI 1988 51–67

PAPER MAKING

See also nos. 219–22

2294 J. Chitty, *Paper in Devon.* (Exeter, Author, 1976) 72p.

2295 A.H. Shorter, 'The historical geography of the paper-making industry in Devon, 1684–1950', *Reps. Trans. Devons. Assoc.* LXXXII 1950 205–16

POSTS AND COMMUNICATIONS

See also nos. 223-5

2296 D.B. Cornelius, 'The twopenny posts in the Plymouth area, 1818–37', *Bull. Postal Hist. Soc.* no. 187 1974 372–5, 383

2297 T.A.Q. Griffiths, *The development of rural postal services with particular reference to Devon, 1790–1905.* (M.Phil. thesis, Exeter University, 1987)

2298 N.C. Oswald, 'Some Devon postmarks', *Reps. Trans. Devons. Assoc.* CXXI 1989 173–93

2299 H.J. Yallop, 'A Devon postal service in 1600', *Devon Cornwall N. & Q.* XXXVI 1989 166–8

POTTERY AND CERAMICS

2300 B. Adams and A. Thomas, *A potwork in Devonshire. The history and products of the Bovey Tracey potteries 1750–1836.* (Bovey Tracey, Sayce Publishing, 1996) 96p. 121 plates

2301 B. Adams, *Wemyss Ware pottery: the Devonshire years.* (Budleigh Salterton, David Thorn, 1990) 58p.

2302 J.P. Allen, *The post-medieval pottery of Exeter 1500–1750* (M.Phil. thesis, Exeter University, 1983)

2303 P. Brannam, *A family business: the story of a pottery.* (Instow, The Author, 1982) 137p.

The firm of C.H. Brannam Ltd, North Devon potters

2304 T. Charbonnier, 'Notes on North Devon pottery of the seventeenth, eighteenth and nineteenth centuries', *Reps. Trans. Devons. Assoc.* XXXVIII 1906 255–60

2305 A. Fox and G.C. Dunning, 'A medieval pottery kiln in Exeter', *Antiq. J.* XXXVII nos. 1, 2 1957 43–53

2306 A.E. Grant, *The North Devon pottery industry of the later seventeenth century.* (Ph.D. thesis, Exeter University, 1981)

2307 A. Grant, *North Devon pottery: the seventeenth century.* (Exeter, University Press, 1983) 156p.

2308 A. Grant, 'The transatlantic trade in north Devon pottery in the seventeenth century', *Devon Archaeol.* I 1983 12–14

2309 T.M. Hall, 'On Barum tobacco pipes and North Devon clays', *Reps. Trans. Devons. Assoc.* XXII 1890 317–23

2310 W.F. Holland, *Fifty years a potter by W.F. Holland.* (Tring, *Pottery Quarterly*, 1958) 105p.

Holland worked at Fremington, Braunston, Clevedon

2311 S. Hunt, 'Two Exeter potteries', *Devon Cornwall N. & Q.* XXXIII 1976 260–1

2312 L. Keen, 'A series of seventeenth- and eighteenth-century lead-glazed tiles from North Devon', *J. Br. Archaeol. Assoc.* XXXII 1969 144–70

2313 T.D. Lloyd, *The old Torquay potteries from castle to cottage.* (Ilfracombe, Stockwell, 1978) 319p.

2314 A. Oswald and J. Barber, 'Marked clay pipes from Plymouth, Devon', *Post-Med. Archaeol.* III 1969 122–42

2315 R.H. Phillips, 'The Bideford pottery industry. Part 1', *Devon Histn.* no. 2 April 1971 11–14; 'Part 2', Oct. 1971 3–11

2316 J. Phillips, 'The potter's art in Devonshire', *Rep. Trans. Devons. Assoc.* XIII 1881 214–17

2317 G.H. Radford, 'Plymouth china', *Rep. Trans. Devons. Assoc.* XLIV 1912 382–93

2318 A. Rippon, 'Ancient Devon tobacco pipes', *Devon Cornwall N. & Q.* IX 1917 113–15

2319 N. Stretton, 'The Indio Pottery at Bovey Tracey', *Trans. Eng. Ceram. Circle* VIII 1972 124–36

2320 H.W. Strong, 'The potteries of north Devon', *Reps. Trans. Devons. Assoc.* XXIII 1891 389–93

2321 R. Terry, *The Barnstaple clay tobacco pipe factory in the nineteenth century.* (Exter, Devon County Council, 1989) 30p.

2322 C.M. Watkins, *North Devon pottery and its export to America in the 17th century.* (Washington, Smithsonian Museum, National Museum Bulletin 225, Paper 13, 1960)

2323 P.J. Weddell and K. Westcott, 'The Bovey Tracey pottery kilns. *Proc. Devon Archaeol. Soc.* no. 44 1986 143–62

A similar title was published by the Exeter Museums Archaeological Field Unit in 1987.

William Cookworthy

2324 T. Compton, *William Cookworthy.* (London, W. Hicks, 1895) 138p.

2325 H. Fox, *The story of William Cookworthy.* (Kingsbridge, Cookworthy Museum, 1972) 30p.

2326 G. Harrison, *Memoir of William Cookworthy, formerly of Plymouth, Devonshire, by his grandson.* (London, Cash, 1854) 207p.

2327 H.R. Hicks, 'William Cookworthy and the Plymouth porcelain factory', *Connoisseur* CXVI no. 497 1945 30–3

2328 F.S. Mackenna, *Cookworthy's Plymouth and Bristol porcelain.* (Leigh-on-Sea,

F. Lewis, 1946) 109p.

2329 F.S. Mackenna, 'William Cookworthy and the Plymouth factory: an updating', *Trans. Eng. Ceramic Circle* XI no. 2 1982 84–98

2330 J. Penderill-Church, *William Cookworthy, 1705–1780: a study of the pioneer of true porcelain manufacture in England.* (Truro, Bradford Barton, 1972) 92p.

2331 N.J.G. Pounds, 'The discovery of china clay', *Econ. Hist. Rev.* 2nd ser. I no. 1 1948 20–33

Much about Cookworthy

2332 J. Prideaux, *Relics of William Cookworthy, discoverer of the Cornish china-clay and stone about A.D. 1755, founder of the British porcelain manufacture about 1760, and an eminent minister of the Society of Friends.* (London, Whittaker & Co., 1853) 31p.

2333 A.D. Selleck, *Cookworthy 1705–80 and his circle.* (Plymouth, Baron Jay Publishers, 1978) 279p.

The title in the book cover is: *Cookworthy: a man of no common clay.*

Based on his London University Ph.D. of 1974–5

2334 C. Staal, 'William Cookworthy and his Plymouth porcelain factory', *J. R. Inst. Cornwall* n.s. VIII 1981 267–74

2335 G. Wills, 'The Plymouth porcelain factory I: letters to Thomas Pitt 1766–69', *Apollo* CXII Dec. 1980 377–85

2336 G. Wills, 'The Plymouth porcelain factory: Part II: letters to Thomas Pitt, 1766–69', *Apollo* CXIII 1981 29–37

2337 R.N. Worth, William Cookworthy and the Plymouth china factory', *Reps. Trans. Devons. Assoc.* VIII 1876 480–96

PRINTING AND PUBLISHING

See also no. 548

2338 M.G. Dickinson, 'Early Exeter printers and booksellers, 1669–1741', *Devon Cornwall N. & Q.* XXIX 1964 164–71

2339 J.I. Dredge, *Devon booksellers and printers in the 17th and 18th centuries.* (Plymouth, W.H. Luke, 1885)

Originally published as a limited edition. Microfiche published by Chadwick-Healey in *The nineteenth century: publishing collection* (1987)

2340 C. Gill, 'The *Western Morning News* 1860–1985', *Reps. Trans. Devons. Assoc.* CXVII 1985 195–226

2341 N. Orme, 'Martin Coeffin, the first Exeter publisher', *Library* 6th ser X no. 3 1988 220–30

2342 H.R. Plomer, 'An Exeter bookseller, his friends and contemporaries', *Library* ser. 3 VIII 1917 128–35

John Gropall alias Lumbard

2343 Lady Radford, 'Early printing in Devon', *Reps. Trans. Devons. Assoc.* LX 1928 51–74

2344 R.N. Worth, 'Notes on the history of publishing in Devon', *Reps. Trans.*

Devons. Assoc. XI 1879 497–515

PUBLIC UTILITIES
See also nos. 228–33
General
2345 A.S. Kingdon, 'Torquay water and electricity', *Trans. Proc. Torquay Nat. Hist. Soc.* VIII no. 3 1940–1 139–45

2346 'Refuse destructor at Torquay', *Engineering* LXVIII 1899 215–16

Electricity
2347 A.F.L. Brayley, *A history of Barnstaple electricity supply industry ... previous to 1st April 1848.* (1982) 23 leaves

Photocopy in West Country Studies Library, Exeter

2348 J.G. Cloke, 'Mary Tavy and Morwellham hydro-electric stations', *Tamar J.* no. 10 1988 44–6

2349 J.H. Fooks Bale, 'The electric lighting of Lynton and Lynmouth', *Elect. Engr.* XXIII Apr. 1899 430–3

2350 W.B. Harris, 'Hydro-electricity in Devon: past, present and future', *Reps. Trans. Devons. Assoc.* CXXVII 1995 259–86

2351 M. Laver, 'Sidmouth and the electric light', *Devon Histn.* no. 41 1990 8–11

2352 R. Pyman, 'Morwellham power-station—a short history', *Tamar J.* no. 5 1983 30–4

2353 D.G. Tucker, 'The early years of hydroelectricity for public supply in Devon', *Devon Histn.* no. 15 21–32

2354 B.E.G. Tyler, 'The West Devon Electric Supply Co. Ltd', *Tamar J.* no. 17 1995 41–7

2355 R. Warburton, 'The history of Newton Abbot power station', *Ind. Archaeol.* XI no. 2 1974 46–52

Gas
2356 A. Bird and H. Nabb, *Stoking up the past: a sketchbook history of the gas industry and the growth of the Gas Workers' Union in Plymouth.* (Bristol, British Gas SW, 1987) 65p.

Water
2357 A. Atkinson, *A brief account of the water supply of Plymouth.* (Plymouth Corporation, 1937) 30p.

2358 J. Coate and J.A. Knight, *To the inhabitants of Axminster on sewage and water supply* (Exeter, *Daily Western Times*, 1876–92) 20p.

Copy in West Country Studies Library, Exeter

Spine title: *Axminster waterworks and sewage*

2359 *Collection of pamphlets concerning the water supply of Plymouth, commencing* with 'An Act for preservation of the haven of Plymouth, 27th Eliz. A.D. 1585' ... and ending with the Harter Controversy, 1850.

Copy in Plymouth Central Library.

2360 Devon County Educational Television Service, *A history of Exeter's water supply*. (Plymouth, Devon County Council) 55p.

2361 D. Hawkings, 'The early water supply of Plymouth: an introduction', *Devon Hist*. XXIV 1982 9–14

2362 R. Hodge, *Report to the Water Committee on the constant supply of water to the Borough of Plymouth*. (1868)

Copy in West Country Studies Library, Exeter

2363 A. Kneel and R. Pickard, 'The modern water supply of Exeter', *Reps. Trans. Devon Assoc*. LXV 1933 337–51

2364 R.E. Middleton, *Honiton water supply*. (1887) 8p.

Copy in West Country Studies Library, Exeter

2365 W. Minchinton, *Life in the city: a social history of Exeter through its water supply*. (Exeter, 1987) 122p.

2366 R.R. Pymm, 'Piped water supplies at Morwellham 1856 to the present day', *Tamar J*. no. 6 1984 28–36

2367 E. Sandeman, *Engineer's report on the water supply of Plymouth*. (Plymouth Corporation, 1891) 53p.

2368 South West Water, *Exeter's water supply*. (South West Water, 1989) 16p.

2369 South West Water, *Plymouth 400: four centuries of water for Plymouth, past and future*. (South West Water, 1987) 14p.

2370 S. Timms, 'Flooding red spider country—the making of Roadford Reservoir', *Reps. Trans. Devons. Assoc*. CXXII 1990 159–78

SHIPBUILDING

See also nos. 234–9

2371 V.C. Boyle, 'R.T. Blackmore, shipwright', *Reps. Trans. Devons. Assoc*. LXXXV 1953 139–44

2372 L.E. Braddick, 'The Port of Topsham, its ships and ship-builders', *Reps. Trans. Devon Assoc*. LXXXV 1953 18–34

2373 K.V. Burns, *Devonport built warships since 1860*. (Liskeard, Maritime Books, 1981) 112p.

2374 K.V. Burns, *The Devonport Dockyard story*. (Liskeard, Maritime Books, 1984) 126p.

2375 J. Coad, 'Architecture and development of Devonport naval base, 1815–1982', *in The new maritime history of Devon* v. 2 167–76 (see no. 2598)

See also no. 1980

2376 J. Coad, 'The development and organisation of Plymouth dockyard, 1689–1815', *in The new maritime history of Devon* v. 1 192–200 (see no. 2598)

2377 J. Derriman, 'A West Looe shipbuilding of 1686', *Devon Cornwall N. & Q*.

XXXV no. 3 1983 117–20

2378 G. Farr, *Shipbuilding in North Devon: containing a list of the ships known to have been built on the North Devon Coasts and rivers ...* (Greenwich, National Maritime Museum, 1976) 72p.

2379 L. Harris, *A two hundred year history of Appledore shipyards.* (Combe Martin, Rotapress-Printers, 1992) 117p.

2380 P. Hildich, 'The dockyard in the local economy', *in The new maritime history of Devon* v. 2 215–25 (see no. 2598)

2381 J.M.P. Hooley, *The growth and development of HM Dockyard, Devonport.* (1939)

Typescript. Copy in Plymouth Central Library

2382 B.D. Hughes, 'North Devon barges', *Marit. S-W* no. 3 1987 37–40

2383 A.D. Lambert, 'The impact of naval technology on warship construction and repair at Devonport, 1815–1986', *in The new maritime history of Devon* v. 2 177–87 (see no. 2598)

2384 A.J. Marsh, 'The local community and the operation of Plymouth dockyard 1689–1763', *in The new maritime history of Devon* v. 1 201–8 (see no. 2598)

2385 R. Morriss, 'Industrial relations at Plymouth dockyard 1770–1820', *in The new maritime history of Devon* v. 1 216–23 (see no. 2598)

2386 M. Nix, 'The timber crisis of 1809 and the north Devon shipbuilding industry', *Devon Histn.* no. 49 1994 28–31

2387 V.J. Northcote, *Morgan Giles Ltd (1920–1964): a pictorial history of the shipyard in Teignmouth.* (Ilfracombe, Stockwell, 1995) 40p.

2388 *Philip & Son Ltd, shipbuilders and engineers 1858–1958: a century of progress,* (Dartmouth, The Firm, 1958) 96p.

2389 *Plymouth's ships of war: a history of naval vessels built in Plymouth between 1694 and 1860.* (Greenwich, National Maritime Museum, Monographs and Reports no. 4, 1972) 152p.

2390 C.N. Ponsford, *ed., Shipbuilding on the River Exe: the memoranda books of Daniel Bishop Davy (1799–1874) of Topsham, Devon: with a biography of Robert Davy (1762–1862).* (Devon & Cornwall Record Society, new ser. v. 31, 1988) 134p.

2391 I. Rogers, *A record of wooden sailing ships and warships built in the port of Bideford from 1568 to 1938 with a brief account of the shipbuilding industry in the town.* (Bideford, Gazette Printing Services, 1947) 48p.

Cover title: *Ships and shipyards of Bideford, 1568–1938.*

2392 D.J. Starkey, 'Devon's shipbuilding industry, 1786–1970', *in The new maritime history of Devon* v. 2 78–90 (see no. 2598)

2393 H. Tapley-Soper, 'Topsham industries—shipbuilding and brickmaking', *Devon Cornwall N. & Q.* XXIII 1947–9 13–15

2394 L.J. Taylor, 'William Froude and the model testing tank at Torquay', *in The new maritime history of Devon* v. 2 188–90 (see no. 2598)

2395 L. Waddell, *A history and bibliography of Devonport Dockyard ...* (Plymouth, College of St Mark & St John Foundation, 1982)

TEXTILES

2396 P.F.S. Amery, 'Sketch of Ashburton and the woollen trade', *Rep. Trans. Devons. Assoc.* VIII 1876 323–50

2397 H. Barnard, *The origin and history of Honiton lace.* (Sid Vale Association, *c.* 1960)

Copy in Exeter City Library

2398 J. Bourke, '"I was always fond of my pillow': the handmade lace industry in the United Kingdom, 1870–1914', *Rural Hist.* V 1994 155–69

2399 S. Chapman ed., *The Devon cloth industry in the eighteenth century: Sun Fire Office inventories of merchants' and manufacturers' property, 1726–1770.* (Devon & Cornwall Record Society, n.s. v. 23, 1976) 160p.

2400 J.R.W. Coxhead, *The romance of the wool, lace and pottery trades in Honiton.* 6th ed. (Honiton, P.H. Thrower, 1968) 43p.

2401 B.F. Cresswell, *Short history of the Worshipful Company of Weavers, Fullers and Shearmen of the city and county of Exeter.* (Exeter, W. Pollard & Co., 1930) 134p.

2402 Devonia, *The Honiton lace book.* (2nd ed. London, 1875?) 83p.

Reprinted by Paul Minet, Chicheley, Bucks., 1972

Devonia was the pen-name of Mrs Mary Whitmore Jones

2403 G.M. Doe, 'Some notes on the woollen and gloving manufactures at Great Torrington', *Rep. Trans. Devons. Assoc.* LXX 1938 223–9

2404 J. Hine, 'The origin of Axminster carpets', *Rep. Trans. Devons. Assoc.* XXI 1889 331–7

2405 P.M. Inder, *Honiton lace.* (Exeter Museum Publication no. 55, 1971) 36p.

2406 B. Jacobs, *Axminster carpets (hand-made) 1755–1957.* (Leigh-on-Sea, F. Lewis, 1970) 79p.

2407 C. Lee, 'Handmade lace and net; ebb and flow', *Reps. Trans. Devons. Assoc.* XXXVI 1904 135–43

2408 J. London, *Some considerations on the importance of the woollen manufactures etc.* (1740)

Copy in Plymouth Central Library

2409 A.P. Moody, *Devon pillow lace: its history and how to make it.* (London, Cassell, 1907) 160p.

2410 D. Seward, 'The Devonshire cloth industry in the early seventeenth century', in R. Burt, ed., *Industry and society in the South-West* (Exeter University Press, Exeter Papers in Economic History, no. 3, 1970)

2411 P. Sharpe, 'Literally spinsters: a new interpretation of local economy and demography in Colyton in the seventeenth and eighteenth centuries', *Econ. Hist. Rev.* XLIV 1991 45–65

Discusses wool-spinning and lacemaking

2412 M. Tomlinson, *Three generations in the Honiton lace trade: a family history.* (Exeter, Author, *c.* 1983) 94p.

2413 Mrs Treadwin, 'Devonshire lace', *Rep. Trans. Devons. Assoc.* XV 1883 231–6

2414 D.E. Varley, 'John Heathcoat 1783–1861: founder of the machine-made lace industry', *Text. Hist.* I no. 1 1969 2–45

2415 D. Warren, 'The woollen trade around Exmoor and a brief successor, crepe', *Somerset Ind. Archaeol. Soc. Bull.* no. 63 1993 9–15

2416 H.J. Yallop, 'The decoration of Honiton lace bobbins', *Rep. Trans. Devons. Assoc.* CXXII 1990 121–31

2417 H.J. Yallop, 'An example of seventeenth-century Honiton lace', *Devon Histn.* no. 29 1984 27–31

2418 M.J. Yallop, 'The history of the Honiton lace industry', *Text. Hist.* XIV 1983 195–211

2419 M.J. Yallop, *The history of the Honiton lace industry.* (Exeter, University Press, 1992) 352p.

2420 H.J. Yallop, *Honiton lace: part 1: The history of the Honiton lace industry. Part 2. The people of the industry.* (Ph.D. thesis, Exeter University, 1987)

2421 H.J. Yallop, 'The making of a myth—the origin of Honiton lace', *Devon Histn.* no. 28 1981 20–4

TRANSPORT
Canals

See also nos. 280–1

2422 R. Clew, *The Exeter canal.* (Chichester, Phillimore, 1984) 112p.

2423 P.C. de la Garde, 'Memoir of the canal of Exeter from 1563 to 1724', *Min. Proc. Instn. Civ. Engrs.* IV 1845 90–102

2424 P.C. de la Garde, 'On the antiquity and invention of the lock canal of Exeter', *Archaeologia* XXVIII 1840 18–19

2425 A. Grant and B. Hughes, *North Devon barges.* (North Devon Trust, 1975) 48p.

2426 D.J. Hawkins, *Water from the moor.* (Exeter, Devon Books, 1987) 90p.

Canals

2427 C. Hedges, *The Tavistock Canal: a short history.* (Totnes, Dartington Amenity Research Trust, 1975) 40p.

2428 E. Hemery, *Walking the Dartmoor waterways: a guide to retracing the leats and canals of the Dartmoor country.* (Newton Abbot, David & Charles, 1986) 128p.

Reprinted by Peninsular Press, 1991

2429 C.G. Henderson, 'Exeter Quay and the Exeter Canal in the sixteenth and seventeenth centuries', *Marit. S-W* no. 4 1988 4–17

2430 S.A. Holland, 'Morwelham and the Tavistock Canal', *Canal & Riverboat* XII no. 12 1989 43–5

2431 B.D. Hughes, 'Aids to recording (6): the Rolle Canal', *Ind. Archaeol.* VII 1970 75–83

2432 A. Patrick, 'The Tamar Manure Navigation: a brief history', *Tamar J.* no. 2 1979–80 21–8

2433 W.B. Stephens, 'The Exeter Lighter canal 1566–1698', *J. Transp. Hist.* III no. 1 May 1957 1–11

2434 J. Taylor, 'Description of the tunnel of the Tavistock Canal, through Morwel Down in the county of Devon', *Trans. Geol. Soc.* 1st ser. IV 1817 146–55

2435 C.H. Thompson, *Exeter canal: how to restore its trade: a letter to the bond holders of the canal.* (1876)

2436 R.W. Toll, 'The Tavistock–Morwelham Canal', *Min. Mag.* LXXIX no. 3 1948 144–8

2437 C.E. Welch, 'Cann Quarry canal and railway', *Reps. Trans. Devons. Assoc.* C 1968 111–23

2438 D.V.H. Wheeler, 'The Exeter canal: the problems of towing ships 1830–1930', *Marit. S-W* no. 1 1985 23–9

2439 G. Worrall, 'Exeter canal: the oldest artificial waterway in England', *Syren & Shipping* CCXL no. 3123 1956

Railways

See also nos. 297–497

2440 E.A. Adams, 'The old Haytor granite railway', *Rep. Trans. Devons. Assoc.* LXXVIII 1946 153–60

This railway had granite 'track'.

2441 G.H. Anthony, *The Tavistock, Launceston and Princetown Railways.* (Lingfield, Oakwood Press, 1971) 102p.

2442 R.S. Apps, *50s to Exeter.* (Silver Link Publications, 1992) 128p.

2443 C.H. Bastin, *Dartmoor steam tramway—the story of the Redlake and Lee Moor Tramways.* (Plymouth, C.H. Bastin Publishing, 1989) 12p.

2444 K.M. Beck and J. Copsey, *The Great Western in South Devon.* (Didcot, Wild Swan, 1990) 248p.

2445 J. Bosham, 'The railways of North Devon', *Rlwy. Mag.* IX 1901 67–73, 177–82

2446 G.A. Brown *and others, The Lynton and Barnstaple Railway.* 2nd ed. (Newton Abbot, David & Charles, 1971) 134p.

2447 F.E. Box, 'The Barnstaple and Ilfracombe Railway', *Rlwy. Mag.* XLV 1919 408–14; XLVI 1920 24–29, 80–4

2448 L.T. Catchpole, *The Lynton and Barnstaple Railway, 1895–1935.* 7th ed. (Oxford, Oakwood Press, 1988) 83p.

2449 J.B.B. Collins, 'Some branch railways in south Devon', *Rlwy. Mag.* XXXII 1913 46–50, 133–38

2450 L. Cozens, *The Axminster and Lyme Regis Light Railway with complementary road passenger services.* (L. Cozens, 1952) 44p.

2451 R. Crombleholme, *The Culme Valley Light Railway: Hemyock Branch.* (1964)

Copy in Exeter Public Library.

2452 M. Dickinson, 'The Duke's men, the Wheal Maria People and others: the story of the Devon Great Consols 'Ghost' railway', *Tamar J.* no. 7 1985 31–40

2453 J. Dilley, 'The High Moor Railway', *Devon Histn.* no. 37 Oct. 1988 21–3

2454 J. Dilley, *Mr Wolston's Little Line: the story of the Torbay and Brixham Railway.* (Paignton, Author, 1990) 48p.

2455 J. Dinwoodie, *Suburban rail demand in eastern Plymouth, 1989.* (Plymouth Polytechnic, Dept. of Shipping and Transport, 1989) 73p.

2456 K.M.C. Ewans, *The Haytor Granite Tramway and Stover Canal.* 2nd ed. (Dawlish, David & Charles, 1966) 72p.

2457 A. Fairclough, *Great Western steam in Devon.* (Truro, Barton, 1973) 96p.

Chiefly illustrations.

2458 A. Fairclough and A. Wills, *More Great Western steam in Devon.* (Truro, Barton, 1975) 96p.

2459 A. Farquharson-Coe, *Devon's railways.* (St Ives, James Pike, 1974)

2460 G. Finch, 'Railways and the balance of trade in Victorian Devon', *Devon Cornwall N. & Q.* XXXVI 1987 85–8

Effects of railways on the Devon economy 1844–1914

2461 E. Forge, C. Asprey and G. Bowie, *Built at Eastleigh: an illustratrd list of steam locomotives built or rebuilt 1910–1961.* (Southampton, Kingfisher, 1985) 40p.

2462 G.L. Gettins, 'The Exmoor Mineral Railway', *Exmoor Rev.* 1967 36–7

2463 R. Gregory, *The South Devon Railway.* (Trowbridge, Oakwood Press, 1982) 128p.

2464 J. Hallett, *Around Princetown's quarries: the Tyrwhitt Railway Trail from Princetown.* (Newton Abbot, Orchard Publications, 1994)

2465 H. Harris, *The Haytor Granite Tramway and Stover Canal: a guide to retracing the route of Dartmoor's Granite from quarry to sea.* (Peninsular Press, 1994) 63p.

A similar title appears in *Tamar J.* no. 17 1995 27–30

2466 W.B. Harris, *When the railways came to Plymouth: an address delivered to the Exeter University Symposium on Railways, March 1970.*

Typescript. Copy in Plymouth Central Library.

2467 E. Hemery, *Walking the Dartmoor railroads.* (Newton Abbot, David & Charles, 1983) 144p.

2468 H.L. Hopwood, 'An early Devonshire tramroad', *Rlwy. Mag.* XLII 1918 181–2

2469 G.L. Huxley, 'By rail through the Exe Valley', *Rlwy. Mag.* June 1951

2470 S.C. Jenkins and L.J. Pomroy, *The Moretonhampstead and South Devon Railway.* (Oxford, Oakwood Press, 1989) 120p.

2471 H.G. Kendall and R.J. Sellick, *The Plymouth and Dartmoor Railway and its forerunners.* (Lingfield, Oakwood Press, 1969) 100p.

2472 A.R. Kingdom, *The Ashburton Branch (and the Totnes Quay Line).* (Oxford, Oxford Publishing Co., 1977) 152p.

2473 A.H. Kingdom, *The Plymouth, Tavistock and Launceston Railway.* (Newton Ferrers, ARK, 1990) 244p.

2474 A.R. Kingdom, *The Yelverton to Princetown Railway.* ([No place], Forest Publishing, 1991) 160p.

A reprint of *The Princetown Branch*

2475 C.E. Lee, 'The Haytor granite tramroad', *Trans. Newcomen Soc.* XXXV 1962–3 237–41

2476 Sir Roper Lethbridge, 'The Bideford and Okehampton Railway of 1831', *Rep. Trans. Devons. Assoc.* XXXIV 1902 168–200

2477 C.A. Lewis, 'Tyrwhitt's North Devon wharf', *Devon Cornwall N. & Q.* XXXV no. 7 1985 256–7

A correction to H.G. Kendall, *The Plymouth & Dartmoor Railway* (1968), J. Hall *Railway landmarks in Devon* (1982) and E. Hemery, *Walking the Dartmoor railroads* (1983)

2478 R. Madge, *Railways round Exmoor.* (Dulverton, Exmoor Press, 1971)

2479 C.G. Maggs, *The Barnstaple and Ilfracombe Railway.* 2nd ed. (Oxford, Oakwood Press, 1988) 80p.

2480 C.G. Maggs, *Branch lines of Devon: Exeter and south, central and east Devon* (Stroud, Alan Sutton, 1995) 146p.

Lavishly illustrated

2481 C.G. Maggs, *Branch lines of Devon: Plymouth, west and north Devon.* (Stroud, Alan Sutton, 1995) 146p.

Lavishly illustrated

2482 C.G. Maggs, *Railway centres: Exeter.* (London, Ian Allan, 1985) 128p.

2483 C.G. Maggs, *Railways to Exmouth.* (Tarrant Hinton, Oakwood Press, 1980) 64p.

2484 C.G. Maggs, *Taunton and Barnstaple line: Devon and Somerset Railway.* (Tarrant Hinton, Oakwood Press, 1980) 59p.

2485 C.G. Maggs, *Taunton steam.* (Bath, Millstream, 1991) 160p.

2486 M. Messenger, *The Culm Valley Light Railway.* (Truro, Twelveheads Press, 1993) 96p.

2487 V. Mitchell, *Branch lines to Exmouth.* (Midhurst, Middleton, 1992) 96p.

2488 V. Mitchell, *Branch lines to Torrington.* (Midhurst, Middleton, 1994)

2489 J. Nicholas, *Lines to Torrington.* (Poole, Oxford Publishing Co., 1984) 192p.

2490 J. Nicholas, *The North Devon line: the Exeter to Barnstaple Railway from inception to the present day.* (Yeovil, Oxford Publishing Co., 1992) 190p.

2492 J. Owen, *The Exe Valley railway.* (Southampton, Kingfisher, 1985) 192p.

The Exeter–Dulverton line and Tiverton Junction branch.

2493 K.S. Perkins, 'Early steampower links with Devonport and Torpoint', *Devon Histn.* no. 33 1986 20–7

2494 J.R. Pike, *Iron horse to the sea: railways in South Devon.* (Bradford-on-Avon, Ex Libris, 1987) 158p.

2495 J.R. Pike, 'Railways in South Devon', *Devon Histn.* no. 31 Oct. 1985 30–2

A chronology

2496 L.W. Pomeroy, *The Teign Valley Line.* (Poole, Oxford Publishing Co., 1984) 36p.

2497 C.R. Potts, *The Brixham branch.* (Oxford, Oakwood Press, c. 1986) 95p.

2498 C.R. Potts, *Railways in and around Newton Abbot and Torbay.* (Stockport, Foxline, 1993) 108p.

2499 J.D.C.A. Prideaux, *The Lynton & Barnstaple Railway remembered.* (Newton

Abbot, David & Charles, 1989) 95p.

2500 H. Rake, 'The London and South-Western Railway's route to Plymouth', *Rlwy. Mag.* XV 1904 56–63, 131–5, 221–5

2501 H. Rake, 'The South Devon Railway. (A railway by the sea)', *Rlwy. Mag.* XI 1902 225–35

2502 K. Robertson, *Devon and Cornwall railways in old photographs.* (Gloucester, Sutton, 1989) 144p.

2503 T.W.E. Roche, *Go Great Western: reminiscences of the G.W.R. main line and branches in Devon.* (West Country Handbooks, 8, 1966)

2504 R.J. Sellick, 'A railway 'Ghost' on Exmoor', *J. Rlwy. Canal Hist. Soc.* XXVIII no. 9 1986 394–9

On the track of an unfinished railway to serve mineral interests on Exmoor

2505 H. Shapcote, 'Recollections of the broad gauge line to Plymouth (England)', *Rlwy. Loco. Hist. Soc. Bull.* XVI 1928 50–60

2506 M. Smith, *The railways of Devon.* (Shepperton, Ian Allan, 1993) 128p.

2507 D. Stuckey, *The Bideford, Westward Ho! and Appledore Railway, 1901–1917.* 2nd ed. (West Country Publications, 1965) 19p.

2508 V. Thompson, *Back along the lines—North Devon railways.* 2nd ed. (Bideford, Badger Books, 1992) 60p.

2509 K. Williams and D. Reynolds, *The Kingsbridge Branch (and the Totnes Quarry Line).* (Oxford, Oxford Publishing Co., 1977) 248p.

2510 B.Y. Williams and C.E. Lee, 'The Plymouth and Dartmoor Railway', *Rlwy. Mag.* Mar. 1934

Roads and Road Transport

See also nos. 499–512

2511 P.C. Anderson and J.M. Anderson, *Quicksilver: a hundred years of coaching, 1750–1850.* (Melbourne, Wren, 1973) 223p.

2512 A. Bates, *Directory of the stage-coach services.* (1896)

Copy in Torquay Central Library

2513 J.J. Beckerlegge, 'Plymouth transport in recent years', *Reps. Trans. Devons. Assoc.* LXXX 1948 177–85

Covers the years 1916–48

2514 D. Brewer, *The Tavistock–Ashburton packhorse track and its guide stones.* (Author, 1991) 48p.

2515 S.W. Brown, 'The medieval Larkbeare bridge, Exeter', *Proc. Devon Archaeol. Soc.* XXXIX 1981 155–8

2516 W. Buckingham, *A turnpike key, or an account of the proceedings of the Exeter turnpike trustees, 1750–1884, with notes.* (1885)

Copies in Exeter Central Library and Exeter University Library.

2517 E.P. Burd, 'Okehampton turnpikes', *Reps. Trans. Devons. Assoc.* 1936 LXVIII 307–23

2518 R. Burnard, 'The great central trackway—Dartmoor', *Reps. Trans. Devons. Assoc.* XXI 1889 431–6

2519 R. Burnard, 'The pack-horse on Dartmoor', *Reps. Trans. Devons. Assoc.* XXXVII 1905 168–74

2520 D. Drake, 'South Molton turnpike roads', *Devon Cornwall N. & Q.* XXII no. 8 1943 188–90

2521 D. Drake, 'The turnpike road from South Molton to Combe Martin', *Devon Cornwall N. & Q.* XXII no. 4 1942 117–19

2522 B. Evans, 'William Stephens of Exeter (1784–1840) coachmaster', *Reps. Trans. Devons. Assoc.* CXII 1980 175–83

2523 A.B. George, 'Highway engineering achievements, Exeter Turnpike Trust 1820–1835', *Devon Histn.* no. 45 1992 3–9

2524 B. George, 'Highway engineering in Devon, 1810–1840', *Panel Hist. Engng. Works Newl.* no. 49 1991

2525 J. Green, *A report on the alteration and improvement of the turnpike road between Exeter and Plymouth through Chudleigh and Ashburton.* (1819) Copy in Exeter Public Library

2526 G.B. Grundy, 'Ancient highways of Devon', *Archaeol. J.* XCVIII 1941 131–64

2527 Rev. Hawker, 'Changes in travelling on the road between Exeter and Plymouth during the last sixty years', *Reps. Trans. Devon Assoc.* XVII 1885 450–7

2528 M. Hawkins, *Devon roads: an illustrated survey of the development and management of Devon's highway network.* (Exeter, Devon Books, 1988) 240p.

2529 L.B. Hutchings, 'Roads in the South Hams, 1760–1840', *Devon Histn.* no. 18 1979 24–9

2530 T.J. Joce, 'The earliest southern way from Exeter', *Rep. Trans. Devons. Assoc.* LIX 1927 271–7

2531 T.J. Joce, 'The Exeter and Dartmouth Road', *Reps. Trans. Devons. Assoc.* XLIV 1912 597–604

2532 T.J. Joce, 'Exeter roads and streets', *Reps. Trans. Devons. Assoc.* LXXV 1943 121–33

2533 T.J. Joce, 'The original main road west of Exeter', *Reps. Trans. Devons. Assoc.* L 1918 411–16

2534 J. Kanefsky, *Devon tollhouses.* (Exeter Industrial Archaeology Group, 1976) 30p.

2535 J. Kanefsky, 'Railway competition and turnpike roads in East Devon', *Reps. Trans. Devons. Assoc.* CIX 1977 59–72

2536 M. Lowe, 'Archival sources for road improvement in 18th-century Devon', *Archives* XX 1992 99–103

2537 M.C. Lowe, 'The Crediton and Chudleigh Turnpike Trust: a mystery', *Devon Cornwall N. & Q.* XXXVI Part X Autumn 1991 369–70

2538 M.C. Lowe, 'The Exeter Turnpike Trust, 1753–1884', *Reps. Trans. Devons. Assoc.* CXXVII 1995 163–88

2539 M.C. Lowe, 'Toll houses of the Exeter Turnpike Trust', *Reps. Trans. Devons. Assoc.* CXXIV 1992 87–99

2540 M.C. Lowe, 'The Totnes North End Turnpike Trust', *Devon Histn.* no. 36 1988 22–7

2541 M.C. Lowe, 'The turnpike trusts in Devon and their roads, 1753–1889', *Reps. Trans. Devons. Assoc.* CXXII 1990 47–70

2542 M.C. Lowe, *Turnpikes and tollgates: a study of the Totnes and Bridgetown Pomeroy turnpike trust, 1759–1881*. (Totnes, Community Archive, 1987) 51p.

2543 M.C. Lowe, 'An unfortunate speculation: the Sidmouth and Cullompton Turnpike Trust', *Devon Histn.* no. 38 1989 16–19

2544 J. Ogilby, *The road from Bristol ... to Exeter: map*. (1671)

Copy in the Devon and Exeter Institution, Exeter

2545 J.B. Perkin, *Exeter and Taunton tramways*. (Midhurst, Middleton, 1994)

2546 J.R. Pike, 'Roads in South Devon', *Devon Histn.* no. 31 Oct. 1985 29–30

2547 PSV Circle, *A history of the Devon General Omnibus and Touring Company, Ltd; jointly compiled by the PSV Circle and the Omnibus Society*. (Shepperton, Ian Allan, 1966) 112p.

2548 *Plymouth tramways: prospectus makers and the public: the Plymouth Tramways case*. (London, J. Cawston & Sons, n.d. [1890])

Copy in Exeter Central Library.

2549 C. Raikes, *Portraits of Devon tollhouses*. (Exeter Industrial Archaeology Group, 1978) 28p.

2550 W.H. Rogers, 'Barnstaple Turnpike Trust', *Reps. Trans. Devons. Assoc.* LXXIV 1942 139–67

2551 R.C. Sambourne, *Exeter: a century of public transport*. (Falmouth, Glasney Press, 1976) 104p.

2552 R.C. Sambourne, *Plymouth: 100 years of street travel*. (Falmouth, Glasney Press, 1972) 104p.

2553 G. Sheldon, *From trackway to turnpike: an illustration from east Devon*. (London, Humphrey Milford, 1928) 178p.

2554 F.H. Starkey and M.H. Meredew, 'The highways of Ilsington', *Devon Cornwall N. & Q*. XXXIV 1980 203–8 and 240–4

2555 H.H. Walker, 'The petition for the making of the Torbay Road, 1836', *Reps. Trans. Devons. Assoc.* XCV 1963 208–18

2556 G. Wilson, 'Public hire chairs in Exeter', *Devon Cornwall N. & Q*. XXXVI 265–9 and 314–24

Bridges

2557 J. Brierley, 'The medieval Exe bridge', *Proc. Instn. Civil Engrs.* Part 1 LXVI 1979 127–39

2558 S.W. Brown, 'The medieval bridge and St Gabriel's Chapel, Bishop's Clyst', *Proc. Devon Archaeol. Soc.* XL 1982 163–9

2559 S. Brown, 'The medieval Larkbeare Bridge, Exeter', *Proc. Devon Archaeol. Soc.* XXXIX 1981 155–8

2560 A.G. Duncan, 'The long bridge of Bideford', *Rep. Trans. Devons. Assoc.* XXXIV 1902 221–64

2561 A.B. George, 'Thorverton Bridge', *Devon Histn.* no. 36 April 1988 28–9

2562 C.G. Henderson and E. Jervoise, *Old Devon bridges*. (Exeter, Wheaton, 1938)

96p.

2563 W.R. Hooper, *Great Torrington's ancient bridges. Notes on their history ...* (*Bideford and North Devon Weekly Gazette*, 1928) 13 leaves

2564 A.T. Markwick, 'Brannon's bridge at Axmouth', *Proc. Devon Archaeol. Soc.* no. 46 1988 153–6

2565 B.W. Oliver, 'The long bridge of Barnstaple. Part 1', *Rep. Trans. Devons. Assoc.* LXX 1938 193–7; 'Part 2', LXXVIII 1946 177–91

2566 G.O. Peard, *A brief history of Bideford bridge.* (Bideford, Coles & Lee, n.d.) 23p.

2567 K.S. Perkins, 'Iron men of Shropshire come to Laira', *Devon Histn.* no. 42 1991 15–19

James Rendel and the building of the Laira bridge.

2568 K.S. Perkins, 'Lord Morley's flying bridge', *Devon Histn.* no. 41 1990 15–20

A form of temporary bridge

2569 K.S. Perkins, 'Opening up South Devon—the Hopkins Connection', *Devon Histn.* no. 45 1992 9–18

2570 K.S. Perkins, 'The Puffing Giant: origins of the Dartmouth floating bridge', *Devon Histn.* no. 30 1985 4–8

2571 K.S. Perkins, 'Rendel's hydraulic drawbridge at Bowcombe Creek', *Devon Histn.* no. 32 1986 15–21

2572 K.S. Perkins, 'Samuel Brown's plan to bridge the Tamar', *Devon Histn.* no. 43 1991 9–14

2573 D.L.B. Thomas, 'Bridges on the Teign rivers', *Reps. Trans. Devons. Assoc.* CXXIX 1997 145–83

2574 D.L.B. Thomas, 'The chronology of Devon's bridges', *Reps. Trans. Devons. Assoc.* CXXIV 1992 175–206

2575 D.L.B. Thomas, 'Devon bridge names', *Devon Histn.* no. 42 1991 9–14

2576 D.L.B. Thomas, 'Fenny Bridges in Fenton and Gittisham', *Devon Histn.* no. 50 4–9

2577 D.L.B. Thomas, 'St Saviour's bridge in Ottery St Mary', *Devon Histn.* no. 47 1993 7–12

2578 D.L.B. Thomas, 'Teignbridge in Teignrace', *Devon Histn.* no. 52 1996 3–11

The remains of one of the oldest masonary bridges in the British Isles

2579 H. Tolson, *Exeter and its bridges.* (Exeter, Devon & Exeter Printing and Publishing Co., n.d.) 15p.

2580 C.E. Welch, 'The iron bridge at Plymouth;', *Reps. Trans. Devons. Assoc.* XCVIII 1966 370–84

2581 F.E. Whiting, 'Bideford bridge', *Reps. Trans. Devons. Assoc.* LXXX 1948 127–36

2582 D. Woolner and A. Woolner, 'Teignbridge and the Haldon Road', *Reps. Trans. Devons. Assoc.* LXXXVI 1954 211–7

'Supplement' XCI 1959 149–51

Ports, Harbours and Shipping

See also no. 1845

2583 F. Argau, 'Sailing barges of the Fal Estuary', *Mar. Mirr.* LXIV 1978 163–8

2584 M. Bouquet, 'The north Devon polaccas', *Mar. Mirr.* XLIX 1963 120–7

2585 J.J. Bourhis, *Le trafic du port de Dartmouth 1599–1641.* (1972)
Copy in Exeter University Library

2586 V.C. Boyle, 'The Bideford polackers', *Mar. Mirr.* XVIII 1932 109–24
A type of sailing ship.

2587 V.C. Boyle and D. Payne, *Devon harbours.* (London, Christopher Johnson, 1952) 224p.

2588 J.B. Bradbeer, 'Barnstaple: a decayed port', *J. Portsmouth Poly. Ind. Archaeol. Soc.* no. 3 1970 10–19

2589 L.E. Braddick, 'The port of Topsham—its ships and shipbuilding', *Reps. Trans. Devons. Assoc.* LXXXV 1953 18–34

2590 P.W. Broughton, *The Wenbury Docks and Railway Proposal of 1909.* (Plymouth, Wenbury Local History Society, 1995) 16p.
A bill for a new dock with railway, rejected by the House of Lords

2591 E.A.G. Clark, *The estuarine ports of the Exe and the Teign, with special reference to the period 1660–1880: a study in historical geography.* (Ph.D. thesis, London University (External), 1957)

2592 E.A.G. Clark, *The ports of the Exe estuary 1660–1860: a study in historical geography.* (University of Exeter, 1960) 247p.

2593 E.A.G. Clark, 'The ports of the Exe estuary, 1701–1972', *in The new maritime history of Devon* v. 2 68–77 (see no. 2598)

2594 J.R.W. Coxhead, 'Axmouth Haven: East Devon's lost harbour', *Devon Cornwall N. & Q.* XXXII 1972

2595 R. Craig, B. Greenhill, J.H. Porter, W.J. Slade, 'Some aspects of the business of Devon shipping in the nineteenth century', *in The new maritime history of Devon* v. 2 99–107 (see no. 2598)

2596 R. Craig, 'Steamship enterprise in Devon, 1852–1920', *in The new maritime history of Devon* v. 2 91–8 (see no. 2598)

2597 E.R. Delderfield, *The Exmouth Docks Company: 100 years of progress and history, 1865–1965.* (1965)

2598 M. Duffy, S. Fisher, B. Greenhill, D. Starkey and J. Youings eds., *The new maritime history of Devon: 1. From early times to the late eighteenth century.* (London, Conway Maritime Press and the University of Exeter, 1992); *2. From the late eighteenth century to the present day* (Conway Maritime Press and University of Exeter, 1994) 2v.

2599 S.E. Ellacott, *Braunton ships and seamen.* (South Molton, Quest (Western) Publications, 1980) 72p.

2600 G.E. Farr, *Ships and harbours of Exmoor.* (The Exmoor Press, 1970) 48p.

2601 G.E. Farr, *The ship registers of the port of Hayle, 1864–1882 compiled ... by Grahame Farr* (London, Trustees of the National Maritime Museum, 1975, Maritime Monographs and Reports no. 20) 143p.

2602 S. Fisher, 'Devon's maritime trade and shipping, 1680–1780', *in The new maritime history of Devon* v. 1 232–41 (see no. 2598)

2603 I. Friel, 'Devon shipping from the Middle Ages to *c*. 1600', *in The new maritime history of Devon* v. 1 73–8 (see no. 2598)

2604 R. Gallup, 'Weir Quay and Holes Hole', *Tamar J.* no. 13 1991 23–34
    The main port for Bere Alston

2605 R. Golding, 'A maritime history of Sidmouth and East Devon', *Marit. S-W* no. 8 1995 101–27

2606 A. Grant, 'Devon shipping, trade and ports, 1600–1689', *in The new maritime history of Devon* v. 1 130–8 (see no. 2598)

2607 A. Grant, 'The North Devon Shipping Company, 1851–1864', *Mar. Mirr.* LVII no. 1 1971 3–16

2608 A. Grant, 'Some Barnstaple sailing ships of the mid-nineteenth century', *Reps. Trans. Devons. Assoc.* CIII 1971 133–45

2609 T. Gray, 'The Duke of Buckingham's survey of South Devon mariners and shipping, 1619', *in The new maritime history of Devon* v. 1 117–18 (see no. 2598)

2610 M.G. Gray, *The history of the port of Millbay: a communications project on the development of Millbay Docks; etc.* (1971)
    Copy in Plymouth Central Library

2611 B. Greenhill and M. Nix, 'North Devon shipping, trade and ports, 1786–1939', *in The new maritime history of Devon* v. 2 48–59 (see no. 2598)

2612 B. Greenhill, 'Towards a new maritime history of Devon', *Reps. Trans. Devons. Assoc.* CXVI 1984 1–12

2613 C.W.S. Hartley, 'Sir Charles Hartley and the improvement of Sutton Harbour in the 1840s', *Reps. Trans. Devons. Assoc.* CXV 1983 133–62

2614 C. Henderson, 'The archaeology of Exeter quay', *Devon Archaeol.* IV 1991 1–15

2615 J.E. Horsley, 'Shipping of the port of Dartmouth in the 19th century', *in* H.E.S. Fisher, ed., *The South-West and the Sea: papers of a seminar on the maritime history of the South-West of England.* (Exeter University, Exeter Papers in Economic History no. 1, 1968) 44–55

2616 M. Jones, 'Two Exeter ship agreements of 1303 and 1310', *Mar. Mirr.* LIII no. 4 1967

2617 P.Q. Karkeek, Notes on the early history of Dartmouth with special reference to its commerce, shipping and seamen in the fourteenth century', *Reps. Trans. Devons. Assoc.* XII 1880 572–90

2618 P.Q. Karkeek, 'The shipping and commerce of Dartmouth in the reign of Richard II', *Reps. Trans. Devons. Assoc.* XIII 1881 186–90

2619 A. Kittridge, *Plymouth: ocean liner port-of-call.* (Truro, Twelveheads Press, 1993) 120p.

2620 M. Kowaleski, 'The port towns of fourteenth-century Devon', *in The new maritime history of Devon* v. 1 62–72 (see no. 2598)

2621 *The local customs accounts of the port of Exeter, 1266–1321.* (Exeter, Devon & Cornwall Record Society, n.s. v. 36, 1993) 243p.

2622 F.A. Mace, 'Devonshire ports in the fourteenth and fifteenth centuries', *Trans. R. Hist. Soc.* 4th ser. VIII 1925

2623 M. Martin, 'Changes to the waterfront of Dartmouth 1000 to 1970', *Mar. Mirr.*LXVI 1980 129–36

2624 I.D. Merry, *The Westcotts and their times*. (Greenwich, National Maritime Museum, 1977) 147p.

Plymouth shipowners *c*. 1870–1938

2625 V.F.L. Millard, 'Plymouth and its ships', *Mar. Mirr.* XXXII 1946 105–14

2626 B. Moseley, *Shipping on the River Dart*. 2nd ed. (Plymouth, B.S. Moseley, 1969) 20p.

2627 M. Murch, D. Murch and L. Fairweather, *Sail and steam in Salcombe Harbour*. (Plymouth, Westaway Publications, *c*. 1987) 40p.

2628 J. Naish, 'Joseph Whidbey and the building of the Plymouth breakwater', *Mar. Mirr.* LXXVIII 1992 37–56

2629 M. Nix, *A maritime history of the ports of Bideford and Barnstaple, 1786–1841*. (Ph.D. thesis, Leicester University, 1991)

2630 M. Nix and M.R. Myers, *Hartland Quay: the story of a vanished port*. (Hartland Quay Museum) 48p.

2631 M.M. Oppenheim, *The maritime history of Devon*. (Exeter, University Press, 1968) 175p.

2632 A. Patrick, 'Coasting vessels at Morwellham in the eighteenth century', *Tamar J.* no. 3 1980–81 7–11

2633 A. Patrick, *The evolution of Morwellham: a Tamar River port*. (M.Phil. thesis, Council for National Academic Awards, 1980)

2634 A. Patrick, 'The growth and decline of Morwellham', *Reps. Trans. Devons. Assoc.* CVI 1974 95–117

2635 A. Patrick, *Morwhellham quay, a history: a Tamar Valley mining quay, 1140–1900*. (Morwhellham Quay Museum Publication no. 13, 1990) 99p.

2636 T. Pawlyn, 'Shipping of the port of Penzance', *in* S. Fisher, *ed., British shipping and seamen, 1630–1960: some studies*. (Exeter University, Exeter Papers in Economic History, no. 16, 1984)

2637 K.S. Perkins, 'Early steampower links Devonpoint and Torpoint', *Devon Histn.* no. 33 1986 20–7

2638 J.R. Pike, *Tall ships in Torbay: a brief maritime history*. (Bradford-on-Avon, Ex Libris, 1986) 142p.

2639 M. Porter, 'Devon's port industry since 1914', *in The new maritime history of Devon* v. 2 235–42 (see no. 2598)

2640 A. Pye, 'Bideford town quay', *Proc. Devon Archaeol. Soc.* no. 50 1992 117–24

2641 P. Russell, 'The building of the New Quay at Dartmouth, 1584–1640', *Reps. Trans. Devons. Assoc.* LXXXII 1950 281–90

2642 P. Russell, *Dartmouth: a history of the port and town*. (London, Batsford, 1950) 184p

2643 A.H. Shorter and E.T. Woodley, 'Plymouth: port and city', *Geography* XXII no. 118 1937 293–306

2644 C.B.M. Sillick, *The city-port of Plymouth*. (Ph.D. thesis, London University, 1938)

2645 W.J. Slade, *Out of Appledore: the autobiography of a coasting shipmaster and shipowner in the last days of wooden sailing ships*. 4th ed. (London, Conway Maritime, 1980)

2646 D.J. Starkey, ed., *Devon's coastline and coastal waters: aspects of man's relationship with the sea*. (Exeter, Exeter University Publications, Exeter Maritime Studies no. 3, c. 1988) 85p.

2647 D.J. Starkey, 'The ports, seaborne trade and shipping industry of South Devon, 1786–1914', *in The new maritime history of Devon* v. 2 32–47 (see no. 2598)

2648 D. Starkey, ed., *Sources for a new maritime history of Devon*. (Exeter, University, Maritime History of Devon Project, c. 1987) 111p.

2649 W.B. Stephens, 'The trade of the port of Barnstaple at the end of the Civil War', *Devon Cornwall N. & Q.* XXXI 1969 167–71

2650 H.J. Trump, 'The Port of Teignmouth and the Teignmouth Harbour Commission 1836–1932', *Maritime Hist.* IV 1974 49–64

2651 H.J. Trump, *Teignmouth: a maritime history*. 2nd ed. (Chichester, Phillimore, 1986) 140p.

2652 H.J. Trump, *Westcountry harbour, the Port of Teignmouth, 1690–1975*. (Teignmouth, Brunswick Press, 1976) 204p.

2653 H.H. Walker, 'Livermead Harbour, Torquay', *Reps. Trans. Devons. Assoc.* XCIX 1967 287–8

2654 H.M. Whitley, 'The maritime trade of Exeter in mediaeval times', *Reps. Trans. Devons. Assoc.* XLIV 1912 530–46

2655 J. Youings and P.W. Cornford, 'Seafaring and maritime trade in sixteenth-century Devon', *in The new maritime history of Devon* v. 1 98–107 (see no. 2598)

Air Transport

2656 G. Worrall, *Exeter Airport in peace and war: a pictorial history*. (Exeter, Devon Books, 1988) 45p.

OTHER INDUSTRIES

2657 E. Besly, 'The Exeter Mint 1643–1646', *Proc. Devon Archaeol. Soc.* no. 50 1992 91–115

2658 S.R. Blaylock, 'Bell and cauldron founding in Exeter', *Hist. Metall.* XXX no. 2 1996 72–82

2659 S.E. Ellacott, *Golden hammer: the history of Garton & King Ltd, incorporating Taylor and Bodley (Exeter) Ltd, 1661–1961*. (1961)

2660 H. Harris, 'A Dartmoor ochre works', *Devon Histn.* no. 43 1991

2661 H. Harris, 'The Sourton Tors Iceworks, north-west Dartmoor, 1874–86', *Reps. Trans. Devons. Assoc.* CXX 1988 177–200

2662 J. Havill, *Eleanor Coade: artificial stone manufacturer, born Exeter 1733 and died London 1821*. (Exeter, J. Havill, 1986) 106p

2663 J. Hayward, 'The Channon family of Exeter and London, chair and cabinet makers', *Victoria and Albert Museum Bull.* II no. 2 1966

2664 J.W. Perkins, 'The Crabtree Limeworks', *Devon Cornwall N. & Q.* XXXI no. 7 1970 199–203

2665 D. Warren, 'Industries associated with the woodlands around Exmoor. Part 1', *Somerset Ind. Archaeol. Soc. Bull.* no. 64 Dec. 1993 5–13

Timber, charcoal and oak bark for tanning.

2666 Wrigley Company Ltd, *Illustrated record of the new Wrigley's factory at Estover, Plymouth, Sept. 30, 1968.*

Copy in Plymouth Central Library.

Dorset

GENERAL

See also no. 555

2667 R. Legg, *Purbeck's heath: claypits, nature and the oilfield.* (Dorset Pub. Co., 1987) 143p.

2668 E.F. J. Mathews, *Economic history of Poole, 1756–1815.* (Ph.D. thesis, London University (External), 1958)

2669 J.V.N. Soane, *The significance of the development of Bournemouth, c. 1840–1940.* (Ph.D. thesis, Surrey University, 1977)

2670 P. Stanier, Dorset's industrial heritage. (Truro, Twelveheads Press, 1989) 47p.

2671 W.B. Stephens, 'The trade fortunes of Poole, Weymouth and Lyme Regis, 1600–40', *Proc. Dorset Nat. Hist. Archaeol. Soc.* XCV 1973 71–3

2672 F.C. Warren, 'Dorset industries of the past', *Proc. Dorset Nat. Hist. Archaeol. Soc.* LIX 1937 32–46

AGRICULTURE

2673 J.R. Baker, 'Tithe rent-charges and the measurement of agricultural production in mid nineteenth-century England and Wales', *Agric. Hist. Rev.* XLI no. 2 1993 169–75

Tithe surveys of Dorset were used.

2674 K. Beales, *The development of steam ploughing techniques in Dorset.* (M.Sc. thesis, Bath University, 1982)

2675 J.H. Bettey, *Agriculture and rural society in Dorset, 1570–1670.* (Ph.D. thesis, Bristol University, 1977)

2676 J.H. Bettey, 'The agriculture and stone industry of the Island of Portland at the beginning of the 19th century', *Proc. Dorset Nat. Hist. Archaeol. Soc.* 1970 XCII 244–9

2677 J.H. Bettey, 'Agriculture of Dorset 1665', *Somerset Dorset N. & Q.* XXX 1975 124

2678 J.H. Bettey, 'Crop returns of 1801 for some Dorset parishes', *Somerset Dorset N. & Q.* XXIX 1970 101

2679 J.H. Bettey, 'The development of the water meadows in Dorset during the seventeenth century', *Agric. Hist. Rev.* XXV 1977 37–43

2680 J.H. Bettey, 'Drovers and the movement of livestock in the seventeenth century', *Somerset Dorset N. & Q.* XXXI 1981 159–61

2681 J.H. Bettey and D.S. Wilde, 'The probate inventories of Dorset farmers 1573–1670', *Loc. Histn.* XII 1977 228–34

2682 J.H. Bettey, 'Land tenure and manorial customs in Dorset, 1570–1670', *S. Hist.* IV 33–54

2683 J.H. Bettey, 'The marketing of agricultural produce in Dorset during the seventeenth century', *Proc. Dorset Nat. Hist. Archaeol. Soc.* XCIX 1977 1–5

2684 J.H. Bettey, 'The revolts over the enclosure of the Royal Forest at Gillingham, 1626–30', *Proc. Dorset Nat. Hist. Archaeol. Soc.* XCVII 1976 21–4

2685 J.H. Bettey, 'Sheep enclosures and watermeadows in Dorset agriculture in the sixteenth and seventeenth century', *in* M. Havinden *ed., Husbandry and marketing in the South-West, 1500–1800*. (Univ. of Exeter, Exeter Papers in Economic History no. 8 1975, 1973)

2686 J.H. Bettey, 'Sheep farming in Dorset during the seventeenth century', *Proc. Dorset Nat. Hist. Archaeol. Soc.* CII 1980 1–5

2687 C.G.S. Bowie, 'Watermeadows in Wessex: a re-evaluation for the period 1640–1850', *Agric. Hist. Rev.* XXXV 1987 151–8

2688 J. Claridge, *General view of the agriculture of Dorset*. (London, 1793)

2689 E.B. Clarke, *Economic changes in the manor of Cranborne (Dorset) in the sixteenth and seventeenth centuries*. (B.Litt. thesis, Oxford University, 1939)

2690 J.S. Cox, 'Cyder making in Dorset in 1815', *Somerset Dorset N. & Q.* XXVIII 1961 28–32

2691 P.J. Dillon, *Agriculture and environment in the Wessex chalklands: the Rawlences, farmers and land agents c. 1810–1901*. (Ph.D. thesis, Exeter University, 1990)

2692 J.P. Dodd, 'Dorset agriculture 1880–1854', *Proc. Dorset Nat. Hist. Archaeol. Soc.* CII 1980 7–13

2693 C.D. Drew, 'Open arable fields at Portland and elsewhere', *Antiquity* XXII no. 86 1948 79–81

Reprinted in *Proc. Dorset Nat. Hist. Archaeol. Soc.* LXIX 1947 51–3

2694 M.J.D.Edgar, 'Occupational diversity in seven rural parishes in Dorset, 1851', *Loc. Pop. Stud.* LII 1994 48–52

2695 G.B. Endacott, *The progress of enclosures in the county of Dorset since 1700*. (B.Litt. thesis, Oxford University, 1938)

2696 J.M.J. Fletcher, 'Dorset vineyards', *Somerset Dorset N. & Q.* XXIII no. 204 1940 105–7

2697 G.E. Fussell, 'A Dorset expert on water meadows: methods at the end of the 18th century', *Dorset County J.* I no. 7 1948 185–6

2698 G.E. Fussell, 'Four centuries of farming in Dorset, 1500–1900', *Proc. Dorset Nat. Hist. Archaeol. Soc.* LXXIII 1951 116–40

2699 G.E. Fussell, 'Land reclamation a century ago: fifteen years work on Durweston common', *Dorset County J.* I no. 5 1947 129–30

2700 G.E. Fussell, 'Red Devon cattle in Dorset', *Dorset County J.* I no. 6 1947 146, 165

2701 P. Horn, 'The Dorset dairy system', *Agric. Hist. Rev.* XXVI 1978 100–7

2702 J.W. Hull, 'Seventy years of farming', *Agriculture* LIV no. 7 1947 302–4

Notes on Dorset farming since the 1870s.

2703 B.W. Ilbery, 'Dorset agriculture: a classification of regional types', *Inst. Br. Geogr. Trans. Pap.* n.s. VI 1981 214–27

2704 J.F. James and J.H. Bettey, *eds., Farming in Dorset: diary of James Warne, 1758; letters of George Boswell, 1787–1805*. (Dorset Record Soc., vol. 13, 1993) 180p.

2705 M.D. Jones, 'Field names in Cerne Abbas and the open-field system', *Proc. Dorset Nat. Hist. Archaeol. Soc.* LXIV 1942 109–74

2706 I. Keil, 'Farming on the Dorset estates of Glastonbury Abbey in the early fourteenth century', *Proc. Dorset Nat. Hist. Archaeol. Soc.* LXXXVII 1965 234–50

2707 B. Kerr, 'The colonization of rural Britain: Sir Robert Edgcumbe and his settlement in Dorset', *Proc. Dorset Nat. Hist. Archaeol. Soc.* XCVIII 1976 25–31

2708 B. Kerr, 'The Dorset agricultural labourer, 1750–1850', *Proc. Dorset Nat. Hist. Archaeol. Soc.* LXXXIV 1962 158–77

2709 B. Kerr, 'Dorset field names and the Agricultural Revolution', *Proc. Dorset Nat. Hist. Archaeol. Soc.* LXXXII 1960 133–42

2710 R. Lavender, *The farmers of Winkton Tithing, 1855–75*. (Dorchester, Dorset County Council, Education Committee, 1977) 15p.

2711 W.E. Minchinton, 'Agriculture in Dorset during the Napoleonic Wars', *Proc. Dorset Nat. Hist. Archaeol. Soc.* LXXVII 1955 162–73

2712 G.E. Mingay, 'The diary of James Warne, 1758', *Agric. Hist. Rev.* XXXVIII 1990 72–8

Warne farmed near Wool.

2713 P.J.A. Perry, 'A note on agricultural trade at Poole and Weymouth, 1815–1914', *Proc. Dorset Nat. Hist. Archaeol. Soc.* XCVII 1976 35–6

2714 P.J.A. Perry and R.J. Johnston, 'The temporal and space incidence of agricultural depression in Dorset, 1868–1902', *J. Interdisc. Hist.* III 1972 297–311

2715 B. Reynolds, *Late medieval Dorset: three essays in historical geography.* (M.A. thesis, London University, 1958)

2716 M.S. Ross, 'Water meadows on the River Stirchel, Dorset', *Proc. Dorset Nat. Hist. Archaeol. Soc.* CXVI 1994 27–32

2717 L.H. Ruegg, 'On the farming of Dorset', *J. R. Agric. Soc.* XV 1854 389–454

2718 T. Squire, 'An eighteenth-century farm inventory', *Somerset Dorset N. & Q.* XXV no. 236 1848 93–4

Of John Iles of Buckland Newton, Dorset, 1734.

2719 W. Stevenson, *General view of the agriculture of Dorset.* (London, 1815)

2720 L.E. Tavener, 'Changes in the agricultural geography of Dorset, 1922–49', *Inst. Br. Geogr. Trans. Pap.* 1952 93–106

2721 L.E. Tavener, 'Dorset farming, 1900–50', *Proc. Dorset Nat. Hist. Archaeol. Soc.* LXXV 1953 91–114

2722 C.C. Taylor, 'Medieval and later fields and field shapes in Dorset', *Proc. Dorset Nat. Hist. Archaeol. Soc.* XC 1969 249–57

2723 F.C. Warren, 'Long continuance of the common-field system: Sutton Waldron', *Proc. Dorset Nat. Hist. Archaeol. Soc.* LXIV 1942 75–83

2724 J. Whitehead, 'The management and land-use of water meadows in the Frome Valley, Dorset', *Proc. Dorset Nat. Hist. Archaeol. Soc.* LXXXIX 1968 257–81

2725 R. Whitlock, *Dorset farming.* (Dovecote Press, 1982) 56p.

2726 J.D. Wilson, 'The medieval deer parks of Dorset. XV', *Proc. Dorset Nat. Hist. Archaeol. Soc.* 1976 6–10

ARCHITECTURE AND BUILDINGS
General

2727 G. Drury, 'The use of Purbeck marble in Medieval times', *Proc. Dorset Nat. Hist. Archaeol. Soc.* LXX 1948 74–98

2728 J. Thomas, 'The building stones of Dorset, Part 1', *Proc. Dorset Nat. Hist. Archaeol. Soc.* CXIV 1992 161–8

Domestic

2729 R. Machin, *The houses of Yetminster*. (University of Bristol, Dept. of Extra-Mural Studies, 1978) 172p.

A study of surviving farmhouses in north Dorset.

Industrial

2730 J. Addison and R. Wailes, 'Dorset watermills', *Trans. Newcomen Soc.* XXXV 1962–3 193–216

'Addendum to Dorset water-mills', *Trans. Newcomen Soc.* XXXVI 1963–4 175–81

'Second addendum to Dorset windmills', *Trans. Newcomen Soc.* XLI 1968–9 139–62

2731 M. Boddy and J. West, 'The Portland breakwaters: a Victorian achievement', *Ind. Archaeol.* XVI 1981 238–54

2732 M. Bone, 'Dorset windmills' *Somerset Dorset N. & Q.* XXXI Mar 1980 11–18; XXXIII part 341 Mar. 1995 360–2

2733 S. Bridges and M. Papworth, 'Hogford Mill, Pamphill', *Proc. Dorset Nat. Hist. Archaeol. Soc.* CXIV 1992 234–7

2734 G.M. Dear, *From watermill to waterworks at Christchurch*. (Bournemouth, Bournemouth Local Studies Publications, 1978) 46p.

2735 H.S.L. Dewar, 'Windmills, watermills and horsemills of Dorset', *Proc. Dorset Nat. Hist. Archaeol. Soc.* LXXXII 1961 109–32; LXXXVI 1964 179–81

2736 A.H. Graham and R. Soames, 'The Old Malthouse, Abbotsbury, Dorset: the medieval watermill of the Benedictine abbey', *Proc. Dorset Nat. Hist. Archaeol. Soc.* CVIII 1987 103–25

2737 R. Hodges, 'Excavations at Daw's Mill', *Proc. Dorset Nat. Hist. Archaeol. Soc.* XCVI 1974 19–44

2738 J.F. James, 'Dorset water mills', *Somerset Dorset N. & Q.* XXX 1979 419–20

2739 H.E.S. Simmons, *Watermills of Dorset*. 1977. 2v.

Volumes in the Simmons Collection relating to British windmills and watermills. A photocopy of the original typescript folders is available in the Science Museum Library, London.

2740 H.E.S. Simmons, *Windmills of Dorset*. 1977.

Part of the volume *The windmills of Devon, Dorset and Durham* in the Simmons Collection relating to British windmills and watermills. A photocopy of the original typescript folders is available in the Science Museum Library, London.

2741 'Watermills on the Kingston Lacy Estate, Dorset', *Ind. Archaeol. Rev.* XVIII no. 1 1995 106–16

Hogford Mill by Martin Papworth; White Mill, Shapwick by Nancy Grace, Martin Watts and Philip Brebner

BREWING

2742 H. Janes, *Hall & Woodhouse 1777–1977: independent family brewers.* (London, Henry Melland Ltd, 1977) 80p.

2743 J. Seekings, *Thomas Hardy's brewer: the story of Eldridge, Pope & Co.* (Dovecote, 1988) 128p.

2744 J. Young, *Old Dorset breweries.* (Rochester Press, 1982)

BRICKMAKING

2745 M.S. Ross, 'Brickmaking at Gillingham and Motcombe in Dorset', *Proc. Dorset Nat. Hist. Archaeol. Soc.* CXIII 1991 17–22

2746 D. Young, 'Brickmaking at Broadmayne', *Proc. Dorset Nat. Hist. Arch. Soc.* LXXXIX 1967 318–24

2747 D. Young, 'Brickmaking at Weymouth, Dorset', *Ind. Archaeol.* IX 1972 188–96

2748 D. Young, 'Brickmaking in Dorset', *Proc. Dorset Nat. Hist. Archaeol. Soc.* XCIII 1971 213–42

BUILDING

2749 C. Hercock, *A history of Burt & Vick Ltd, Poole.* (Poole, Local History Publication, no. 2 1980) 24p.

A building firm.

2750 *The Home of Willis, 1904–1954.* (The Firm, 1954) 22p.

A building firm.

CLOCK AND WATCHMAKING

2751 R.G. Barklot, 'Dorset clocks and clockmakers', *Proc. Dorset Nat. Hist. Field Club* XLVIII 1927 86–102

2752 T. Tribe, *comp., Dorset clock and watchmakers.* (Sturminster Newton, Dorset, The Compiler, 1970) 12p.

2753 A. White, *The chain makers: a history of the watch fusee chain industry.* (Christchurch, The Author, 1967) 38p.

An industry centred on Christchurch for the production of fusee chains, used in watchmaking.

ENGINEERING

2754 A.J. Cooksey, 'The Wren & Hopkinson horizontal cross compound engine, *c.* 1870', *Ind. Archaeol.* VII 1970 165–70

At J.J. Sydenham, Poole, Dorset

2755 E. Course, 'The Rolt Memorial Lecture, 1994: Engineering in rural areas', *Ind. Archaeol. Rev.* XVIII no. 2 1996 151–64

Includes case-studies in Hampshire and Dorset

2756 R. Wear and E. Lees, *Stephen Lewin and the Poole Foundry.* (London, Industrial Railway Society, 1978) 101p.

2757 R.A. Whitehead, *A century of service: an illustrated history of Eddison Plant Hire Limited.* (Eddison Plant, 1968) 50p.

The firm started business in Dorset in 1870.

FISHERIES

2758 H.J.S. Clark, 'The salmon fishery and weir at Wareham', *Proc. Dorset Nat. Hist. Archaeol. Soc.* LXXII 1950 99–110

LIMEBURNING

2759 P.H. Stanier, 'Dorset limekilns: a first survey', *Proc. Dorset Nat. Hist. Archaeol. Soc.* CXV 1993 33–49

2760 P.H. Stanier, 'More Dorset limekilns', *Proc. Dorset Nat. Hist. Archaeol. Soc.* CXVII 1995 91–4

QUARRYING

2761 E. Benfield, *Purbeck shop: a stoneworker's story of stone.* (Cambridge, University Press, 1940) 186p.

Reprinted by Ensign Publications, 1990

2762 W.P. Hunter, 'Rough notes made during a visit to the freestone quarries of the Isle of Portland, on Wednesday, August 25, 1825', *Mag. Nat. Hist.* IX 1836 97–101

2763 R. Leach, *An investigation into the use of Purbeck marble in medieval England.* 2nd ed. (Crediton, Privately published, 1978) 86p.

2764 M. McGarvie, 'Purbeck quarries in 1893', *Somerset Dorset N. & Q.* XXXIV Mar 1996 37–40

2765 J. Phillips, 'Quarr houses on the Isle of Purbeck, Dorset', *Mining Hist.* XIII no.

2 1996 155–62

Quarr sheds are associated with the Purbeck limestone industry

2766 L. Popplewell, *Ironstone canyon: the Hengistbury Head Mining Company*. (Bournemouth, Melledgen, 1986) 40p.

A similar title in *Dorset Yrbk.* 1985 42–9

2767 D. Pushman, *Precious stone of Dorset*. (Sherborne, Dorset Publishing Co., 1987) 128p.

2768 R.J. Saville, *Ancient order of Purbeck marblers and stonecutters. Articles of agreement transcribed and annotated* ... (Langton Matravers Local History and Preservation Society, Booklet no. 10, 1973) 16p.

2769 R.J. Saville, ed., *A Langton quarryman's apprentice 1826–1837. James Corben's autobiography*. (Langton Matravers, n.d.) 64p.

2770 R.J. Saville, *The stone quarries of Langton Matravers*. 2nd ed. (Langton Matravers Local History and Preservation Society, Booklet no. 15, 1986) 48p.

2771 *South Western Stone Co. Ltd, Portland stone*. (The Company, 1933) 40p.

2772 P. Stanier, 'The quarried face: evidence from Dorset's cliffstone quarries', *Mining Hist.* XIII no. 2 1996 1–9

2773 A.M. Wallis, 'The Portland stone quarries', *Proc. Dorset Field Club* XII 1891 187–94

2774 J. Walton, 'The English stone-slater's craft', *Folk Life* XIII 1975 38–53

POSTS AND COMMUNICATIONS

2775 A.J.A. Cooksey, *The development of communications in the Dorset area*. (Dorset County Council, Education Committee, available from The Teachers' Centre, 40, Lowther Road, Bournemouth) 9 parts

Part III. *Waggon mail and stage coaches in Dorset*.

Part VI. *Electric telegraph in Dorset*. (Booklet no. 608, 1974) 18p.

Part VII. *The coming of the telephone to the Dorset area*. (Booklet no. 609, 1974) 31p.

Part VIII. *Wireless telegraphy in Dorset*. (Booklet no. 610, 1975) 12p.

2776 J.A. Young, *An outline of postal services in Bournemouth, 1839–1899*. (Dorchester, Dorset County Council, Education Committee, 1977) 17p.

POTTERY AND CERAMICS

2777 D. Algar, A. Light and P. Treherne, *The Verwood & District Potteries. A Dorset industry*. (C.J. Newsome & Associates, 1979) 45p.

2778 J.E. Acland, 'Note on early clay tobacco pipes', *Proc. Dorset Nat. Hist. Field Club* XLVII 1926 lvii–lviii

2779 D.R. Atkinson, 'Clay tobacco pipes found in Shaftesbury', *Proc. Dorset Nat. Hist. Archaeol. Soc.* XCI 1970 206–15

2780 Carter, Stabler and Adams, *Poole pottery; with an introductory note by Joseph*

Thorp. (Poole, Careter, Stabler and Adams, 192–) 16p.

2781 A.J.A. Cooksey, 'Jennings South Western Pottery, Parkstone: a preliminary survey report', *Ind. Archaeol.* VI 1969 164–71

2782 A.J.A. Cooksey, *The Poole clay tobacco pipes*. (Bournemouth, Bournemouth Local Studies Publications, 1980) 22p.

2783 A.J.A. Cooksey, 'Tobacco-pipe makers of Poole', *Somerset Dorset N. & Q.* XXX no. 229 1974 28–30

2784 P. Copland-Griffiths and C. Butterworth, 'Excavation of the 17th-century kiln at Horton, Dorset', *Proc. Dorset Nat. Hist. Archaeol. Soc.* CXII 1991 23–32

2785 G.J. Davies, 'Tobacco-pipe-clay in Poole's coastal trade', *Somerset Dorset N. & Q.* XXXI Sept. 1982 235–8

2786 J. Draper, 'An 18th-century kiln at Hole Common, Lyme Regis, Dorset', *Proc. Dorset Archaeol. Nat. Hist. Soc.* CIV 1982 137–42

2787 J. Draper, 'Inventory of Ann Shergold, ceramic dealer in Blandford, Dorset', *Post-Med. Archaeol.* XVI 1982 85–92

2788 J. Hawkins, *The Poole potteries*. (London, Barrie & Jenkins, 1980) 224p.

2789 J.P.M. Latham, 'Dorset clay to Staffordshire pot', *Trans. Eng. Ceram. Circ.* X no. 2 1977 109–17

2790 Pike & Fayle Ltd, *Clay mines of Dorset, worked by Pike Bros. and Fayle & Co. Ltd of Wareham 1760–1960*. (Harley Pub. Co. Ltd, 1960) 30p.

2791 P. Spoerry and V. Hart, 'Documentary and other evidence for medieval and post-medieval ceramic production in Dorset', *Proc. Dorset Nat. Hist. Archaeol. Soc.* CX 1988 29–35

2792 E. Watkins, 'Clay pipes found in Dorset', *Proc. Dorset Nat. Hist. Archaeol. Soc.* LXXXVIII 1966 216–33

2793 E. Watkins, 'Clay tobacco pipes of Bridport, Gleve', *Proc. Dorset Nat. Hist. Archaeol. Soc.* XCVI 1974 63–4

2794 D. Young, 'The Architectural Pottery', *Proc. Dorset Nat. Hist. Archaeol. Soc.* XCII 1970 212–13

ROPE MAKING

2795 J. Pahl, 'The rope and net industry of Bridport: some aspects of its history and geography', *Proc. Dorset Nat. Hist. Archaeol. Soc.* LXXXII 1961 143–54

SHIPBUILDING

2796 A.E. Cocksedge, *Bridport harbour: ships built 1769–1879*. (Bridport, Hindson & Partners, 1992) 228p.

2797 P. Ferguson, 'Shipbuilding at Bridport', *Marit. S-W* no. 5 1991 78–116

TEXTILES

2798 J.H. Bettey, 'Cloth production in Dorset 1570–1670', *Somerset Dorset N. & Q.* no. 315 Mar. 1982 209–11

2799 M. Bone, 'The Bridport flax and hemp industry', *BIAS J.* XVIII 1985 19–31

2800 M.R. Bone, 'Bridport textile industry, 1814–1945', *Somerset Dorset N. & Q.* XXXI 1981 141–54

2801 H.S.L. Dewar, 'Flax, hemp and their growers in West Dorset', *Proc. Dorset Nat. Hist. Archaeol. Soc.* XCI 1969 216–19

2802 P.P. Roberts, 'Richard Roberts, flax spinner', *Proc. Dorset Nat. Hist. Archaeol. Soc.* ICIX 1977 11–18

2803 J. Seymour, 'Bridport textile industry: a family view', *Somerset Dorset N & Q.* XXXIV Mar. 1996 31–36

2804 E.B. Short, 'The Bridport textile industry', *Somerset Dorset N. & Q.* XXXI Mar.1982 no. 315 205–9

2805 H. Symonds, 'The silk industry in Wessex. 1. The throwing mills at Sherborne and their owners; 2. Domestic economics in the 18th century', *Proc. Dorset Nat. Hist. Field Club* XXXVII 1916 66–93

TRANSPORT
Railways

2806 M.H.C. Baker, *The Waterloo to Weymouth line.* (Patrick Stephens, 1987) 200p.

2807 M.H.C. Baker, 'Whither Weymouth', *Rlwy. Mag.* CXIX 1973 436–9

2808 Dorset Archives Service, *Railway records in the Dorset Record Office.* (Dorset County Council, 1997) 65p.

2809 J. Draper, 'An early railway proposal for Dorset—Dorchester to Weymouth 1834', *Proc. Dorset Nat. Hist. Archaol. Soc.* CXVIII 1996 160–1

2810 W.E. Edwards, 'The Bridport Railway', *Rlwy. Mag.* XLVII 1920 241–4

2811 W.E. Edwards, 'Weymouth as a railway centre', *Rlwy. Mag.* XXII 1908 230–8, 396–403

2812 C. Howe, 'Railways in Gillingham', *Dorset Yrbk* 1985 75–8

2813 B.L. Jackson, *The Abbotsbury branch.* (Didcot, Wild Swan, 1989) 190p.

2814 R.W. Kidner, *The railways of Purbeck.* (Lingfield, Oakwood Press, 1973. Locomotion Papers, no. 68) 47p.

2815 G. Lanning, 'The Wool–Bovington Railway', *Somerset Dorset N. & Q.* XXXII Mar. 1988 679–82

2816 H.O. Lock, 'The first railway line to enter Dorset', *Somerset Dorset N. & Q.* XXVII no. 262 1956 65–8

The Southampton and Dorchester Railway.

2817 J.H. Lucking, *The Great Western at Weymouth: a railway and shipping history.* (Newton Abbot, David & Charles, 1971) 253p.

2818 J.H. Lucking, *Railways of Dorset: an outline of their establishment, development and progress from 1825.* (Lichfield, Railway Correspondence & Travel Society, 1969) 67p.

2819 J.H. Lucking, *The Weymouth Harbour tramway*. (Poole, Oxford Publishing, 1986) 128p.

2820 C.G. Maggs, *Branch lines of Dorset*. (Stroud, Sutton, 1996) 160p.

2821 V. Mitchell and K. Smith, *Branch line to Lyme Regis*. (Midhurst, Middleton Press, 1987) 96p.

2822 V. Mitchell and K. Smith, *Bournemouth to Weymouth* (Midhurst, Middleton Press, 1988) 96p.

2823 V. Mitchell and K. Smith, *Branch lines around Weymouth from Abbotsbury, Easton and the Quay*. (Midhurst, Middleton, 1989) 196p.

2824 V. Mitchell and K. Smith, *Branch lines around Wimborne*. (Midhurst, Middleton Press, 1992)

2825 L. Oppitz, *Dorset railways remembered*. (Newbury, Countryside Books, 1989) 112p.

2826 P.J. Perry, 'Sea coal and railway coal in Dorset', *Proc. Dorset Nat. Hist. Archaeol. Soc.* XCIII 1971 243–6

2827 L. Popplewell, *Bournemouth railway history: an exposure of Victorian engineering fraud*. (Sherborne, Dorset Publishing Co., 1974) 224p.

2828 A. Smith, 'A plan of the railway at Dorchester South', *Somerset Dorset N. & Q.* XXXIV Mar. 1998 174–5

2829 O.J. Smith, 'History of the London–Bournemouth train services', *Rlwy. Mag.* XXX 1912 323–7

2830 F.C. Warren, 'Early railway days in Dorset', *Proc. Dorset Nat. Hist. Archaeol. Soc.* LV 1933 77–85

2831 J.A. Young, *Main line to Bournemouth: 1885–88*. (Bournemouth Local Studies Publications, 1985) 36p.

2832 J.A. Young, *The nineteenth-century railways of Bournemouth and Christchurch*. (Bournemouth Local Studies Publications, no. 646, 1979) 40p.

2833 J.A. Young, *The Ringwood, Christchurch and Bournemouth Railway*. Rev. ed. (Bournemouth Local Studies Publications, no. 718, 1992) 38p.

Roads and Road Transport

2834 R.C. Anderson, *The history of the tramways of Bournemouth and Poole*. (Light Railway Transport League, 1964) 120p.

2835 D. Gerhold, 'A Dorset carrier in 1830', *Proc. Dorset Nat. Hist. Archaeol. Soc.* CXV 1993 29–32

2836 R.D. Good, *The old roads of Dorset*. 2nd ed. (Bournemouth, Horace G. Common, 1967)

First published 1940.

2837 J. Mawson, *Bournemouth Corporation transport*. (Advertiser Press, 1967) 276p. plus maps

2838 W.P. Meikle, 'Highway repairs in the 18th century', *Trans. Newcomen Soc.* XXI 1940–41 123–8

Concerns the parish of Langton, Long Blandford, Dorset.

2839 A.J. Miller, *Poole Turnpike Trust 1756–1882*. (Poole Teachers' Centre)

2840 C. Morris, *Hants. and Dorset: a history*. Rev. ed. (Croydon, DTS, *c.* 1996) 161p.

History of the Hants. & Dorset Motor Services Ltd.

2841 W.P. Ransom, *The story of Bournemouth Corporation transport*. (Bournemouth Local Studies Publications)

Part 1. *The trams*. (1982)

Part 2. *Trolleybus era*. (1982)

2842 R.T.C. Street, *Victorian high-wheelers: the early social life of the bicycle where Dorset meets Hampshire*. (Sherborne, Dorset Publishing Co., 1979) 60p.

2843 D. Viner, 'The Wimborne and Puddletown Turnpike Trust 1841–1878 and the toll-house at Athelhampton', *Proc. Dorset Nat. Hist. Archaeol. Soc.* CIV 1982 25–32

Bridges

2844 A.J. Wallis, *Dorset bridges*. (Sherbourne, Abbey Press, 1974) 96p.

Ports, Docks and Shipping

2845 D. Chalk, *Any more for the Skylark? The story of Bournemouth's pleasure boats: including a complete history of J. Bolson & Son Limited and Croson Limited*. (Bournemouth, The Author, 1980) 50p.

2846 G.J. Davies, 'Poole shipping in the eighteenth century', *Proc. Dorset Nat. Hist. Archaeol. Soc.* CXVI 1994 21–5

2847 G.J. Davies, 'Shipping in Weymouth, 1775–83', *Somerset Dorset N. & Q.* XXXI 1980 1–4

2848 G.W. Hannah, 'The evolution of Bridport harbour', *Proc. Dorset Nat. Hist. Archaeol. Soc.* CVIII 1986 27–31

2849 I. Horsey, 'Poole—the development of a medieval waterfront', *Marit. S-W* no. 4 1988 18–24

2850 R.C. Jarvis, 'Eighteenth-century Dorset shipping', *Proc. Dorset Nat. Hist. Archaeol. Soc.* XCII 1971 250–8

2851 D. Payne, *Dorset harbours*. (London, Christopher Johnson, 1953) 156p.

2852 P.J. Perry, 'Bridport harbour and the hemp and flax trade, 1815–1914', *Proc. Dorset Nat. Hist. Archaeol. Soc.* LXXXVI 1964 231–4

2853 P.J. Perry, 'The development of cross-Channel trade at Weymouth, 1794–1914: geographical and operational factors', *Transp. Hist.* II no. 3 1969 244–57

2854 P. Perry, 'The Dorset ports and the coming of the railways', *Mar. Mirr.* LIII 1967 243–9

2855 P.J. Perry, *A geographical study of the trade of the Dorset ports, 1815–1914*. (Ph.D. thesis, Cambridge University, 1963)

2856 R. Tittler, 'The vitality of an Elizabethan port: the economy of Poole, *c.* 1550–1600', *S. Hist.* VII 1985 95–118

2857 A. Tully, *Ferries of East Dorset*. (Bournemouth Local Studies Publication, 1981) 24p.

2858 W.B. Weinstock, 'Bridport shipping', *Somerset Dorset N. & Q* XXIX 1974

183–4

2859 D. Williamson, *The mariners of ancient Wessex: a brief maritime history of Central Southern England to the reign of King Henry VIII*. (Privately published, 1998) 148p.
Copy in Dorchester Local History Library

OTHER INDUSTRIES

2860 N. du Q. Bird, 'The goldsmiths of Dorset', *Somerset & Dorset N. & Q.* XXXIII Sept. 1993 235–60

2861 G.J. Davies, 'Dorset's trade in tobacco', *Somerset & Dorset N. & Q.* XXXI Mar. 1982 216–18

2862 J.P. Ferris, 'Alum at Kimmeridge', *Somerset & Dorset N. & Q.* XXIX 1969 81–5

2863 J.P. Ferris, 'The saltpetreman in Dorset 1635', *Proc. Dorset Nat. Hist. Archaeol. Soc.* LXXXV 1963 158–63

2864 F.E. Hansford, 'Eleanor Coade of Lyme Regis', *Dorset Yrbk.* LIV 1961 23–8
Development of artificial stone, 1708–96

2865 J.N. Hare, 'The growth of the roof tile industry in later medieval Wessex', *Med. Archaeol.* XXXV 1991 86–103

2866 L. Keen, 'Medieval salt-working in Dorset', *Proc. Dorset Nat. Hist. Archaeol. Soc.* CIX 1987 25–8

2867 D. Sherry, *Oil in Dorset.* 3rd ed. (Bournemouth Teachers' Centre, Bournemouth Local Studies Pubs. no. 641, 1981) 10p.

2868 A.H. Shorter, 'Paper mills in Dorset', *Somerset & Dorset N. & Q.* XXV no. 239 1948 114–18

2869 J.E. Skyrme, *A Casterbridge ironmonger: Thurmans of Dorchester, 1863–1966.* (Sutton Poyntz, Rowbotham, 1993) 53p.

Gloucestershire

GENERAL

2870 R. Anstis, *The industrial Teagues and the Forest of Dean*. (Gloucester, Alan Sutton, 1989) 204p.

2871 R. Beard, 'Changing patterns of employment in the Forest of Dean', *Geography* LVI no. 1 1971 43–6

2872 D.E. Bick, *The old industries of Dean*. (Newent, Pound House, 1980) 80p.

2873 D.E. Bick, *Old Leckhampton: quarries, railways, riots, Devil's Chimney*. 2nd ed. (Cheltenham, Runpast, 1996) 72p.

2874 A. Chatwin, 'Old industrial Tewkesbury', *GSIA J*. 1971 85–8

2875 *The Cotswolds: a new study, edited by Charles and Alice Mary Hadfield*. (Newton Abbot, David & Charles, 1973) 322p.

Chapters on farming and industry, transport and wool, woolmen and weavers.

2876 C. Cox, 'A walk up the Washbrook', *GSIA J*. 1984 39–42

2877 D. Evans, 'Gloucester's Civil War trades and industries 1642–46', *Trans. Bristol Glos. Archaeol. Soc*. CX 1992 137–47

2878 H.P.R. Finberg, *The Gloucestershire landscape*. (London, Hodder & Stoughton, 1975) 141p.

Originally published in 1955 entitled: *Gloucestershire: an illustrated essay on the history of the landscape*.

2879 Gloucestershire Community Council, Local History Committee, *I remember, the day's work in Gloucestershire villages, 1850–1950, compiled by M. Darvill*. (Gloucester, Gloucestershire Community Council, 1978) 44p.

2880 I.E. Gray, 'Some 17th-century token issuers', *Trans. Bristol Glos. Archaeol. Soc*. LXXXIV 1965 101–9

2881 C. Hart, *The Forest of Dean: new history 1500–1818*. (Stroud, Alan Sutton, 1995) 330p.

2882 C. Hart, *The industrial history of Dean: with an introduction to its industrial archaeology*. (Newton Abbot, David & Charles, 1971) 466p.

2883 *A guide to the industrial archaeology in Gloucestershire*. 3rd ed. (Gloucestershire Society for Industrial Archaeology and Association for Industrial Archaeology, 1992) 52p.

2884 *Industrial Gloucestershire* (Gloucester, Chance & Bland, 1904) 81p.

2885 P. Jump, 'The Cotswold countryside: an engineer's thoughts on the past and present', *Trans. Newcomen Soc*. XXXV 1962–3 225–36

2886 R.J. Mansfield, *Industrial sites in the Vale of Castiard*. (Gloucester, Community Council, 1974) 20p.

2887 G.N. Myatt, 'Industry in Cranham', *GSIA J*. 1980 49–50

2888 J. Nisbet, 'The history of the Forest of Dean, in Gloucestershire', *Eng. Hist. Rev*. XXI 1906 445–59

2889 K.J. Noyes, *Changes in the economic geography of the vale of Gloucester since the First World War*. (M.A. thesis, Manchester University, 1958)

2890 H.W. Paar, *An industrial tour of the Wye Valley and the Forest of Dean.* (West London Industrial Archaeology Society, 1980) 24p.

2891 P. Ripley, 'The economy of the City of Gloucester 1660–1740', *Trans. Bristol Glos. Archaeol. Soc.* XCVIII 1980 135–54

2892 P. Ripley, 'The trade and social structure of Gloucester 1600–1640', *Trans. Bristol Glos. Archaeol. Soc.* XCIV 1976 117–23

2893 P. Ripley, 'Village and town: occupation and wealth in the hinterland of Gloucester 1660–1700', *Agric. Hist. Rev.* XXXII 1984 170–8

2894 D.P. Rollison, *The intensification of community, society and economy in seventeenth- and eighteenth-century Gloucestershire (England).* (Ph.D. thesis, New South Wales University, 1982)

2895 R.L. Rose, 'The industrial history of Dudbridge', *GSIA Newsl.* no. 8 1966 25–40

2896 S. Rudder, 'A new history of Gloucestershire', *GSIA J.* 1972 42–7; 1973 34–40; 1974 41–50; 1975 66–71; 1976 13–16; 1977–78 40–3

Extracts dealing with industry from Rudder's *A New History of Gloucestershire* (1779)

2897 I. Standing and S. Coates, 'Historical sites of industrial importance on Forestry Commission land in Dean', *GSIA J.* 1979 16–20

2898 I. Standing, 'The industrial heritage of Bixhead and Bixslade in the Forest of Dean', *GSIA J.* 1987 17–32

2899 G. Stapleton, 'Industrial archaeology of Moreton-in-Marsh, Gloucestershire', *GSIA J.* 1977–78 25–9

2900 J.C. Stuttard, *The historical geography of the Forest of Dean during the 17th century.* (M.Sc. thesis, Cambridge University, 1941)

2901 H. Torrens, 'A forgotten book on early Gloucestershire patent history', *GIAS J.* 1983 17–23

An article on old time inventions

2902 D. Viner, 'Industrial archaeology in Gloucestershire', *in* A Saville, ed., *Archaeology in Gloucestershire: from the earliest hunters to the industrial age.* (Cheltenham, Cheltenham Art Gallery & Museum and Bristol & Gloucestershire Archaeological Society, 1984) 317–42

2903 L.F.J. Walrond, 'Industrial archaeology in the Stroud area', *Trans. Bristol Glos. Archaeol. Soc.* LXXXVI 1967 173–82

2904 J. Whitaker, *The Best: a history of H.H. Martyn & Co.* (Cheltenham, John Whitaker, 1985) 372p.

H.H. Martyn & Co., Cheltenham, 1888–1971. Architectural decorators and craftsmen in all materials. Includes a valuable chapter on the founding of the Gloster Aircraft Company, pp. 152–85.

2905 T.D. Whittet, 'Gloucestershire apothecaries' tokens and their issuers', *GSIA J.* 1985 21–8

2906 R. Wilson, 'The IA of Woodchester Park—an interim note', *GSIA J* 1994 27–32

2907 J.P. Wilton, 'Gloucester tokens of the seventeenth, eighteenth and nineteenth centuries', *Trans. Bristol Glos. Archaeol. Soc.* XIII 1888–9 130–45

2908 J.W. Wyatt, 'Some observations on industry in Gloucestershire, 1608', *Glos. Hist. Stud.* X 1979 12–19

2909 J.W. Wyatt, 'Trades and occupations in Gloucester, Tewkesbury and Cirencester in 1608', *Glos. Hist. Stud.* VII 1976 2–12

AGRICULTURE

See also no. 3020

2910 H.H. Albino, 'Clay draining. The craft of the old field drainer', *Glos. Countryside* V no. 4 1944 77–8

2911 J.R.L. Allen, 'A short history of salt-marsh reclamation at Slimbridge Warth and neighbouring areas, Gloucestershire', *Trans. Glos. Archaeol. Soc.* CIV 1986 139–55

2912 S.F. Baldock, 'The cider industry in Gloucestershire', *Glos. Hist. Stud.* III 1969 26–36

2913 S.F. Baldock, 'The development and decline of the cider industry with particular reference to Gloucestershire', *Glevensis* XIII 1979 13–17

2914 D. Barber, 'A rural ride through Gloucestershire farming country', *J. R. Agric. Soc.* CXXXIV 1973 57–65

2915 J. Bravender, 'On the farming of Gloucestershire', *J. R. Agric. Soc.* XI 1850 116–77

2916 D. Charnock, *Oldacre: a Gloucestershire family and business 1881–1986.* (Lewes, Book Guild, 1990) 320p.

Animal feed merchants

2917 E.M. Clifford, 'Working oxen at Cirencester', *Trans. Bristol Glos. Archaeol. Soc.* LXIII 1942 168–71

2918 R. Davis and others, 'The inclosure of Upton St Leonards', *Glos. Hist. Stud.* X 1979 64–79

2919 J.P. Dodd, 'Gloucestershire agriculture, 1801–54', *Trans. Bristol Glos. Archaeol. Soc.* XCVII 1980 101–16

2920 P.A. Franklin, *Thornbury Manor in the Age of the Black Death: peasant society, land-holding and agriculture in Gloucestershire 1328–1352.* (Ph.D. thesis, Birmingham University, 1982)

2921 G.E. Fussell, 'Hard times a century: a Gloucestershire farmer's position in 1833', *Glos. Countryside* VI no. 2 1947 39–40

Joseph Stallard of Red Marley

2922 I.A. Gray, 'A Gloucestershire postscript to the 'Domesday of Inclosures'', *Trans. Bristol Glos. Archaeol. Soc.* XCVII 1979 75–80

2923 G.B. Grundy, 'The ancient woodland of Gloucestershire', *Trans. Bristol Glos. Archaeol. Soc.* LVIII 1936 65–155

2924 C.E. Hart, *The history of the Forest of Dean as a timber producing forest.* (Ph.D. thesis, Leicester University, 1964)

2925 C.E. Hart, *Royal Forest: a history of Dean's woods as producers of timber.* (Clarendon Press, 1966) 367p.

2926 J.V. Garrett and T. Hodgkins, 'Stone built sheepwashes in Gloucestershire', *Glos. Hist.* 1995 11–14

2927 D. Hooke, 'Early Cotswold woodland', *J. Hist. Geog.* IV no. 1 1978 333–41

2928 *Inclosure in Gloucester.* (Gloucestershire County Record Office, 1976) 30p.

2929 W. Marshall, *The rural economy of Gloucestershire; including its dairy: together with the dairy management of North Wiltshire and the management of orchards and fruit liquor in Herefordshire.* 2nd ed. *(1796)* (Gloucester, Alan Sutton, 1979)

A reprint of the 1796 edition.

2930 C. Miller ed., *The account books of Thomas Smith, Ireley Farm, Hailes, Gloucestershire, 1865–1871.* (Bristol, Bristol & Gloucestershire Archaeological Society, 1985) 196p.

2931 C.A. Miller, *Farming, farm work and farm workers in Victorian Gloucestershire.* (Ph.D. thesis, Bristol University, 1980)

2932 C. Miller, 'The hidden workforce: female field workers in Gloucestershire 1870–1901', *S. Hist.* VI 1984 139–61

2933 C. Miller, 'The model farms of Victorian Gloucestershire', *Glos. Hist.* IV 1990 11–13

2934 W.E. Minchinton, 'Agriculture in Gloucestershire during the Napoleonic wars', *Trans. Bristol Glos. Archaeol. Soc.* LXVIII 1949 165–83

2935 C. Morris, *Dairy farming in Gloucestershire.* (Gloucester Folk Museum, 1983)

2936 C. Morris, *Farming in Gloucestershire c. 1800–1914.* (Gloucester Folk Museum, 1984) 75p.

2937 J.C. Morton, 'On the farming of Gloucestershire', *J. Bath & W. Eng. Soc.* XII 1864 1–24

2938 V.C. Nielsen, 'Cheese-making and cheese chambers in Gloucestershire', *Ind. Archaeol.* V 1968 162–70

The same author and title also appears in *Glos. Hist. Stud.* no. 1 1967 5–10

2939 C. Nielsen, 'The history and practice of cheese-making in Gloucestershire', *Glevensis* no. 29 1996 35–6

2940 J. Pearson, 'Farming in Oxenhall, 1755–1912', *Glos. Hist. Stud.* IV 1970 34–6

2941 T. Rudge, *General view of the agriculture of the County of Gloucester drawn up for the consideration of the Board of Agriculture* (1807)

2942 W.E. Tate, 'Gloucestershire enclosure acts and awards', *Trans. Bristol Glos. Archaeol. Soc.* LXIV 1943 1–70

2943 G. Turner, *General view of the agriculture of the county of Gloucester with observations on the means of its improvement, drawn up for consideration of the Board of Agriculture.* (1794)

2944 A.M. Urdank, 'The consumption of rental property: Gloucestershire plebians and the market economy, 1750–1860', *J. Interdisc. Hist.* XXI no. 2 1990 261–81

2945 C.E. Watson, 'Cheese-making in Gloucestershire Records of 600 years ago', *Glos Countryside* IV no. 3 1941 59–60

2946 G. Whittington, 'Strip lynchets in the Gloucestershire Cotswolds', *Trans. Bristol Glos. Archaeol. Soc.* LXXIX 1960 Part 2 212–20

2947 T. Wright, *The art of floating land as is practised in the county of Gloucester ... with particular examination of what Mr Boswell, Mr Davis, Mr Marshall and others have written on the subject: minute and plain directions are afterwards given for the formation of a floated meadow.* (London, 1799) 95p.

AMMUNITION

2948 B. Edwards, 'National Filling Factory no. 5, Quedgeley', GSIA J 1994 32–52
A shell filling factory, 1915–18

2949 B. Edwards, 'The Slimbridge Munitions depot', *GSIA J.* 1995 13–21

2950 R. Howes, 'Making ammunition in the English Civil War', *GSIA J.* 1992 37–9

2951 M.J. Walters, 'The gun and shot-founding industries in the Forest of Dean during the seventeenth century', *Dean Archaeol.* no. 4 1991 27–37

ARCHITECTURE AND BUILDINGS
General

2952 F. Derrick, *Cotswold stone.* (London, Chapman & Hall, 1948) 96p.

Domestic

2953 P. Ariss, 'The dovecotes of Gloucestershire', *J. Hist. Farm Bldgs. Gp.* VI 1992 3–34

2954 R.K. Howes, 'Farm buildings in the early nineteenth century', *Glos. Hist. Stud.* VI 1974–75 55–7

2955 A.J. Isherwood, 'Dock company housing, Sharpness, Gloucestershire', *GSIA J.* 1976 30–50

2956 T.R. Slater, 'The Cirencester Improved Dwellings Co., 1880–1914', *Bus. Archives* XL 1974 23–32

Also appears in A McWhirr ed., *Studies in the archaeology and history of Cirencester* (British Archaeology Reports, 30, 1976) 171–97

Industrial

See also no. 3131

2957 A. Adlard, *A short history of the Postlip Mill, Winchcombe.* (Evans, Adlard & Co., 1949) 31p.

2958 D.E. Bick, 'An atmospheric engine house in Gloucestershire', *GSIA Newsl.* no. 14 1970 14–16

2959 P. Borne, 'Brockworth Mill: Mill Lane, Brockworth Parish, Gloucester', *Glevensis* no. 15 1981 14–20

2960 B.V. Cave, 'Draught chimney at Fairplay Mine', *GSIA J.* 1980 3–6

2961 B.V. Cave, 'Mill sites on the Longhope–Flaxley–Westbury streams', *GSIA J.* 1974 9–31

2962 F.W.B. Charles and W. Horn, 'The cruck-built barn of Frocester Court farm,

Gloucestershire, England', *J. Soc. Archit. Histns.* XLII 1983 211–37

2963 A. Chatwin, 'Cheltenham Mills', *GSIA J.* 1993 3–15

2964 H. Conway-Jones, 'Flour milling in Gloucester', *Glos. Hist. Stud.* XII 1981 3–8

2965 A.H. Conway-Jones, 'The north warehouse at Gloucester docks', *Glevensis* no. 15 1981 6–9

2966 A.H. Conway-Jones, 'The warehouses at Gloucester Docks', *GSIA J.* 1977–8 13–19

2967 S.D. Coates and D.G. Tucker, *Water-mills of the Middle Wye Valley; the River Wye and its tributaries.* (Monmouth Museum, 1983)

2968 G.M. Davies, 'Mills of the Dean Forest Borders', *GSIA Newsl.* no. 14 1970 21–5

2969 G.M. Davies, 'Mills of the River Leadon and tributaries', *GSIA Newsl.* no. 7 1966 26–43

2970 G.M. Davies, 'Mills of the Severn Vale', *GSIA Newsl.* no. 10 1967 5–15

2971 J.M. Eastwood, 'Huntley Mill', *Glos. Hist. Stud.* XI 1980 50–5

2972 K.A. Falconer, 'Mills of the Stroud Valley', *Ind. Archaeol. Rev.* XVI 1993 62–81

2973 M.G. Fulford, 'A post-medieval mill at Woolaston', *Trans. Bristol Glos. Archaeol. Soc.* CX 1992 123–8

2974 J. Garrett, 'Coombend Bone Mill, Elkstone', *GSIA J.* 1986 21–2

2975 C. Haine, 'Skinner's Mill', *GSIA J.* 1986 26–8

2976 C. Haine, 'Wool drying stoves along the Painswick stream', *GSIA J.* 1981 30–1

2977 H. Lebherz, 'Schinkel and industrial architecture', *Archit. Rev.* CLXXXIV Aug. 1988 41–6

Including the influence on him of Stanley Mill, Gloucestershire

2978 R.A. Lewis, 'Whitminster Mills', *GSIA Newsl.* no. 12 1968 26–8

2979 'The malt house in Red Lane, Tewkesbury', *GSIA J.* 1972 39–41

2980 W.G. Medlam, 'Kilcott Mill', *GSIA J.* 1977–8 20–4

2981 W.G. Medlam, 'Kilcott Mill restored', *GSIA J.* 1981 3–8

2982 S. Mills and P. Riemer, *Gloucestershire mills in camera.* (Quotes, 1991) 80p.

2983 S. Mills and P. Riemer, *The mills of Gloucestershire.* (Barracuda Books, 1989) 160p.

2984 S. Mills, 'A note on Stowell Mill', *GSIA J* 1990 43–8

2985 S. Mills, 'An unrecorded mill site near Slad?', *GSIA J.* 1993 23–6

2986 E.A.L. Moir, 'The cloth mills of the Stroud Valley', *Hist. Today* IX 1959 319–25

2987 N.J.Moore, 'Arlington Row, Bibury, Gloucestershire: early conversion of an industrial building', *Vernac. Archit.* XXV 1994 20–4

2988 J.E.C. Peters, 'An unusual type of barn in north-east Gloucestershire', *Vernac. Archit.* XXVII 1996 25–7

2989 F. Richmond, 'Stoke Orchard Mill', *GSIA J.* 1979 39–49

2990 B.J. Roberts, 'Windmills in Gloucestershire', *Glos. Hist. Stud.* IV 1970 2–9

2991 H.E.S. Simmons, *Watermills of Gloucestershire.* 1977. 2v.

Volumes in the Simmons Collection relating to British windmills and watermills. A photocopy copy of the original typescript folders is available in the Science Museum Library, London.

2992 M. Stratton and B. Trinder, 'Stanley Mill, Gloucestershire', *Post-Med. Archaeol.* XXII 1988 143–80

2993 M. Stratton and B. Trinder, *Stanley Mill—an evaluation* (Institute of Industrial Archaeology, Research Paper no. 12, Mar. 1987)

2994 C. Swynnerton, 'The Priory Mill of Stanley St Leonard', *Trans. Bristol Glos. Archaeol. Soc.* XLVI 1924 145–7

2995 C. Swynnerton, 'The water-mill of the Abbots of Gloucester in Stonehouse', *Trans. Bristol Glos. Archaeol. Soc.* XLVI 1924 149–68

2996 J. Tann, 'Some problems of water power—a study of mill siting in Gloucestershire', *Trans. Bristol Glos. Archaeol. Soc.* LXXXIV 1965 53–77

2997 D. Vinter, 'A Gloucestershire bone mill', *Ind. Archaeol.* V 1968 72–81

2998 R. Walls, 'Langley's Mill, Cirencester', *Cirencester Archaeol. Hist. Soc. Ann. Rep.* no. 28 1986 4–17

2999 M. Westerling, 'Gloucestershire tithe barns', *Glos. Countryside* III no. 10 1940 540–2

3000 R. Wilson, 'Circular wool drying towers', *GSIA J.* 1989 32–5

3001 R. Wilson, 'Dunkirk Mills, Nailsworth: a new chapter', *GSIA J.* 1988 30–1; 'A progress report', *GSIA J.* 1989 36–8; 'Chapter Three', *GSIA J.* 1990 60–2; 'Dunkirk Mills, Nailsworth, in the doldrums', *GSIA J.* 1991 48–50;

BELL FOUNDING

3002 H.B. Walters, 'The Gloucestershire bell foundries. (I)', *Trans. Bristol Glos. Archaeol. Soc.* XXXIV 1911 110–19

3003 H.B. Walters, 'The Gloucestershire bell foundries. (II): The Bristol foundry', *Trans. Bristol Glos. Archaeol. Soc.* LI no. 1 1918 49–86

BREWING

3004 M.G. Jones, 'The malt house in Red Lane, Tewkesbury', *GSIA J.* 1972

3005 A. Chatwin, '39–40, High Street, Tewkesbury', *GSIA J.* 1980 7–17

A house used for brewing and hosiery manufacture.

3006 D. Viner, 'Tetbury brewery and Cirencester maltings', *GSIA J.* 1984 34–6

CLOCK AND WATCHMAKING

3007 F. Buckley and G.B. Buckley, 'Clock and watch makers of the 18th century in Gloucestershire and Bristol', *Trans. Bristol Glos. Archaeol. Soc.* LI 1929 305–19

3008 G. Dowler, *Gloucestershire clock and watch makers*. (Chichester, Phillimore,

1984) 230p.

ENGINEERING

3009 C. Bowen, 'A Gloucester engine in Scotland', *GSIA J.* 1981 72–3
See also *Ind. Archaeol Rev.* I 1976 19–27

3010 R.K. Close, 'A short history of Newman Hender & Co.', *GSIA J.* 1994 11–23
An engineering firm.

3011 S. Davies, 'Kells of Gloucester and Ross: agricultural implement makers', *Trans. Bristol & Glos. Archaeol. Soc.* XCIX 1981 157–66

3012 D.E. Evans, *Lister's: the first hundred years.* (Gloucester, Sutton Publishing, 1979) 256p.
Manufacturers of gas, petrol and diesel engines and other agricultural engineering products.

3013 N. Kingsley, 'Boulton and Watt engines supplied to Gloucestershire: a preliminary list', *GSIA J.* 1990 49–53

3014 C. Miller, 'The Gloucestershire Steam Plough Company 1860–2', *Trans. Bristol Glos. Archaeol. Soc.* XCIX 1981 141–56

3015 S. Mills, 'Fielding and Platt, an innovative Gloucester engineering company. The first 100 years, 1866–1966', *GSIA J.* 1992 8–17

3016 A. Pope, 'The Lightmoor Colliery winding engine', *GSIA J.* 1982 7–12

3017 E.G. Price, 'Whitelaw & Stirrat turbines at Frocester Court, Glos.', *Trans. Bristol Glos. Archaeol. Soc.* LXXXIX 1970 156–66

3018 H.A. Randall, 'Some mid-Gloucestershire engineers and inventors', *Trans. Newcomen Soc.* XXXVIII 1965–6 89–96

3019 R.L. Rose, 'Some textile machinery makers of Stroud', *GSIA Newsl.* no. 14 1970 3–13

3020 M. Thexton, *Steam thrashing in the Cotswolds: being an account of the history and operation of Blackwell's of Northleach, the steam thrashing contractors.* (London, Regency Press, 1986) 115p.

3021 T.G. Tucker, 'Power at Lower Redbrook on Wye in the early 19th century', *GSIA J.* 1971 59–66

3022 T. Youles, 'The Nailsworth engineers. Part 1. 1875 to the early twentieth century', *GSIA J.* 1989 22–31; 'Part 2', *GSIA J.* 1990 2–13

GLASS MAKING

3023 J.S. Daniels, 'The Huguenot glass house of Woodchester *c.* 1590–1615', *Proc. Huguenot Soc. London* XVIII no. 6 1952 464–72

3024 J.S. Daniels, *The Woodchester glasshouse: a record of the work of the Huguenot glass workers with descriptions of the glass produced at the Woodchester site.* (Gloucester, Bellows, 1950) 28p. 17 plates
Reprint of the 1900 edition.

3025 H. Penn, 'Glassmaking in Gloucestershire', *GSIA J.* 1983 3–16

3026 W. St. Clair Baddeley, 'A glass house at Nailsworth (16th and 17th century)', *Trans. Bristol Glos. Archaeol. Soc.* XLII 1920 89–95

3027 A. Vince, *Newent glasshouse: a late 16th-century and 17th-century glasshouse and late 17th- and 18th-century pottery.* (Committee for Rescue Archaeology in Avon, Gloucestershire and Somerset Occ. Pap. 2 1977)

GOLD

3028 C.E. Hart, 'Gold in Dean Forest', *Trans. Bristol Glos. Archaeol. Soc.* LXV 1944 98–104

3029 A.J.H. Sale, 'Goldsmiths of Gloucestershire, 1500–1800', *Trans. Bristol Glos. Archaeol. Soc.* CVIII 1990 135–70

IRON AND STEEL

3030 R. Anstis, *Man of Iron—Man of Steel: the lives of David and Robert Mushet.* (Coleford, Albion House, 1997) 216p.

3031 F.T. Baber, 'The historical geography of the iron industry in the Forest of Dean', *Geography* XXVII 1942 54–62

3032 D.E. Bick, 'Darkhill ironworks and the Mushet Family', *Glos. Hist. Stud.* IV 1970 60–3

The same author and a similar title appears in *GSIA J.* 1971 67–73

3033 D. Bick, 'Early iron production from the Forest of Dean and district', *Hist. Metall.* XXIV no. 1 1990 39–42

3034 D.E. Bick, 'A Mushet mystery', *GSIA J.* 1986 23–5

A Mushet mining operation in Wales.

3035 D.E. Bick, 'Remnants of Newent Furnace', *GSIA J.* 1980 19–37

3036 N.P. Bridgewater and G.R. Morton, 'Bromley Hill furnace, Oakwood, Forest of Dean', *Bull. Hist. Metall. Gp.* II no. 1 1968 43–6

3037 N.P. Bridgewater, 'Iron mining and working sites in and around the Forest of Dean', *Bull. Hist. Metall. Gp.* II no. 1 1968 27–32

3038 A. Chatwin, *Cheltenham's oramental ironwork.* 2nd ed. (The Author, Elston Boutique, 6–7 Montpellier Street, Cheltenham, 1984) 93p.

3039 I.Cohen, 'History of iron working in and near the Forest of Dean', *Trans. Woolhope Nat. Field Club* XXXIV 1954 161–77

3040 D. Court and I.J. Standing, 'A ventilation furnace on the Findall iron mine, Soudley, Forest of Dean', *GSIA J.* 1979 9–15

3041 T.G. Grey-Davies, 'A metallurgical history of the Valley of the Wye', *Metallurgia* LXXII 1965 153–8

3042 H.J. Ellis, 'Iron working at Flaxley Abbey', *GSIA J.* 1991 34–44

3043 C. Evans, 'Failure in a new technology: smelting iron with coke in South Gloucestershire in the 1770s', *Trans. Bristol Glos. Archaeol. Soc.* CIX 1991 199–206

3044 G. Hammersley, *The history of the iron industry in the Forest of Dean region, 1562–1660*. (Ph.D thesis, University of London, 1972)

3045 C.E. Hart, 'Charcoal burning in the Forest of Dean', *Bull. Hist. Metall. Gp.* II 1968 33–39

3046 C.E. Hart, 'A résumé of the history of the Forest of Dean's ironworking industries', *Bull. Hist. Metall. Gp.* II 1968 7–15

3047 R. Jenkins, 'Iron-making in the Forest of Dean', *Trans. Newcomen Soc.* VI 1925–6 42–65

3048 B.L.C. Johnson, 'New light on the iron industry of the Forest of Dean', *Trans. Bristol Glos. Archaeol. Soc.* LXXII 1953 129–43

3049 R.I. Kemp, 'A seventeenth-century royal forge in the Forest of Dean, Gloucestershire', *Post-Med. Archaeol.* XXI 1987 127–46

3050 R.F. Mushet, *Bessemer Mushet process or manufacture of cheap steel.* (Eindhoven, De Archaeologische Pers, 1984) 64p.

Originally published in 1883 by the author.

3051 R. Newman, 'The origins of the Cinderford coke iron furnace', *GSIA J*. 1982 12–16

3052 H.G. Nicholls, *Nicholls's Forest of Dean, edited by Cyril Hart*. (Newton Abbot, David & Charles, 1966) 402p.

A combined reprint of *The Forest of Dean* (1858) and *Iron making in the olden times in the Forest of Dean* (1866)

3053 F.M. Osborn, *The story of the Mushets*. (T. Nelson & Sons, 1951) 195p.

3054 R.J. Piggott, 'Some notes on the geology of the coal and iron deposits in the Forest of Dean', *Bull. Hist. Metall. Gp.* II no. 1 1968 16–26

3055 H. Powle, 'An account of the ironworks in the Forest of Dean', *Phil. Trans. R. Soc.* XII 1677–8 931–5

3056 B. Rendell and K. Childs, *Our industrial heritage: the tinplaters of Lydney and Lydbrook*. (Review Graphics, 1985) 86p.

3057 H.R. Schubert, 'The King's Ironworks in the Forest of Dean, 1612–1674', *J. Iron Steel Inst.* CLXXIII 1953 153–62

3058 R.A. Stiles, 'Elmbridge Furnace, Oxenhall: the economics of a Gloucestershire blast furnace in the seventeenth century', *Glos. Hist. Stud.* V 1972 2–11

3059 I. Standing, 'The Whitecliff Ironworks in the Forest of Dean', *GSIA J*. 1980 18–28; 'Dear Mushet: a history of Whitecliff Ironworks. Part Two 1808–1810', *GIAS. J*. 1981 32–71; 'Part Three', *GSIA J*. 1986 2–20

3060 D. Wainwright, *Men of steel: a history of Richard Thomas and his family.* (London, Quiller Press, 1986) 149p.

Richard Thomas & Baldwins, steel manufacturers.

3061 G. Wyrall, 'Observations on the iron cinders found in the Forest of Dean and its neighbourhood', *Trans. Bristol Glos. Archaeol. Soc.* II 1878 216–34

LEATHER AND FOOTWEAR

3062 C.R. Elrington, 'Records of the Cordwainers' Society of Tewkesbury,

1562–1941', *Trans. Bristol Glos. Archaeol. Soc.* LXXXV 1966 164–74

3063 S. Mills, 'Leonard Stanley Tannery: a preliminary report', *GSIA J.* 1991 2–12

LIMEBURNING

3064 D. Bick, 'Lime-kilns in North-West Gloucestershire', *GSIA J.* 1984 2–12

3065 D. Bick, 'Lime-kilns on the Gloucestershire–Herefordshire border', *Ind. Archaeol. Rev.* VII no. 1 1984 85–93

3066 G.L. Good, 'An 18th–19th-century limekiln at Water Lane, Temple, Bristol', *Bristol Avon Archaeol.* no. 6 1987 66–9

3067 M. Wilkinson, 'A field survey of lime-kilns in the Forest of Dean. Part I', *Dean Archaeol.* V 1992 37–49

MATCHMAKING

3068 P. Campion, 'The match industry in Gloucester', *GSIA J.* 1994 53–6

3069 P. Campion, *Matches from Gloucester: William Taylor and the other match makers of the island: a history of these match makers of the 1870s, including a chapter on Gloucester Fire Brigades.* (Cheltenham, P.J. Campion, c. 1986) 40p.

MINING AND QUARRYING

See also nos. 164–8

3070 M.V. Bent, *The last deep mine of Dean.* (Ruardean Hill, Glos., M.V. Bent, 1988) 173p.

3071 D. Bick, 'Early iron ore production in the Forest of Dean and district', *Hist. Metall.* XXIV no. 1 1990

3072 D.E. Bick, *The mines of Newent and Ross.* (Newent, Pound House, c. 1987) 88p.

3073 D.E. Bick, 'The Newent coalfield', *Glos. Hist. Stud.* V 1972 75–80

3074 D.E. Bick, 'Records of the Newent coalfield', *GSIA J.* 1979 1–8

3075 C.R. Bowen, 'Swallow holes and mine drainage in the Forest of Dean', *GSIA J.* 1991 17–27

The same title is also published in *Br. Mining* no. 43 1991 139–48

3076 C.R. Bowen, 'Wigpool Iron Mine, surface drainage', *GSIA J.* 1988 21–7

3077 'Celestine production in Gloucestershire', *Mine Quarry Engng.* XXVI 1960 362–73

3078 D. Court and I. Standing, 'A ventilation furnace on the Findall Iron Mine, Soudley, Forest of Dean', *GSIA J.* 1979 9–15

3079 C. Fisher, *Custom, work and market capitalism: the Forest of Dean colliers, 1788–1888.* (London, Croom Helm, 1981) 203p.

3080 W.H. Fryer, 'Notes on the iron ore mines of the Forest of Dean, and of the history of their working', *Trans. Bristol Glos. Archaeol. Soc.* XXIX 1906–7 311–16

3081 C.E. Hart, 'Coal ownership in the Forest of Dean', *Trans. Bristol Glos. Archaeol. Soc.* LXV 1944 220–1

3082 C. Hart, *The free miners of the Royal Forest of Dean and Hundred of St Briavels.* (Gloucester, British Publishing Co., 1953) 527p.

3083 D. Mullin, 'Some millstone quarry locations in the Forest of Dean', *New Regard* IV 1988 53–9

3084 R. Newman, 'Coal mining at Dymock', *GSIA J.* 1984 37–8

3085 A.G. Parker, *Dean Forest coalfield: a study in employment transition.* (M.Sc. thesis, University of Wales (UWIST), 1970)

3086 A. Price, 'Frank Simmonds recalls his quarrying and building career', *GSIA J.* 1995 3–12

3087 A.J. Price, 'Underground quarry workings at Quarry Wood, Sherborne Park, Gloucestershire', *GSIA J.* 1994 23–6

3088 R. Reece, 'Early medieval quarries at Ewen 1971–2'. *Trans. Bristol Glos. Archaeol. Soc.* XCIII 1974 131–5

3089 W. Smith, 'The Forest of Dean stone quarries', *Quarry* I 1890 191–2

3090 B. Smith, 'The origin of Newent coal mining', *GSIA J.* 1976 5–6

3091 I.J. Standing, 'The mining of coal in the Coleford District before 1850', *GSIA J.* 1980 38–48

PAPER MAKING

3092 B. Harley and R.T. Holmes, *Papermaking in Little Barrington* (Tolsey Museum, Tolsey Paper no. 7, 1996)

3093 F.J.T. Harris, 'Gunsmill as a paper mill', *GSIA J.* 1974 33–9

3094 F.J.T. Harris and J.L. Angel, 'A history of paper making in and near Winchcombe, Gloucestershire, England', *GSIA J.* 1975 9–65

3095 F.J.T. Harris, 'Paper and board mills in or near Gloucestershire', *Trans. Bristol Glos. Archaeol. Soc.* XCIII 1974 124–35

3096 A.H. Shorter, 'Paper mills in Gloucestershire', *Trans. Bristol Glos. Archaeol. Soc.* LXXI 1952 145–61

PIN MAKING

3097 J. Davies, *Pinmaking.* (Gloucester Folk Museum, 1979)

3098 S.R.H. Jones, 'Hall, English and Co. 1813–41: a study of entrepreneurial response in the Gloucester pin industry', *Bus. Hist.* XVIII no. 1 1976 35–65

3099 S. Mills, 'The Stroud pin makers', *GSIA J.* 1995 37–42

POTTERY AND CERAMICS

3100 S. Atkin, 'Clay tobacco pipes in Gloucester', *Glevensis* XXII 1988 42–6

3101 E.M. Jope, 'Regional character in West Country medieval pottery, illustrated from Gloucester, Brockworth and Bourton on the Water, with notes on the use of spectrographic analyses of medieval glazes', *Trans. Bristol Glos. Archaeol. Soc.* LXXI 1952 88–97

3102 A. Peacey, *Clay tobacco pipes in Gloucestershire*. (Bristol, Committee for Rescue Archaeology in Avon, Gloucestershire and Somerset, 1980) 34p.

3103 A. Vince, 'The medieval and post-medieval ceramic industry of the Malvern region: the study of a ware and its distribution' *in* D.P.S. Peacock, *ed., Pottery and early commerce: characterization and trade in Roman and later ceramics*. (London, Academic Press, 1977) 257–305

3104 I.C. Walker, 'Eight Gloucestershire pipe-makers', *Trans. Bristol Glos. Archaeol. Soc.* XCII 1973 139–44

POSTS AND COMMUNICATIONS

3105 G. Cole, 'Postal reforms and Gloucestershire's postal history', *Glos. Hist.* VII 1993 14–36

3106 P. Copeland, *Gloucester's postal history*. (Gloucester, P. Copeland, 1988) 77p.

3107 A. Dodd, *History of the telephone service in Gloucester 1887–1987*. (Gloucester, British Telecom, 1987) 62p.

PRINTING AND PUBLISHING

3108 R. Austin, 'Gloucester Journal, 1722–1922', *N. & Q.* ser. 12 X 1922 260–4, 283–5

3109 R. Austin, 'Robert Raikes, the elder, & the Gloucester Journal', *Library* ser. 3 VI 1915 1–24

3110 F.A. Hyett, 'Notes on the first Bristol and Gloucestershire printers', *Trans. Bristol Glos. Archaeol. Soc.* XX 1895–7 38–51

PUBLIC UTILITIES

3111 R. Acock, *Electricity comes to Cheltenham: a hundred years of light and power*. (Cheltenham, Glenside Press, 1995) 172p.

3112 A.W. Excell, 'Blockley and the electric light', *in* H.E.M. Icely, *Blockley through twelve centuries*. (Paradigm Press for Blockley Antiquarian Society, 1974) 217–19

'Blockley has a quite well-founded claim to be the first village to have electric light'.

3113 A. Chatwin, 'Early years of the Cheltenham Gas Light & Coke Company and the beginnings of the Tewkesbury Gas Light Company', *GSIA J.* 1972 10–35

3114 R.J. Lyon Smith, 'The lighting of Tewkesbury's streets', *Glos. Comm. Council*

Loc. Hist. Bull. no. 51 1985 9–11

3115 S. Mills, 'A note on some early water turbines and hydroelectric generating schemes: (with reference to Chatsworth House HEP scheme)', *GSIA J.* 1990 53–9

3116 'Water supply of the City of Gloucester', *Proc. Cotteswold Nat. Field Club* XVII pt. 3 1912

3117 R. Wilson, 'Early public electricity supply at Stroud', *GSIA J.* 1995 43–6

3118 R. Wilson, 'Electricity generation at Longford's Mill', *GSIA J.* 1992 18–26

3119 R. Wilson, 'Record of tidal outfall at Hill Pill', *GSIA J.* 1993 37–43

SHIP AND BOAT BUILDING

See also nos. 535, 541, 542, 547

3120 R. Barker, 'A Severn trow at Lydney, Glos.', *Wilkinson Stud.* I 1991 49–52

3121 R. Barker, 'The Lydney trow—1991', *Wilkinson Stud.* II 1992 93

3122 F.H. Harris, 'Lydney ships', *Trans. Bristol Glos. Archaeol. Soc.* LXVI 1947 238–45

17th-century shipbuilding in the Forest of Dean.

3123 A.M. Langford, 'Steamboat-builders of Brimscombe', *GSIA J.* 1987 33–41; 1988 3–20

A detailed history of the boatyards on the Thames and Severn Canal 1884–1931

3124 P.J. Stuckey, 'The Severn and its trows', *Marit. S-W.* no. 7 1994 133–9

TEXTILES

3125 E.M. Carus-Wilson, 'Evidences of industrial growth on some fifteenth-century manors', *Econ. Hist. Rev.* 2nd ser. XII 1959 190–205

Surveys the woollen industry of Castle Combe in Wiltshire and Stroudwater in Gloucestershire

Reprinted in E.M. Carus-Wilson, *Essays in economic history* v. 2 (London, Edward Arnold, 1962) 151–67

3126 A. Chatwin, 'Hampen flax mill', *GSIA J.* 1976 17–25

3127 *The cloth trade in Gloucestershire.* (Gloucester Record Office, 197–)

A teaching aid.

3128 H. Conway-Jones, 'The silk industry in the Chalford Valley', *Glos. Hist. Stud.* XI 1980 44–9

3129 T. Exell, *Brief history of the weavers of the County of Gloucester, being the substance of a letter, addressed to her Majesty's commissioner appointed to enquire into the condition of the hand-loom weavers.* (1838)

Copy in Gloucester Local History Library.

3130 S. Gonnsen and S. White, *A handbook of textile terms of the Stroud Valley.* (Stroud, Mid-Gloucester Technical College, 1988) 12p.

3131 C. Haine, 'The cloth trade along the Painswick Stream: from earliest times to 1700', *Glos. Hist. Stud.* X 1979 2–11; 'From 1700 to 1800', XI 1980 22–31; 'The nineteenth century', XII 1981 24–36; 'The cloth mills (part 1)', XIII 1982 3–18; 'Cloth mills along the Painswick Stream—mills near the centre of Painswick (Part II)', *GSIA J.* 1982 17–34; 'The cloth mills. Part III' *GSIA J.* 1983 24–37; 'Part IV', 1984 19–33; 'Part I'*(sic; recte* V) 1985 2–20

3132 I. Mackintosh, 'Exploring Stroud's origin—an introduction', *GSIA J.* 1984 13–18

3133 I. Mackintosh, 'Laying the foundation: Stroud in the 16th century', *GSIA J.* 1985 29–37

3134 I. Mackintosh, 'The metropolitan town of the clothing trade', *GSIA J.* 1986 29–40

3135 N.M. Marshall, *Blockley and the silk trade.* (Shipston on Stour, P. Drinkwater, 1979) 43p.

3136 S. Mills, 'Beards Mill and the mender's shop (Leonard Stanley)', *GSIA J.* 1991 28–33

3137 W.E. Minchinton, 'The beginnings of trade unionism in the Gloucestershire woollen industry', *Trans. Bristol Glos. Archaeol. Soc.* LXX 1951 126–41

3138 W.E. Minchinton, 'The petitions of the weavers and clothiers of Gloucestershire in 1756', *Trans. Bristol Glos. Archaeol. Soc.* LXXIII 1954 216–27

3139 E.A.L. Moir, 'The gentlemen clothiers: a study in the organization of the Gloucestershire cloth industry, 1750–1835', *in* H.P.R. Finberg, *ed., Gloucestershire studies.* (Leicester University Press, 1957) 225–66

3140 E.A.L. Moir, 'Marling & Evans, King's Stanley and Ebley Mills, Gloucestershire', *Text. Hist.* II no. 1 1971 28–56

3141 R. Perry, 'The Gloucestershire woollen industry, 1100–1690', *Trans. Bristol Glos. Archaeol. Soc.* LXVI 1945 49–137

3142 R. Perry, *The Gloucester woollen industry in the eighteenth and nineteenth centuries.* (Ph.D. thesis, London University (External), 1947)

3143 T. Rath, 'The Tewkesbury hosiery industry', *Text. Hist.* VII 1976 140–53

3144 F.C. Raggatt, *Woollen trade and industry in the rural areas of Gloucestershire.* (M.A. thesis, Bristol University, 1933)

3145 J.J. Simpson, 'The wool trade and the woolmen of Gloucestershire', *Trans. Bristol Glos. Archaeol. Soc.* LIII 1931 65–97

3146 J. Tann, *Aspects of the development of the Gloucestershire woollen industry.* (Ph.D. thesis, Leicester University, 1964)

3147 J. Tann, *Gloucestershire woollen mills: industrial archaeology.* (Newton Abbot, David & Charles, 1967) 254p.

3148 A.M. Urdank, Economic decline in the English Industrial Revolution: the Gloucester wool trade, 1800–1840', *J. Econ. Hist.* XLV June 1985 427–33

3149 L.F.J. Walrond, 'Early fulling stocks in Gloucestershire', *J. Ind. Archaeol.* I no. 1 1964 9–16

3150 R. Wilson, 'Hosiery manufacture at Dunkirk Mills, Nailsworth', *GSIA J.* 1990 32–42

TRANSPORT
General

3151 E.H. Duckworth, 'Transport in Gloucestershire', *Proc. Cotteswold Nat. Field Club* XXXV no. 4 1970

Canals and Rivers

3152 D.E. Bick, *The Hereford and Gloucester Canal.* New ed. (Oxford, Oakwood Press, 1994) 104p.

3153 D.E. Bick, 'The Oxenhall branch of the Herefordshire and Gloucestershire Canal', *GSIA J.* 1972 3–9

The same title appears in *Rlwy. Canal Hist. Soc. J.* XVIII 1972 71–5

3154 R.S. Brewster, *The Port of Gloucester.*

Unpublished typescript in Gloucester Reference Library

3155 British Waterways Board, *Sharpness: centenary of the New Dock, 1874–1974.* (1974) 16p.

3156 British Waterways Board, Amenity Services Division, *A brief history of the engineers engaged in the construction of the Gloucester & Sharpness Canal & its trade.* (Gloucester, The Board, 1979)

3157 S. Bryan and J. Hague, '*Harriet*: last of the Kennet barges', *GSIA J.* 1992 27–33

3158 H. Conway-Jones, *Gloucester docks: an illustrated history.* (Alan Sutton and Gloucestershire County Library, 1984) 181p.

3159 H. Conway-Jones, 'Gloucester quay 1780–1820', *Glos. Hist. Stud.* XIII 1982 19–22

3160 A.H. Conway Jones, 'The development of Gloucester docks', *Glos. Hist. Stud.* X 1979 56–8

3161 H. Conway-Jones, 'The classical bridge houses on the Gloucester and Sharpness Canal', *GSIA J.* 1994 3–9

3162 H. Conway-Jones, 'The origins of Gloucester's canals', *GSIA J.* 1992 2–7

3163 G.N. Crawford, 'The Gloucester & Berkeley Canal manuscripts in the Telford Collection', *GSIA J.* 1981 9–29

3164 G.N. Crawford, 'Thomas Telford and the Gloucester and Berkeley Canal', *Ind. Archaeol. Rev.* XI no. 2 1989 155–70

3165 E. Cuss and S.J. Gardiner, *Stroudwater and Thames & Severn Canals in old photographs.* (Gloucester, Alan Sutton, 1988) 159p.

3166 R.D. Field, *The Grand Scheme—history of the construction of the Gloucester & Berkeley Canal 1793–1827.* (Winchcombe, The Author, 1977) 16p.

Copy in Gloucester Reference Library

3167 M.G. Fulford and others, 'The medieval quay at Woolaston Grange, Gloucestershire', *Trans. Bristol Glos. Archaeol. Soc.* CX 1992 101–22

3168 Gloucester & Berkeley Canal Co., *The Gloucester & Berkeley Canal.* (Gloucester, Walker & Sons, 1826) 13p.

3169 M. Handford, *Stroudwater Canal.* (Gloucester, Alan Sutton, 1979) 93p.

3170 M. Handford and D. Viner, *Stroudwater & Thames and Severn canals towpath guide*. (Gloucester, Alan Sutton, 1984) 224p.

3171 P.A. Howard and B.S. Smith, *Gloucestershire waterways*. (Gloucester Record Office, 1977) 30p.

A teaching aid.

3172 J. James, 'The construction of the Stroudwater Canal', *Glos. Hist. Stud*. V 1972 47–54

3173 R.A. Lewis, 'The navigation to Stroud', *GSIA Newsl*. no. 6 1965 34–49

3174 C.R. Penny, 'The Herefordshire and Gloucestershire Canal', *GSIA J*. 1995 26–33

3175 F. Pratt, *Sharpness: centenary of the New Dock, 1874–1974*. (British Waterways Board, 1979) 16p.

3176 G.P.J. Preece, 'Railway and canal coal-drops at Sharpness docks',*Ind. Archaeol*. XI no. 4 1977 43–8

An article with the same author and title also appears in *Ind. Archaeol. Rev*. II no. 1 1977 78–84

3177 A. Richardson, 'Locks and water levels on the Gloucester and Berkeley Canal', *J. Rlwy. Canal Hist. Soc*. XXIX 1987 144–9

3178 Sharpness Docks and Gloucester & Birmingham Navigation Co., *The port of Gloucester: 'The ocean port for the Midlands': shipping, manufacturing, mining*. (Gloucester, 1936) 64p.

3179 M. Stimpson, *The history of Gloucester docks and its associated canals and railways*. (Potters Bar, West London Industrial Archaeology Society, 1980) 24p.

3180 R.A. Taylor, 'The construction of the Stroudwater', *Glos. Hist. Stud*. III 1969 37–42

3181 P.T. Underdown, 'The navigation of the River Severn, 1750–1950', *Trans. Worcester Archaeol. Soc*. IX 1984 95–100

3182 J. Upton, *Observations on the Gloucester and Berkeley Canal by John Upton, engineer*. (London, Institution of Civil Engineers, Tract no. 8, 1815)

Copy in Gloucester Local History Library

3183 D.J. Viner, *Cirencester and the Thames and Severn Canal*. (Cirencester, Corinium Museum, 1974) 6p.

3184 D. Viner, 'The Thames and Severn Canal in Cirencester, *in* A. McWhirr *ed., Studies in the archaeology and history of Cirencester*. (Oxford, British Archaeological Reports, 30, 1976) 126–44

3185 A.P. Wakelin, *Pre-industrial trade on the River Severn: a computer-aided study of the Gloucester port books, c. 1640–c. 1770*. (Ph.D thesis, Woverhampton Polytechnic, 1991)

3186 C.P. Weaver and C.R. Weaver, *The Gloucester & Sharpness Canal*. (Birmingham, Railway & Canal Historical Society, 1967) 42p.

3187 T.S. Willan, 'The river navigation and trade of the Severn Valley 1600–1750', *Econ. Hist. Rev*. VIII 1937 no. 1 68–79

3188 R. Wilson, 'Scenes at Sharpness Docks by Samuel Loxton', *GSIA J*. 1993 27–9

Sketches of the docks by Loxton, 1880–1920

3189 R. Wilson, 'Stroudwater Canal cranes (Part One)', *GSIA J* 1994 57–62; '(Part Two): the Dudbridge crane', 1995 21–5

Railways

3190 R. Anstis, 'The Birch Hill tramroad', *New Regard* no. 2 1986 52–3

3191 B. Ashworth, *The last days of steam in Gloucestershire*. (Alan Sutton, 1983) 137p.

3192 W. Awdry, 'Eastgate Station R.I.P.', *GSIA J*. 1975 76–83

3193 B. Baxter, 'The route of the Gloucester and Cheltenham Railway', *Rlwy. Mag.* XCIX

3194 D.E. Bick, *The Gloucester and Cheltenham tramroad and the Leckhampton Quarry lines*. 2nd ed. (Cheltenham, Runpast, 1996) 92p.

3195 D.E. Bick, 'Tramplates of the Gloucester and Cheltenham Railway', *Ind. Archaeol.* III 1966 201–8

3196 G.W. Bishop, 'The Norris engines on the Birmingham and Gloucester Railway', *Bull. Rlwy. Loco. Hist. Soc.* X 1925 46–52; XII 1926 41–2

3197 S.E. Brown, 'Gloucester Railway Carriage and Wagon Company Limited', *Bus Archives* LXVI 1993 1–15

3198 R.G. Burtt, 'The GWR comes to Gloucestershire. Recollections of 100 years ago', *Glos. Countryside* V no. 9 1945 186–90

3199 M. Christensen, 'The Gloucester Wagon Co. Ltd', *Br. Rlwy. J.* I 1983–5 178–89, 244–59, 352

Manufacturers of railway wagons and equipment

3200 G. Clissold and I. Standing, 'Mr Teague's Railway: some new information', *GSIA J*. 1980 51–60

The first tramroad to be built in the Forest of Dean.

3201 H. Conway-Jones, 'The excavation of a tramroad siding at Gloucester Docks', *GSIA J*. 1983 38–42

3202 G.J. Field, *Gloucester Railway Carriage & Wagon Co. Centenary history*. (1960)

3203 H. Household, *Gloucestershire railways in the twenties*. (Gloucester, Sutton, 1984) 137p.

3204 M. Hoy, 'The Stonehouse & Nailsworth Railway and the Midland branch to Stroud', *GSIA J*. 1987 2–16

3205 R. Huxley, *The rise and fall of the Severn Bridge Railway: an illustrated history*. (Gloucester, Alan Sutton & Gloucester County Library, 1984) 172p.

The railway ran from Sharpness to Lydney.

3206 P.J. Long and W.V. Awdry, *The Birmingham and Gloucester Railway*. (Gloucester, Sutton, 1987) 305p.

3207 C.G. Maggs, *The Birmingham Gloucester Line*. (Cheltenham, Line One, 1986)

3208 C. Maggs, *Branch lines of Gloucestershire*. (Stroud, Sutton, 1991)

3209 K. Montague, *Private owners wagons from the Gloucester Railway Carriage & Wagon* Co. Ltd. (Oxford, Oxford Publishing Co., 1981) 182p.

3210 T.E.R. Morris, 'The Forest of Dean tramroads', *Loco. Rlwy. Carr. Wagon Rev.*

XXXVII 1931 26–9, 59–60, 96–7, 128–30

3211 S. Mourton, *Steam routes around Cheltenham.* (Cheltenham, Runpast Publications, 1993) 96p.

3212 J. Nims, 'The Tewkesbury and Malvern Railway', *J. Rlwy. Canal Hist. Soc.* XXIX 1987 30–9

3213 H.W. Parr, 'The Forest railways and their industrial associations', *Bull. Hist. Metall. Gp.* II no. 1 1968 40–2

3214 H.W. Paar, 'The Redbrook Tramway Incline, in the Wye Valley', *GSIA J.* 1977–8 30–3

3215 H.W. Paar, *A history of the railways of the Forest of Dean* (Newton Abbot, David & Charles) 2v.

Part 1. *The Severn & Wye Railway* 2nd ed. (1973)

Part 2. *The Great Western Railway in Dean.* (1971)

See also I. Pope

3216 I. Pope and P. Karau, *Severn & Wye Railway: v. 3 Forest of Dean.* (Didcot, Wild Swan, 1988) 217p.

3217 Pope, B. How and P. Karau, *An illustrated history of the Severn & Wye Valley Railway.* (Upper Buckleberry, Wild Swan, 1983–8) 3v.

3218 E.N. Preedy, *ed., Steam around Gloucester.* (Stroud, Watts, 1985) 80p.

Mostly illustrations.

3219 S. Randolph, *An illustrated history of the Tetbury branch, Great Western Railway* (Upper Bucklebury, Wild Swan, *c.* 1985) 114p.

3220 P. Smith, *An historical survey of the Midland in Gloucestershire: station layouts and illustrations.* (Poole, Oxford Publishing, 1985) 160p.

3221 I. Standing, 'Forest of Dean tramroads: some notes on construction and rails', *GSIA J.* 1982 43–7

3222 I. Statham, 'Bullo Pill Tramroad—an exposure near Bilson', *GSIA J.* 1982 35–7

3223 R. Tutton, 'The steam rail motor cars built by the Gloucester Railway Carriage and Wagon Company Limited for the Great Western Railway', *GSIA J.* 1993 29–36

Roads and Road Transport

3224 D.H. Aldred, 'Country carriers, Cheltenham, 1880', *Glos. Comm. Council Loc. Hist. Bull.* no. 36 1977 8–10

3225 J.F. Bayes, 'Gloucester and Hereford Turnpike Trust', *Glos. Hist. Stud.* IV 1970 21–3

3226 J.F. Bayes and J. Roberts, 'Turnpike roads from Gloucester to Cheltenham and Tewkesbury', *GSIA J.* 1971 74–84

The same authors and title appear in *Glos. Hist. Stud.* III 1969 58–68

3227 R.R. Chaplin, 'Notes on the Chepstow and District Turnpike Trust', *Glos. Hist. Stud.* III 1969 47–57

3228 C. Cox, 'Building the Nailsworth Turnpike', *GSIA J.* 1979 21–38

3229 C. Cox, *The development and decline of the turnpike system in the Stroudwater* area of Gloucestershire, 1725–1875. (Ph.D. thesis, London University (London School of Economics), 1987)

3230 C. Cox, 'Milestones of the Stroud District', *Trans. Bristol Glos. Archaeol. Soc.* LXXXIII 1964 119–42

3231 C. Cox, 'Network: turnpike roads in the Stroudwater area in the eighteenth century', *GSIA J.* 1990 14–25

3232 G.N. Crawford, 'The Bibury Turnpike Trust 1753–1803', *Glos. Hist. Stud.* IX 1978 31–40

The same author and similar title appears in *GSIA J.* 1977–8 1–12

3233 D.E. Evans, *The ingenious Mr Pederson.* (Dursley, Allan Sutton, 1978)

The cycle industry.

3234 W. Fawcett, 'Coaching days in the Cotswolds', *Glos. Countryside* III no. 10 1940 536–8

3235 A.E. Fielder, 'The tramways of Gloucestershire: a brief history', *GSIA J.* 1973 17–30

3236 J.C. Frost, 'Over Bridge, Gloucester', *Glos. Hist. Stud.* II 1968 36–40

3237 M. Freeman, 'Popular attitudes to turnpikes in early eighteenth-century England', *J. Hist. Geog.* XIX no. 1 Jan. 1993 33–47

Focuses on the Vales of Tewkesbury and Evesham, and the West Riding of Yorkshire.

3238 J.V. Garrett, 'Charles Baker of Painswick and Cheltenham and the development of roads around Stroud and Cheltenham in the early part of the 19th century', *GSIA J.* 1989 2–8

3239 *Gloucestershire turnpike roads.* (Gloucestershire Record Office, 197–)

A teaching aid

3240 C. Haine, 'Main roads through Painswick', *GSIA J.* 1987 42–9

3241 N. Herbert, ed., *Road travel and transport in Gloucestershire: extracts from the Gloucester Journal.* (Gloucester, Alan Sutton, 1985) 160p.

3242 B. Kearney, 'Cheltenham toll roads in the 19th century', *Cheltenham Loc. Hist. Soc. J.* X 1994 20–5

3243 W. Mackenzie, 'Account of the bridge over the Severn, near the Town of Tewkesbury in the County of Gloucester, designed by Thomas Telford and erected under his superintendence', *Trans. Instn. Civ. Engrs.* II 1838 1–14

3244 R.J. Owens, 'The Newent turnpike road', *Glos. Hist. Stud.* V 1972 19–23

3245 N. Spry, 'The Northgate turnpike', *GSIA J.* 1971 1–58

3246 D.G. Tucker, 'The trolleybus proposal at Stroud, Glos. in 1903: the Stroud District and Cheltenham tramways bill', *J. Transp. Hist.* IV 1977 40–6

3247 R. Wilson, 'GWR omnibus services and garage at Stroud', *GSIA J.* 1991 13–16

OTHER INDUSTRIES

3248 A. Chatwin, 'Cycle industry in Cheltenham', *GSIA J.* 1971 89–92

3249 A. Conway-Jones, *Price Walker and Company: 250 years of timber trading in*

Gloucester. (Gloucester, The Company, 1986) 24p.

3250 T. Southgate, 'A history of Van Moppes—IDP Ltd. (Formerly Impregnated Diamond Products Ltd)' *GSIA J.* 1995 34–5

3251 D.G. Tucker, 'Millstone making in Gloucestershire. Wm Gardner's Gloucester Millstone Manufactory with a note on Hudsons of Penallt and Redbrook', *GSIA J.* 1973 6–16

3252 A.R. Williams, 'The Gloucestershire tobacco trade', *Virginia Mag. Hist. & Biog.* LXXIX 1971 145–52

Somerset

GENERAL

3253 J. Astell, *Somerset at work: 1870 to 1950*. (Bristol, Redcliffe Press, 1986)
A photographic collection.

3254 M. Atkinson ed., *Exmoor's industrial archaeology*. (Tiverton, Exmoor Books, 1997) 192p.

3255 R. Atthill, *Mendip: new study*. (Newton Abbot, David & Charles, 1976) 204p.

3256 R. Atthill, *Old Mendip*. (Dawlish, David & Charles, 1971) 204p.

3257 N. du Q. Bird, 'Token currency in Bath, 1636–1675', *Somerset Dorset N. & Q.* XXXIV Sept. 1996 82–6

3258 B. Buchanan, 'Aspects of capital formation: some insights from north Somerset 1750–1830', *S. Hist.* VIII 1986 73–93

3259 B.J. Buchanan, *Capital investment in a regional economy: some aspects of the sources and employment of capital in north Somerset*. (Ph.D thesis, University of London (External), 1992)

3260 R.A. Buchanan, *The industrial archaeology of Bath*. (Bath University Press, 1969) 20p.

3261 G.P. Davis, *Social and economic change in a Somerset village, Newton St Loe 1801–1871*. (M.Sc. thesis, Bath University, 1975)

3262 J. Fussell, 'The view of Dulcote—a changing scene', *BIAS J.* no. 25 1992 16–17

3263 C.M. Gerrard, *Trade and settlement in medieval Somerset,* (Ph.D thesis, Bristol University, 1987)

3264 M. Havinden, *The Somerset landscape*. (London, Hodder & Stoughton, 1981) 272p.

3265 F. Hawtin, 'Industrial archaeology at Charterhouse-on-Mendip', *Ind. Archaeol.* VII 1970 171–5

3266 V. Heal, 'Investigation and management of industrial sites within Exmoor National Park', *Mining Hist.* XIII no. 2 1996 130–6

3267 S. Minnitt, 'Cox's of Taunton and their penny token', *SIAS J.* no. 3 1981 18–19

3268 R.S. Neale, 'The industries of the City of Bath in the first half of the nineteenth century', *Proc. Somerset Archaeol. Nat. Hist. Soc.* CVIII 1964 132–44

3269 D. Warren, *ed., Somerset's industral heritage: a guide and gazetteer*. (Somerset Industrial Archaeology Society, Survey no. 8, 1996) 68p.

3270 T.D. Whittet, 'Somerset apothecaries' tokens and their issuers', *Proc. Somerset Archaeol. Nat. Hist. Soc.* CXXX 1985–6 127–33

AGRICULTURE

See also no. 52

3271 T.D. Acland, 'On the farming of Somerset', *J. R. Agric. Soc.* XI 1850

3272 T.D. Acland and W. Sturge, *The farming of Somerset.* (1851)

3273 P.J. Ashford, *The structure of land ownership and occupation in the Vale of Porlock (Somerset), 1760–1850.* (B.Phil. thesis, Open University, 1985)

3274 M. Aston, 'The development of medieval rural settlement in Somerset', *in* R. Higham, *ed., Landscape and townscape in the South West.* (Exeter, University, Exeter Studies in History no. 22, 1989) 19–40

3275 J.H. Bettey, 'Agriculture in Somerset in the sixteenth century', *Somerset Dorset N. & Q.* XXX 1979 401–4

3276 J. Billingsley, *A general view of the agriculture in the County of Somerset.* (1794) 320p.

Billingsley also wrote the 2nd ed. of 1798.

3277 B.J. Buchanan, 'The financing of parliamentary waste land enclosure: some evidence from North Somerset, 1770–1830', *Agric. Hist. Rev.* XXX 1982 112–26

3278 F. Coles, *The life of a farmer's boy.* (Ilfracombe, Stockwell, 1950) 24p.

Covers the period 1891–1902.

3279 N.J. Corcos, *Shapwick: the enclosure of a Somerset parish, 1515–1839.* (M.A. dissertation, Leicester University, 1982)

3280 M.D. Costen, 'Rimpton in Somerset—a late Saxon estate', *S. Hist.* VIII 1985 13–24

3281 A. Court, *The wind of change in Somerset: Somerset County Branch National Farmers' Union, 1963–88.* (Taunton, The Branch, 1990)

3282 P.E.C. Croot, *Aspects of agrarian society in Brent Marsh, Somerset 1500–1700.* (Ph.D. thesis, Leeds University, 1982)

3283 J. Darby, 'The farming of Somerset', *J. Bath W. Eng. Soc.* V 1873 154

3284 G. East, 'Land utilization in Somerset at the end of the eighteenth century', *Somerset Yrbk.* no. 36 1937 60–5

3285 H.S.A. Fox, 'The alleged transformation from two-field to three-field systems in medieval England', *Econ. Hist. Rev.* XXXIX 1986 526–48

With an analysis of the Somerset manor of Podimore

3286 G.E. Fussell, 'Agricultural depression 100 years ago: an Ilminster landowner's views', *Somerset Countryman* XV no. 9 1947 100–1

3287 G.E. Fussell, 'Die Landwirtschaft in Somersetshire von 1500–1900', *Zeit. Agrargesch. und Agrarsoziol.* XXII 1974 41–58

3288 G.E. Fussell, 'A Somerset grazier in the eighteenth century: Robert Brown of Hill Farm, 1759', *The Somerset Yrbk* XXX 1931 54–6

3289 G.E. Fussell, 'Somerset men and 'Ruby' cattle', *Somerset Countryman* XVI no. 1 1948 20–1

3290 G.E. Fussell, 'The Vale of Taunton a century ago: capital, costs and returns of farming', *Somerset Countryman* XV no. 11 1947 208–9

3291 A.A. Gibson, 'Farming on the Somerset levels and moors', *J. R. Agric. Soc.*

CXLVIII 1987 66–73

3292 O. Hallam, 'Vegetation and land use on Exmoor', *Proc. Somerset Archaeol. Nat. Hist. Soc.* CXXII 1978 37–51

3293 J. Hardwick, Strip lynchets: the case study of South Cadbury, Somerset', *Proc. Somerset Archaeol. Nat. Hist. Soc.* CXXII 1977–8 29–35

3294 J.H. Harvey, 'Templar holdings in East Somerset', *Somerset Dorset N. & Q.* XXI 1981 135–41

3295 A. Heeley and M. Brown, *Victorian Somerset: John Hodges, a farm labourer.* (Glastonbury, Somerset Rural Life Museum, 1979) 52p.

3296 P.J. Helm, 'The Somerset levels in the middle ages 1086–1539', *J. Br. Archaeol. Assoc.* 3rd ser. XII 1949 37–52

3297 B. Hook, A.P. Ward and B.J. Murless, 'Horse gins in Somerset', *SIAS J.* no. 1 1975 31–4

3298 S.G. Kendall, *Farming memories of a Westcountry yeoman.* (London, Faber, 1944) 247p.

3299 R. Lennard, 'The desmesnes of Glastonbury Abbey in the eleventh and twelfth centuries', *Econ. Hist. Rev.* 2nd ser. VIII no. 3 1956 355–63

3300 M. McGarvie, *Memoirs of a Victorian farmer: Richard White of Mells, Norridge and Zeals.* (Frome, Frome Society for Local Study, 1990) 132p.

3301 I. Miles ... *Bogs and inundations* ... , (Somerset Industrial Archaeology Society and Westonzoyland Engine Trust, Survey no. 7, 1993) 40p.

A brief history of efforts to drain the Somerset Levels.

3302 K.D. Moddever, *Farmhouse cheese making in Somerset.* (1966)

3303 S.C. Morland, 'The making of the field pattern of Somerset', *in* T. Stuart-Menteath, *The land of Britain: Somerset.* (1938)

3304 T. Munckton, *Chancellors farm accounts, 1766–1767.* (Weston-super-Mare, Harry Galloway, 1994)

Farm income of a family farm at West Harptree.

3305 M.M. Postan, 'Glastonbury estates in the twelfth century', *Econ. Hist. Rev.* V no. 3 1953 358–67

3306 R.G. Scott, 'Population and enclosure in the mid-nineteenth century: the example of Exmoor', *Loc. Pop. Stud.* XIII 1974 31–40

3307 M. Siraut, 'A Somerset farming account book', *Proc. Somerset Archaeol. Nat. Hist. Soc.* CXXIX 1984–5 161–70

John Kinglake (d. 1809)

3308 W.E. Tate, *Somerset enclosure acts and awards.* (Frome and London, 1948)

3309 M. Whitfield, 'The medieval fields of South-East Somerset', *Proc. Somerset Archaeol. Nat. Hist. Soc.* CXXV 1981 17–29

3310 M. Williams, *The draining of the Somerset levels.* (Ph.D. thesis, University of Wales, 1960)

3311 M. Williams, *The draining of the Somerset levels.* (Cambridge, Cambridge University Press, 1970) 288p.

3312 M. Williams, 'The draining and reclamation of the Somerset levels, 1770–1833', *Inst. Br. Geogr. Trans. Pap.* no. 33 1963 163–79

3313 M. Williams, 'The enclosure and reclamation of the Mendip Hills, 1770–1870', *Agric. Hist. Rev.* XIX 1971 65–81

3314 M. Williams, 'The enclosure of waste land in Somerset, 1700–1900', *Trans. Inst. Br. Geog.* no. 57 1972 99–123

3315 M. Williams, 'The 1801 crop returns for Somerset', *Proc. Somerset Archaeol. Nat. Hist. Soc.* CXIII 1968–9 69–85

3316 G.H. Woodward, 'The disposal of chantry lands in Somerset', *S. Hist.* V 1983 95–114

ARCHITECTURE AND BUILDINGS

See also nos. 627–44

Domestic

3317 C. Austin and Sir R. de Z. Hall, 'A cruck-roofed house in North Cadbury, Somerset', *Proc. Somerset Archaeol. Nat. Hist.* CXIV 1969–70 63–8

3318 C. Austin and Sir R. de Z. Hall, 'The medieval houses of Stocklinch', *Proc. Somerset Archaeol. Nat. Hist.* CXVI 1972 86–100

3319 M. Batt, 'Broom's cottage: a cob building at Latcham, near Widmore, Somerset (ST 449471)', *Proc. Somerset Archaeol. Nat. Hist. Soc.* CXX 1976 106–8

3320 R.G. Gilson, 'South Somerset jointed crucks: some problems', *Proc. Somerset Archaeol. Nat. Hist. Soc.* CXX 1976 51–5

3321 Sir R. de Z. Hall, 'A preliminary catalogue of cruck-roofed buildings in Somerset', *Proc. Somerset Archaeol. Nat. Hist. Soc.* CXIV 1969–70 48–63

3322 Sir R. de Z. Hall, 'A preliminary catalogue of curing chambers in Somerset', *Proc. Somerset Archaeol. Nat. Hist.* CXV 1970–1 45–7

3323 Sir R. de Z. Hall, 'A further catalogue of Somerset crucks', *Proc. Somerset Archaeol. Nat. Hist. Soc.* CXVII 1973 102–6

3324 R. Leech, *Early industrial housing: the Trinity area of Frome.* (HMSO, Royal Commission on Historical Monuments, Supplementary Series no. 3, 1981) 44p. plus plates

3325 M. MacDermott, 'Little Poundisford farmhouse', *Proc. Somerset Archaeol. Nat. Hist. Soc.* CXX 1976 104–5

3326 M.B. McDermott, 'Single-storeyed medieval houses: two examples from West Somerset', *Proc. Somerset Archaeol. Nat. Hist. Soc.* CXXVI 1981–2 93–101

3327 Somerset and South Avon Vernacular Buildings Research Group, *Somerset villages. The houses, cottages and farms of Chiselborough.* (Glastonbury, Somerset Rural Life Museum, 1993) 104p.

3328 R. Taylor, 'Town houses in Taunton, 1500–1700', *Post-Med. Archaeol.* VIII 1974 62–79

3329 L.F.J. Walrond, 'An early jointed cruck building at South Bradon, Langport Rural District' *Proc. Somerset Archaeol. Nat. Hist. Soc.* CXIV 1969–70 68–73

3330 E.H.D. Williams, 'Bacon-curing chambers: some recent discoveries', *Proc.*

Somerset Archaeol. Nat. Hist. Soc. CXXII 1978 53–6

3331 E.H.D. Williams, 'Base crucks in Somerset—I', *Proc. Somerset Archaeol. Nat. Hist. Soc.* CXXI 1976–7 55–66; 'Part II', CXXIII 1978–9 27–53; 'Part III and allied roof forms', CXXV 1980–1 45–66

3332 E.H.D. Williams, 'The building materials of Somerset's vernacular houses', *Proc. Somerset Archaeol. Nat. Hist. Soc.* CXXXV 1991 123–34

3333 E.H.D. Williams, 'Corn drying kilns', *Proc. Somerset Archaeol. Nat. Hist. Soc.* CXVI 1971–72 101–3

3334 E.H.D. Williams, 'Curing chambers and domestic corn drying kilns', *Proc. Somerset Archaeol. Nat. Hist. Soc.* CXX 1975–6 57–61

3335 E.H.D. Williams, 'Some two-unit houses in Somerset', *Proc. Somerset Archaeol. Nat. Hist. Soc.* CXVIII 1973–4 28–38

Industrial

3336 R. Atthill, 'The Nettlebridge valley', *BIAS J.* no. 3 1970 9–10

Concentrates on water power in the valley

3337 M. Bodmin, 'Mills of the Upper Chew', *BIAS J.* no. 22 1990 12–22

3338 M. Bodman, 'Mills on the Cam and Midford brooks', *BIAS J.* no. 29 1997 2–13

3339 C.A. Buchanan, 'Shapwick windmill', *SIAS J.* no. 1 1975 16–17

3340 J.S. Buckland, 'Stembridge tower mill, High Ham, Somerset', *Somerset Dorset N. & Q.* XXIX 1970

3341 M. Chapman, 'The chimney in Milk Street, Bath', *BIAS J.* no. 28 1995 39–42

3342 A.J. Coulthard and M. Watts, *Windmills of Somerset and the men who worked them.* (London, Research Publishing Co., 1979)

3343 P. Daniel, 'Waterside Mill, Radstock', *Somerset Ind. Archaeol. Soc. Bull.* no. 63 Aug. 1993 16–19

3344 J. Day, 'The last of the dyewood mills', *Ind. Archaeol.* III 1966 119–26

Near Keynsham in North Somerset

3345 P. England, 'Dunkirk Mill, Freshford', *SIAS J.* no. 1 1975 35–38

3346 A.J. Higgs-Coulthard, 'Windmills in Somerset', *Somerset Dorset N. & Q.* XXVI Aug. 1952 84–87; Dec. 1952 107–8; Apr. 1953 130–2; Dec. 1953 161–3

3347 'Horse gins in Somerset', *SIAS J.* I 1975 31–4

3348 M.H. Jones, 'Simonsbath sawmill', *Somerset Ind. Archaeol. Soc. Bull.* no. 77 Apr. 1998 2–13

3349 I. Keil, 'Building a post windmill in 1342', *Trans. Newcomen Soc.* XXXIV 1961–2 151–4

The building account of a mill built at Walton, Somerset

3350 M. Lewcun, 'Excavations on the site of an aerated water manufactory at Empire Hotel Bath, 1995', *BIAS J.* no. 28 1995 30–4

3351 I. Miles, 'Westzoyland pumping station', *SIAS J.* no. 3 1981 26–7

3352 M. Miles, 'Halse Maltings, Somerset', *Ind. Archaeol. Rev.* XI no. 2 1989 136–40

3353 A.H. Shorter, 'Paper and board mills in Somerset', *Somerset Dorset N. & Q.* XXV 1950 245–57

3354 H.E.S. Simmons, *Watermills of Somerset.* 1977. 2v.

Volumes in the Simmons Collection relating to British windmills and watermills. A photocopy of the original typescript folders is available in the Science Museum Library, London.

3355 R. Stiles, 'Bishop Sutton mill', *BIAS J.* IV 1971 12–13

3356 O. Ward, 'Priston Mill', *BIAS J.* VII 1974 29–31

3357 O. Ward, *Priston Mill near Bath, Avon—a working corn mill powered by a large water wheel.* (Bristol, Avongraphics, 1975) 14p.

Produced mainly from material previously published in *BIAS J.*

3358 D. Warren, 'Nethercot Farm malthouse', *Somerset Ind. Archaeol. Soc. Bull.* no. 56 1991

3359 D. Warren, 'Report on Bridge Mill, Bishop's Hull ST 206250', *Somerset Ind. Archaeol. Soc. Bull.* no. 77 Apr. 1998 22–4

3360 D. Warren, 'Water power on farms in West Somerset', *SIAS J.* no. 1 1975 5–12

3361 M. Watts, *Somerset windmills.* (Bristol, Agraphicus Publications, 1975) 14p.

3362 M. Watts, 'Documentary evidence of windmills at Walton', *SIAS J.* no. 2 1977 31–2

3363 M. Watts, 'Windmills of Somerset', *BIAS J.* VI 1973 21–31

BREWING AND CIDER MAKING

3364 M. Miles, *Hancock's Brewery, Wiveliscombe.* (Somerset Industrial Archaeology Society Survey no. 2, 1986) 32p.

3365 F. Hawtin and P. Hawtin, 'Stogumber brewery, 1840–1973', *SIAS J.* no. 2 1973 15–19

3366 E.V.M. Whiteway, *Whiteway's cider: a company history.* (Newton Abbot, David & Charles, 1990) 160p.

3367 R. Wilcox, 'Bath breweries in the latter half of the eighteenth century', *in* his *A Second North Somerset miscellany.* (1971) 23–31

BRICKMAKING

3368 R.J.E. Bush, 'A Somerset brickmaker of 1680', *SIAS J.* no. 3 1981 17

3369 B.J. Murless, 'The Bath brick industry at Bridgwater: a preliminary survey', *SIAS J.* I 18–28

3370 B.J. Murless, 'Taunton brickyards', *SIAS J.* no. 3 1981 28–35

3371 I. Parrott and L. Isaac, *Brickmaking in Wellington: a history of the Poolle Brickworks of William Thomas & Co. Ltd of Wellington, Somerset.* (Wellington, Wellington Museum Society, 1995) 43p.

3372 E. Wide, 'Brick making at Bishop's Hull, 1940–1950', *SIAS Bull.* no. 68 April

1995 4–14

CLOCK AND WATCHMAKING

3373 R.G. Bartelot, 'Old clocks of Wessex', *Proc. Somerset Archaeol. Soc. Bath Branch* VIII no. 3 1941 121–8

3374 M. Glenny, 'Ingenious and efficient: the Wells Cathedral clock', *Country Life* 18 Sept. 1986 852–4

3375 G.W. Saunders, 'Somerset clockmakers. Thomas Stocker of Martock', *Somerset Dorset N. & Q.* XXIV no. 218 1943 39–40

ENGINEERING

3376 R. Bell, 'A horizontal steam engine in the centre of Bath', *BIAS J.* no. 26 1993 30–2

An engine used to power the printing press of Isaac Pitman, pioneer of shorthand.

3377 S. Burroughs, 'Enterprise in precision engineering: the early years of the Horstmann family of Bath', *BIAS J.* no. 27 1994 30–4

A German clockmaking family which settled in Bath. Later became a precision engineering firm.

3378 D. Chapman, 'Richard Clyburn and his screw spanner', *Somerset Ind. Archaeol. Soc. Bull.* no. 75 Apr. 1997 2–5

3379 *Claverton Pumping Station: a definitive study.* (Bristol, Kennet & Avon Canal Trust, 1984) 67p.

3380 J. Cornwell and R. Stiles, 'Fussell's ironworks, Mells, Somerset', *BIAS J.* VIII 1975 14–15

3381 D. Jones, 'The Stothert and Pitt steam Fairbairn type crane', *BIAS J.* VIII 1975 20–4

3382 M.H. Jones, 'The excavation of Smoky Bottom engine house', *Ind. Archaeol. Rev.* XI 1988 86–92

3383 B. Luker and J. Hasler, 'An industrial site at Wookey', *Proc. Somerset Archaeol. Nat. Hist. Soc.* CXXXVII 1993 119–21

A possible iron mill

3384 I. Miles, 'A Cornish boiler at Highbridge', *SIAS J.* no. 1 1975 29–30.

3385 I. Miles, 'The Thermalume petrol-air gas generator', *Somerset Ind. Archaeol. Soc. Bull.* no. 76 Dec. 1997 12–19

3386 M. Miller, 'Claverton pump', *Engineering* CCXIV 1974 1014–16

3387 D. Rivers, 'Claverton pumping station', *BIAS J.* VI 1973 14–17

A waterwheel-powered pumping station.

3388 H. Torrens, 'The early years of Stothert and Pitt', *BIAS J.* IX 1976 24–30

3389 H. Torrens, *The evolution of a family firm: Stothert and Pitt of Bath.* (Bath, Stothert & Pitt, 1978) 86p.

3390 D. Warren, 'The Buckland St. Mary Rake and Gate Manufactory', *Somerset Ind. Archaeol. Soc. Bull.* no. 76 1997 2–9

3391 D.W. Warren, 'Chidgley's Foundry, Watchet', *SIAS J.* no. 3 1981 6–9

John Chidgley's brass foundry and millwright.

3392 D. Warren, *Dening of Chard: agricultural engineers 1828–1965.* (Somerset Industrial Archaeology Society Survey no. 6, 1989) 44p.

3393 D. Warren, *A village industry: W.H. Pool and Sons, Engineers, Chipstable.* (Somerset Industrial Archaeology Society Survey no. 4, 1988) 44p.

3394 C.P. Weaver, 'Claverton pumping station', *J. Rlwy Canal Hist. Soc.* XXV 1979 141–53

3395 F. Wilmott, 'C. & J. Clark's power plant history 1910–1958', *Int. Stationary Steam Engine Soc. Bull.* XIII no. 3 1991 23–8

The three preserved steam engines at the Street works are described.

FOOTWEAR AND LEATHER

3396 L.H. Barber, *Clarks of Street, 1825–1950.* (Street, C. & J. Clark Ltd, 1950) 177p.

3397 K. Hudson, *Towards precision shoemaking. C. & J. Clark Limited and the development of the British shoe industry.* (Newton Abbot, David & Charles, 1968) 109p.

3398 M. McGarvie, *Bowlingreen Mill: a centenary history* (Avalon Leatherboard Co., 1982) 153p.

Leather industry, Street, Somerset

3399 G.B. Sutton, *C. & J. Clark 1833–1903: a history of shoemaking in Street, Somerset.* (York, Ebor Press, 1979) 208p.

3400 G.B. Sutton, 'The marketing of ready made footwear in the 19th century: a study of the firm of C. & J. Clark', *Bus. Hist.* VI no. 2 1964 93–112

GUNPOWDER

3401 B.J. Buchanan and M.T. Tucker, 'The manufacture of gunpowder: a study of the documentary and physical evidence relating to the Woolley Powder Works near Bath', *Ind. Archaeol. Rev.* V no. 3 1981 185–202

3402 B. Buchanan, 'The study of gunpowder making', *BIAS J.* XIX 1986 39–40

3403 B.J. Buchanan, 'The technology of gunpowder making in the eighteenth century: evidence from the Bristol region', *Trans. Newcomen Soc.* LXVII 1995–6 125–59

IRONWORKING

3404 J.P. Ferris, 'The Iron Lady of Somerset', *Somerset Dorset N. & Q.* XXXI Mar. 1984 351–3

Rachel, Lady Hopton. Information on the Witham ironworks.

3405 M. McGarvie, 'Iron smelting at Witham Friary, Trudoxhill and Nunnery', *Somerset Dorset N. & Q.* XXXI Mar. 1984 353–5

3406 M. McGarvie, 'Somerset iron', *Somerset Dorset N. & Q.* XXXI Sept. 1985 445–7
Letters giving information on the Witham ironworks

LIMEBURNING

See also nos. 755, 756, 3426

3407 P. Daniel and B.J. Murless, 'A limekiln complex at Down End, Puriton', *Somerset Ind. Archaeol. Soc. Bull.* no. 65 April 1994 15–22

3408 P. Daniel and B. Murless, 'Limekilns at Warren Bay', *Somerset Ind. Archaeol. Soc. Bull.* no. 62 April 1993 2–8

3409 P. Daniel, 'Limeburning and geology in Somerset', *Somerset Ind. Archaeol. Soc. Bull.* no. 55 1990

3410 E. Taylor, 'Limekilns on Mendip', *BIAS J.* XVIII 1985 10–11

3411 A.P. Ward, 'A limekiln near Fitzhead', *SIAS J.* no. 1 1975 39–43

MINING AND QUARRYING

See also nos. 3552, 3558, 3569, 3573

3412 C. Alabaster, 'The minerals of Mendip', *Somerset Mines Res. Group J.* I no. 4 1982 1–52

3413 S. Beadle, *Economic changes and the population of coalfields in the early nineteenth century with specific reference to the Somerset and St Helens coalfield.* (Ph.D. thesis, Liverpool University, 1984)

3414 S. Beadle, 'Tracing coal mining in Somerset and south-west Lancashire: some pitfalls', *Loc. Histn.* XVIII no. 1 1988 5–12

3415 R.K. Bluhm, 'The Somerset coalfield, 1790–1820', *in A Second North Somerset miscellany.* (1971) 52–60

3416 R. Bluhm, 'The Somerset Coal Combination—a further note', *BIAS J* no. 25 1992 11
See no. 3472

3417 P.M. Bonsall, *Industrial decline in the Somerset coalfield 1947–1973.* (Radstock, Midsomer Norton and District Museum Society, 1993)

3418 P. Bonsall, 'The Somerset coalfield, 1947–73: attitudes and responses to pit closures in the post-nationalization era', *S. Hist.* XI 1989 114–30

3419 P.M. Bonsall, *The Somerset and Lothian miners 1919–c. 1947: changing attitudes to pit work in the twentieth century.* (Ph.D. thesis, Warwick University, 1990)

3420 S.W. Brice, *The coal-field of north Somersetshire* (London, Bemrose & Lothian, 1867) 83p.

3421 J. Brooke, 'Elborough Mine', *Somerset Mines Res. Group J.* I no. 1 1980 2–3

3422 R.W.G. Bryant, *Early history of the Somerset coalfield.* (M.Sc.(Econ.) thesis, London University)

3423 J.A. Bulley, *The development of the coal industry in the Radstock area of Somerset from the earliest times to 1830.* (M.A. thesis, London University (External), 1952)

3424 J. Bulley, 'To Mendip for coal—a study of the Somerset coalfield before 1830. Part 1. Output, marketing and techniques of mining', *Proc. Somerset Archaeol. Nat. Hist. Soc.* XCVII 1952 46–78; 'Part 2. Masters and men', XCVIII 1953 17–54

3425 R.L. Burgess, F. Hawtin and C. Richards, 'Mendip survey', *BIAS J.* IV 1971 5–9

3426 R. Burton, 'A brief history of Newland lime quarries, Exford', *Somerset Ind. Archaeol. Soc. Bull.* no. 75 Apr. 1997 6–9

3427 P. Collier, *Colliers' way: history and walks in the Somerset coalfield.* (Bradford-on-Avon, Ex Libris, 1986) 157p.

3428 N. Corcos, 'Worle, Woodspring and Wallop: the calamine connection', *Proc. Somerset Archaeol. Nat. Hist. Soc.* CXXXII 1988 193–208

3429 H. Cossham, *On the northern end of the Bristol coalfield.* (Reprinted from *Trans. N. Eng. Inst. Min. Engrs.* 1861) 12p.

3430 T. Cox, 'A Mendip mining law', *Br. Caver* XLIX 1968 59–60

3431 C. Crook, 'Observations on surface features at Middlehope, Kewstoke which indicate possible mine workings', *Somerset Mines Res. Group J.* I no. 2 1981 21–2

3432 G. Davis, 'Coal mining at Newton St Loe', *BIAS J.* X 1977 27–33

3433 M.W. Doughty, 'Samborne Palmer's diary: technological innovation by a Somerset coal-mine owner', *Ind. Archaeol. Rev.* III no. 1 1978 17–28

3434 C.G. Down and A.J. Warrington, *The history of the Somerset coalfield.* (Newton Abbot, David & Charles, 1971) 283p.

3435 'Early coal mining in Midsomer Norton', *Somerset Dorset N. & Q.* XIV 1915 13–14

3436 J. Evans, 'Man and mining on and around Mendip: notes on the display in Woodspring Museum, Weston-super-Mare', *Somerset Mines Res. Group J.* I no. 2 1981 23–8

3437 B.D. Ferriman, *An historical geography of coal mining in the Radstock Basin.* (M.Sc. thesis, Bristol University, 1978)

3438 F. Flower, *Somerset coalmining life: a miner's memories.* (Bath, Millstream, 1990) 141p.

3439 M. Glosson, 'Rules and laws governing lead and calamine mining in Backwell, 1709', *Somerset Mines Res. Group J.* I no. 3 1982 43–5

3440 J.W. Gough, *Mendip mining laws and Forest bounds.* (Somerset Record Soc. vol. 45, 1930) 214p.

3441 J.W. Gough, *The mines of Mendip.* 2nd ed. (Newton Abbot, David & Charles, 1967) 269p.

First published by Oxford University Press in 1930

Mainly concerned with lead mining.

3442 S. Gould, 'Coke ovens at Vobster Breach Colliery', *Ind. Archaeol. Rev.* XVII no. 1 1994 79–85

Same title appears in *SIAS Bull.* no. 69 Aug. 1995 20–4

3443 S. Gould, 'The collieries of North Somerset', *Mining Hist.* XIII no. 1 1996 16–26

3444 G.C. Greenwell, 'Notes on the coalfield of east Somerset', *Trans. N. Eng. Inst. Min. Engrs.* II 1864 258–66

3445 G.C. Greenwell, 'On the ironstone of Wilts. and Somerset', *Proc. S. Wales Inst. Engrs.* I 1859 307–23

3446 G.C. Greenwell and J. McMurtrie, *On the Radstock portion of the Somerset coal field.* (Newcastle, 1864)

3447 G.C. Greenwell, 'On the Somersetshire section of the Bristol coalfield', *Trans. N. Eng. Inst. Min. Engrs.* X 1862 106–16

3448 G.C. Greenwell, 'On the south eastern portion of the Somersetshire coalfields', *Trans. Manchr. Geol. Soc.* V 1864 34–40

3449 G.C. Greenwell, 'On the southern portion of the Somersetshire coalfields', *Proc. S. Wales Inst. Engrs.* I 1858 147–61

3450 J.R. Hamilton and J.F. Lawrence, *Men and mining on the Quantocks.* (Bracknell, Town & Country Press, 1970) 78p.

3451 M. Hannam, 'Mendip mining', *Br. Caver* XXIX 1958 31–4, 63–5

3452 G.M. Huggins and R.F. Pickford, *Bath stone. A short history.* (Bath, Geological Museum, 1975) 16p.

3453 J.L. Jones, 'Forgotten mines of Mendip', *Country Life* CXIX 16 Feb. 1956 260–1

3454 M. Jones, 'Excavations at Chargot Wood and Langham Hill', *SIAS Bull.* no. 70 Dec. 1995 9–13

Two ironstone working sites in the Brendon Hills.

3455 'Lead mining on Mendip', *Br. Caver* XLIX 1968 20–2

3456 J. McMurtrie, 'On the Somersetshire coalfield and the method of working thin seams in the Radstock district', *Proc. S. Wales Inst. Engrs.* XII 1881 424–54, 543–53

3457 T. Morgans, 'Notes on the lead industry of the Mendip Hills', *Trans. Fed. Instn. Min. Engrs.* XX 1900–1 478–95

3458 J.W. Perkins, A.T. Brooks and A.E. McR. Pearce, *Bath stone, a quarry history.* (Cardiff, University College, and Bath, Kingsmead Press, 1979) 54p.

3459 D. Pollard, 'Digging Bath stone', *BIAS J.* no. 21 1989 28–36

3460 J. Powell, 'Fullers earth from Midford', *BIAS J.* no. 11 1978 22–5

3461 J. Presto, *Five years of colliery life; or The adventures of a collier boy in a Somersetshire coal mine.* (Manchester, J. Heywood, 1884) 62p.

3462 J. Randall, 'Bath freestone', *The Builder* 1 Oct. 1864 719–21

3463 C. Richards, 'Singing River Mine: a coalmine working at Shipham', *BIAS J.* IV 1971 7–9

3464 H.C. Salmon, 'Lead smelting on the Mendips', *Mining & Smelting Mag.* VI

1864 321–8

3465 C.J. Schmitz, 'An account of Mendip calamine mining in the early 1870s', *Proc. Somerset Archaeol. Nat. Hist. Soc.* CXX 1976 81–3

3466 Somerset County Council, *Quarrying in Somerset: a survey of the history, practice and prospects of the quarrying industry in North Somerset and an examination of conflicting interests.* (Taunton, 1971) 349p.

3467 W.I. Stanton and A.G. Clarke, 'Cornish miners at Charterhouse-on-Mendip', *Proc. Univ. Bristol Spelaeol. Soc.* XVII 1984 no. 1 29–54

3468 F.J. Stephens, 'Mining in the Mendip Hills', *Ann. Reps. R. Cornwall Polytech. Soc.* Rep. 59 1891 108–16

3469 P.A.E. Stewart, 'Mendip: Emborough adit', *Br. Caver* XXVII 1956 55–7

3470 E.A. Stewart, 'Report on an investigation of mine shafts on Sandford Hill, Mendips', *Br. Caver* XXXII 1959 51–5

3471 R. Stiles, 'Some documentary evidence of calamine working at Shipham Manor, Somerset, in the eighteenth century', *Somerset Mines Res. Group J.* II no. 1 1983 1–7

3472 R. Stiles, 'The Somerset coal combination', *BIAS J.* XX 1988 23–8

An agreement by coalpit owners in 1828 to maintain artificially high prices for coal.

3473 D.W. Warren, 'Newland Quarry', *SIAS J.* no. 2 36–39

3474 W.C. Wells, *Historical review of the Bristol and Somerset coalfields.* (Midsomer Norton, Mardon Flexible Packaging, 1977)

3475 W.J. Williams, *Coal mining in Bishop Sutton, North Somerset, c. 1799–1929.* (The Author, 1978)

3476 H.B. Woodward, 'The lead and zinc mines of Mendip', *Mining Mag. & Rev.* Mar. 1872 196–202

3477 P. Wooster, 'The stone industry at Bath', *BIAS J.* XI 1978 5–13

PAPER MAKING

3478 N. Edwards, 'Paper making at Watchet', *Somerset Ind. Archaeol. Soc. Bull.* no. 62 April 1993

3479 W.W. Jervis and S.J. Jones, 'The paper-making industry in Somerset', *Geography* XV 1929–30 625–9

3480 M. Watts, 'Wookey Hole Paper Mill', *BIAS J.* VII 1974 26–7

POSTS AND COMMUNICATIONS

3481 M.J.H. Ellis, *The early history of the telephone in Bath.* (Bristol, British Telecom, Severnside District Office, 1986) 90p.

The same author and title appear in *BIAS J.* XIX 1986 21–31

3482 J.W.M. Stone, *Old-Down.* (Dorchester, Somerset & Dorset Postal History Group, c. 1984) 25p.

3483 N. Wilson, 'The Washford transmitting station', *Somerset Ind. Archaeol. Soc. Bull.* no. 73 1996 2–10

POTTERY AND CERAMICS

3484 P.S. Brown and J.M. Sneddon, 'Clay tobacco pipes from Bath', *Somerset Dorset N. & Q.* XXIX no. 298 1973 294–6

3485 B.J.H. Brown, 'The Royal Potteries, Weston-super-Mare, 1836–1961', *Ind. Archaeol.* VIII 1971 5–13

3486 P.S. Brown and D. Brown, 'Tobacco-pipe makers of Bath in the nineteenth century', *Somerset Dorset N. & Q.* XXX no. 299 1974 24–8

3487 R.J.C. Coleman-Smith, *Donyatt Pottery 11th century–1939.* (Somerset Industrial Archaeology Society, Survey no. 9, 1996) 32p.

3488 R. Coleman-Smith and T. Pearson, *Excavations in the Donyatt Potteries.* (Chichester, Phillimore, 1988) 428p.

3489 R. Coleman-Smith, 'Two pottery kilns and a workshop of the late 17th to early 18th century, excavated at Site 13, Donyatt, Somerset', *Trans. Eng. Ceram. Circle* XVI no. 1 1996 70–5

3490 M.J. Lewcun, 'The clay tobacco pipe making industry of Bath', *Bath Hist.* V 1994 125–46

3491 R. Maggs, 'George But, clay pipe maker', *Proc. Somerset Archaeol. Nat. Hist. Soc.* CXXXVI 1992 184–5

3492 B. Murless, 'Chilton Tile Factory', *Somerset Ind. Archaeol. Soc. Bull.* no. 67 1994 16–17

3493 M.B. Owen, 'Clay tobacco pipes from Bath', *Proc. Somerset Archaeol. Nat. Hist. Soc.* CXI 1967 51–5

3494 *The Royal Potteries of Weston-super-Mare.* (Weston-super-Mare, Woodspring Museum, 1987) 44p.

3495 I.C. Walker, 'A clay tobacco pipe from Bath', *Proc. Somerset Archaeol. Nat. Hist. Soc.* CXIV 1970 100

3496 I.C. Walker, 'Three Somerset pipemakers', *Proc. Somerset Archaeol. Nat. Hist. Soc.* CXVI 114–15

PUBLIC UTILITIES
Electricity

3497 W.E. Eyles, *Electricity in Bath 1890–1974.* (Bath City Council and S.W. Electricity Board, 1974) 65p.

3498 D. Gledhill and P. Lamb, *Electricity in Taunton 1807–1948.* (Somerset Industrial Archaeology Society Survey no. 3, 1986) 32p.

3499 D. Gledhill, 'Gas engines and waterwheels in Somerset power stations', *Ssomerset Ind. Archaeol. Soc. Bull.* no. 70 Dec. 1995 2–8

3500 P.N. Roche, 'The story of Bath power station', *Western Power* I no. 2 Feb. 1962

Gas

3501 D. Gledhill, 'The gas engines at the Westford Water Pumping Station', *Somerset Ind. Archaeol. Soc. Bull.* no. 73 Dec. 1996 13–16

3502 D. Gledhill, 'A history of gas and electricity in Banwell', *Somerset Ind. Archaeol. Soc. Bull.* no. 64 Dec. 1993 2–4

3503 D. Gledhill, *Taunton gas 1816–1949.* (Somerset Industrial Archaeology Society Survey no. 5, 1989) 44p.

3504 D. Gledhill and P. Daniel, 'Wedmore gasworks', *Somerset Ind. Archaeol. Soc. Bull.* no. 66 Aug. 1994 2–9

Water

3505 A. Hardiman, 'Servicing the houses of Bath 1714–1830: water supply', *BIAS J.* no. 27 1994 11–18

3506 A. Hardiman, 'Servicing the houses of Bath 1714–1830: sewage and rainwater disposal', *BIAS J.* no. 29 1997 14–22

3507 F. Hawtin, 'An early water system on the Quantocks', *Ind. Archaeol.* IX 1972 412–20

A 17th-century water system to supply the settlement at Cushuish.

3508 'Rural water supply', *Somerset Ind. Archaeol. Soc. Bull.* no. 64 Dec. 1993 19–24

3509 Rev. C.W. Shickle, *The early water supply of Bath.* (Bath, *Bath Chronicle*, 1917) 17p.

3510 D.W. Warren, *Rural water supply in Somerset (Devon & Dorset).* (Somerset Industrial Archaeology Society Survey no. 10, 1998) 40p.

SALT

3511 S. Farrer and B. Murless, 'Dunball Salt Works', *Somerset Ind. Archaeol. Soc. Bull.* no. 74 1997 16–27

3512 A. Whittaker, 'The salt industry at Puriton, Somerset', *Proc. Somerset Archaeol. Nat. Hist. Soc.* CXIV 1970 96–9

TEXTILES

3513 N. von Behr, 'The cloth industry of Twerton from the 1780s to the 1820s', *Bath Hist.* VI 1996 88–107

3514 'Cloth trade in Somerset', *Somerset Dorset N. & Q.* XXIV no. 225 1945 191–3

Text of an agreement made in 1578

3515 J.H. Fox, *The woollen manufacture in Wellington, Somerset: compiled from the records of an old family business.* (1914) 121p.

3516 E. Green, 'On some Flemish weavers settled at Glastonbury A.D. 1551', *Proc. Somerset Archaeol. Nat. Hist. Soc.* XXVI pt. 2 1880

3517 T.J. Hunt, 'Some notes on the cloth trade in Taunton in the thirteenth century'

Proc. Somerset Archaeol. Nat. Hist. Soc. CI–CII 1956–7 89–107

3518 E. Moir, 'Benedict Webb, clothier', *Econ. Hist. Rev.* 2nd ser. X no. 2 1957 257–64

A clothier of Taunton in the reign of James I.

3519 H.C. Oram, *The Industrial Revolution and the textile industries of Somerset.* (M.A. thesis, Bristol University, 1930)

3520 K. Ponting, 'Clothing villages on the Frome', *Ind. Archaeol.* III 1966 256–60

Centres on the village of Tellisford

3521 D. Warren, 'Holyrood lace mill, Chard', *Somerset Ind. Archaeol. Soc. Bull.* no. 75 1997 18

TRANSPORT
Canals

3522 N. Allsop, *The Somersetshire Coal Canal rediscovered.* Rev. ed. (Bath, Millstream Books, 1993) 96p.

3523 R.A. Atthill, 'The Somerset Coal Canal', *Country Life* CIX 1951 1014–15

3524 R.K. Bluhm, 'The Radstock branch of the Somerset Coal Canal, with a note on William Ashman's locomotive', *Ind. Archaeol.* III 1966 245–50

3525 A.M. Boyd, 'The Glastonbury Navigation and Canal', *J. Rlwy. Canal Hist. Soc.* XXIII 1977 42–55

3526 B.J. Buchanan, 'The Avon Navigation and the inland port of Bath', *Bath Hist.* VI 1996 63–97

3527 C.A. Buchanan, *The Bridgwater and Taunton Canal.* 2nd ed. (Somerset Industrial Archaeology Society Survey no. 1, 1994)

3528 R.A. Buchanan, 'Coombe Hay Caisson Lock, Somersetshire Coal Canal: a BIAS project report', *BAIS J.* II 1969 27–9

3529 M. Chapman, 'The Somerset Coal Canal: a cartographical survey', *BIAS J.* XX 1988 4–22

3530 K.R. Clew, *The Somersetshire Coal Canal and railways.* (Newton Abbot, David & Charles, 1970) 176p.

3531 E. Corrie, 'The Bridgwater and Taunton Canal', *Waterways Wld.* XXI no. 6 June 1992

3532 J.M. Eyles, 'A further study of the early maps of the Somersetshire Coal Canal', *Cartographic J.* XII 1975 47–8

3533 B.J. Murless, *Bridgwater docks and the River Parrett.* (Bridgwater, Somerset County Library, 1983) 50p.

3534 'The Somersetshire Coal Canal', *Engineer* CIII 1907 520–2

3535 F. Stratford, *A plan for extending the navigation from Bath to Chippenham. In a letter to the Worshipful Company of Merchants in the City of Bristol.* (Bristol, E. Farley, 1765)

Copy in Wiltshire Archaeological Society Library, Tract no. 73

3536 H. Torrens, 'Early maps of the Somersetshire Coal Canal', *Cartographic J.* XI 1974 45–7

3537 H. Torrens, 'Further comments on the maps of the Somersetshire Coal Canal', *Cartographic J.* XII 1975 49

3538 H. Torrens, 'The Somersetshire Coal Canal caisson lock', *BIAS J.* VIII 1975 4–10

3539 M. Westerling, 'The Chard Canal in 1966', *Ind. Archaeol.* IV 1967 148–57

3540 A.T. Wicks, 'The Somerset Coal Canal', *Somerset Dorset N. & Q.* XXIV no. 223 1944 151–2

Railways

3541 M. Arlett and I. Peters, *Steam around Bath.* (Millstream, 1987)

3542 A.W. Arthurton, 'The Camerton and Limpley Stoke Railway', *Rlwy. Mag.* XXIX 1911 33–7

3543 L.H. Barber, *A family and a railway.* (Street, C. & J. Clark Ltd, 1955) 48p.
Centenary history of Somerset Central Railway, 1854–1954.

3544 R. Bluhm, 'The first railway locomotive in the West of England', *BIAS J.* XI 1978 34–5
On the tramroad of the Somerset Coal Canal Co.

3545 R.A. Bye and T.H. Lovell, 'A proposed extension of the West Somerset Mineral Railway to Eisen Hill', *SIAS J.* no. 2 1977 24–6

3546 C.R. Clinker, 'The Wrington Vale Light Railway', *Rlwy. Mag.* CV 1959 741–4, 790

3547 B. Coomer, *History of the Somerset & Dorset Railway.* (Wimborne, Bill Coomer, 1997) 144p.

3548 T. Cubitt, *The West Somerset Railway: official guide.* 5th ed. (West Somerset Books, *c.* 1988) 32p.

3549 C.G. Down and A.J. Warrington, *The Newbury Railway.* (Warrington, Industrial Railway Society, 1979)
A mineral railway built to carry coal from Newbury Colliery near Radstock.

3550 C. Dunmall, *Transport of delight: a pictorial celebration of the West Somerset Railway.* (Dulverton, Exmoor Press, 1990) 100p.

3551 W.E. Edwards, 'The East Somerset Railway', *Rlwy. Mag.* XLIX 1921 29–34

3552 A. Elton, 'The pre-history of railways, with special reference to the early quarry railways of north Somerset', *Proc. Somerset Archaeol. Nat. Hist. Soc.* CVII 1963 31–59

3553 M. Farr, *The Wrington Vale Light Railway.* (Bristol, Avon-Anglia Publications, 1978) 29p.

3554 R.B. Fellows, 'Templecombe Junction, 1860–1932', *Rlwy. Mag.* LXXI 1932 410–12

3555 R.G. Gilson and G.W. Quartley, 'Some technical aspects of the Somerset Coal Canal tramways', *J. Ind. Archaeol.* V 1968 140–61

3556 A. Hammond, *Stories of the Somerset and Dorset.* (Bath, Millstream Books, 1995) 88p.
Reminiscences of railway men.

3557 H.L. Hopwood, 'The West Somerset Mineral Line', *Rlwy. Mag.* XLIV 1921

151–6

3558 M.H. Jones, 'The prehistory of the West Somerset mineral railway', *SIAS J.* no. 2 1977 4–14

3559 C.G. Maggs, *Branch lines of Somerset.* (Stroud, Sutton, 1993) 154p.

3560 C.G. Maggs, *The Clevedon branch.* (Didcot, Wild Swan, c. 1987) 67p.

3561 C.G. Maggs, *The East Somerset Railway, 1858–72.* (Bristol, Avon-Anglia Publications for the East Somerset Railway Co., 1977) 28p.

3562 C.G. Maggs, 'The Hallatrow–Limpley Stoke line', *Rlwy. Mag.* XCIX 1953 265–9

3563 R. May and others, 'New approach at Somerset and Avon', *Rlwy. Mag.* CXXXVII 1991 282–5

Somerset & Avon Railway Co. Ltd.

3564 V. Mitchell and K. Smith, *Frome to Bristol.* (Midhurst, Midddleton, 1986) 96p.

3565 V. Mitchell and K. Smith, *Yeovil to Dorchester.* (Midhurst, Middleton, 1990) 96p.

3566 J. Owen, *Life on the railway.* (Bath, Millstream, 1989) 199p.

History and description of Bath (Green Park) Station

3567 I. Peters, *The Somerset & Dorset: an English cross-country railway.* (Oxford Publishing Co., 1974) 128p.

See also nos. 487–97

3568 D. Phillips, *Working Somerset & Dorset steam, including the Highbridge Branch.* (Yeovil, Fox & Co., 1990) 96p.

3569 D. Pollard, 'Bath stone quarry railways 1795–1830', *BIAS J.* XV 1982 13–19

3570 H. Rake, 'The railways of Somerset', *Rlwy. Mag.* XXXIV 1914 402–10

3571 C. Redwood, *The Weston, Clevedon and Portishead Railway: the detailed study of an independent light railway.* (Weston-super-Mare, Sequoia, 1981) 183p.

See also no. 498

3572 R.J. Sellick, *The Old Mineral Line—an illustrated survey of the West Somerset Mineral Railway from Watchet to the Brendon Hills as it was and is today.* (Dulverton, Exmoor Press, 1976) 90p.

3573 R.J. Sellick, *The West Somerset mineral railway and the story of the Brendon Hills Iron Mines* 2nd ed. (Newton Abbot, David & Charles, 1970) 128p.

3574 *The Taunton to Minehead railway: a short history and description of the line; compiled by members of Minehead & District Round Table.* (1970)

3575 M. Vincent, *Reflections on the Portishead Branch.* (Poole, Oxford Publishing Co., 1983) 224p.

3576 M. Vincent, *Through countryside and coalfield: the GWR's Bristol and North Somerset Railway.* (Yeovil, Foulis, 1990) 256p.

3577 D. Warnock, *The Bristol and North Somerset Railway, 1863–84.* (Bristol, Temple Cloud Publications, 1978) 17p.

3578 *West Somerset Railway: stock book.* (Devizes, West Somerset Books on behalf of the West Somerset Railway Association, 1989) 63p.

3579 K. White, 'Bath station in Broad Gauge days', *Broadsheet* no. 14 1985 16–19

3580 'Wrington Vale Light Railway', *Rlwy. Mag.* X 1902 82–5

Roads and Road Transport

3581 P. Bell, 'Ropeway, Kennesome Hill–Langham Hill pits', *Somerset Ind. Archaeol. Soc. Bull.* no. 55 Dec. 1990

Drawings of an aerial ropeway, carrying iron ore from the pit to the main line railway.

3582 J. Bentley and P. Daniel, 'Investigation of turnpike road north of Shepton Mallet', *Somerset Ind. Archaeol. Soc. Bull.* no. 77 Apr. 1998 15–17

3583 J.B. Bentley and B.J. Murless, *Somerset roads—the legacy of the turnpikes.*

Phase 1. Western Somerset. (Somerset Industrial Archaeology Society, 1985) 112p.

Phase 2. East Somerset. (Somerset Industrial Archaeology Society, 1987)

3584 A. Buchanan and D. Browning, 'A note on Bath roads', *BIAS J.* I 1968 14–16

3585 B.J. Buchanan, 'The Great Bath Road 1700–1830', *Bath Hist.* IV 1992 71–94

3586 C.A. Buchanan, 'The Shepton Mallet Turnpike Trust', *Somerset Ind. Archaeol. Soc. Bull.* no. 77 Apr. 1998 17–21

3587 C.A. Buchanan, 'The Langport, Somerton and Castle Cary Turnpike Trust: an introduction', *SIAS J.* no. 2. 1977 20–3

3588 C.A. Buchanan, 'A patent road scraper', *SIAS J.* no. 2 1977 34–5

3589 C.A. Buchanan, 'The Wells Turnpike Trust', *SIAS J.* no. 3 1981 10–16

3590 S. Chislett, *Buses and trams of Bath.* (Bath, Millstream Books, 1986) 96p.

3591 C.R. Clear, *John Palmer of Bath, mail coach pioneer.* (London, Blandford Press, in conjunction with the Postal History Society, 1955) 109p.

3592 T. Fawcett, 'Chair transport in Bath: the sedan era', *Bath Hist.* II 1988 113–38

3593 G.B. Grundy, 'The ancient highways of Somerset', *Archaeol. J.* XCVI no. 2 1939 226–97

3594 C.G. Maggs, *The Bath tramways.* 2nd ed. (Oxford, Oakwood Press, 1992) 104p.

3595 C.G. Maggs, *The Weston-super-Mare tramways.* 2nd ed. (Lingfield, Oakwood Press, 1974) 37p.

3596 F. Neale, 'The Blagdon tollhouse', *Somerset Dorset N. & Q.*, XXIX 1970 291

3597 R.D. Reid, 'The Wells Turnpike Trust', *Proc. Somerset Archaeol. Soc. Bath Branch* VIII no. 6 1944 316–23

3598 R.H. Spiro, 'John Loudon McAdam in Somerset and Dorset', *Somerset Dorset N.& Q.* XXVII no. 263 1956 85–92

3599 W.A. Webb, *The early years of stage coaching on the Bath road.* (Ealing, 1922)

3600 E.F. Williams, 'The Luxborough–Roadwater Road', *Somerset. Dorset N. & Q.* XXX 1978

Bridges

3601 R.A. Buchanan, 'The bridges of Bath', *Bath Hist.* III 1990 1–21

3602 A.J.H. Coulthard, 'Somerset pack horse bridges', *Somerset Dorset N. & Q.* XXIV no. 218 Sept. 1943 55

3603 D.J. Greenfield, 'The County Bridge papers', *SIAS J.* no. 2 1977 27–30

3604 D.J. Greenfield, 'Silk Mills Canal bridge', *SIAS J.* no. 3 1981 20–2

3605 D. Hague, 'Victoria Bridge, Bath', *BIAS J.* XII 1979 27–8

3606 G. Wallis and A. Wilkinson, 'Restoration of Cleveland Bridge in Bath: work undertaken by Dorothea Restorations Limited', *BIAS J.* no. 27 1994 35–6

3607 A.T. Wicks, 'Somerset pack horse bridges', *Somerset Dorset N. & Q.* XXIV no. 221 1944 116–17

Piers, Ports, Ships and Shipping

3608 B.J.H. Brown, 'Clevedon Pier: a note in its Centenary year', *BIAS J.* no. 2 1969 18–19

3609 N.J. Burgess, *An appraisal of the structural design of Clevedon Pier, Somerset. (1838).* (M.Phil. thesis, Brunel University, 1975)

3610 D.B. Clement, 'Three Bridgwater ships', *Marit. S-W* no. 3 1987 29–36

The *Charles*, the *Arthur* and the *Young Fox*

3611 N. Coombes, *Striding boldly: the story of Clevedon Pier.* (Clevedon Pier Trust, 1995) 64p.

3612 C.D. Curtis, 'The Port of Uphill', *Somerset Dorset N. & Q.* XXIX 1973 265–6

3613 G.E. Farr, *Somerset harbours, including the port of Bristol.* (Christopher Johnson, 1954) 160p.

3614 S. Lamb, 'The waterborne trade of Huntspill, Somerset', *Marit. S-W* no. 5 1991 17–24

3615 K. Mallory, *Clevedon Pier.* (Bristol, Redcliffe Press, 1981) 77p.

3616 J.G. McKee, 'The Weston-super-Mare flatner', *Mar. Mirr.* LVII 1971 25–39

A type of sailing boat.

3617 M. Miles, 'Eroding boats', *Somerset Ind. Archaeol. Soc. Bull.* no. 66 1994 14–20

Describes the *Persevere*, last of the eroding boats built for the Somerset Rivers Catchment Board.

3618 M. Miles, 'The dream fulfilled (?)' *Somerset Ind. Archaeol. Soc. Bull.* no. 64 Dec. 1993 14–18

3619 P. Newman, *Grandeur and decay: a salvaged history of Clevedon Pier.* (Bristol, Engart Press, 1981)

3620 P. Stuckey, 'The lovely ketch 'Irene'', *BIAS J.* XVII 1984 9–11

Launched at Bridgwater.

3621 A.P. Ward, 'A willow boat from Curload, Stoke St Gregory', *SIAS J.* no. 2 1977 33

OTHER INDUSTRIES

3622 N. Bird, 'The goldsmiths of Wells', *Somerset Dorset N. & Q.* XXXIII Mar. 1993 206–10

3623 K. Burge, ed., *The story of a community and its newspaper: Somerset County Gazette 150 years*. (Taunton, South West Counties Newspapers, 1986) 96p.

3624 H. St G. Gray, 'Salmon fishing on the coast of Somerset', *Somerset Dorset N. & Q.* XXIII pt. 204 Mar. 1940 97–8

3625 C.W.J. Harris, *100 years of bookbinding in Bath.* (Bath, Chivers, 1978)

3626 F. Hawtin and B.J. Murless, 'Bridgwater glasshouse', *SIAS J.* no. 3 1981 2–5

3627 A.P. Ward, 'A withy boiler at Burrow Bridge', *SIAS J.* no. 1 1975 13

Wiltshire

GENERAL

3628 M.C. Corfield, *ed., A guide to the industrial archaeology of Wiltshire.* (Wiltshire County Council, Library & Museum Service, for Wiltshire Archaeological & Natural History Society, 1978) 73p.

3629 C. Dale, *Wiltshire apprentices and their masters, 1710–1760.* (Wilts. Archaeological & Natural History Society. Records Branch v. 17 1961) 224p.

3630 M.F. Davies, *Life in an English village. An economical and historical survey of the parish of Corsley in Wiltshire.* (London, T. Fisher Unwin, 1909) 319p.

3631 P.S. Goodhugh, 'The Poor Law in Amesbury', *Wilts. Ind. Archaeol.* no. 2 1970 6–12

3632 N. Moore, 'Cast iron monuments', *Wilts. Ind. Archaeol.* no. 1 1969 25

3633 A. Pentelow, 'Recollections of the Rural Industries Bureau in Wiltshire', *Wilts. Folklife* no. 15 1987 3–11

3634 K. Ponting, *ed., The industrial archaeology of Wiltshire.* 2nd ed. (Devizes, Wiltshire Archaeological & Natural History Society, 1973) 28p.

3635 K.H. Rogers, 'County records', *Wilts. Ind. Archaeol.* no. 3 1971 20

Their value for industrial archaeology.

3636 K.H. Rogers and J.H. Chandler, *eds., Early trade directories of Wiltshire.* (Wilts. Record Soc. XLVII, 1992) 215p.

3637 C.M. Rowe, *Salisbury's local coinage.* (Salisbury, Tisbury Printing Works, 1966) 88p.

Salisbury trade tokens.

3638 *Victoria County History of Wiltshire* (London, Institute of Historical Research) v. 4 is devoted largely to economic history. For detailed references therein see R.A.M. Green *A bibliography of printed works relating to Wiltshire 1920–1960* (Wiltshire Library & Museum Service, 1975)

3639 T.D. Whittet, 'Wiltshire apothecaries' tokens and their issuers', *Wilts. Archaeol. Nat. Hist. Soc. Mag.* LXXXI 1987 74–79

3640 N.J. Williams, *ed., Tradesmen in early Stuart Wiltshire: a miscellany.* (Wiltshire Archaeological & Natural History Society, Records Branch v. 15, 1959) 146p.

AGRICULTURE

See also nos. 52, 3702, 3713, 3716

3641 G. Atwood, 'A study of the Wiltshire water meadows', *Wilts. Archaeol. Nat. Hist. Mag.* LVIII 1963 403–13

3642 W.E. Barber, 'Flax-growing in England', *Country Life* XCVI 1944 766–8

Decribes the processing of flax at Devizes flax mill.

3643 J.H. Bettey, 'The cultivation of woad in the Salisbury area during the late sixteenth and seventeenth centuries', *Text. Hist.* IX 1978 112–17

3644 J.H. Bettey, 'Some evidence for livestock traffic in Wiltshire during the seventeenth century', *Wilts. Archaeol. Nat. Hist. Soc. Mag.* LXXXI 1987 133–7

3645 A. Court, *Seedtime to harvest: a farmer's life.* (Bradford-on-Avon, Ex Libris, 1987)

3646 M. Cowan, *Floated water meadows in the Salisbury area.* (S. Wilts. Industrial Archaeology Society, Historical Monographs no. 9, 1982) [12p.]

3647 E. Coward, 'Notes on farming families of the 19th century in Wiltshire', *Wilts. Archaeol. Nat. Hist. Soc. Mag.* XLV 1930–2 336–41

3648 R.M. Cruse, 'The Cruse family of Imber: their dew ponds', *Wilts. Folklife* no. 2 1980–1 19–24

3649 T. Davis, *General view of the agriculture of the County of Wiltshire with observations on the means of its improvements.* (Board of Agriculture, 1794)

3650 T. Davis, *General view of the agriculture of Wiltshire ...* (Board of Agriculture, 1811) 208p.

3651 B.R. Dittmer, *An agricultural geography of north-west Wiltshire, 1773–1840.* (M.A. thesis, London University, 1963)

3652 J.P. Dodd, 'Wiltshire agriculture in 1854. The value of the Board of Trade returns', *S. Hist.* IV 1982 145–65

3653 J.R. Ellis, *Parliamentary enclosure in Wiltshire.* (Ph.D. thesis, Bristol University, 1972)

3654 J.R. Ellis, 'Parliamentary enclosure in Wiltshire by public general acts', *Wilts. Archaeol. Nat. Hist. Mag.* LXXII–LXXIII 1977–8 155–65

3655 J.R. Ellis, 'The parliamentary enclosure of Aldbourne', *Wilts. Archaeol. Nat. Hist. Mag.* LXVIII 1973 89–108

3656 D.L. Farmer, 'Two Wiltshire manors and their markets', *Agric. Hist. Rev.* XXXVII 1989 1–11

3657 E.H. Goddard, 'A terriar of the common fields belonging to Broad Town & Thornhill in the County of Wilts. 1725', *Wilts. Archaeol. Nat. Hist. Mag.* XLVI 1932–4 366–79

3658 J. Hare, 'Change and continuity in Wiltshire agriculture in the later middle ages', in W. Minchinton, *ed., Agricultural improvement: medieval and modern.* (Exeter University, Exeter Papers in Economic History, no. 14, 1981) 1–18

3659 J.N. Hare, 'The demesne lessees of fifteenth-century Wiltshire', *Agric. Hist. Rev.* XXIX 1981 1–15

3660 J. Hare, *Lord and tenant in Wiltshire, c. 1380–c. 1520, with particular reference to regional and seigneurial variations.* (Ph.D. thesis, London University, 1976)

3661 B. Harrison, 'Field systems and demesne farming on the Wiltshire estates of Saint Swithun's Priory, Winchester, 1248–1340', *Agric. Hist. Rev.* XLIII pt. 1 1995 1–18

3662 H.C.K. Henderson, 'The 1801 crop returns for Wiltshire', *Wilts. Archaeol. Nat. Hist. Mag.* LIV no. 194 1951 85–91

3663 G.B. Hony, 'Sheep farming in Wiltshire with a short history of the Hampshire Down breed', *Wilts. Archaeol. Nat. Hist. Mag.* XLIII 449–64

3664 A.J. Hosier and F.H. Hosier, *Hosier's farming system*. (London, Crosby Lockwood, 1951) 244p.

An account of large-scale farming in Wiltshire.

3665 D. Howell, *Smallbrook Farm, Warminster 1905–1965*. (Warminster, Wylye Valley Publications, 1988) [76]p.

3666 W.H. Hudson, *A shepherd's life*. (Tisbury, Compton Press, 1978) 215p.

First published 1910. Various editions of this view of rural life have been published.

3667 J.L. Jones, 'A farming revolution', *Country Life* CXXII 1957 972–3

Corn growing on the Wiltshire chalk downs.

3668 E.W.J. Kerridge, *The agrarian development of Wiltshire, 1540–1640*. (Ph.D. thesis, London University, 1952)

3669 E. Kerridge, 'The floating of the Wiltshire water meadows', *Wilts. Archaeol. Nat. Hist. Mag.* LV 1953 105–18

3670 E. Kerridge, 'The notebook of a Wiltshire farmer in the early seventeenth century', *Wilts Archaeol. Nat. Hist. Mag.* LIV 1952 416–28

Robert Wansborough of Shrewton

3671 E. Kerridge, 'The revolts in Wiltshire against Charles I', *Wilts. Archaeol. Nat. Hist. Mag.* LVII 1958–60 64–75

Revolts against enclosure proposals.

3672 E. Kerridge, 'The sheepfold in Wiltshire and the floating of the water-meadows', *Econ. Hist. Rev.* 2nd ser. VI 1954 282–9

3673 E. Lisle, *Observations in husbandry*. 2v. (1757)

Describes farming in south Hampshire and Wiltshire 1690–1740

3674 E. Little, 'On the farming of Wiltshire', *J. R. Agric. Soc.* V 1844 161–80

3675 J.E. Manners, 'Shepherds of the plain', *Wilts. Folklife* no. 11 1984 2–7

3676 F.W. Morgan, 'Woodland in Wiltshire at the time of the Domesday Book', *Wilts. Archaeol. Nat. Hist. Mag.* XLVII 1935–7 25–33

3677 J. Morrison, 'Philip Wittaker and the Bratton farm books', *Wilts. Folklife* no. 20 1990 3–8

Details of farming by Wittaker at Bratton.

3678 J.R. Pierrepont, 'The Manor of Brixton Deverill: a custumal and an extent of the thirteenth century', *Wilts. Archaeol. Nat. Hist. Mag.* LXXVIII 1983 55–61

3679 K. Ponting, 'Sheep in Wiltshire', *Wilts. Folklife* II no. 3 1979 18–30

3680 R.F.S., 'Hosier milking bail', *Wilts. Folklife* no. 11 1984 30–2

3681 R.E. Sandell, ed., *Abstracts of Wiltshire inclosure awards and agreements*. (Wiltshire Record Society, XXV 1969) 216p.

3682 R.C. Scott, *Agrarian conditions on the Wiltshire estates of the duchy of Lancaster, the Lords Hungerford and the bishopric of Winchester in the 13th, 14th and 15th centuries*. (Ph.D. thesis, London University, 1940)

3683 B. Spreadbury, *Farmer's boy: shepherding, farming and village life in east Wiltshire between the wars*. (Avebury, Wiltshire Life Society, 1992) 65p.

3684 A.G. Street, *Ditchampton Farm*. (London, Eyre & Spottiswoode, 1946) 207p.

3685 A.G. Street, *Farmer's glory*. New ed. (London, Faber & Faber, 1959) 287p.

3686 A.G. Street, *Hitler's whistle*. (London, Eyre & Spottiswoode, 1943) 297p.
Farming in South Wiltshire in wartime.

3687 C.C. Taylor, 'Three deserted medieval settlements in Whiteparish', *Wilts. Archaeol. Nat. Hist. Mag.* LXIII 1968 39–45

3688 D. Taylor, *The development of English dairy farming, 1860–1930, with special reference to Wiltshire*. (D.Phil. thesis, Oxford University, 1971)

3689 W.E. Tate, 'A hand-list of Wiltshire enclosure acts and awards', *Wilts. Archaeol. Nat Hist. Mag.* LI 1945 127–73

3690 J.R.N. Thwaite, *The history of the Wiltshire Horn breed of sheep*. (Holcombe, The Author, 1978)

3691 H.M. Trethowan, 'Farming in South Wiltshire 1920–40', *Wilts. Folklife* no. 20 1990 12–17

3692 A.R. Wilson, *Cocklebury: a farming area and its people in the vale of Wiltshire*. (Chichester, Phillimore, 1983) 120p.

3693 A. Wilson, *Forgotten harvest: the story of cheesemaking in Wiltshire*. (Privately published, 1995; available from Thatcher Distributing Group, 10 Azalea Close, Calne SN11 0QT)

ARCHITECTURE AND BUILDINGS
Domestic

3694 N.B. Chapman and P.M. Slocombe, 'A domestic cruck building at Potterne', *Wilts. Archaeol. Nat. Hist. Mag.* LXXVI 1981 105–8

3695 M. Cowan, 'Mid 19th-century 'Ideal Homes' in Salisbury?', *Wilts. Folklife* no. 15 1987 12–16

3696 N. Davey, 'Medieval timber buildings in Potterne', *Wilts. Archaeol. Nat. Hist. Mag.* LXXXIII 1990 57–69

3697 A.M. Foster, 'Bee boles in Wiltshire', *Wilts. Archaeol. Nat. Hist. Mag.* LXXX 1986 176–83
Bee boles are apertures in house or garden walls which held straw bee hives.

3698 S.R. Jones and J.T. Smith, 'A medieval timber-framed house in Cricklade', *Wilts. Archaeol. Nat. Hist. Mag.* LV 1953–4 344–52

3699 J. Morrison, 'Labourers' 'ideal homes'', *Wilts. Folklife* no. 13 1985 2–20

3700 P. Slocombe, *Medieval houses of Wiltshire*. (Alan Sutton, 1992)

3701 P.M. Slocombe, 'Two medieval roofs in West Wiltshire', *Wilts. Archaeol. Nat. Hist. Mag.* LXXX 1986 170–5

3702 P.M. Slocombe, *Wiltshire farmhouses and cottages 1500–1850*. (Devizes, Wiltshire Buildings Record, 1988) 72p.

3703 M. Waley, 'A very ordinary village house or, see how they grow', *Wilts. Archaeol. Nat. Hist. Mag.* LXXVII 1982 93–101

Industrial

3704 M. Cowan, 'Wiltshire ice houses', *Wilts. Folklife* no. 22 1991 18–21

3705 D.A.E. Cross, 'Preserving a Wiltshire windmill', *Ind. Archaeol.* IX no. 3 1972 315

3706 I. Edelman, 'The Great Barn', *Wilts. Folklife* no. 12 1984 34–7; no. 14 1986 28–9

3707 A. Ifor, 'Wilton windmill', *Wilts. Folklife* I no. 1 1976 13–15

3708 J.K. Major, *The windmills of John Wallis Titt*. (International Molinological Society, 1977) 36p.

Titt was born in Wiltshire but installed mills throughout the country.

3709 'The medieval tithe barn, Bradford-on-Avon. Report on the work of repair', *Wilts. Archaeol. Nat. Hist. Mag.* XXXIX 1915–17 485–90

3710 J.G. W. Musty, 'Water-mills on the river Bourne, south Wiltshire; the excavation of the site of Gomeldon Mill, with a note on local post-medieval pottery', *Wilts. Archaeol. Nat. Hist. Mag.* LXIII 1968 46–53

3711 P. Nicholson, 'The old cider mill at Avebury', *Wilts. Folklife* II no. 1 1978 2–3

3712 R.P. de B. Nicholson, 'Two Wiltshire windmills', *Wilts. Ind. Archaeol.* no. 3 1971 21–9

3713 P. Nicholson, 'Wiltshire buildings I: An Avon valley 'Furze House'', *Wilts. Folklife* I no. 2 1977 33–35; II: Farm buildings', *Wilts. Folklife* I no. 3 1977 43–8; 'III: Barns', *Wilts. Folklife* II no. 1 1978 21–8; 'IV: Barns, granaries and staddle stones', *Wilts. Folklife* II no. 3 1979 49–55

3714 S.E. Rigold, 'The Cherhill barn', *Wilts. Archaeol. Nat. Hist. Mag.* LXIII 1968 58–65

3715 H.E.S. Simmons, *Watermills of Wiltshire*. 1977.

A volume in the Simmons Collection relating to British windmills and watermills. A photocopy of the original typescript folders is available in the Science Museum Library, London.

3716 P.M. Slocombe, *Wiltshire farm buildings 1500–1900*. (Devizes Books Press, Wiltshire Buildings Record, 1989) 80p.

3717 K. Werran, 'Limpley Stoke Mill', *BIAS J.* no. 26 1993 15–19

3718 M. Watts, 'Littleton Wood mill and its hopper boy', *in Transactions of the 4th Symposium of the International Molinological Society, Matlock, Sept. 1977*. (London, Society for the Protection of Ancient Buildings, 1978) 327–9

3719 M. Watts, *Wiltshire windmills*. (Wiltshire Library and Museum Service, 1980) 48p.

3720 J. Weller, 'The Great Barn', *Wilts. Folklife* no. 13 1985 32–7

3721 E.T. Whyte, 'Tithe Barn, Place Farm, Tisbury', *Wilts. Archaeol. Nat. Hist. Mag.* XXXV 1907–8 21–2

3722 R.W.H. Willoughby, 'Watermills in west Wiltshire', *Wilts. Arch. & Nat. Hist. Mag.* LXIV 1969 71–99

BUILDING & CIVIL ENGINEERING

3723 J. Illston, *One man and his construction company: Reed and Mallik, 1937 to 1968*. (S. Wilts Industrial Archaeology Society, Historical Monograph no. 13 1995) 22p.

Concerns William Edward Reed

CLOCK AND WATCHMAKING

3724 W.G.C. Backinsell, *The medieval clock in Amesbury Abbey*. (Salisbury, S. Wilts. Industrial Archaeology Society, Historical Monograph no. 3, 1979) 4p.

3725 W.G.C. Backinsell, *The medieval clock in Salisbury cathedral*. (Salisbury, S. Wilts. Industrial Archaeology Society, Historical Monograph no. 2, 1977) 8p.

3726 B.H. Cunnington, 'Clock and watch makers of Wiltshire in the 17th and 18th centuries', *Wilts. Archaeol. Nat. Hist. Mag.* XLVIII 1937–9 313–17; L no. 177 1942 92–4

3727 E. Kite, 'Some old Wiltshire clocks and clockmakers', *Wilts. N. & Q.* VI 309–21

3728 M. Krognes, 'Some Wiltshire watch and clockmakers', *Wilts. Folklife* III no. 1 1979 14–22

3729 M. Snell, 'William Monk turret clocks', *Antiq. Horol.* XV Dec. 1985 583–601

Monk worked at Berwick St John

ENGINEERING AND IRONMAKING

3730 W.G.C. Backinsell, *Medieval engineering in Salisbury Cathedral*. (South Wiltshire Industrial Archaeology Society, Historical Monograph no. 10, 1986) 12p.

3731 W.G.C. Backinsell, *Medieval windlasses at Salisbury, Peterborough and Tewkesbury*. (Salisbury, S. Wiltshire Industrial Archaeology Society, Historical monograph no. 7, 1980) [8p.]

3732 H.R. Bristow, 'The village genius: Wm. Lander, brazier of Mere', *Wilts. Ind. Archaeol.* no. 3 1971 9–17

3733 R.J. Cogswell, *The Westbury Ironworks*. (Typescript in the Wiltshire Record Office, 1988)

3734 'Crofton pumping engines', *Ind. Archaeol.* V no. 4 1968 415–16

3735 R. Day, 'The iron industry in Wiltshire, 1856–1939', *BIAS J.* XII 1979 29–40

3736 R.Day and W.K.V.Gale, 'Wiltshire iron: 1855–1949' *Hist Metall.* XV 1981 18–38

3737 P. Elkins, 'The Iron Duke', *Wilts. Ind. Archaeol.* no. 2 1970 16–17

A rubber calendaring machine.

3738 J.P. Farrant, *Scout Motors of Salisbury: a history of the motor engineering firm, 1902–21*. (Salisbury & South Wiltshire Industrial Archaeology Group, 1967) 24p.

3739 D. Howell, *The Wiltshire Foundry, Warminster, 1816–1909*. (Warminster,

Wylye Valley Publications, 1987) 52p.

3740 E.G.H. Kempson, 'The wheelwright's shop', *Wilts. Archaeol. Nat. Hist. Mag.* LVI 1955–6 62–65

Wheelwright's bill of 1730–1, giving the contemporary name of many items.

3741 Kennet & Avon Canal Trust, *Crofton pumps*. (Kennet & Avon Canal Trust, Booklet no. 6, 1971) 13p.

3742 J. Morrison, 'R. & J. Reeves—agricultural implement makers', *Wilts. Folklife* I no. 1 1976 4–7

3743 J.C. Sawtell, 'Institutional steam power', *Wilts. Ind. Archaeol.* no. 2 1970 18–25

3744 P. Stokes, 'The Crofton beam engines', *J. Watford Dist. Ind. Hist.* Soc. no. 5 1975 5–21

3745 P. Stokes, 'Crofton and the Kennet & Avon Canal. The application of mid 19th-century Cornish technology, and the James Sims compound engine', *J. Trevithick Soc.* no. 18 1991 29–50

3746 C.P. Weaver and C.R. Weaver, *The Crofton pumping engines, Savernake: an illustrated account of two engines, one of which may well be the oldest surviving steam engine in commercial service in the world*. (Farnborough, Railway Enthusiasts Club, 1958) 9p.

The engines were built in 1801 and 1813.

GUNMAKING

3747 M.J.F. Fowler and H.J. Needham, 'Gun-flint industries in the Salisbury region', *Wilts Archaeol. Nat. Hist. Mag.* LXXXVIII 1995 137–41

3748 C.N. Moore, 'Salisbury gunsmiths', *Wilts. Ind. Archaeol.* no. 4 1972–3 21–3

3749 D.K. Neal, 'Gunmaking in Warminster 1800–1860', *Wilts. Folklife* II no. 3 1979 31–9

MINING AND QUARRYING

See also nos. 3452, 3458, 3462

3750 'Bath stone' *Builder* LVIII 1895 273–78, 291–5

3751 'Box Hill and its Bath stone quarries' *Builder* 1862 XX 613–16

3752 'Building stone from underground', *Quarry Managers J.* XLVI 1962 175–84

3753 Cotham Caving Group, *Box freestone mines, Wiltshire*. (1967)

3754 *A guide to the history and geology of Bath stone*. (Kingston Minerals, 1970)

3755 C.J. Hall, *'Tanky' Elms—Bath stone quarryman*. (Corsham, Wilts., C.J. Hall, 1984) 119p.

Reminiscences of Frank Elms, compiled from a series of tape recordings

3756 K. Hudson, *The fashionable stone*. (Bath, Adams & Dart, 1971) 120p.

3757 N.E. King, 'The Kennet Valley sarsen industry', *Wilts. Archaeol. Nat. Hist. Mag.* LXIII 1968 83–93

Quarrying and working sarsen stone.

3758 Pictor & Sons, *Bath stone quarries, Box.* (1883)

3759 R.J. Tucker, 'Box quarries, Wiltshire', *Ind. Archaeol.* V no. 2 1968 178–83

3760 R.J. Tucker, R.J. Bates and R.W. Mansfield, 'Box Stone 'Mines'' *Mem. Cotham Spelaeological Soc.* IV 1968–9 9–29

3761 R.J. Tucker, *Scripta legenda (Box quarries, Wiltshire) v. 1 Lower Hill Series* (Free Troglophile Association, 1976) 40p.
Copy in Swindon Reference Library

3762 R.J. Tucker, *Some notable Wiltshire quarrymen.* (Free Troglophile Association, 1973) 38p.
Copy in Swindon Reference Library

POTTERY AND CERAMICS

3763 D.R. Atkinson, 'Clay tobacco pipes and pipemakers of Marlborough', *Wilts. Archaeol. Nat. Hist. Mag.* LX 1965 85–95

3764 D.R. Atkinson, 'Clay tobacco pipes and pipemakers of Salisbury, Wiltshire', *Wilts. Archaeol. Nat. Hist. Mag.* LXV 1970 177–89

3765 D.R. Atkinson, 'Further notes on clay tobacco pipes and pipemakers from the Marlborough and Salisbury districts', *Wilts. Archaeol Nat. Hist. Mag.* LXVII 1972 149–56

3766 D. Atkinson, 'More Wiltshire clay tobacco pipe varieties', *Wilts. Archaeol Nat. Hist. Mag.* LXXII–LXXIII 1977–8 67–74

3767 D.R. Atkinson, 'Jeffry Hunt pipes', *Wilts. Archaeol. Nat. Hist. Mag.* LXVI 1971 156–61

3768 D.R. Atkinson, 'Tobacco pipes and pipemakers of Marlborough', *Wilts. Archaeolog. Nat. Hist. Mag.* LX 1965 85–95

3769 M.R. McCarthy, 'The medieval kilns of Nash Hill, Lacock, Wilts.', *Wilts. Archaeol. Nat. Hist. Soc. Mag.* LXIX 1974 97–160

3770 N. Moore, 'Wiltshire brown ware', *Wilts. Ind. Archaeol.* no. 1 1969 34

3771 J. Musty, D.J. Algar and P.F. Ewence, 'The medieval pottery kilns at Laverstock, near Salisbury, Wiltshire', *Archaeologia* CII 1969 (2nd ser. LII) 83–150

3772 J. Musty, 'A preliminary account of a medieval pottery industry at Minety, North Wiltshire.', *Wilts Archaeol. Nat. Hist. Mag.* LXVIII 1973 79–88

3773 I.C. Walker, 'Note on a Wiltshire pipemaker', *Wilts. Archaeol. Nat. Hist. Mag.* LXVII 1972 163

PRINTING AND PUBLISHING

3774 W. Partridge, *Iron printing presses: early survivors working in South Wiltshire.* (S. Wiltshire Industrial Archaeology Society, Historical Monograph no. 6, 1980) 8p.

3775 'Wiltshire newspapers—past and present. Part I by J.J. Slade', *Wilts. Archaeol.*

Nat. Hist. Mag. XL 1917–19 37–74; 'Part II', XL 1917–19 129–41; 'Part III by Mrs H. Richardson', XL 1917–19 318–51, XLI 1920–1 53–69, 479–501, XLIII 1925–7 26–38; 'Part IV by J.J. Slade', XLII 1922–4 231–41; 'Part V by J.J. Slade', XLII 1922–4 313–24

PUBLIC UTILITIES
Electricity
3776 D.A.E. Cross, 'Hydro-electricity from the Salisbury Avon and tributaries', *Wilts. Ind. Archaeol.* I 1969 26–9; IV 1972–3 24–9

3777 'Salisbury Electric Light Station', *Elect. Engr.* XXII 23 Dec. 1898 818–22

Gas
3778 J.H. Watts, *Salisbury gasworks: The Salisbury Gas Light & Coke Company.* (S. Wiltshire Industrial Archaeology Society, Historical monograph no. 12, 1991) 26p.

Water
3779 P.C. Hunt, 'Before the mains', *Wilts. Folklife* no. 13 1985 38–45

Rural water supply.

3780 M.J. Lansdown, *Trowbridge's fight for pure water, 1804–1874.* (Devizes, West Wiltshire Branch of the Historical Association, 1968) 24p.

3781 J. Watts, 'A history of Salisbury water works', *Wilts. Ind. Archaeol.* no. 4 1972–3 14–20

3782 J. Watts, 'Salisbury and Winchester sewage works', *Wilts. Ind. Archaeol.* no. 5 1974 19–25

TEXTILES
See also nos. 240–67 and 3125

3783 R.P. Beckinsale, ed., *The Trowbridge woollen industry, as illustrated by the stock books of John and Thomas Clark, 1804–24.* (Devizes, Wilts. Archaeol. Nat. Hist. Soc., Records Branch, Publication no. 6, 1950) 249p.

3784 J. Blanchard, *Malmesbury lace.* (London, Batsford, 1990)

3785 H.R. Exelby, *The industrial revolution in the textile industries of Wiltshire.* (M.A. thesis, Bristol University, 1928)

3786 W. Gaby, 'William Gaby, his booke, 1656', *Wilts. Archaeol. Nat. Hist. Mag.* XLVI 1932–4 50–7

A clothier of Netherstreet, near Devizes. His notebook, dealing with the wool trade.

3787 M. Gibson, 'The Downton lace industry', *Wilts. Folklife* III no. 3 1982 23–5

3788 E.F. Glyn, *Downton lace industry.* (Salisbury, Tisbury Printing Works, 1961)

3789 S. Hartley and P. Parry, *Downton lace: a history of lace making in Salisbury and the surrounding area.* (Salisbury, Salisbury & South Wiltshire Museum, 1991) 20p.

3790 J. de L. Mann, 'Clothiers and weavers in Wiltshire during the eighteenth century', *in* L.S. Pressnell, *ed., Studies in the Industrial Revolution: presented to T.S. Ashton* (Athlone Press, 1960) 66–96

3791 J. de L. Mann, *Documents illustrating the Wiltshire textile trades in the eighteenth century.* (Wilts. Archaeol. Nat. Hist. Soc., Records Branch, v. 19, 1964) 191p.

3792 J. de L. Mann, A Wiltshire family of clothiers: George and Hester Wansey, 1683–1714', *Econ. Hist. Rev.* 2nd ser. IX no. 2 1956 241–53

3793 *The Miseries of the Miserable, or, an essay towards laying open the Decay of the Fine Woollen Trade and the unhappy condition of the poor Wiltshire Manufacturers. By a Gentleman of Wilts.* (1739)

3794 R.A. Pelham, 'The application of steam power to the Wiltshire textile industry in the early 19th century', *Wilts. Archaeol. Nat. Hist. Mag.* LIV 1951 no. 194 92–103

3795 W. Perrett, 'Three centuries of Wilton's carpet trade', *Hatcher Rev.* XXIV 1987 159–65

3796 K. Ponting, 'Clothiers' pattern books', *J. Ind. Archaeol.* II no. 4 1965 147–49

3797 K.G. Ponting, *The decline of the woollen industry in the Trowbridge and Bradford-on-Avon areas in the nineteenth century.* (M.Litt. thesis, Bristol University, 1974)

3798 K.G. Ponting, 'The weavers and fullers of Marlborough', *Wilts. Archaeol. Nat. Hist. Mag.* LIII no. 190 1949 113–17

3799 K.G. Ponting, 'Wiltshire woollen mills: insurance returns 1753–1771', *Wilts. Archaeol. Nat. Hist. Mag.* LXIX 1974 161–72

3800 K.G. Ponting, *Wool and water: Bradford-on-Avon and the River Frome.* (Bradford-on-Avon, Moonraker Press, 1975) 66p.

3801 K.G. Ponting, 'The woollen mill at Staverton: its later history', *Wilts Archaeol. Nat. Hist. Soc. Bi-Annual Bull.* no. 18 1975 10–18

3802 G.D. Ramsey, *The Wiltshire woollen industry, chiefly in the sixteenth and early seventeeth centuries.* (D.Phil. thesis, Oxford University, 1939)

3803 G.D. Ramsay, *The Wiltshire woollen industry in the sixteenth and seventeenth centuries.* 2nd ed. (London, Frank Cass, 1965) 165p.
Originally published by Oxford University Press, 1943

3804 K. Rogers, *The book of Trowbridge.* (Barracuda Books, 1984) 156p.
Largely concerned with the woollen industry

3805 K.H. Rogers, 'Trowbridge clothiers and their houses, 1660–1800', *in* N.B. Harte and K.G. Ponting, *eds., Textile history and economic history; essays in honour of Miss Julia de Lacy Mann.* (Manchester, Manchester University Press, 1973) 138–62

3806 C.D. Ross, 'The Wiltshire woollen industry', *Wool Knowledge* IV no. 1 1957 5–8; no. 2 1957 20–3

3807 K.C. White, 'Bratton woollen mills', *Wilts. Folklife* no. 14 1986 8–10

3808 *Wool encouraged without exportation, or, Practical Observations on Wool and* the Woollen manufacture. In 2 parts. Pt I, Strictures on Appendix no. IV to a Report. Pt II. Brief history of Wool and the Nature of the Woollen Manufacture. By a Wiltshire Clothier. New ed. (c. 1801)

First published 1791

Author was Henry Wansey of Warminster

TRANSPORT
Canals

3809 D.L. Banfield, 'The Wilts. & Berks. Canal, Part I', *CBA Group 9 Bull*. Apr. 1969; Part II July 1969

3810 H.S. Braun, 'The Salisbury canal: a Georgian misadventure', *Wilts. Archaeol. Nat. Hist. Mag.* LXVIII 1962 171–80

3811 D.A.E. Cross, 'The Salisbury Avon Navigation', *Ind. Archaeol.* VII 1970 121–130

An article with the same title also appears in *Wilts. Archaeol. Nat. Hist. Mag.* LXV 1970 172–6

3812 L.J. Dalby, *The Wilts. and Berks. Canal.* (Lingfield, Oakwood Press, 1971) 70p.

3813 W. Ford, 'The Devizes wharf', *Wilts. Folklife* I no. 3 1977 36–42

Built to provide wharfage facilities on the Kennet & Avon Canal.

3814 R.A. Pelham, 'The projected Marlborough Canal in the 18th century', *Wilts. Archaeol. Nat. Hist. Mag. Notes* LV 1953–4 83–4

3815 M. Smith, *Swindon and the construction of the Wilts. and Berks. Canal.* (1968)

Typescript. Copy in Swindon Reference Library.

3816 E. Welch, *The bankrupt canal: Southampton and Salisbury, 1795–1808*. 2nd ed. (Southampton Record Office, Southampton Paper no. 5, 1978)

3817 T.S. Willan, 'Salisbury and the navigation of the Avon', *Wilts. Archaeol. Nat. Hist. Mag.* XLVII 1937 592–4

Railways

3818 W.G.C. Backinsell, *The Salisbury Railway & Market House Company.* (S. Wiltshire Industrial Archaeology Society, Historical Monograph no. 1, 1977) [8p.]

3819 D. Brooke, 'Box Tunnel and railway navvies', *Wilts. Folklife* no. 22 1991 3–10

3820 T. Bryan, *Return to Swindon.* (Swindon, Avon-Anglia and the GWR Museum, 1990) 28p.

An account of Swindon and its works in the Golden Age of the GWR.

3821 H.C. Casserley, *Wessex* (Newton Abbot, David & Charles, 1975) 96p.

Railway History in Pictures Series

3822 J. Cattell and K. Falconer, *Swindon: the legacy of a railway town.* (HMSO, 1995) 186p.

3823 D. Cobbold, *A survey of Salisbury railways and market house.* (1980)

Southampton University undergraduate dissertation. Copy in Wiltshire Local History Library, Trowbridge.

3824 D.E.C. Eversley, 'The Great Western Railway and the Swindon Works in the Great Depression', *Univ. Birmingham Hist. J.* V 1951–2 167–90

3825 J. Farrant, 'A railroad to Salisbury: the proposal of 1834', *Wilts. Ind. Archaeol.* I 1969 10–13

3826 D.M. Fenton, *The Malmesbury Branch.* (Didcot, Wild Swan, 1990) 258p.

3827 D.M. Fenton, *The Malmesbury Railway: to commemorate the centenary of its opening, 1877–1977.* (Blandford, Oakwood Press, 1977) 57p.

3828 H.A. Freebury, *Great Western apprentice: Swinton in the thirties.* (Trowbridge, Wiltshire Library Service, 1985) 163p.

3829 *GWR Locomotive factory at Swindon. 1852.* (Reprint from *Borough News*, Swindon)

3830 T. Gale, *A brief account of the making and working of the Great Box Tunnel.* (Bath, 1884) 16p.

3831 K. Gibbs, *Reminiscences as office boy and apprentice at Swindon railway works, 1944–51: the sights, sounds, smells, personalities and jobs remembered with nostalgia from steam days.* (Poole, Oxford Publishing, 1986) 192p.

3832 Great Western Railway Co., *Swindon Works and its place in Great Western Railway history.* (GWR, 1947) 64p.

Reprinted by the Borough of Thamesdown, 1985.

3833 Great Western Railway, *The town and works of Swindon with a brief history of the Broad Gauge.* (Swindon, 1892) 47p.

3834 D. Harper, *Wilts. & Somerset: a railway landscape.* (Bath, Millstream, 1987) 111p.

3835 Holt Magazine, *Holt Junction: the story of a village railway station, based upon research by many persons and information from many sources.* (1966)

3836 K. Hudson, 'The early years of the railway community in Swindon', *Transp. Hist.* I no. 2 1968 130–151

3837 E.J. Larkin and J.G. Larkin, *The railway workshops of Britain, 1823–1986.* (London, Macmillan, 1988) 266p.

3838 C.G. Maggs, *The Calne Branch.* (Dicot, Wild Swan, 1990) 112p.

3839 C.G. Maggs, *Rail centres: Swindon.* (London, Ian Allan, 1983) 128p.

3840 V. Michell and K. Smith, *Salisbury to Westbury.* (Midhurst, Middleton, 1994) 96p.

3841 V. Michell and K. Smith, *Salisbury to Yeovil.* (Midhurst, Middleton, 1992) 96p.

3842 B. Morrison, *Great Western steam at Swindon works.* (Truro, Bradford Barton, 1975) 96p.

3843 E.R. Mountford, *Swindon GWR reminiscences.* (Truro, Barton, 1982) 112p.

3844 L.H. Ruegg, *The Salisbury and Yeovil Railway: a centenary reprint of 'The history of a railway' with an introduction by David St John Thomas.* New ed. (Dawlish, 1960) 66p.

3845 A.F. Saunders, 'The little trains of Chilmark', *Rlwy. Mag.* CXXII 1976 116–18

3846 T.J. Saunders, 'Railways to Devizes', *Rlwy. Mag.* CIII 1957 673–9

3847 J.C. Sawtell, '34002 Salisbury', *Wilts. Ind. Archaeol.* I 1969 30–3

3848 Southern Railway, *Ashford Works Centenary 1847–1947.* (1947)

3849 *Swindon signals from the past. GWR 1835–1985.* (Swindon Chamber of Commerce, 1985) 159p.

3850 *Swindon works and its place in British railway history.* (Swindon, British Rail Engineering, 1975) 40p.

3851 'Swindon Works: British Railways, Western Region', *Br. Machine Tool Engng.* XXXII no. 160 Apr.–June 1950 67–146

3852 A.N. Malan, *Swindon and the Broad Gauge in 1893.* (Belfast, Cuan Pubs., 1985) 65p.

3853 A.S. Peck, *The Great Western at Swindon works.* (Poole, Oxford Publishing, 1983) 278p.

3854 G.H.J. Tanner, *The Calne branch.* (Oxford, Oxford Publishing Co., 1972) 64p.

3855 D.W.J. Thody, 'Railway reveries', *Wilts. Ind. Archaeol.* V 1974 35–40

3856 R. Tomkins and P. Sheldon, *Swindon and the GWR.* (Gloucester, Sutton, 1990) 144p.

3857 B. Trinder, 'Swindon—an unfulfilled opportunity', *Ind. Archaeol. Rev.* V no. 1 1980 15–18

3858 A.P. Voce, 'The Murhill tramroad', *Wilts Ind. Archaeol.* I 1969 14–19

3859 A. Williams, *Life in a railway factory: work in the GWR Swindon works around 1915.* (Gloucester, Alan Sutton, 1984) 286p.

Originally published in 1915

Roads and Road Transport

3860 J. Chandler, 'Accommodation and travel in pre-turnpike Wiltshire', *Wilts. Archaeol. Mag.* CXXXIX 1991 83–95

3861 J.H. Chandler, *The Amesbury Turnpike Trust.* (Salisbury, S. Wiltshire Industrial Archaeology Society, Historical monograph no. 4, 1979) 12p.

3862 J. Chandler, 'The rise and fall of the Wiltshire carrier', *Wilts. Folklife* no. 17 1988 3–12

3863 J.H. Chandler, *Stage coach operation through Wiltshire.* (Salisbury, S. Wilts. Industrial Archaeology Society, Historical monograph no. 8, 1980) 8p.

3864 C. Cochrane, *The lost roads of Wessex.* (Newton Abbot, David & Charles, 1969) 199p.

3865 L.J. Dalby, *The Swindon tramways and electricity undertaking.* (Lingfield, Oakwood Press, 1973) 44p.

3866 A. Greening, 'Nineteenth-century country carriers in North Wiltshire', *Wilts. Archaeol. Nat. Hist. Mag.* LXVI 1971 162–76

3867 R.I.E. Haynes, 'Wiltshire milestones', *in* Wiltshire County Council, *Leisure in Wiltshire.* 2nd ed. (1968) 52–7

3868 F.H. Hinton, 'The roads and bridges of the Parish of Laycock, Wilts.: their management, maintenance and condition from 1583 to the end of the seventeenth century', *Wilts. Archaeol. Nat. Hist. Soc. Mag.* L 1942–4 119–35

3869 R.H. Lane, 'A Wiltshire waggon', *Rep. Marlborough Coll. Nat. Hist. Soc.* no.

81 1932 49–53

A farm waggon.

3870 T.E. Morland, 'The Great Western post road', *Wilts. Ind. Archaeol.* no. 2 1970 26–7

3871 T.E. Morland, 'Second hand milestones', *Wilts. Ind. Archaeol.* no. 1 1969 8–9

3872 T.E. Morland, 'Two Wessex roadways', *Wilts. Ind. Archaeol.* no. 5 1974 30–4

3873 S. Mullins, ''And old Mrs Ridout and all': a study of Salisbury's county carriers', *Wilts. Folklife* II no. 1 1978 29–35

3874 II.W. Timperley and E. Brill, *Ancient trackways of Wessex*. 2nd ed. (Shipston-on-Stour, P. Drinkwater, 1983) 148p.

3875 K.G. Watts, *Droving in Wiltshire: the trade and its routes*. (Avebury, Wiltshire Life Society, 1990) 93p.

3876 G. Wright, *Roads and trackways of Wessex*. (Moorland Publishing Co., 1988) 191p.

Aviation

3877 N.C. Parker, *Aviation in Wiltshire: a historical survey*. (South Wiltshire Industrial Archaeology Society, Historical monograph no. 5, 1982) 8p.

OTHER INDUSTRIES

3878 I.M. Brock, 'Looking back at the harness trade', *Wilts. Folklife* III no. 1 1979 23–6

3879 M.E. Cunnington, 'The straw plaiting industry in Wiltshire', *Wilts. Archaeol. Nat. Hist. Mag.* XLVII 1935–7 281–2, 538

3880 G.J. Eltringham, 'Salisbury companies and their ordinances with particular reference to the woodworking crafts', *Wilts Archaeol. Nat. Hist. Mag.* LIV no. 195 1951 185–91

3881 P.S. Goodhugh, 'Marconi on Salisbury plain', *Wilts. Ind. Archaeol.* no. 5 1974 26–9

3882 D. Jackson, *Maltings in Salisbury*. (South Wiltshire Industrial Archaeology Society, Historical monograph no. 11, 1986) [16p.]

3883 J.K. Major, 'Brickmaking', *Wilts. Ind. Archaeol.* no. 3 1971 6–8

3884 J.K. Major, 'A survival of the Wiltshire paper industry', *J. Ind. Archaeol.* I 1964 17–20

The Rag Mill, Slaughterford

3885 C.N. Moore, 'The Salisbury cutlery industry', *Wilts. Ind. Archaeol.* no. 4 1972–3 7–13

3886 C.N. Moore, 'Salisbury pewterers', *Wilts. Ind. Archaeol.* no. 4 1972–3 30–31

3887 H. Shortt, 'A thirteenth-century 'steelyard' balance from Huish', *Wilts. Archaeol. Nat. Hist. Mag.* LXIII 1968 66–71

3888 W. Woodruff, 'Origins of an early English rubber manufactory', *Bull. Bus. Historical Soc.* XXV no. 1 1951 31–51

Stephen Moulton's firm at Bradford-on-Avon, Wiltshire

Index of Authors and Personal Names

This index lists all personal names, whether as author or subject of books or articles. Corporate names are listed only if the body is the author of a publication. Numbers refer to titles, not pages.

Abbott, D. 418
Acland, J.E. 2778
   T.D. 3271–2
Acock, R. 3111
Acton, B. 1375
Acworth, R. 2290
Adams, A.R. 645
   B. 2300–1
   E.A. 2440
Addison, J. 2730
   P. 1020
Adlard, A. 2957
Aiken, S.R. 2127
Alabaster, C. 3412
Albino, H.H. 2910
Alcock, N.W. 1871–2, 1951–5, 1965
Aldred, D.H. 3224
Alford, B.W.E. 551, 731, 888–9
Algar, D.J.. 2777, 3771
Allan, J.P. 226
Allen *family* 1443
   A.A. 820
   C.J. 329
   G.C. 1319–20
   G.F. 297
   J.P. 2302
   J.R.L. 2911
   J.S. 2032–4, 2053
Allsop, N. 3522
Amery, P.F.S. 2396
Anderson, J.M. 2511
   P.C. 2511
   R.C. 499–500, 2834
Andrew, C.K.C. 1321
   J.H. 2060
Andrews, J. 1816
   W.K. 1294
Angel, J.L. 3094
Angove, R. 1106
Angwin, A. 1650
Anstie, J. 164, 240–1
Anstis, R. 2870, 3030, 3190
Antell, R. 465

Anthony, G.H. 1709, 2441
Appleby, J.B. 934
Appleyard, H.S. 1796
Apps, R.S. 2442
Archer, A.B. 242–3
Argau, F. 1765–6, 2583
Ariss, P. 2953
Arlett, M. 298, 3541
Armstrong, P. 299
Arnold, C.J. 227
Arthur, M. 1295
Arthurton, A.W. 912, 3542
Arx, R. von 1322–4, 2128–30
Ashcroft-Healey, V.R.G. 2121
Ashford, E.C.B. 487
   P.J. 3273
Ashman, W. 3524
Ashworth, B. 3191
Asprey, C. 2461
Astell, J. 3253
Aston, M. 3274
Atkin, S. 3100
Atkinson, A. 129, 1326–31, 1525, 2131, 2357
   B.J. 552
   C. 1325
   D.R. 2779, 3763–8
   M. 211, 1332, 2132–4, 3254
   R.L. 170, 1333
Atthill, R. 488–9, 3255–6, 3336
   R.A. 3523
Attwood, B. 790, 791
   J.S. 548
Atwood, G. 3641
Austin, C. 3317–18
   D. 1334
   R. 3108–9
   S. 300
Avon County Council 913–14
Awdry, C. 330

   W. 3192
   W.V. 3206

Baber, F.T. 3031
Backinsell, W.G.C. 3724–5, 3730–1, 3818
Baddeley, W. St Clair 3026
Bainbridge, B.C.L. 1335
Bainsmith, B.F. 1336
Baker, C. 3238
   C.M.A. 1873
   G.F. 23
   J.R. 2673
   M.H.C. 2806, 280
   O.A. 146, 171, 1337, 2135
   W.G. 172
Balchin, W.G.V. 1034
Baldock, S.F. 1876, 2912–13
Ball, A. 849
Ballantyne, R.M. 2003
Ballard, M. 956
Bamber, G.C. 882
Banfield, D.L. 3809
Bannister, G.F. 331
Barber, D. 2914
   J. 2314
   L.H. 3396, 3543
   W.E. 3642
Barclay, C.F. 1338
Barford, K.E. 244
Barham, L.F. 1758–9
Baring-Gould, S. 2093
Barker, R. 3120–1
Barklot, R.G. 2751
Barlow, F. 1832
   W.H. 946
Barman, C. 332
Barnard, H. 2397
Barnes, C.H. 646–7
Barrett, A. 1299
   D. 480
Barrie, D.S. 327, 481, 490,

1710
Barron, R.A. 2062
Bartelot, R.G. 3373
Bartholomew, D. 482
Bartlett, J. 631
  S. 1339–40
Barton, D.B. 173–4,
  1135–6, 1341–5,
  1711
  K.J. 800–2
  P. 2074
  R.M. 1296
Bastin, C.H. 2443
Bate, T.W. 1260
Bateman, D. 821–3
Bates, A. 2512
  R.J. 3760
Batt, M. 3319
Bawden, M. 2136
Baxter, B. 3193
Bayes, J.F. 3225–6
Bayles, R. 1137–9, 2137
Beadle, S. 3413–14
Beagrie, N. 1124, 1346
Beale, D. 491
  G. 333, 407
Beales, K. 2674
Beamish, R. 82
Beard, R. 2871
Beare, T. 1347
Beche, H.T. 1874
Beck, K.M. 2444
Becker, C.O. 2035
Beckerlegge, J.J. 1212,
  2513
Beckett, D. 83
Beckey, I. 807
Beckinsale, R.P. 245, 3783
Beer, K.E. 2138
Behr, N. von 868, 3513
Bell, P. 3376, 3581
Bellchambers, J.K. 2019
Bemrose, C. 792
Benbrook, I. 957
Benfield, E. 2761
Bennett, A. 1712–14
  J. 1348
  W.J. 1035
Benney, D.E. 1107
Benson, J. 24
Bent, M.V. 3070
Bentley, J.B. 3582–3
Bento, J.S. 1817
Berridge, P.S.A. 513, 1715
Besly, E. 2657
Bettey, J.H. 25, 553–4,
  2675–86, 2704, 2798,
  3275, 3643–4
Bevan, J.C.D. 1348

Beynon, V.G. 1875
Bick, D.E. 2139, 2872–3,
  2958, 3033–5,
  3064–5, 3071–4,
  3252, 3153, 3194–5
Biddle, G. 1716
Billingsley, J. 3276–7
Binding, J. 1717
Bird, A. 2356
  D. 480
  E. 1652
  J. 958
  N. 3622
  N. du Q. 555, 2860,
    3257
  R. 1766
  R.H. 175
Bishop, G.W. 3196
Bizley, A.C. 1349
Blackmore, R.T. 2371
Blake, J. 850
Blanchard, J. 3784
Blaylock, S.R. 2658
Blenkinsop, R.J. 334
Blewett, H. 1277
Blight, J. 1213, 1350
Bluhm, R. 3544
  R.K. 3415–16, 3524
Blunden, J.R. 1351–2,
  1877
Boalch, G. 117
  G.T. 2090
Boase, H. 1214
  J.R. 1353
Boddy, M. 2731
Bodman, M. 121, 556,
  632–4, 752, 3337–8
Body, G. 301, 302, 915,
  947, 1719
Bone, M. 693, 1818, 2732
  M.R. 2799–2800
Bonney, D.J. 1878
Bonsall, P.M. 3417–19
Booker, F. 1–2, 233, 335,
  2292
Boorer, M. 1021
Booth, L.G. 106
Bootsgezel, J.J. 2036
Borlase, W.C. 1354
Born, A. 1879, 2293
Borne, P. 2959
Bosham, J. 2445
Boucher, C.T.G. 694
Boulay, J. du 1768
Bouquet, M. 2584
  M.R. 516
Bourhis, J.J. 2585
Bourke, J. 2398
Bourne, J.C. 336

Bowcott, J.E.L. 682
Bowen, C. 3009
  C.R. 3075–6
  T. 716
Bowie, G.G.S. 26, 2687
  G. 2461
Bowman, W.D. 959
Bowring, B. 2020
Bowyer, V. 269
Box, F.E. 2447
Boyd, A.M. 3525
Boyle, V.C. 234, 2371,
  2586–7
Bradbeer, J.B. 2588
Braddick, L.E. 2372, 2589
Bradley, A. 905
  D.L. 463, 475
  P.C. 2111
Braithwaite, J.L. 1819
Brannam, P. 2303
Braun, H.S. 3810
Bravender, J. 2915
Brayley, A.F.L. 2347
Brayshaw, M. 223, 501
Brayshay, M. 1956–7
Brears, P.C.D. 1674
Brebner, P. 2741
Breckon, D. 337
Brent, D. 1078
Brereton, R.P. 1720
Brewer, D. 2514
Brewster, R.S. 3154
Brice, S.W. 3420
Bridgeman, B. 480, 483
Bridges, J. 948
  S. 2733
Bridgewater, N.P. 3036–7
Brierley, J. 2557
Briggs, D. 793
Brighouse, U.W. 1978
Brill, E. 3874
Brindley, J. 694
Briscoe, G. 635
Bristol Times & Mirror
  557–8
Bristow, C.M. 152
  H.R. 3732
British Waterways Board
  3155–6
Britton, J.N.N. 559
Brock, D. 338
  I.M. 3878
  J.H. 1355–6
Bromley, R.D.F. 1820
Brooke, D. 303, 339, 3819
  J. 176, 177, 1357–71,
    1767, 2140–8, 3421
Brooks, A.T. 3458
  A.W. 1372–3

INDEX OF AUTHORS AND PERSONAL NAMES 231

Broome, J. 636
Broughton, D.G. 1374, 2149–51
P.W. 2590
Brown, B.J.H. 960, 3485, 3608
C.G. 1821
D. 3486
G.A. 2446
H.M. 1809
K. 77, 1140–2, 1375–6
L.G. 1377
M. 3295
P. 776
P.S. 3484, 3486
R. 3288
S. 2572
S.E. 3197
S.W. 1958–9, 2515, 2558–9
Browning, D. 3584
Brunel, I.K. 82–113, 513, 696–8, 921, 963, 1715, 1717, 2028
Sir M.I. 82, 90, 94, 100, 103, 107, 111
Bryan, S. 3157
T. 341, 3820
Bryant, J. 1022, 1378
R.W.G. 3422
Buchanan, A. 85, 961, 3584
B.J. 3258–9, 3277, 3401–3, 3526, 3585
C.A. 3, 3339, 3527, 3586–9
R.A. 3, 86, 106, 560–2, 696–8, 962–4, 2060, 3260, 3528, 3601
Buck, A. 87
Buckingham, W. 2516
Buckland, J.S. 3340
J.S.P. 2004, 2037
W. 165
Buckley, A. 1379–80, 1387
F. 120, 733, 3007
G.B. 3007
J.A. 1381–6, 1388, 1390, 1396, 1431
J.F. 1389
S.E. 88
Budge, E. 2063
Bullen, L.J. 1391
Bulley, J.A. 2113, 3423–4
Burd, E.P. 2517
Burge, K. 3623
Burgess, N.J. 3609
R.L. 3425

Burke, G.M. 1392–5
Burlison, R. 1721
Burnard, R. 2152, 2518–19
Burnley, R. 130, 1400
Burns, K.V. 2373–4
Burritt, E. 1898
Burroughs, S. 3377
Burrow, J.C. 1396–7
Burt, R. 4, 130, 139, 147–9, 178, 212, 1615, 1332, 1398–1402, 2133–4
R.O. 1403
W. 1822
Burton, A. 270
R. 3426
Burtt, R.G. 3198
Bush, R.J.E. 3368
Bushell, T. 1415
But, G. 3491
Butler, T.H. 683
Butterworth, C. 2784
Bye, R.A. 3545

Caff, W.R.M. 78
Caldwell, J.B. 106
Calley, J. 2036
Camm, G.S. 1435
Campbell, J.M. 89
S.M. 1769
Campion, P. 3068–9
Cane, C.R. 563
Cannon, J. 551
Carne, J. 1405–9
Carpenter, R. 342
Carswell, J. 1410
Carter, C. 1108, 1411, 1770–1
Carus-Wilson, E.M. 564–7, 1823, 3125
Caseldine, C.J. 1067
Casserley, H.C. 464, 3821
Castle, P. 1979
Catchpole, L.T. 2448
Cattell, J. 3822
Caunter, F.L. 1412
Cave, B.V. 2960–1
T.S. 1363
Cawthorne, R. 1413
Central Electricity Generating Board 228
Chadwick, R. 179
Chalk, D. 2845
Champion, R. 813
W. 766, 769
Chance, Sir H. 734–5
Chandler, J.H. 3636, 3860–3
Channon, G. 343–4, 668,

916
Chanter, J.F. 2094–5
Chaplin, R.R. 3227
Chapman, D. 3378
G.M. 1880
M. 777, 3341, 3529
N.B. 3694
S. 2399
S.D. 1960
Charbonnier, T. 2304
Charles, F.W.B. 2962
Charleston, R.J. 803
Charlton, T.M. 106
Charnock, D. 2916
Chatwin, A. 568, 2874, 2963, 3005, 3038, 3113, 3126, 3248
Chesher, F.J. 1100, 1102
V. 1068
V.M. 1100–1
Chester, J. 1267
Chilcott, G.H. 1414
Childs, K. 3056
W.R. 517, 1824
Chiplin, R.F.T. 27
Chislett, S. 3590
Chitty, J. 2294
M. 1825
Chope, R.P. 1415, 1881
Christensen, M. 3199
Christiansen, R. 304
Christie-Miller, J. 1023
Chudley, R. 1948
Church, J.L.P. 2115
Churchward, G.J. 434–5
City Docks Working Group 965
Clammer, R. 271
Clapp, B. 1961
Claridge, J. 2688
Clark *family* 3783
E.A.G. 1826, 2591–3
H.J.S. 2758
R.H. 345
T. 1760
Clarke, A.G. 3467
A.J. 1416
E.B. 2689
W. 333
Claughton, P.F. 2153–60
Clear, C.R. 3591
Clement, D.B. 3610
E. 2027
Clements, P. 90
Clew, J.R. 699
K.R. 272–4, 3530
R. 2422
Clifford, E.M. 2917
Clinker, C.R. 322, 388,

490, 917, 918,
  1722–4, 3546
Clissold, G. 3200
Cloke, J.G. 2348
Close, R.K. 3010
Clyburn, R. 3378
Coad, J. 1980, 2375–6
Coade, E. 2662, 2864
Coate, J. 2358
Coates, H. 1762
  S. 2897
  S.D. 2967
Cobbold, D. 3823
Cochrane, C. 3864
Cock, D. 637, 1297
Cocks, E.J. 758
  J.V.S. 346, 2122, 2161
Cocksedge, A.E. 2796
Coeffin, M. 2341
Cogswell, R.J. 3733
Cohen, I. 3039
Cole, G. 3105
Coleman-Smith, R. 1835
  R.J.C. 3487–9
Coles, F. 3278
Collier, P. 3427
  Sir R.P. 131
  W.F. 1827
Collins, C.M.E. 1675–6
  J.B.B. 1725, 2449
  J.H. 132–5, 180–2, 213,
    214, 1298, 1417,
    1534, 1654
Combes, C. 1418
Commin, J.G. 520
Compton, T. 2324
Connell, J.E. 1150
Conway-Jones, A. 3249
  A.H. 2964–6, 3158–62
  H. 275, 3128, 3201
Conybeare, C.A.V. 1299
  W.D. 29, 165
Cook, R.M.L. 2162
Cooke, F.E. 966
  M.H. 1249–50
Cooksey, A.J.A. 2754,
  2775, 2781–3
Cookworthy, W. 749, 811,
  2324–37
Coombe, M.O. 1036
Coombes, N. 967, 3611
Coomer, B. 3547
Coon, J.M. 153–5, 1300
Cooper, A.B. 700
  B.K. 347, 465
Copeland, P. 3106
Copeland-Griffiths, P. 2784
Copley, J. 425, 2102, 2444
Copus, A.K. 30

Corbyn, A. 1420
Corcos, N. 3428
  N.J. 3279
Corfield, M. 276
  M.C. 3628
Corin, J. 1421
Corlett, E.C.B. 851–2
Cornelius, D.B. 224, 2296
Cornford, P.W. 2655
Cornish Chamber of Mines
  1422
Cornish, J.B. 1125
Cornwall Archaeology Unit
  1037, 1145, 1302,
  1312, 1424–5, 1580,
  1653, 1726
Cornwall Record Office
  1701
Cornwell, J. 569, 642,
  778–9, 3380
Corrie, E. 3531
Cossham, H. 3429
Cossons, N. 5, 561–2, 937
Costen, M.D. 3280
Cotham Caving Group
  3753
Cotterell, H.H. 549
Cotton, W. 1828
Cottrell, A.E. 949
Couch, J. 1069, 1268
Coulthard, A.J.H. 3342,
  3602
Course, E. 2755
Court, A. 3282, 3645
  D. 3040, 3078
Courtenay, J.S. 1038
Cousins, J. 886
Cowan, M. 3646, 3695,
  3704,
Coward, E. 3647
Cowles, R. 305
Cox, C. 2876, 3228–31
  J.S. 2690
  N. 570
  T. 3430
Coxhead, J.R.W. 2400,
  2594
Cozens, L. 2450
Craddock, P.T. 1690
Craig, R. 2595–6
  R.S. 235, 521
Crane, M. 1031
Crawford, A. 717
  G.N. 3163–4, 3232
Cresswell, B.F. 2401
Cromblehome, R. 1727,
  2451
Crook, C. 3431
Croot, P.E.C. 3282

Cross, D.A.E. 3705, 3776,
  3811
Crossing, W. 1829
Cruse *family* 3648
  R.M. 3648
Cubitt, T. 3548
Cullum, D.H. 1039
Cumming, A.A. 2325
Cunningham, L.J. 780
Cunnington, B.H. 3726
  M.E. 3879
Curnow, W.H. 1040
Curtis, B.A. 1146
  C.D. 968, 3612
  M.S. 938–40
  R.C. 1772
Cuss, E. 3165

Daff, T. 122
Dalby, L.J. 3812, 3865
Dale, C. 3629
Damer Powell, J.W. 969
Daniel, P. 3343, 3407–9,
  3502, 3582
Darby, A. 570
  H.C. 6
  J. 3283
Dart, M. 306
Darvill, M. 2879
Darwin, B.R.M. 824
Daubeny *family* 720–1
Davey, H. 1147, 2038
  N. 3696
  P.C. 1428
Davidson, J. 684
Davies, A. 1773
  C.J. 1691
  D.W. 1215
  G.J. 2785, 2846–7,
    2861, 2968–70
  J. 3097
  M.F. 3630
  S. 3011
Davis, C.P. 701
  G. 3432
  G.P. 3261
  J. 1216
  J.F. 166
  P. 702
  R. 2918
  T. 3649–50
Davison, E.H. 156–7, 1429
Davy, D.B. 2390
  J. 502
  R. 2390
Day, J. 571, 617, 638,
  3344
  J.M. 759–64
  L. 348

INDEX OF AUTHORS AND PERSONAL NAMES 233

R. 675, 919, 977
  3735–6
Day-Lewis, S. 349
Deacon, B. 1041, 1430
Deakin, P.R. 1431
Dear, G.M. 2734
Dearing, J. 1882
De La Beche, Sir H.T. 31
Delabole Slate Ltd 1655
Delderfield, E.R. 2597
Delta *pseud.* 1148
Denham, P.V. 1883
Derrick, F. 2952
Derriman, J. 2377
  J.A. 1692
Devon County Educational
  Television Service
  2360
Devonia *pseud.* 2402
Dewar, H.S.L. 2735, 2801
Dewey, H. 215
Diaper, S. 718
  S.J. 881
Dickinson, H.W. 1149,
  1217, 2039
  M.G. 1433, 2064, 2075,
    2163, 2338, 2452
  N. 216
  S.V. 890
Dicks, T.R.B. 32
Dilley, J. 2453–4
Dillon, P.J. 2691
Dines, H.G. 183
Dinwoodie, J. 2455
Dittmer, B.R. 3651
Dixon, C. 2076
  D. 1434
  D.G. 2164
  T. 2105, 2107
Dodd, A. 3107
  J.P. 2692, 2919, 3652
Doe, G.M. 2403
Dominy, S.C. 1435
Dommett, H.C. 781
  H.E. 736
Donald, M.B. 1436
Donvan, E. 869
Dorset Archives Service
  2808
Douch, H.L. 71, 1109–10,
  1290–1, 1437–8,
  1677–9, 1699, 1774
Doughty, M. 671
  M.W. 3433
Douglass, J.N. 1111, 1775
  W.T. 2005
Dowler, G. 3008
Down, C.G. 3434, 3549
Drake, D. 2520–1

Draper, J. 2786–7, 2809
Dredge, J.I. 2339
Drew, C.D. 2693
  G.J. 1150
  J.H. 1702
Drewe, B. 1830
Drury, G. 2727
Duckworth, C.L.D. 522
  E.H. 3151
Duffy, M. 2598
Dumpleton, B. 853
Duncan, A.G. 2560
Dungey, C.J. 1373
Dunmall, C. 3550
Dunning, G.C. 2305
Durning-Lawrence, Sir E.
  1126
Dyer, R. 1886

Eardley-Wilmot, H. 503
Earl, B. 7, 150, 184, 205
  1265, 1387, 1439–40,
  2165
Earle Marsh, D. 442
East, G. 3284
Eastwood, J.M. 2971
Edelman, I. 3706
Edgar, M.J.D. 2694
Edgcumbe, Sir R. 2707
Edginton, C. 1831
Edmonds, E.W.A. 1441
Edwards, B. 2948–9
  E.P. 2006
  J. 1470
  N. 3478
  W.E. 2810–11, 3551
Eliot, E.A.S. 2077
Elkin, P. 572, 941, 970
Elkins, P. 3737
Ellacott, S.E. 2599, 2659
Ellis *family* 1774
  C.H. 466
  H.J. 3042
  I. 246
  J.R. 3653–5
  M. 283
  M.J.H. 794–5, 3481
  W. 1065
Elms, F. 3755
Elrington, C.R. 3062
Elston, W. 1816
Elton, A. 3552
Eltringham, G.J. 3880
Endacott, G.B. 2695
  L. 307
England, P. 3345
Enys, J.S. 1656
Esau, M. 308, 350
Espley, J.G. 277

Evans, B. 2522
  C. 3043
  C.J. 1442
  D. 33, 126, 2877
  D.E. 3012, 3233
  H.R. 1443
  J. 3436
Eveleigh, D. 765
Everard, C.E. 1444
Everett, A.W. 1981
Eversley, D.E.C. 3824
Ewans, K.M.C. 2456
Ewence, P.F. 3771
Excell, A.W. 3112
Exelby, H.R. 3785
Exell, T. 3129
Exley, C.S. 152
Eyles, J.M. 1218, 3532
  W.E. 3497

Fairclough, A. 1728–9,
  2457–8
  T. 309, 351
Fairley, W. 167
Fairweather, L. 2627
Falconer, J. 91
  K.A. 2972, 3822
Falla, T.J. 2014
Falmouth, Viscount 1127
Farmer, D.L. 3656
Farnsworth, G. 703
Farquharson-Coe, A. 2459
Farr, E.J. 971
  G.E. 854–7, 972–6,
    523–4, 2378, 2600–1,
    3613
  M. 3553
Farrant, J. 3825
  J.P. 3738
Farrer, S. 3511
Faulkner, A.H. 278
  D.O. 1755
  J.N. 467
Fawcett, A.E. 3234
  T. 3592
Fay, S. 468
Feakes, L.F. 826
Fearon, P. 648
Fedden, Sir R. 649
Fellows, R.B. 3554
Fenton, D.M. 3826–7
  M. 352
Ferguson, J. 1445
  N.A. 628
  P. 2797
Ferriman, B.D. 3437
Ferris, J.P. 2862–3, 3404
Ferrner, B. 766
Field, G.J. 3202

R.D. 3166
Fielder, A.E. 3235
Finberg, H.P.R. 1833,
　　1887–8, 2166–8,
　　2878
Finch, G. 1889, 2460
　G.P. 1834
Finn, R.W. 6
Firestone, M. 2078
Fisher, C. 3079
　H.E.S. 525–30
　H.W. 1446
　S. 8, 2598, 2602
　T. 704, 977–8
Fitton, W.H. 1301
Fleming, A. 1890–1
Fletcher, J.M.J. 2696
Flinn, D. 1219
Flower, F. 3438
　P.W. 1447
Fogwill, E.G. 1892
Fooks Bale, J.H. 2349
Forbes, J. 1448, 1449
Ford, W. 3813
Forge, E. 2461
Foster, A.M. 3697
Fowell *family* 1264
Fowler, D. 92
　M.J.F. 3747
Fox, A. 2305
　C.L. 1269
　F.F. 885
　H. 114, 1190, 2325
　H.S.A. 35–6, 1894–6,
　　1982, 3285
　J.H. 3515
　J.J. 1042
　J.J.A. 34
　R.W. 1450
Frankis, G.G.A. 499–500
Franklin, P.A. 2920
Fraser, A. 1151
　D. 353
　R. 1070, 1897
Freebury, H.A. 3828
Freeman, J. 1663
　M. 3237
Friel, I. 2603
Frohling, W. 93
Frost, J.C. 3236
Froude, W. 2394
Fryer, W.H. 3080
Fulford, M.G. 2973, 3167
Fulligar, R. 669, 845
Furze, S. 1451, 1452
Fussell, G.E. 37, 38, 1071,
　　1898–9, 2697–700,
　　2921, 3286–90
　J. 3262

Fyfield-Shayler, B.A. 1152,
　　1453

Gaby, W. 3786
Gale, T. 3830
　W.K.V. 1043, 1454,
　　3736
Gallup, R. 39, 2604
Gamlen, W.H. 1900
Garde, P.C. de la 2423–4
Gardiner, D. 531
　S.J. 3165
Gardner, J. 354
Garnett, E. 94
Garrett, J. 2974
　J.V. 2926, 3238
Gaskell-Brown, C. 1835
Gasson, G.H. 355
Gawne, E. 1901
　H.E. 1962
Geen, M. 1270
Gentry, P.W. 505
George, A.B. 2523–4,
　　2561
　H. 310
Gerhold, D. 504, 2835
Gerrard, C.M. 3263
　G.A.M. 1334, 1455–6
　S. 186, 1457–60,
　　2169–71
Gettins, G.L. 2462
Gibbs, G.H. 356
　K. 3831
Gibson, A.A. 3291
　J.C. 357
　M. 3787
Gilbert, D. 1060, 1153,
　　1206
Gilg, A. 40
Gill, C. 1836, 2340
Gillet, S. 650
　T.E. 1461
Gillis, R.H.C. 1776–7
Gilman, J.M. 532
Gilson, R.G. 3320, 3555
Gladwyn, Lady C. 98
Glanvill, P. 2172
Gledhill, D. 3498–504
Glenny, M. 3374
Glosson, M. 3439
Gloucester & Berkeley
　　Canal Co. 3168
Gloucestershire Commun-
　　ity Council, Local
　　History Committee
　　2879
Gloucestershire Record
　　Office 3127, 3171,
　　3239

Glyn, E.F. 3788
　G.C. 319
Goddard, E.H. 3657
Golding, R. 2605
Gomme, A. 627
Gonnsen, S. 3130
Gooch, D. 358, 408
Good, G.L. 979, 3066
　R.D. 2836
Goodhugh, P.S. 3631,
　　3881
Goodman, W.L. 573,
　　1024–5
Goodridge, J.A. 187
　J.C. 1462–3, 2173
Goold-Adams, R. 858, 859
Gough, J.W. 3440–1
Gould, S. 3442–3
Grace, N. 2741
Grafton, P. 359
Graham, A.H. 2736
Grant, A. 719, 2425,
　　2606–8
　A.E. 2306–8
　G. 1027
　J. 1902
Gray, G. 2262
　H. St G. 737–8, 3624
　I.A. 2922
　I.E. 2880
　M.G. 2610
　T. 41, 533, 2079, 2609
　V. 1983
Great Western Railway Co.
　　3832–3
Greaves, C. 2070
Green, A.B. 2065
　B. 1778
　D. 353
　E. 3516
　F.H.W. 506
　G. 651, 652
　J. 279, 282, 574, 2065,
　　2525
Greenfield, D.J. 3603,
　　3604
Greenhill, B. 534–6, 545,
　　910, 1779, 1782,
　　2595, 2598, 2611–12
　B.J. 739
Greenhow, D. 1984
Greening, A. 3866
Greenman, D. 653
Greenwell, G.C. 3444–9
Greenwood, J.W. 1026
Greeves, E. 2184
　T. 188
　T.A.P. 1334, 2162,
　　2171, 2174–92

INDEX OF AUTHORS AND PERSONAL NAMES

Gregor, H. 860
Gregory, K.J. 18
　M. 1665
　R. 2463
Grey, V. 2193
Grey-Davies, T.G. 3041
Griffin, P.K. 886
Griffith, D. 366
　F. 2194
Griffiths, D. 861, 1837
　J. 1192
　R. 367
　T.A.Q. 2297
Grinsell, L.V. 575
Gropall, J. 2342
Grundy, G.B. 1761, 2526, 2923, 3593
Gurney, Sir G. 1257
Gwyn-Smith, S. 1027

Hadfield, A.M. 2875
　C. 2875
　E.C.R. 280–2
Hafner, R. 655
Hague, D. 3605
　J. 3157
Haine, C. 2975–6, 3131, 3240
Hale, M. 368
Hall, C.J. 3755
　I.V. 720–5
　L. 629
　Sir R de Z. 3317–18, 3321–3
　T.M. 2195, 2309
Hallam, O. 3292
Hallett, J. 2464
Hamilton, J.R. 2196, 3450
Hammersley, E. 672
　G. 3044
Hammond, A. 3556
Handford, M. 3169–70
Handford Worth, R. *see* Worth, R.N.
Hannah, G.W. 2848
Hannam, M. 3451
Hansford, F.E. 2864
Hanson, J. 1072
　P. 1072
Hardiman, A. 3505–6
Harding, Sir H. 106
Hardingham, R. 469
Hardwick, J. 3293
Hare, J. 3658–60
　J.N. 2865
Haresnape, B. 369
Harker, R.S. 1464
Harley, B. 3092
　J.B. 42

S.F. 1985
Harlow, I.S. 767
Harper, C.G. 507–8
　D. 3834
　E.K. 1220
　P. 898
Harris, C.W.J. 3625
　F.H. 3122
　F.J.T. 3093–5
　G.F. 206, 1657
　H. 283–4, 1838, 2066, 2123, 2197, 2465, 2660–1
　H.B.M. 2198
　J. 617
　J.R. 1465–6, 2060
　K. 1271
　L. 2379
　M. 370
　P. 920
　T.R. 1128, 1202, 1252–3, 1256–8, 1266–70
　W. 674, 922
　W.B. 2350, 2466
Harrison, B. 3661
　G. 726, 1471. 2326
　G.V. 43
　R.K. 1602
Hart, C. 2881–2, 3052
　C.E. 2924–5, 3028, 3045–6, 3081–2
　V. 2791
Harte, N.B. 256
　W.J. 1839
Hartley, Sir C. 2613
　C.W.S. 2613
　S. 3789
Harvey, C. 702, 904, 906–8
　C.E. 576
　C.J. 207
　H.N. 1154
　J.H. 3294
　N. 44
Hasler, J. 3383
Haswell, E.G.F. 371
Hatcher, J. 189, 1074
　M.J.J.R. 1044–6, 1472
Hatton, D.E. 1155
Havill, J. 2662
Havinden, M. 8–9, 1906, 3264
　M.A. 40, 45–6
Hawk, W. 1073, 1078
Hawker, Revd 1903–4, 2527
Hawkings, D. 2361
Hawkins, C. 372, 1473

D.J. 2426
J. 1474–5, 1573, 2788
M. 492, 2528
Hawkshaw, J. 999
Hawtin, F. 3265, 3365, 3425, 3507, 3626
　P. 3365
Hay, P. 95–6
Haynes, R.G. 1905
　R.I.E. 3867
Hayward, J. 2663
　K. 654
Hazard, R. 2199
Heal, V. 3266
Heape, W. 2080
Hearn, J.R. 1780
Heath *family* 1231
Heathcoat, D.E. 2414
Hedges, C. 2427
　E.S. 1476
Heeley, A. 3295
Heffer, P. 1477
Helm, P.J. 3296
Hemery, E. 2428, 2467
Henderson, C. 1762, 2614
　C.G. 1112, 2429, 2562
　H.C.K. 3662
　J.S. 1478–9
Henrywood, R.K. 804
Henwood, G. 190, 1480, 1583
　W.J. 1156–61, 1481
Herbert, N. 3241
　S. 1482
Hercock, C. 2749
Herring, P. 1483
　P.C. 1302
Hicks, G. 2200
　H.R. 2327
　N. 47
Higgans, J. 1484
Higgs-Coulthard, A.J. 3346
Higham, R. 35
Hildich, P. 2380
Hill, H.O. 537, 1781, 1782
　J.C.G. 862, 980
Hills, J.G.B. 1221
　R.L. 11191, 2040
Hilton, N. 1075
Hindley, D.J.B. 1840
Hine, J. 723, 2404
　M. 2041
Hinton, F.H. 3868
Hitchens Unwin, A. 1113
Hitchings, J.O. 1907
Hoaen, A. 1521
Hoare, M.C.B. 1885
Hobbs, J. 655
Hobday, P.W. 981

236 INDEX OF AUTHORS AND PERSONAL NAMES

Hockin, C. 1810
Hocking, J. 1485
　J.A. 158
　S. 1254
Hodge, H.R. 1811
　J. 1129–30, 1134,
　　1222–6
　R. 2362
Hodges, J. 3295
　R. 2737
Hodgkins, T. 2926
Holcroft, H. 373–4
Holdridge, D.A. 2117
Holland, R. 686–90
　S.A. 2430
　W.F. 2310
Hollingsworth, B. 375
Hollister-Short, G.J. 2042
Hollowood, A.B. 1259
Holman, E.B. 1200
　T. 1162
Holmes, R.T. 3092
Holt Magazine 3835
Holt, H. 1076
Homer, R.F. 2096–8, 2201
Homfrey, S. 1218
Honnywell, W. 1914
Hony, G.B. 3663
Hook, B. 3297
　D.R. 1690
Hooke, D. 2927
Hooley, J.M.P. 2381
Hooper, W.R. 2563
　W.T. 1131, 1210–11,
　　1486–7
Hopkins, H.B. 639–40
Hopton, Lady 3404
Hopwood, H.L. 493,
　　1730–2, 2468, 3557
Horn, P. 2701
　W. 2962
Hornblower *family* 1202–8
　J. 1203–8
Horsey, I. 2849
Horsley, J.E. 2615
Horstmann *family* 3377
Hosegood, J.G. 376
Hosier, A.J. 3664
　F.A. 509
　F.H. 3664
Hoskins, W.G. 247, 1488,
　　1841–4, 1908–11,
　　1963–4
Hoskyns, G. 1843
Household, H. 3203
　H.G.W. 285–7
Houston, W.J. 1489
How, B. 3217
　G.E.P. 1028

Howard, B. 1490
　P.A. 3171
　T. 982
Howe, C. 2812
Howell, D. 3665, 3739
Howes, R. 2950
　R.K. 2954
Hoy, M. 3204
Hubbard, J. 377
Hudleston, C.R. 691–2
Hudson, K. 10, 11, 48,
　　159, 1304, 3397,
　　3756, 3836
　W.H. 3666
Huggins, G.M. 3452
Hughes, B. 2425
　B.D. 2382, 2431
Hull, J.W. 2702
　P.L. 1783
Hulland, C. 1953
Hunt, J. 3767
　P.C. 3779
　S. 2311
　T.J. 2517
Hunter, J. 1491, 2202–3
　W.P. 2762
Hussey, D.P. 983
Hutchings, L.B. 2529
Huxley, G.L. 2469
　R. 3205
Hyett, F.A. 3110

Ifor, A. 3707
Ilbery, B.W. 2703
Iles, J. 2718
Illston, J. 3723
Ince, L. 1227
Inder, P.M. 2405
Isaac, L. 3371
Isherwood, A.J. 2955

Jackson, B.L. 2813
　D. 3882
　P. 805, 898–9
　R.G. 805–7, 894, 898–9
Jacobs *family* 741
　B. 2406
James, C.C. 1493–4
　J. 3172
　J.F. 2704, 2738
　R.H. 580
Janes, H. 2742
Jarman, I. 1852
Jarrett, G. 50
Jars, G. 1495
Jarvis, R.C. 2850
Jeffery, F.D.C. 984
Jenkin, A.K.H. 1193,
　　1496–1502, 2204

Jenkins, C.C. 1492
　D. 99
　H. 99
　R. 100, 191, 768, 769,
　　1132, 1204, 1228,
　　1255, 1503, 2043–7,
　　3047
　S.C. 2470
Jenner, M. 627
Jervis, W.W. 3479
Jervoise, E. 514, 2562
Jewell, A. 51
Joce, T.J. 2530–3
Johnson, B.L.C. 3048
Johnston, R.J. 2714
Jones, D. 12, 704, 727,
　　977, 3381
　F.C. 846
　J.L. 3453, 3667
　M. 2616, 3454
　M.D. 2705
　M.G. 3004
　M.H. 2205–7, 3348,
　　3382, 3558
　M. Whitmore 2402
　O. 740
　R.H. 985
　S. 236
　S.J. 581–2, 887, 3479
　S.K. 85
　S.R. 1953, 3698
　S.R.H. 3098
　W.H. 1260
Jope, E.M. 3101
Jordan, E. 986
Joseph, P. 1504–5
Josephs, Z. 741
Judge, C.W. 494
Jump, P. 2885

Kain, R. 1076
Kanaris, M.D. 583
Kanefsky, J. 2534–5
Karau, P. 378, 425,
　　3216–17
Karkeek, P.Q. 2617–18
　W.F. 1077
Kearney, B. 3242
Keast, J. 1047
Keen, L. 2312, 2866
Keil, I. 2706, 3349
Kelley, P.J. 510
Kemp, R.I. 3049
Kempson, E.G.H. 3740
Kendall, H.G. 2471
　S.G. 52, 3298
Kennedy, R. 379
Kennet & Avon Canal
　Trust 3741

INDEX OF AUTHORS AND PERSONAL NAMES 237

Kent, J.M. 1658
  O. 898
Kerr, B. 2707–9
Kerridge, E.W.J. 3668–72
Kew, J.E. 1912
Kidner, R.W. 2814
Kilvington, C. 2162
King, A. 863
  C.M. 46
  N.E. 3757
Kingdom, A.R. 380, 2472–4
Kingdon, A.S. 2345
Kinglake, J. 3307
Kingsley, N. 3013
Kingston, J.T. 2208
Kinvig, R.H. 248
Kiss, K. 85
Kitchenside, G. 363
Kite, E. 3727
Kittridge, A. 271, 288, 1693, 1784–6, 2619
Klapper, C.F. 312
Kneebone, D.A. 1048
Kneel, A. 2363
Knight, D.H. 1305
  J. 722
  J.A. 2358
Kowaleski, M. 1845–7, 2620
Kranich, B. 1436
Krause, I. 381
Krognes, M. 3728
Kropotkin, P. 1922
Kudo, N. 1398

Lacy Mann J. de *see* Mann J. de L.
Laithwaite, J.M.W. 1959, 1965–8
Lamb, J.B. 1787
  P. 229, 3498
  P.G. 836–8
  S. 3614
Lambert, A.D. 2383
Lander, W. 3732
Lane, R. 723
  R.H. 3869
Langford, A.M. 3123
Langley, M. 538
Langmuir, G.E. 522
Langsford, A. 53
Lanning, G. 2815
Lansdown, M.J. 3780
Large, D. 847, 987
Larkin, E.J. 3837
  J.G. 3837
Larn, B. 1788
  R. 1788

Latham, J.P.M. 2789
Latimer, J. 584
Lavender, R. 2710
Laver, M. 2351
Law, R.J. 1229, 1505
Lawrence, Sir E.D. 1163
  J.F. 3450
Lawry, J.W. 1078
Laws, P. 1049, 1061, 1164
Laycock, C.H. 1969
Le Boutillier, N.G. 1507
Le Marchant, R. 1508–12, 2029
Le Mesurier, B. 1829
Leach, R. 2763
Lead, P. 1230, 1231
Lean, T. 1165
Lebherz, H. 2977
Lee, C. 2407
  C.E. 2475, 2510
Leech, R. 3324
Leek, M.E. 864
Lees, E. 2756
Legg, R. 2667
Leifchild, J.R. 1513
Leigh, C. 382–5
Lemon, Sir C. 1514
  Sir W. 1767
Lennard, E.W. 585
  R. 54, 3299
Letcher, J.T. 1527
Lethbridge, Sir R. 1913, 2476
Levitt, S. 808
Lewcun, M.J. 3350, 3490
Lewis, C.A. 2477
  G.R. 192
  J. 407
  M.J.T. 1733
  R.A. 2978, 3173
Lidstone, T. 2048
Light, A. 2777
Lillingston, E.B.C. 587
Linday, D.T.A. 882
Lindqvist, S. 2060
Lineham, C.D. 2210
Lisle, E. 38, 3673
Little, B. 627
  E. 3674
Littlefield, D. 656
Llewellyn, B. 1515
Lloyd, T.D. 2313
Loam, E. 1261
  M. 1261
Lock, H.O. 2816
Lockett, N. 386
London, J. 2408
Loney, H. 1521
Long, C.J. 951

  E.C. 2211
  P.J. 3206
Loomie, J. 588
Lord, J. 988
Louis, H. 1516
Lovell, T.H. 3545
Lovering, J. 657
Lowe, M.C. 2536–43
Loxton, S. 3188
Lucking, J.H. 2817–19
Luff, D. 658
Luker, B. 3383
Lund, B. 817
Lundberg, M. 806
Luxton, H.W.B. 1832
Lyon Smith, R.J. 3114
Lyons, E.T. 387

Macan, H. 2106
MacCaffrey, W.T. 1848
MacDermot, E.T. 388
MacDermott, M.B. 3325–6
MacDonald, N. 389
Mace, F.A. 1849, 2622
MacGregor, D.R. 1779
Machin, R. 2729
MacInnes, C.M. 870, 992
Mackenna, F.S. 2328–9
Mackenzie, J.B. 993
  W. 3243
Mackintosh, I. 3132–4
Maclean, J. 1517
Maddock, L. 117
Madge, R. 2478
Maggs, C.G. 313, 323, 326, 390, 484, 495, 498, 923–6, 2479–85, 2820, 3207–8, 3559–62, 3594–5, 3838–9
  R. 3491
Major, J.K. 2068, 3708, 3883–4
Maker, L. 1078
Malan, A.H. 391, 3852
Malcolmson, R.W. 782
Mallet, J.V.G. 811
Mallett, W.R. 1986
Mallory, K. 3615
Mankee, H. 1386
Mann J. de L. 249–50, 3790–2
Manners, J.E. 3675
Mansfield, R.J. 2886
  R.W. 3760
Marconi Company 1670–1
Marcy, P.T. 942
Mardon, H. 827
Markwick, A.T. 2564

Marochan, K. 812
Marsh, A.J. 2384
  D.E. see Earle Marsh, D.
Marshall, E. 2007
  N.M. 3135
  P. 871–2
  W. 55, 2929
Marten, C. 1885
Martin, E.W. 1914
  M. 2623
Mason, W.W. 1734
Mathews, E.F.J. 2668
Matschloss, C. 2049
Matthew D. 123
  G. 123
Matthews, H.E. 880
  K. 115
  L.H. 865
Maudsley, H. 107
Maunder, G. 1841
Mawson, J. 2837
Maxted, I. 1851
Maxwell, I.S. 1079
May, R. 3563
Mayer, P. 1518
Maynard, J. 1519
Mayo, R. 594
McAdam, J.L. 3598
McCarthy, M.R. 3769
McCaughan, M. 1694
McClelland, B.J.A. 989
McCombe, C. 2067
McDonnell, G. 1521
McGarvie, M. 2764, 3300, 3398, 3405–6
McGrail, D. 1850
McGrath, P. 551, 589–93
  P.V. 990–1
McGuinness, T.W. 1050–1, 1522–4
McKee, J.G. 3616
McKenna, F.S. 809
  N. 1525
McMurtrie, J. 3446, 3456
McWilliams, F.H. 1272
Measom, G. 324, 392–3, 471
Medlam, W.G. 2980–1
Meik, H.H. 472
Meikle, W.P. 2838
Mercer, S. 1232
Meredew, M.H. 2554
Merrett, C. 595
  L.H. 289
Merry, I.D. 539, 2624
  S. 1233
Messenger, M. 2486
  M.J. 1526, 1703–6, 1735–8, 2118, 2212
Mettler, A.E. 2015
Meynell, L.W. 101
Michell, F.B. 1262, 1528–33
  F.W. 1166
  S. 1133, 1196, 1263, 1527, 1813
Middleton, R.E. 2364
Mildren, J. 233
Miles, I. 3301, 3351, 3384–5
  M. 3352, 3364, 3617–18
Millard, V.F.L. 540, 2625
Miller, A.J. 2839
  C. 625, 3014
  C.A. 2930–3
  L. 1680
  M. 853, 3386
  W. 817
Mills, H.H. 1292
  M.T. 2213
  S. 2982–5, 3015, 3063, 3099, 3115, 3136
Minchinton, W.E. 13–14, 56–7, 70, 72, 102, 127, 529, 550, 596–7, 994–5, 1832, 1852-4, 1915, 1987–92, 2365, 2711, 2934, 3137–8
Mingay, G.E. 2712
Minnitt, S. 3267
Mitchell, D. 2121
  V. 2487–8, 2821–4, 3564–5, 3840–1
Moddever, K.D. 3302
Moir, E. 3518
  E.A.L. 2986, 3139–40
Moissenet, M.L. 1534
Monk, W. 3729
Montague, K. 395, 3209
Moody, A.P. 2409
Moore, C.N. 3748, 3885–6
  L.R. 168
  N. 3632, 3770
  N.J. 2987
Morgan, F.W. 1855, 3676
  J.E. 1535
  K. 598, 943
Morgans, T. 3457
Morland, S.C. 3303
  T.E. 3870–2
Morley, Lord 2568
Morris, C. 2840, 2935–6
  J.R. 251
  T.E.R. 3210
  W.A. 1537
Morrison, B. 3842
  G. 459
  J. 3677, 3699, 3742
  T.A. 1536, 1538
Morriss, R. 2385
Morton, G.R. 3036
  H.E. 691
  J. 1539
  J.C. 2937
Moseley, B. 2626
Mosse, J. 396–7, 641, 770, 927
Mostyn, J. 728
Mote, G. 541
Mott, R.A. 2050
Moulton, S. 3888
Mounfield, P.R. 124
Mountford, E.R. 3843
Mourton, S. 3211
Mowat, C.L. 928
Moyle, M.P. 1540
Mudd, D. 1789
Mudge, T. 2027
Mullin, D. 3083
Mullins, S. 3873
Munro, C.A.J. 1373
Munckton, T. 3304
Murch, D. 2627
  M. 2627
Murdoch, W. 1192
Murless, B. 3492, 3511
  B.J. 3297, 3369–70, 3407–8, 3533, 3583, 3626
Mushet *family* 3030, 3032, 3034, 3050, 3053
  R.F. 3050
Musty, J. 3771–2
  J.G.W. 3710
Myatt, G.N. 2887
Myers, M.R. 2630

Nabb, H. 232, 841–3, 2356
Naish, J. 2628
Nance, R.D. 2030
  R.M. 542, 1273, 1790–2
  R.W.M. 2030
Nankervis, J. 1114
Nasmyth, J. 2069
Navillus, C.H. 2008
Neal, D.K. 3749
Neale, F. 3596
  R.S. 3268
  W.G. 996–8
Neaverson, P. 1552, 1553
Needham, H.J. 3747
Newcomen, T. 2032–61
Newell, E. 1541–3
Newman, P. 193, 2189, 2214–18, 3619
  R. 3051, 3084

INDEX OF AUTHORS AND PERSONAL NAMES

Newton, E.W. 1544
  P.H. 1993
Nicholas, B. 1385
  C. 137
  J. 2489–90
Nicholls, B. 1681, 2219
  D. 1274
  H.G. 3052
  L.M. 1856
Nicholson, P. 3711, 3713
  R.P. de B. 3712
Nielsen, V.C. 2938–9
Nims, J. 3212
Nisbet, J. 2888
Nix, M. 2386, 2611, 2629–30
Noall, C. 1167–7, 1275–6, 1545–51, 1694, 1740, 1763, 1793, 1794
Noble, Lady C.B. 103
Nock, O.S. 106, 398–406, 473, 489
Norris, J. 328, 407
Northcote, V.J. 2387
Northway, A.M. 2081, 2083
Norton, C.P. 1453
Norway, A.H. 1795
Nott, H.E. 692
Noyes, K.J. 2889

O'Brien, T. 883
O'Callaghan, J. 866
O'Donoghue, K.J. 1796
O'Hea, J.D. 1857
Oakley, M. 929
Odgers, J.F. 1234
Ogden, R. 1916
Ogilby, J. 2544
Oldacre *family* 2916
Oliver, A.S. 1695
  B.W. 2565
Ollerenshaw, P. 574
Opie, W.G. 1614
Oppenheim, M.M. 2631
Oppitz, L. 2825
Oram, H.C. 3519
Ordish, H.G. 1168–9
Orme, N. 2341
Orwin, C.S. 58
Osborn, F.M. 3053
Osler, E. 1739
Oswald, A. 2314
  A.H. 895
  N. 2082
  N.C. 1917–18, 2298
Otter, R.A. 15
Overton, M. 1080, 1915
Owen, H. 813

  J. 2492, 3566
  J.B.B. 106
  M.B. 3493
Owens, R.J. 3244
Oxenford, P. 2220
Oxford, A.W. 818

PSV Circle 2547
Paar, H.W. 2890
Page, T. 999
Pahl, J. 2795
Paige, R.T. 237
Painting, M.H. 844
Paisley, T.B. 1264
Paley, G. 2099
Palmer, J. 1068, 3591
  M. 1552–3
  S. 3433
Pamment, J. 2221
Papworth, M. 2733, 2741
Paris, J.A. 1306, 1554
Parish, C.W. 2291
Parker, A.G. 3085
  N.C. 3877
Parr, H.W. 3214–15
Parris, H. 408
Parrott, I. 3371
Parry, P. 3789
Parsons, A.H. 783
  D. 69
  H. 1994, 2222
  J. 1277
  N. 1277
  R.M. 1000–1
  S.R. 1858
  T. 1170
Partridge, W. 252, 3774
Pascoe, D.W. 1797
  W.A. 1556–7
  W.H. 1555, 2223
Patrick, A. 195, 543, 2224, 2432, 2632–5
Pattison, S.R. 2225
Pawlyn, T. 1696, 2636
Payne, B. 1919
  D. 2587, 2851
  F.G. 1081
  H.M.C. 1082
Paynter, W. 1694
  W.H. 1558
Peacey, A. 896, 3102
Peacock, D.P.S. 227, 1682
Pearce, A.E. McR. 3458
  S. 1920
  T. 196
Peard, G.O. 2566
Pearse, R. 1798
Pearson, A. 1689
  J. 2940

  T. 3488
Peck, A.S. 3853
Pederson, Mr 3233
Pedlar, N. 1235
Pelham, R.A. 3794, 3814
Pemberton, M. 1307
Penderill-Church, J. 2330
Pendred, L. St L. 1236, 2051
Penhale, J. 1559
Penhallurick, R.D. 1560
Penn, H. 3025
Penn, S.A.C. 599, 676
Pennington, R.R. 197, 1171, 1506, 1561–2
Penny, C.R. 3174
  J. 1032
Pentelow, A. 3633
Perkin, J.B. 2545
Perkins, J. 72, 1987
  J.W. 1991, 2664, 3458
  K.S. 2069–70, 2493, 2567–72, 2637
  W.T. 474
Perrett, W. 3795
Perrott, H. 732
Perry, G. 409
  P.J. 2826, 2852–5
  P.J.A. 2713–14
  R. 3141–2
Peskett, H.M. 1859
Peters, I. 3541, 3567
  J.E.C. 2988
Pethybridge, G.H. 1083
Pezzack, W. 1278
Philbrick, E.M. 1764
  M.E. 1672
Philips, J. 2765
Phillips, A.D.M. 1921
  D. 3568
  J. 2316
  M.C. 1995
  R.H. 2315
Photos, E. 205
Pickard, R. 2363
Pickford, R.F. 3452
Pidgeon, J. 1958
Pierrepoint, J.R. 3678
Piggott, R.J. 3054
Pigot & Co. 16
Pike, J.R. 198, 2494–5, 2546, 2638
Pippard, S.B. 673
Pitt, T. 2335–6
Platt, A. 410
Plomer, H.R. 2342
Pole, F.J.C. 411
  W. 1172
Polkinghorne, J.P.R.

2226–7
Pollard, D. 3459, 3569
Pomeroy, L.W. 2496
Pomroy, L.J. 2470
Ponsford, C.N. 2020–4, 2390
Ponting, K. 3520, 3634, 3679
   K.G. 253–9, 3796–801
Pool, P.A.S. 1091, 1790, 1799
Pope, A. 3016
   I. 3216–17
   P. 226
Popplewell, L. 314–15, 496, 2766, 2827
Port of Bristol Authority 1002, 1008
Porter, J.H. 1922–4, 2084, 2595
   M. 2085, 2639
Porter Goff, R.F.D. 952
Portman, D. 1970–1
Postan, M.M. 3305
Postles, D. 2016
Potter, J. 17
Potts, C.R. 345, 412, 494, 2497–8
   R. 1084
   R.A.J. 1686
Pounds, N.J.G. 69, 160, 1052–4, 1085–7, 1293, 1563–4, 1707, 1800–1, 1812, 2331
Pountney, W.J. 814
Powell, A.C. 742
   A.G. 820
   C. 630
   C.G. 677–80
   J. 600, 978, 1003, 3460
   R. 104
Powle, H. 3055
Pratt, F. 3175
Preece, G.P.J. 3176
Preedy, E.N. 3218
Press, J. 576, 702, 754, 904–8, 1004
Presto, J. 3461
Prew, W.J. 2228
Price, A.J. 3086–7
   E.G. 3017
   L.L. 1565
   R. 805, 815
   R.H. 894, 897–9
Prideaux, J. 2332
   J.D.C.A. 2499
Pritchard, J.E. 830, 900
Proctor, F.B. 816
Provis, J. 1567

Pryce, W. 1568
Pudney, J. 105
   J.S. 659
Pugsley, Sir A. 106
   A.G. 706
   A.J. 601
Pulman, G.P.R. 29
Pushman, D. 2767
Pye, A. 2640
   A.R. 2031, 2103–4, 2107–8, 2110
Pyman, R. 2352
Pymm, R.R. 59, 1925, 2229, 2366

Quartley, G.W. 3555
Queniart, J. 40

Rabjohns, E.W. 1416
Rack, E. 44
Radford, G.H. 2317
   Lady 2230, 2343
Raggatt, F.C. 3144
Raikes, C. 2549
   R. 3109
Railway Correspondence and Travel Society 413, 475
Raistrick, A. 1569
Rake, H. 325, 497, 1741, 2500–1, 3570
Ramsden, J.V. 2231–3
Ramsey, G.D. 3802–3
Randall, A.J. 260
   H.A. 3018
   J. 3462
Randolph, S. 3219
Ransom, W.P. 2841
Rapson, J. 1659
Rashleigh, J. 1281
Raspe, R.E. 1505
Rath, T. 3143
Rattenburg, G. 1742
Ravenhill, W.L.D. 18
Ravensdale, J.R. 1308–9
Rawson, R.R. 60
Redgrave, B. 2234
Redwood, C. 3571
Reece, R. 3088
Reed, W.E. 3723
Rees, D.G. 873
   E.A. 1683
   H. 602
   P. 415–16
   S.A. 944
Reichel, O.J. 61
Reid, H. 603
   R.D. 3597
   W.N. 1005

Rendel, J. 2567, 2571
   J.M. 515
Rendell, B. 3056
   J. 290
Rendle, R.S. 2100
Renouard, Y. 604
Retter, F. 1926
Reynolds, B. 2715
   D. 2509
Ribbins, P.A. 2086
Rich, J. 1006
Richards *family* 1434
   C. 3425, 3463
   D. 2052
Richardson, A. 292, 3177
   H. 3775
   I. 2071
   J.M. 291
   P. 1392
   P.D. 874–9
   P.H.G. 2235–42
Richmond, F. 2989
Ricketts *family* 748
Riddell, J. 1708
Riddle, C. 1088
Riekstins, R.T. 1431
Riemer, P. 2982–3
Rigold, S.E. 3714
Riley, R.C. 316
Ring *family* 898
Ripley, P. 2891–3
Rippon, A. 2318
Roach, W. 2087
Roberts, B.J. 2990
   J. 3226
   P. 2072, 2243, 2245–6
   P.P. 2802
   R. 2802
   R.O. 1466
   S. 2244
   W. 1279
Robertson, A.W. 225
   K. 317, 417–18, 476, 2502
Robins, J.A.C. 2247–51
Robinson, R. 1927, 2103
Robson, J. 784
Roche, P.N. 3500
   T.W.E. 419–20, 1743–4, 2503
Rocksborough-Smith, S. 318
Rodda, J.T. 1173
Rogers, F.R. 605–6
   I. 2025–6, 2391
   K.H. 80, 261–2, 3636, 3804–5
   W.H. 2550
Rollison, D.P. 2894

INDEX OF AUTHORS AND PERSONAL NAMES 241

Rolls-Royce Heritage Trust 661
Rolt, L.T.C. 84, 108, 1239, 2053–4, 2119
Rose, R.L. 2895, 3019
Rose-Troup, F. 62–3
Ross, C.D. 263, 3806
  M.S. 2716, 2745
Ross-Johnson, D. 1007
Rottenbury, F.J. 2252–4
Rouckleiffe, J. 2027
Round, F. 847
Rouse, G.D. 1832
Rowe, C. 1174
  C.M. 3637
  G.A. 199, 2255–6
  J. 1057, 1089, 1240, 1570–1
  J.H. 1196, 1263, 1813
  M.M. 2099
  W.J. 1055–6
Rowland, K.T. 867
Rowledge, J.W.P. 421
Rowse, A.L. 1058, 1310, 2088
Rudder, S. 2896
Rudge, T. 2941
Ruegg, L.H. 2717, 3844
Rule, J. 116
  J.G. 1572
Rumbold, R. 217
Russell, A. 663, 1573
  D.A. 662
  J. 293
  J.H. 422–8
  P. 2089, 2641–2
  P.M.G. 2257

Sacks, D.H. 607–8
Sainsbury, P. 1928
Sale, A.J.H. 3029
Salmon, H.C. 3464
Salter, C. 200
  R.J. 109
Sambourne, R.C. 2551–2
Sampson, P. 1860
Sandall, R.E. 3681
Sandeman, E. 2367
Sanders, A.F. 1134
Sands, T.B. 485
Saunders, A.F. 3845
  E.G.S. 2027
  G.W. 3375
  T.J. 3846
Savery, T. 2037, 2044, 2047, 2055
Saville, R.J. 2768–70
Sawtell, J. 707
  J.C. 3743, 3847

Sawyer, W.D. 1175
Scantlebury, J. 1280–2
Schmitz, C.J. 201, 1574, 2124, 2132, 2258–61, 3465
Schofield, J. 1115
Schubert, H.R. 773, 3057
Schwind, A.P. 750
Scott, B. 353
  C. 2073
  J. 2262
  R.C. 3306, 3682
  W.J. 429
Seekings, J. 2743
Sekon, G.A. *pseud*. 430, 477
Selleck, A.D. 161, 2333
Sellick, R.J. 58, 2471, 2504, 3572–3
Sellman, R.R. 110
Semmens, P.W.B. 431, 1745
Semple, Sir W. 588
Serjeant, C.E. 1299
Sessions, W.K. 831
Sevier, W.E. 1575
Seward, D. 2410
Seymour, J. 2803
Shambrook, H.R. 1176, 1576–9
  R. 2263
Shapcote, H. 2505
Sharman, M. 432, 478
Sharpe, A. 1177, 1311, 1379, 1458, 1580
  P. 2411
Shaw, T. 2264
Sheldon, G. 2553
  L. 1996–7
  P. 3856
Shelton, G. 319
Shepherd, E. 309
  F.W. 1090
Sheppard, P.A. 1116
Sherborne, J.W. 1009
Shergold, A. 2787
Sheridan, A. 1929
Sherry, D. 2867
Shickle, C.W. 3509
Shiel, N. 1816
Shipsides, F. 1010–11
Shirley-Smith, Sir H. 106
Short, E.B. 2804
Shorter, A.H. 18, 64, 73, 125, 219–21, 1667–9, 1931–2, 2295, 2643, 2868, 3095, 3353
Shortt, H. 3887
Sillick, C.B.M. 2644

Simmonds, F. 3086
Simmons, H.E.S. 117, 1118, 1998–9, 2739–40, 2991, 3354, 3715
  J. 356, 433, 1746
Simpson, J.J. 3145
Sims, J. 1256, 1581
Sinclair, J. 1933
Siraut, M. 3307
Sivewright, D.J. 19
Skillen, B.S. 1582–3
Skinner, P. 848
Skyrme, J.E. 2869
Slade, J.J. 3775
  W.J. 545, 2595, 2645
Slader, J.M. 2265
Slater, B. 2221
  T.R. 2956
Slee, A.H. 1861, 1930
Slocombe, P.M. 3694, 3700–2, 3716
Smale, V. 1584
Small, E. 538
Smart, D. 1284
  I.H. 2056
Smeaton, J. 2009–11
Smedley, J. 1700
Smerdon, R. 2266
Smiles, S. 111
Smith, A. 2060, 2828
  B. 3090
  B.S. 3171
  D. 1585
  E.C. 2057
  J.R. 1302, 1312, 1747
  J.T. 3698
  K. 2821–4, 3564–5, 3840–1
  M. 2506, 3815
  O.J. 2829
  P. 3220
  R. 202, 1586
  T. 2930
  W. 1218, 3089
Smyth, W. 1587
Sneddon, J.M. 3484
Snell, J.T.R. 1748
  M. 3729
Soames, R. 2736
Soane, J.V.N. 2669
Somerset and South Avon Vernacular Buildings Research Group 3327
Somerset County Council 3466
Somerville, J. 884
Soole, G.H. 353
South West Water 2368–9

INDEX OF AUTHORS AND PERSONAL NAMES

South Western Electricity
    Board 230
Southam, J. 988
Southgate, T. 3250
Southward, A. 117
    A.J. 2090
Southway, M.J.H. 785
Soyres, B. de 81, 772
Spargo, T. 138, 1588
Spink, G. 1589
Spiro, R.H. 3598
Spoerry, P. 2791
Spooner, D.J. 20
Spreadbury, B. 3683
Spry, N. 3245
Squire, T. 2718
Staal, C. 1684, 2334
    S. 1590
Stafford, H. 2017
Stallard, J. 2921
Stammers, M. 546
Stanbrook, E. 1934
Standing, I. 2897–8, 3059,
    3200, 3221
    I.J. 3040, 3078, 3091
Stanes, R. 1862
    R.G.F. 65, 1935–7,
    2125, 2267
Stanier, P. 1119, 1591,
    2670, 2772
    P.H. 203, 208–10,
    1660–3, 1802–3,
    2759–60
    Sir W. 434–5
Stanton, W.I. 3467
Stanyer, J. 40
Stapleton, G. 2899
Starkey, D. 2598
    D.J. 238–9, 2091, 2392,
    2646–8
    F.H. 2554
Statham, I. 3222
Steele, A.K. 436
Stembridge, P.K. 609
Stengelhofen, J. 1599
Stephan, J. 264
Stephens, F.J. 1592–8,
    3468
    P. 1599
    W. 810, 2522
    W.B. 118, 222, 610,
    1804, 1863–6, 2433,
    2649, 2671
Stephenson, B. 437
Stevens, J. 1091
    J.R. 1012
Stevenson, W. 2719
Steward, S.F. 231
Stewart, P.A.E. 3469–70

Stiles, J. 708
    R. 729, 796, 1013,
    3355, 3380, 3471–2
    R.A. 3058
Stimpson, M. 3179
Stock, C.S. 1749
Stocker, T. 3375
Stokes, P. 3744–5
Stone, G. 665
    J.W.M. 3482
Stowers, A. 2058–9
Stoyel, A. 1120, 1600
Straight, M. 2092
Stratford, F. 953, 3535
Stratton, M. 2992–3
Street, A.G. 3684–6
    D. 1029
    R.T.C. 2842
Stretton, N. 2319
Strong, H.W. 1867, 2320
Stuart, E.A. 42
Stuckey, D. 486, 2269,
    2507, 3620
    P.J. 547, 3124
Sturge, W. 3272
Stuttard, J.C. 2900
Styles, R. 786
Sutton, G.B. 3399–400
Swynnerton, C. 2994–5
Symonds, H. 2805

Talbot, C.R.M. 415
Tamblin, J.L. 1868
    W.J. 1938
Tames, R. 112
Tangye, M. 1059, 1285
    N. 1687–8
Tann, J. 265, 1194, 1205,
    2060, 2996, 3146–7
Tanner, G.H.J. 3854
    H. 1939
Tapley-Soper, H. 2393
Tate, W.E. 2942, 3308,
    3689
Tavener, L.E. 2720–1
Taylor, C. 2270
    C.C. 2722, 3687
    D. 3688
    E. 128, 755, 3410
    F.J.D. 1673
    J. 139, 885, 1178–9,
    1402, 1601–2, 2434
    J.N. 119
    K. 1602
    L.G. 611
    L.J. 2394
    R. 3328
    R.A. 3180
    W. 3069

Telford, T. 3164
Terry, R. 2321
Tew, D.H. 1180–1
Thexton, M. 3020
Thirsk, J. 43
Thody, D.W.J. 3855
Thomas *family* 3060
    A. 2300
    A.C. 1092
    C. 140–1, 884, 1241,
    1603
    D. St J. 320, 438–9,
    458, 3844
    D.L.B. 2573–8
    H. 1604
    J. 1605, 2728
    J.G. 1606
    K. 930
    M. 612
    M.A. 626
    R. 2126
    R.A. 1607
    S.E. 2101
    W. 1397, 1608
    W.T. 1371
Thompson, C.H. 2435
    M. 67
    V. 2508
Thornton, W.H. 1869
Thorp, J. 2780
    J.R.L. 1972–3
Thorpe, J. 2000
Thurlow, C. 162, 1313
Thwaite, J.R.N. 3690
Till, R. 893
Tilly, V.J. 1609
Timbrell, M. 148–9
Timms, S. 2370
Timperley, H.W. 3874
Titley, A. 1217, 1242–3,
    1610, 2035
Titt, J.W. 3708
Tittler, R. 2856
Todd, A.C. 1060–1, 1182,
    1206
Toll, R.W. 151, 2001,
    2109, 2271–3, 2436
Tolson, H. 2579
Tombs, R.C. 797–8
Tomkins, R. 3856
Tomlinson, M. 2412
Tonkin, C. 1314–15
    J.W. 1103
Toop, R.E. 441
Toppin, A.J. 817
Torrens, H. 1230–1, 2901,
    3388–9, 3536–8
    H.S. 709–10, 774,
    1207–8, 1244

INDEX OF AUTHORS AND PERSONAL NAMES

Totterdill, J.W. 931
Touchard, H. 1870
Townsend, C. 1014
Trapnell, A. 818
Treadwin, Mrs 2413
Tredinnick, R. 142, 1611
Treffry, J.T. 1047
Treherne, P. 2777
Treloar, P.Q. 442
Trethewey, W. 1316
Trethowan, D.M. 1805
  H.M. 3691
Trevithick, F. 1245
  J.H. 1246
  R. 1212–48, 1734, 1750
  R. *senior* 1610
Trew, A.R.F. 932
Tribe, T. 2752
Triewald, M. 2060
Trinder, B. 2992–3, 3857
Trinick, G.M.A. 1612
Tristram, W.O. 511
Trivett, R. 1613
Trounson, J.H. 204, 1183–5, 1614–22
Trudgian, A.R. 1814
  J. 1814
Trueman, A.E. 168
Trump, H. 2028
  H.J. 2650–2
Tucker, D.G. 839, 1623, 2353, 2967, 3246, 3251
  J. 1093
  M. 1623
  M.T. 3401
  R.J. 3759–62
  T.G. 3021
Tully, A. 2857
Tunzelman, G.N. von 1186
Tuplin, W.A. 443–5
Turk, F.A. 1094
Turner, G. 2943
  J.F. 1624
  M. 832
Tutton, R. 3223
Tyack, N.C.P. 613, 892
Tylecote, R.F. 205, 1440, 1625–6
Tyler, B.E.G. 2354

Ugawa, K. 1940
Underdown, P.T. 3181
Unwin, A.H. 1121–3
Upton, J. 3182
Urdank, A.M. 2944, 3148

Vaisey, D. 832
Vale, E. 1198

Vallance, H.A. 1751
Valletin, R. 1286–8
Vancouver, C. 1941
Vanes, J. 1015
  J.M. 614–15
Varcoe, P. 1317
Varley, D.E. 2414
Vaughan, A. 113, 446–56
  J.A.M. 321, 1752–3
Verran, W.H. 1697
Vince, A. 3027, 3103
Vincent, C. 1664
  M. 933, 3575–6
Viner, D. 268, 2843, 2902, 3006, 3170
  D.J. 294, 3183–4
Vinter, D. 787–8, 2997
Vipan, P.G.L. 218
Vivian, J. 1627
  W. 1585
Voce, A.P. 3858

Waddell, L. 2395
Wade, E.A. 1754, 2120
Wagner, G. 730
Wailes, R. 1247, 2730
Wainwright, D. 3060
Waite, P. 130, 1400, 1615, 2133–4
Wakelin, A.P. 3185
  P. 617
Walden, I.N. 2060
Waley, M. 3703
Walker, F. 616, 618, 1016
  Sir H. 312
  H.H. 1942, 2555, 2653
  I.C. 901–2, 3104, 3495–6, 3773
  T.A. 457
Wall, R. 1011
Wallis, A.J. 2844
  A.M. 2773
  G. 3606
Walls, E. 911
  R. 2998
Walrond, L.F.J. 266, 2903, 3149, 3329
Walters, B. 758
  H.B. 3002–3
  M.J. 2951
Walton, J. 2774
  K.M. 1030
Wansey, H. 3808
Warburton, R. 2355
Ward, A.P. 3297, 3411, 3621, 3627
  J. 276
  J.D.U. 74
  J.R. 681

  O. 642–4, 671, 674, 711, 3356–7
Ward-Jackson, C.H. 1698, 1806–7
Wardley, P. 574
Warn, I.M. 799
Warne, J. 2712
Warner, R.B. 1628
Warnock, D. 3577
Warren, D. 2415, 2665, 3269, 3358–60, 3521
  D.W. 3390–3, 3473, 3510
  F.C. 2672, 2723, 2830
Warrington, A.J. 3434, 3549
Waterhouse, R. 2274
Watkins, C.M. 2322
  E. 2792–3
  G. 712, 840
Watson, C.E. 2945
  J.Y. 1629–30
Watt, A. 1943
Watton, W.J. 1815
Watts, J.H. 3778, 3781–2
  K.G. 3875
  M. 713, 2002, 2071, 2741, 3342, 3361–3, 3480, 3718–19
Way, J.P. 819
Wear, R. 2756
Weaver, C.P. 3186, 3394, 3746
  M.E. 1104–5
Webb, B. 3518
  D.J. 1017
  F.G. 743
  W.A. 3599
  W.W. 954
Webber, R. 619, 1666
Webb-Geach 1631
Weddell, P. 2194
  P.J. 1974, 2108, 2110, 2323
Wedgwood, J. 1680
Weeden, C. 744–50
Weinstock, W.B. 2858
Welch, C.E. 1095, 1950, 2437, 2580
  E. 3816
Weller, J. 3720
Wellington, J. 143, 1187
  J.F. 75
Wells, A.P. 1632
  C. 1018
  W.C. 3474
Werran, K. 3717
West, J. 2731
  W. 1249–51

Westcott, K. 2323
K.A. 2031
Westerling, M. 2999, 3539
Westlake & Laws 136
Weston, R.H. 2012
Westward Television 21
Wheeler, D.V.H. 2438
Whetmath, C.F.D. 486, 1755
Whetter, J.C.A. 1062–4, 1096, 1808
Whidbey, J. 2628
Whitaker, J. 2904
White, A. 2753
Sir G. 904–9
G.B. 1065
K. 3579
K.C. 3807
R. 3301
S. 3130
Whitehead, J. 1635, 2724
R.A. 2757
Whitehouse, D.B. 903
P. 438, 458
Whiteley, J. 459
Whiteways, E.V.M. 2018, 3366
Whitfield, M. 3309
Whiting, F.E. 2581
Whitley, H.M. 2654
Whitlock, R. 2725
Whitson, J. 589
Whittaker, A. 3512
Whittet, T.D. 2905, 3270, 3639
Whittington, G. 2946
Whyatt, G.K. 1097
Whyte, E.T. 3721
Wicks, A.T. 3540, 3607
Wicksteed, T. 1188, 1189
Wide, E. 3372
Wilcox, R. 3367
Wilde, D.S. 2681
Wilkes, R. 630
Wilkie, I. 212
Wilkinson, A. 3606
F. 1944
M. 3067

N. 1289
W.F. 1636
Willan, T.S. 295, 3817
Williams *family* 2099
A. 460, 3859
A.F. 1019
A.R. 3252
B.Y. 2510
C.L. 461
E.F. 3600
E.H.D. 76, 1975, 3330–5
G. 1637–48, 2275
H.V. 1649
K. 2509
M. 698, 3310–15
N.J. 3640
R.A. 467, 479
W.J. 3475
Williamson, D. 2859
Willoughby, R.W.H. 3722
Wills, A. 351, 2458
G. 2335–6
H.M. 1033
Wilmot, S.A.H. 68
Wilmott, F. 3395
Wilson, A. 3693
A.R. 3692
G. 2556
J.D. 2726
N. 3483
R. 2906, 3000–1, 3117–19, 3150, 3188–9, 3247
R.B. 358, 462
R.E. 1945, 1976, 1995
T. 1190
Wilson-North, R. 2276
Wilton, J.P. 2907
Wiltshire, L. 670
Winstone, J. 620
R. 945
Winter, D.M. 1946
Winwood, J. 1203
Withiel, G. 42
Witt, C. 750–1
Wittaker, P. 3677
Wood, P.D. 1098

W.H. 2013
Woodcock, G. 2277–8
L.H. 1248
Woodfin, R.J. 1756
Woodland, P.T.M. 621
Woodley, E.T. 2643
Woodrow, A. 1650
Woodruff, W. 3888
Woodward, G.H. 3316
H.B. 3476
Woolf, A. 1159, 1219, 1229, 1252–5
Woolner, A. 2582
D. 2582
Woolrich, A.P. 22, 623, 789, 833
T. 622, 766
Wooster, P. 3477
Wordsworth, A. 624
Worgan, G.B. 1099
Worrall, G. 2439, 2656
Worth, R.N. 144, 163, 311, 1066, 1251, 1685, 1977, 2279–88, 2337, 2344
Wright, D. 849
G. 3876
G.N. 512
T. 2947
Wroe, D.J. 1757
Wurtzburg, R. 1947
Wyatt, J.W. 2908–9
Wylie, J.A.H. 2099
Wyrall, G. 3061

Yallop, H.J. 2299, 2416-21
Yeates, G.M. 756
Youell, R.F. 2289
Youings, J. 1832, 2598, 2655
Youles, T. 3022
Young, D. 2746–8, 2794
H.R. 145, 1651
J. 2744
J.A. 2776, 2831–3
W.A. 715, 2061
W.E.D. 277, 296

Subject Index

This index should be used in conjunction with the Contents list, which contains broad subject headings under each county. Numbers refer to titles, not pages.

1851 Exhibition, Bristol 622

alum, Dorset 2862
Anderton, tin mine 2211
Angarack, smelting house 1484
Appledore, shipbuilding 2379
apprentices, Bristol 555, 573, 577–9, 1025
arsenic see Contents
Ashburton, woollen trade 2396
Avon Navigation 3526
Avonmouth, zinc working 757, 758
Avonside Ironworks 701
Axminster, carpets 2404, 2406
    water supply 2358
Axminster & Lyme Regis Light Railway 2450

Bal maidens 1395, 1545
ballooning, Bristol 1031–33
barges see under SHIPBUILDING; TRANSPORT, Ports and Shipping
barns see under ARCHITECTURE & BUILDINGS: Industrial
Barnstaple, clay tobacco pipes 2321
    clocks 2025
    electricity supply 2347
    industrial archaeology 1818
    pewterers 2101
    port see under DEVON, TRANSPORT. Ports, Harbours and Shipping
Barnstaple & Ilfracombe Railway 2447, 2479
Barnstaple Goldsmiths Guild 2094
barytes industry, Devon 2226–7, 2258–9
Basset Mines 1552
Bath, bookbinding 3625
    breweries 3367
    bridges see under SOMERSET, TRANSPORT, Bridges
    communications 3481
    electricity supplies 3497, 3498
    engineering see under SOMERSET, ENGINEERING
    industrial archaeology 3260, 3268
    railways see under SOMERSET, TRANSPORT, Railways
    road transport see under SOMERSET, TRANSPORT, Roads and Road Transport
    tobacco Pipes see under SOMERSET, POTTERIES AND CERAMICS
    water supplies 3505, 3506, 3509
Bath and West Society 44, 48, 49
Bath stone 3452, 3458–9, 3462, 3477, 3750–62
bee boles, Wiltshire 3697
beekeeping, Devon 1916
Bere Alston, mining 1518, 2131, 2200
    slate quarrying 2292
Bere Ferrers, mining 2154
Bibury Turnpike Trust 3232
Bideford, maritime history 1778
    potteries 2315
    shipbuilding 2391
Birch Tor mining complex 1374
Blackmore Vale, agriculture 27
Blasting, mining 1384
Blockley, electric lighting 3112
    silk trade 3136
blowing houses 1994, 2222, 2266, 2280–5
Bodley Bros & Co. Ltd 2067
Bodmin, mining 1331, 1498
Bodmin & Wadebridge Railway 1722, 1755
bookbinding, Bath 3625
booksellers, South–west England 548
Bordeaux 604
Boscean United Mining Co. Ltd 1633
Botallack, mining 1353, 1504, 1525, 1546
Boulton & Watt 693, 1190–4, 3013
Bournemouth, economic history 2669
    railways see under DORSET, RAILWAYS
    road transport see under DORSET, ROADS AND ROAD TRANSPORT
Bovey Tracey, clay mining 2112
    lignite industry 2291
    potteries 2300, 2319, 2323
Brannam, C.H. Ltd 2303
brass working, Bristol 759–61, 763–5, 767, 771–2, 775
Breage, mining 1498
breakwaters, Portland 2731
Brendon Hill 2205, 2206
brewing, St Austell 1810
brickmaking, Wiltshire 3883

246　SUBJECT INDEX

Bridford, baryte mine 2226–7
　economic history 1857
Bridge Iron Foundry 2063
Bridgwater, brickmaking 3369
Bridgwater & Taunton Canal 3527, 3531
Bridport, shipbuilding 2796, 2697
　textile industry 2799–2805
Bristol, 1851 Exhibition 622
　apprentices 555, 573, 577–9, 1025
　ballooning 1031–3
　cabinet–making 1030
　chocolate 718, 730
　cotton industry 887
　goldsmiths 1028
　Guild of Weavers 885
　Huguenots 587, 594
　locomotive building 701, 702
　match making 1027
　musical instrument makers 1025
　newspapers 820
　packaging 821, 824, 832
　pewterers 1021
　pin–making 1029
　ropemakers 1022
　shot tower 635, 641
　sugar 719–29
　wire–drawers 773
Bristol & Gloucestershire Railway 932
Bristol & Portishead Pier & Railway 928
Bristol Commercial Vehicles 940
Bristol Gas Light Company 842
Bristol Industrial Museum 572
Bristol Mint 575, 1026
Bristol Omnibus Co. Ltd 935
Bristol Port Railway 917, 924
Bristol Tramway & Carriage Co. 936
Bristol Typographical Society 822, 823
Bristol United Breweries 667
Bristol Wagon & Carriage Works Co. Ltd. 695
Brixham, fishing industry 2089, 2092
　iron mines 2140
Bubble Company 1357
Bude, mining 1498
　railways 1757
Bude Canal 283, 290
Bulkamore Iron Mine 2212
Burt & Vick Ltd 2749
Butler, Wm & Co. Ltd 683

cabinet–making, Bristol 1030
calamine mining 3428, 3465
Calenick, mining 1625
Callington, mining 1331, 1413, 1440, 1498
　railways 1727, 1748
Calstock, mining 1331, 1498, 1518
Camborne, mining 1488, 1498, 1588, 1595, 1600

　trams 1758
Camelford, mining 1498
Camerton & Limpley Stoke Railway 912
Cann Quarry Canal 2437
Canons Marsh goods shed 919
Cape Cornwall Mine 1323
capital formation, mining 201
　South–west England 13
Caradon, mining 1404, 1526, 1576, 1589, 1631
Carn Brea, mining 1606
carpenters' nails 1024
Castiard, Vale of, industrial history 2886
Cordwainers Society of Tewkesbury 3062
Chagford, tin mining 2151
Chard, lace making 3521
Chard Canal 3539
Charfield Blockworks 674
Charles, mining 2158
Charleston, maritime history 1788
Charterhouse–on–Mendip, industrial archaeology 3265
Cheltenham, cycle industry 3248
　electricity supply 3111, 3113
　roads see under GLOUCESTERSHIRE, ROADS AND ROAD TRANSPORT
Chepstow and District Turnpike Trust 3227
China clay see Contents
chocolate, Bristol 718, 730
Christopher Thomas & Brothers Ltd 881, 883–4
Chumleigh, industrial history 1820
cider industry, Gloucestershire 2912–13
　South–west England 550
Cirencester Improved Dwellings Co. 2956
Clark, C. & J. Ltd 3395–400, 3543
Claverton Pumping Station 3379, 3386–7, 3394
clay pipes see under POTTERY AND CERAMICS
Clevedon Pier 3608–9, 3611, 3615, 3619
Clifton hydraulic power scheme 694
Clifton Suspension Bridge 946–54
clocks and clockmakers, Cornwall 1809
Clutton, coal mining 780
coal mining see Contents
Coalbrookdale 570, 600, 609
coinage, Bristol 575
　Cornwall 1544
　Exeter 1816
Colchester 605
Combe Martin, mining 2159, 2254, 2269
Company of Soapmakers 880
copper mining see Contents
copper slag block industry 1445
Copper Standard, Cornwall 1543
Copperhouse Foundry and Engine Works 1468

corn kilns, South–west England 76
Cornish Copper Company 1467–8, 1539, 1555
Cornish Metal Company 1466, 1561
Cornish Riviera Ltd 1719, 1743
cost book system, mining 1392, 1394, 1398, 1496, 1516
Cotswolds, industrial history 2875, 2885
   railways 313
   transport 268
   woollen industry 245–6
Cox's of Taunton 3267
cotton industry, Bristol 887
Cranham, industrial history 2887
crepe industry, Exmoor 2415
Crift Farm Project 1387, 1521
Crofton Pumping Engine 3734, 3741, 3744–6
cruck houses *see under* ARCHITECTURE AND BUILDINGS, DOMESTIC
Culm Valley, economic history 1862
Culme Valley Light Railway 2451, 2486
Culmstock, industrial history 1860
Cumberland Basin, ports 961
curing chambers, Somerset 3322, 3330, 3334
   South–west England 76
cutlery industry, Wiltshire 3885
cycle industry, Cheltenham 3248

Dart River, passenger cteamers 271
Dartington, housing 1951
Dartmoor, agriculture 1878, 1882, 1890, 1891, 1905, 1944
   blowing houses 1994
   industrial history 1829, 1836–1838
   mining 2128, 2133, 2149–50, 2152, 2163, 2165, 2170, 2202, 2215–16, 2218, 2239, 2284–8
   ochre works 2197
   railways 2467
Dartmouth, economic history 1856
   shipbuilding 2388
   whaling trade 2074
Delabole Slate Ltd 1655, 1658, 1664
Dening of Chard 3392
Devon Great Consols Mine 2029, 2107, 2137, 2143, 2145, 2147, 2173, 2199, 2242, 2255–6, 2278
Devon Great Consols Railway 2452
Devon United Mines 2141
Devonport, industrial history 1817
   shipbuilding 2373–5, 2380–1, 2383, 2395
Diesel engines, Penzance 1134
Ding–Dong Mine 1537, 1639–40
Dolcoath Mine 1379, 1469, 1603, 1605
Donyatt Potteries 3487–9

Dorset & Somerset Canal 272
Douglas Motor Cycle Co. 699
dovecotes, Gloucestershire 2953
Downton, lace industry 3787–9
dredgers, steamships 868
Drift Moor, mining 1405
drought, South–west England 233
Druid Mine 2129
Dudbridge, industrial history 2895
Dulcote, industrial history 3262
Dunheved Ironworks 1260
Dymock, mining 3084

East Buckland, mining 2158
East Cornwall Mineral Railway 1723
East Cornwall Silver Mining Company 1348
East Pool Mine 1477, 1530
East Trevell Mine 1324
East Wheal Rose Mine 1438
Eldridge, Pope & Co. 2743
elver fishing, South–west England 119
English China Clays Ltd 159, 1294, 1304
English Clays, Lovering, Pochin & Co. Ltd 2115–16
eroding boats, Somerset 3617
Ewen, quarrying 3088
Exe Bight Oyster Fishery & Pier Company 2084
Exe Valley Railway 2492
Exeter, bookselling 2338, 2342
   clockmaking 2024
   coinage 1816
   economic history 1823–6 1828, 1832, 1844–8, 1851, 1863–4, 1869
   engineering 2067, 2073
   housing 1970, 1971
   Merchant Adventurers Guild 1828, 1859
   pewterers 2096, 2098
   potteries 2302, 2305, 2311
   printing 2338, 2341
   railways *see under* DEVON, RAILWAYS
   water supply 2360, 2363, 2365, 2368
   wool trade 2401
Exeter Canal 2422–4, 2429, 2435, 2438–9
Exeter Cathedral, economic history 1840
Exeter Goldsmiths Guild 2095
Exeter Lighter Canal 2433
Exeter Mint 2657
Exeter Whale Fishery Co. 2076
Exmoor, agriculture 58, 3293
   industrial archaeology 3254, 3266
   mining 2139, 2156, 2196, 2253, 2265
   railways 2504
   ships 2600
   woollen and crepe industry 2415
Exmouth Docks Company 2597

Fal River, passenger steamers 1785
Falmouth, coal gas industry 1689
  harbour 1797
  mining 1331, 1498
  oyster cultivation 1286
  ships 1766, 1773, 1782, 1789, 1795
feltmaking 1023
field systems, South–west England 36, 60, 61, 63
Fielding & Platt Ltd 3015
Finch Brothers Foundry 2062, 2068, 2071
Firefly Project 396–7
fisheries, Somerset 3624
flax growing, Devizes 3642
flour milling, Gloucestershire 2964
flower growing, Tamar Valley 53
Forest of Dean, agriculture 2924–5
  ammunition industries 2951
  goldmining 3028
  industrial history 2870–1, 2881–2, 2888, 2890, 2898, 2900
  iron working *See under* GLOUCESTERSHIRE, IRON AND STEEL
  mining *See under* GLOUCESTERSHIRE, MINING AND QUARRYING
  shipbuilding 3122
Fowells of St Ives 1264
Fowey, shipbuilding 1698
  ships 1806
Frampton Cotterell, mill 640
Frome River, mills 639, 643
fruit growing, Tamar Valley 59
Fry, J.S. & Sons 718, 730
Fullabrook Mine 2153
fuller's earth 3460

Gawton Mine and Arsenic Works 2105, 2108, 2110
Geevor Mine 1373, 1529, 1547, 1575, 1635
George and Charlotte Mine 1510, 1511
Georgeham, mining 2157
Georges & Co. 666, 668
Georgia Consols 1641
German miners, in Cornwall 1563
Giew Mine 1642
Glastonbury Navigation & Canal 3525
Gloucester, Docks *see under* GLOUCESTERSHIRE, CANALS AND RIVERS
  industrial history 2877, 2896
  match industry 3068, 3069
Gloucester & Berkeley Canal 3163–4, 3166, 3168, 3177, 3182
Gloucester & Cheltenham Railway 3193–5
Gloucester & Hereford Turnpike Trust 3225
Gloucester & Sharpness Canal 3156, 3161, 3186
Gloucester Journal 3108–9
Gloucester Railway Carriage & Wagon Co. Ltd 3197, 3199, 3202, 3209, 3223
Gloucestershire Steam Plough Co. 3014
Godolphin Ball Mine 1495
gold mining 2142
  Cornwall 1473
goldsmiths, Bristol 1028
  Dorset 2860
  Somerset 3622
Goonhilly Project 1673
Grand Western Canal 279, 282, 284, 289
granite quarrying *see* Contents
Great Britain, SS 849–53, 856, 858–60, 864–7
Great Dowgas Mine 1441
Great Western, SS 857, 861
Great Wheal Vor Mine 1493, 1499
Guildhall, London, mining records 1399
Guild of Weavers, Bristol 885
Gunnislake, mines 1337
Gwennap, mining 1331, 1498
Gwinear, mining 1331, 1498, 1616
Gwithian, mining 1331, 1498

Hain of St Ives 1796
Hall & Woodhouse, 2742
Hall, English & Co. 3098
Hancock's Brewery 3364
Hants. & Dorset Motor Services 2840
Harlow, R. & Son Ltd 767
harness trade, Wiltshire 3878
Hartland Quay 2630
Harvey's of Hayle 1195–8
Hayle, industrial history 1036
  mining 1331, 1498
  shipbuilding 1696
Haytor, iron mining 2208
  mining 2128
  quarrying 2122
Haytor Granite Tramway 2440, 2456, 2465, 2475
Hereford & Gloucester Canal 3152–3, 3174
herring fishing, South–west England 117
Hollybrook Brick Co. Ltd 673
Holman Bros Ltd 1130, 1199–1201, 1423
Honiton, lace industry 2397–8, 2400, 2402, 2405, 2407, 2409, 2412–21
  water supply 2364
Huguenots, Bristol 587, 594
Hunt, Octavius Ltd 1027

ice houses, St Austell 1116
  Wiltshire 3704
iceworks, Devon 2661
Illogan, mining 1498, 1593
Imperial Tobacco Company 890

SUBJECT INDEX

Imperial Smelting Corporation 757, 758
Impregnated Diamond Products Ltd 3250
Indio Pottery 2319
iron mining *see* Contents

Kells of Gloucester 3011
Kelly Iron Mine 2132
Kennet & Avon Canal 269–70, 273, 276, 291–3, 3734, 3741, 3744–6, 3813
King Edward Mine 1372
Kings, C.J. & Sons 1000

lace industry, Wiltshire 3784, 3787–9
  Devon *see under* DEVON, TEXTILES
Lady Elizabeth Mine 2219
Land's End, mining 1588
Lanhydrock Atlas 1087
Lanivet, mining 1458
Launceston, mining 1331, 1498
  railways 2441, 2473
lead mining *see* Contents
Levant Mine 1353, 1421, 1548
limeburning industry, Devon 1879, 1906, 1945
limekilns, South–west England 127, 128
Liskeard, mining 1331, 1339, 1498, 1593, 1631
Liskeard & Caradon Railway 1736, 1737
Liskeard & Looe Canal 1704, 1705
Liskeard & Looe Railway 1731
Lister's Ltd 3012
Little Barrington, papermaking 3092
Lizard, mining 1331, 1498
locomotive building, Bristol 701–2
Looe, mining 1526
  shipbuilding 1692
Lovell's Shipping 986
Lundy, copper mining 2213
  quarrying 2124
Lynmouth, electric lighting 2349
Lynton, electric lighting 2349
Lynton & Barnstaple Railway 2446, 2448, 2499
Lysaght Co. Ltd 705

maltings, Wiltshire 3882
man engines *see under* ENGINEERING: Engines and Engine Houses
manganese mining 212, 2198, 2257, 2271
Marazion, mining 1498, 1596, 1612, 1616
Marconi Company 1670, 1671, 3881
Mardon, Son & Hall 827, 828
Marlborough Canal 3814
Martyn, H.H. & Co. 2904
Mary Tavy, mines 2238
match making, Bristol 1027
Mayflower, SS 863
Mendips, mining *see under* SOMERSET, MINING AND QUARRYING
Menheniot, mines 1340
Mercers' and Linen Drapers' Company 585
Merchant Adventurers Guild, Exeter 1828, 1859
Merchant Vventurers of Bristol 564, 584, 590, 592–3, 611, 991, 994
Meredith, J. & Co. 715
Merrivale Bridge Mine 2181
Mevagissey, mining 1331, 1498
millstone making, Gloucestershire 3251
Mineral Tramways Project 1726
mining records, Guildhall, London
Minions Survey 1037
Molland, mining 2164
Moreton in Marsh, industrial archaeology 2896
Moretonhampstead & South Devon Railway 2470
Morgan Giles Ltd 2387
Morval Barton, limekiln 1293
Morwellham, power supply 2348, 2352
  water supply 2366
  port *see under* DEVON, PORTS, HARBOURS AND SHIPPING
Mount Batten, shipbuilding 1693
Mount Wellington Mine 1427
Mounts Bay, mining 1331, 1498, 1588
musical instrument makers, Bristol 1025

Nailsea, coal mining 781
  industrial history 612
  cider making 716
Nailsworth, agriculture 626
  engineering 3022
  glassmaing 734–9, 3026
  hosiery manufacture 3150
  turnpike 3228
Netham Chemical Co. Ltd 689
New Chiverton Mine 1349
New Quay, archaeology 1835
Newcomen engine, South–west England 80
Newent, glassmaking 3027
  mining *See under* GLOUCESTERSHIRE, MINING AND QUARRYING
Newham, tin working 1478
Newman Hender & Co. 3010
Newquay, mining 1331, 1498
  railways 1753
  shipbuilding 1697
newspapers, Bristol 820
North Cliff, mines 1329
North Devon Shipping Company 2607
North Molton, mining 2164

ochre industry, Winford 1020
  Dartmoor 2197

oil, Dorset 2867
organ manufacture, Cornwall 1814
Over Bridge 3236, 3243
oyster cultivation, Falmouth 1286

packaging, Bristol 821, 824, 832
Padstow, mining 1331, 1498
paper industry, Dorset 2868
  Wiltshire 3884
Parbola Mine 1643
Partridge & Love Ltd 829
passenger steamers, Dart River 271
  Tamar River 288
Pednandrea Mine 1495
Pentewan Railway 1721, 1733
Penzance, diesel engines 1134
  harbour 1799
  industries 1049
  mining 1331, 1405, 1498
Perran Foundry 1209–11
Perranporth, mining 1327, 1331, 1498
Perranuthnoe, mining 1596
pewter industry, Wiltshire 3886
pewterers, Bristol 1021
  South–west England 549
Philip & Son Ltd 2388
Phillack Parish, mining 2223
Phoenix, mining 1576
Phoenix Glassworks 731
Phoenix United Mines 1577
photography, underground 1815
Pike Bros. 2790
pilchard fishing, South–west England 114
pin–making, Bristol 1029
Plymouth, fishing industry 2080, 2086–8
  gas supply 2356
  industrial history 1817, 1819, 1821–2, 1827, 1865, 1867
  port see under DEVON, PORTS, HARBOURS AND SHIPPING
  postal service 2296
  potteries 2317, 2324–37
  railways 2455, 2466
  shipbuilding 2376, 2384, 2385, 2389
  water supply 2357, 2359, 2361–2, 2367, 2369
Plympton, economic history 1850
Polackers 2584, 2586
Polrose Mine 1644
Pool, W.H. & Sons 3393
Poole, economic history 2668, 2671
population, Cornwall 1042, 1050, 1054, 1522–4, 1563, 1564
Porkellis, mining 1331, 1530
port books, Cornwall 1062
Porth, maritime history 1777
Porthleven, harbour 1805
Portishead, port 960

Portreath, industrial history 1059
  mines 1330
  ships 1771
post–horse routes, South–west England 501
potato crop, South–west England 23
powdermills, Dartmoor 2103–4
Price Walker & Co. 3249
Princetown, railways 2441, 2464, 2474
printers, South–west England
Proctor Chemical Works 687
Providence Mine 1566
Purbeck marble 2727, 2761–74

Quantocks, mining see under SOMERSET, MINING AND QUARRYING

radium 216, 1584, 1665
Redlake China Clay Works 1754, 2120
  tramway 2443
Redruth, bacon curing 1811
  mining 1488, 1489, 1498, 1588, 1595
  trams 1758
Redruth & Chasewater Railway 1711, 1749
Reed & Malik Ltd 3723
Retallack Mine 1459
Robinsons of Bristol 824, 832
Rogers & Co. 708
Rolle Canal 2431
Rolls Royce, aircraft manufacture 650, 660, 661
roof tiles, Wessex 2865
ropemakers, Bristol 1022
Roskrow United Mine 1602
Royal Albert Bridge, Saltash 1715, 1720
Royal Blue Express Services 499
Royal Cornwall Show 1088
Royal Portbury Docks, Bristol 1002
Royal Potteries, Weston–super–Mare 3485, 3494
rubber industry, Wiltshire 3888
Russell, T. & Co. 504

St Agnes, mining 1331, 1417, 1425, 1498, 1593, 1606
St Austell, brewing 1810
  China clay industry 1302
  ice house 1116
  mining 1331, 1444, 1498
St Columb, mining 1331, 1498
St Columb Canal 1708
St Erith, sand pits 1666
St Erth, mining 1616
St Germans Quay Tramway 1738
St Hilary, mining 1498, 1623
St Ives, boatbuilding 1694
  engineering 1264
  fishing 1270, 1283
  mining 1331, 1498, 1616

St Ives Mining District 1549
St Just, mining 1407, 1633
St Just Mining District 1368, 1424, 1550, 1580, 1608, 1616
St Just United Mine 1505
St Stephen, mining 1441
Salisbury, cutlery industry 3885
　electricity supply 3777
　gas supply 3778
　gunmaking 3748
　water supply 3781, 3782
Salisbury Avon Navigation 3810–11, 3817
Salisbury Cathedral, clocks 3725, 3730
Saltash, mining 1331, 1498
saltpetre, Dorset 2863
sarsen industry, Wiltshire 3757
Scilly Isles, agriculture 1090
　pilot gigs 1776
　shipbuilding 1691
　wrecks 1768
Scout Motors 3738
Severn Bridge Railway 925
Severn Railway Tunnel 301, 305
Severn Valley Navigation 295, 3181, 3185, 3187
Sharpness, Docks see under GLOUCESTERSHIRE, CANALS AND RIVERS
sheep, South–west England 67
Shortwood Brickworks 671
Shot Tower, Bristol 635, 641
Sidmouth, electric lighting 2351
silver mining 1406, 1440, 1518, 2261, 2269, 2272
　see also Contents
Somerset & Avon Railway 317
Somerset County Gazette 3623
Somersetshire Coal Canal see under SOMERSET, TRANSPORT, CANALS
South Croft Mine 1356, 1373, 1389, 1391, 1431, 1435, 1461, 1507
South Devon United Mine 2240
South Molton, mining 2164
South Terras Mine 1584, 1665
South Western Electricity Board 230, 231
South Wheal Rancis Mine 1562
Southampton & Salisbury Canal 3816
stamping mills 1457–8, 1485, 1489
Stannaries 172, 176–7, 185, 192, 194, 196–7
　Cornwall 1446, 1471, 1490, 1506
　Devon 2161, 2166–8, 2178–9, 2209, 2230, 2237, 2279
Stapleton, mills 631, 632
statistics, China clay mining 1306
　copper and tin mining 178
　Cornish mining 1409, 1419
　Cornwall 1038, 1042, 1050, 1062

fishing 1279
mining 1318, 1514
steam engine, South–west England 77, 79–80
steatite industry, Cornwall 1812
Stonehouse, industrial history 1817
Stothert & Pitt 3381, 3388–9
Stover Canal 2456, 2465
straw plaiting industry, Wiltshire 3879
Stroud, industrial archaeology 2903
　pin–making 3099
　roads see under GLOUCESTERSHIRE, ROADS AND ROAD TRANSPORT
　textile industry 3019, 3130, 3132–4
Stroudwater, turnpikes 3229, 3231
Stroudwater Canal 3165, 3169–70, 3172, 3180, 3189
sugar, Bristol 719–29
Swanpool Mine 1487
Swedish visitors, to South–west England 22
Swindon, railways see under WILTSHIRE, TRANSPORT, Railways
　trams 3865

Tamar Firebrick & Clay Company 1681
Tamar Manure Navigation 2432
Tamar River, passenger steamers 288, 1786
　shipping 539, 543
Tamar Valley, agriculture 33, 39
　copper production 2224
　flower growing 53
　fruit growing 59
　industrial archaeology 1–2, 12
　mining 195, 199, 2239, 2255
　shipbuilding 237
　viticulture 39
Tamerton, mining 2135
Taunton, brickmaking 3370
　electricity supply 3503
　gas supply 3501
　railways 2484–5
　textiles 3517–18
Tavistock, agriculture 1883
　brewing 2015
　foundries 2066
　mining 2127, 2136
　railways 2441, 2473
　Stannaries 2161, 2167
Tavistock Abbey, industrial history 1833
Tavistock–Morwelham Canal 2427, 2430, 2434, 2436
Teign Valley, economic history 1857
　mining 2231, 2233, 2260–1
Teign Valley Line 2496
Teignmouth, engineering 2028
　shipbuilding 2387
Temple Meads Station, Bristol 927, 931
Tewkesbury, Cordwainers Society 3062

industrial history 2874
Thames & Severn Canal 275, 277–8,
  285–7, 294, 296, 3165, 3170, 3183–4
Thomas, William & Co. Ltd 3371
tidemills, South–west England 72
  see also under ARCHITECTURE &
  BUILDINGS: Industrial
timber trading, Gloucester 3249
tin bounders 1443
tin Mining see Contents
tin streaming 1335, 1364, 1405, 1453,
  1460, 1483, 1512, 1599
Tindene Mine 1645
tithe barns, South–west England 74
Tiverton, clockmakers 2021
  industrial archaeology 1831, 1870
  industrial housing 1957
tobacco pipes see under POTTERY AND
  CERAMICS
tobacco trade, Bristol See Contents
  Dorset 2861
  Gloucestershire 3252
tokens, Bath 3257
  Cornwall 1066
  Gloucestershire 2880, 2905
  Somerset 3270
  Taunton 3267
  Wiltshire 3637, 3639
Tolgus Tin Stamping Co. Ltd 1489
Topsham, shipbuilding 2372, 2390, 2393
Torbay, road transport 1759
Torbay & Brixham Railway 2454
Torquay, potteries 2313
  public utilities 2345–6
Totnes, economic history 1856
Tregembo Mine 1646
Tregurtha Down Mine 1612
Trethowel, China clay industry 1311, 1314
Trowbridge, woollen industry 3783, 3797,
  3804–5
trows, 535, 541, 547, 910, 3120–1, 3124
Truro, mining 1498, 1593
  pottery 1674
  textiles 1699
  tin working 1478
tungsten mining, South–west England 182
Twerton, cloth industry 3513
Twitchen, mining 2164

Underfall Yard, ports 977, 984
Uphill, ports 96, 3612
Upper Merrivale, mining 2185
  tin blowing 2171
  tin mill 2274
uranium mining 216, 1584

Van Moppes, IDP Ltd 3250
viticulture, South–west England 24, 39, 62

vitifer mining complex 1374

Wadebridge, mining 1498
Wareham, potteries 2790
warehouses, Gloucester 2965–6
Warminster, gunmaking 3749
  foundry 3739
watch fusee chain industry 2753
watermills see under ARCHITECTURE &
  BUILDINGS: Industrial
Wellington (Somerset), brickmaking 3371
  textiles 3515
Wemyss Ware 2301
Wendron, forge 1152
  mining 1331, 1364, 1502, 1598, 1616
Wessex, clocks 3373
  maritime history 2859
  railways 308
  roads 3864, 3872, 3874
  roof tiles 2865
  silk industry 2805
West Colliford, tin working 1456
West Cornwall Mines Investment Company
  1360
West Devon Electric Supply Co. Ltd 2354
West Godolphin Mine 1647
West Great Work Mine 1648
West Looe, shipbuilding 2377
West of England Bacon Co. 1811
West Wheal Basset Mine 1562
Westbury Ironworks 3733
Western Counties Agricultural
  Co–operative 637
Western Morning News 2340
Western National 500
Weston, Clevedon & Portishead Railway
  3571, 3575
Weston–super–Mare, potteries 3485, 3494
Weymouth, brickmaking 2747
  railways see under DORSET, RAIL-
  WAYS
Wheal Alfred Mine 1500
Wheal Betsy Mine 2031, 2234
Wheal Buller Mine 1366
Wheal Coates Mine 1425
Wheal Cumpston Mine 2192
Wheal Fortune Mine 1367, 2181
Wheal Friendship Mine 2172
Wheal Grenville Mine 1416
Wheal Guskus Mine 1623
Wheal Hermon Mine, 1368
Wheal Jane Mine 1361, 1491, 1632
Wheal Langford Mine 1440
Wheal Lopes Mine 2130
Wheal Owles Mine 1464, 1633
Wheal Prosper 2191
Wheal Prosper Tin Stamps 1458
Wheal Reeth Mine 1637–8

Wheal Reeth Tin Ltd 2275
Wheal Robins Mine 1362
Wheal Spernon Mine 1495
Wheal Vor Mine 1369, 1616
Wheal Zion Mine 1370, 2148
Wherry Mine 1579
Whiteways Cyder 2018
Williams Perran Foundry Co. 1209–11
Wills, W.D. & H.O. 889, 891–3
Willsbridge, mill 644
Wiltshire & Berkshire Canal 3809, 3812, 3815
Wiltshire Foundry 3739
Winchcombe, papermaking 3094
windmills *see under* ARCHITECTURE & BUILDINGS: Industrial
Winford, ochre industry 1020

Winwood & Co. 710–11
wire–drawers, Bristol 773
Wolf Rock Lighthouse 1111
Woodchester, glassmaking 3023–4
Worshipful Company of Weavers, Fullers and Shearmen 2401
Wright, J. & Sons 834–5
Wrigley Co. Ltd 2666
Wrington Vale Light Railway 3546, 3553, 3571, 3580

Yelverton–Princeton Railway 2474
Yeo River, mills 633
Yetminster, houses 2729

zinc mining *see* Contents
zinc working, Bristol 757–8, 766, 769